DARE to Say No

JUSTICE, POWER, AND POLITICS

Heather Ann Thompson and Rhonda Y. Williams, editors

The Justice, Power, and Politics series publishes new works in history that explore the myriad struggles for justice, battles for power, and shifts in politics that have shaped the United States over time. Through the lenses of justice, power, and politics, the series seeks to broaden scholarly debates about America's past as well as to inform public discussions about its future.

A complete list of books published in Justice, Power, and Politics is available at https://uncpress.org/series/justice-power-politics.

DARE to Say No

Policing and the War on Drugs in Schools

Max Felker-Kantor

The University of North Carolina Press CHAPEL HILL

Set in Merope Basic by Westchester Publishing Services
Manufactured in the United States of America

Library of Congress Cataloging-in-Publication Data
Names: Felker-Kantor, Max, author.
Title: DARE to say no : policing and the war on drugs in schools / Max Felker-Kantor.
Other titles: Justice, power, and politics.
Description: Chapel Hill : The University of North Carolina Press, [2024] | Series: Justice, power, and politics | Includes bibliographical references and index.
Identifiers: LCCN 2023045911 | ISBN 9781469676364 (cloth) | ISBN 9781469679044 (paperback) | ISBN 9781469676371 (epub) | ISBN 9798890887207 (pdf)
Subjects: LCSH: Drug Abuse Resistance Education (Program)—History. | Drug abuse—Study and teaching—United States—History. | Drug abuse—United States—Prevention—History. | Drug control—United States—History. | BISAC: HISTORY / United States / 20th Century | SOCIAL SCIENCE / Ethnic Studies / American / African American & Black Studies
Classification: LCC HV5808 .F45 2024 | DDC 362.29/30973—dc23/eng/20231031
LC record available at https://lccn.loc.gov/2023045911

Cover illustration: School locker by Jose Gil / stock.adobe.com.

Portions of this book were previously published in a different form and are used here with permissions. Throughout is included material from "Arresting the Demand for Drugs: DARE and the School–Police Nexus in Los Angeles," *Journal of Urban History* 49, no. 5 (2023): 1108–29; "DARE to Say No: Police and the Cultural Politics of Prevention in the War on Drugs," *Modern American History* 5, no. 3 (November 2022): 313–37.

This book will be made open access within three years of publication thanks to Path to Open, a program developed in partnership between JSTOR, the American Council of Learned Societies (ACLS), the University of Michigan Press, and the University of North Carolina Press to bring about equitable access and impact for the entire scholarly community, including authors, researchers, libraries, and university presses around the world. Learn more at https://about.jstor.org/path-to-open/.

For my parents

Contents

Illustrations

FIGURES

GRAPHS

DARE to Say No

INTRODUCTION

A Challenge to Arm the Nation's Youth

In the fall of 1983, ten uniformed police officers entered fifth-grade classrooms across Los Angeles as instructors. Their very presence was, for the Los Angeles Police Department (LAPD), an admission of failure. Militarized drug raids, mass sweeps, specialized units, joint task forces, and undercover operations had long been their tactics of choice for preventing drugs from reaching America's streets—but as chief of police Daryl Gates acknowledged in 1987, the police had, for all intents and purposes, failed at their most basic mission to prevent the supply of drugs from reaching America's streets. "Efforts by federal, state and local law enforcement agencies have been unable consistently to interrupt the ever-increasing flow of illicit drugs," Gates wrote. "The demand for these drugs supported in part by public apathy and casual acceptance of drug abuse, has correspondingly increased."[1]

Something had to change—and what Gates envisioned was a program that would turn children themselves into frontline soldiers in the war on drugs. It would do so by turning the police into teachers. Children, in the minds of the police, needed to be armed to resist drugs. And the police, not classroom teachers, were the ones who could best ensure their students would be armed to resist drug use. Gates concluded, "Law enforcement administrators must spearhead the effort to teach the children of this country to 'DARE to Say No' to drugs."[2]

It began with stints of fifteen (later expanded to seventeen) weeks to deliver the Drug Abuse Resistance Education (DARE) curriculum in fifty classrooms. Police officers, many educators and law enforcement officials believed, would be ideal instructors of drug education because they had credibility with students due to their real-world experience with the negative consequences of drug abuse. "The officers," Gates recalled in his memoir, "spinning tales of the streets, enthralled the children, who discovered they actually liked these guys."[3] Deploying veteran police officers as instructors to work the classroom beat, the program designers believed, would help students learn how to say no to drugs, develop positive self-esteem, and take personal responsibility for their choices. For many law enforcement officials, DARE became a shining example of how the police, and their political backers, were positively and proactively combating the drug war in the nation's schools through prevention rather than enforcement. And they hoped to bring the program to every student in the country.

Within a decade, DARE became the largest and most visible drug prevention program in the United States. At its height, police officers taught DARE to fifth- and sixth-grade students in more than 75 percent of American school districts as well as in dozens of countries around the world. Alongside the students receiving the full seventeen-week curriculum, millions of other students ranging from kindergarten to high school received variations of DARE. At the end of the 1990s, altogether DARE reached an estimated 50 million students globally.[4] Everyone involved—parents, students, educators, police officers, Congress members, and presidents—praised the program as a model of drug prevention. In the two decades after its introduction, DARE brought the war on drugs directly into the nation's schools, and education became an additional weapon in the police arsenal.

This is the first full history of the DARE program. It traces DARE's rapid growth from Los Angeles to schools across the country and how, through savvy marketing and public relations, DARE became a cultural icon and symbol of the drug war. More centrally, it shows how the police used DARE in an attempt to legitimize themselves by empowering officers to enter children's lives as teachers, friends, and mentors. In the process, this history reveals that DARE was never solely about drug education but fundamentally about the expansion of police power and authority in America.

If DARE became the darling of drug warriors, it also embodied the drug war's paradoxes. It originated in police failure but relied on cops as instructors. It hoped to humanize the police while reinforcing a law-and-order, zero-tolerance message. DARE administrators hoped that a calculated public relations campaign enlisting athletes and celebrities alongside the presence of DARE officers in classrooms would facilitate trust between children and the police. For many students, DARE did just that, getting the zero tolerance for drug use message into their heads, often with dire consequences. The most high-profile instances occurred when students told their DARE officers about their parents' drug use, which led to the arrest of the child's family members. Through DARE and its infamous Question Box, where students could provide anonymous information or concerns to their DARE officer, children unwittingly became the eyes and ears of the police. Other students, in contrast, saw through the façade, treating the role-playing and skits where they acted out drug sale interactions as a game to make their friends laugh. The image of fifth graders trying to convince their friends to try drugs or DARE officers telling young students horror stories exposed, for many, the absurdity of DARE. Finally, and perhaps most notably, for all the political commitment and funding behind DARE, it did not prevent youth drug use. DARE, in turn, became yet another failed police experiment-billed-as-reform that expanded police authority under the guise of prevention.

Viewed from a different vantage point, however, DARE was a success. Its near ubiquity in schools, widespread political support, and cultural visibility underscores the ways it normalized the police in all aspects of American life. The intentional use of police officers as instructors aimed to influence young minds to support the police mission and accept cops as commonsense in their educational spaces. The ability of the police to refashion their image in the minds of kids, parents, educators, policymakers, and the police themselves was the metric of success. Within the context of a militarized war on drugs on the streets of America's cities, DARE officials hoped to provide a countermeasure to the image of the aggressive cop banging down doors, tearing homes apart, and conducting mass arrests, especially in communities of color. From this perspective, DARE was a solution to problems of law enforcement's own making.[5] Using a law enforcement officer to teach antidrug education, DARE connected the drug war's soft side of prevention with its hard side of enforcement of drug laws. Quite simply, DARE enabled the police to move fluidly between schools and the streets and, in doing so, shaped policing to this day.

Police, Drug Education, and the Carceral State

Examining how seemingly nonpunitive institutions, such as schools, became part of the carceral state demonstrates the ways police used antidrug education to broaden their authority during the Reagan era. Scholars of the war on drugs have focused on policing, punitive policies, and prison expansion.[6] Such an emphasis is important but leaves the understanding of the scope of the drug war incomplete. Indeed, the drug war encompassed much more than formal law enforcement functions or the extension of get-tough logics to a range of institutions outside the criminal punishment system.[7] As some scholars have shown, it also relied on a widespread public relations offensive ranging from Nancy Reagan's Just Say No to the Partnership for a Drug-Free America advertising campaigns.[8] Centering DARE adds a layer of nuance to the story of the drug war and reveals the ways the public relations efforts to deglamorize drug use worked intimately with the application of police authority to act as educators and mentors in the nation's schools. DARE demonstrates the ways the hard and soft sides of the drug war were mutually reinforcing and broadens the understanding of the development of the carceral state by showing how the police maneuvered to define social issues as problems to be solved by law enforcement rather than health, education, or social welfare.[9]

Law enforcement needed DARE. Traditional methods of combating drugs had actively undermined trust in the police throughout the 1980s, especially among youth of color who witnessed the overpolicing and underprotection of their neighborhoods.[10] DARE administrators and proponents hoped that using cops as teachers would transform the image of the police officer. In turn, DARE was as much a community policing project aimed to legitimize the police within the context of an aggressive drug war as it was a drug prevention program. The effort to humanize the police by transforming them into friends and mentors instead of a uniformed enemy was a key building block of police power and insularity in the late twentieth century.

Relying on police officers as teachers enabled DARE to simultaneously transform both the police and schools.[11] Police had engaged in youth and school programs throughout the twentieth century with particularly devastating consequences for Black and Latinx youth.[12] Indeed, Los Angeles schools had become enmeshed in the carceral system in the post–World War II period as educators both adopted punitive discipline policies and formally established the Los Angeles School Police Department in 1983.[13] Examining DARE provides a different perspective. It shows how the carceral state was not merely imposed on schools but also developed from within them. By enabling officers to assert expertise as teachers of drug education, DARE expanded law enforcement authority to wage the drug war, whether it was enforcing drug laws on the streets of America's cities or teaching kids to say no in schools. DARE not only made the police a regular presence in schools but, by defining cops as teachers, aimed to transform the image of the police officer from a threatening enemy to a friend and mentor. As institutions that embodied the state's supposed protective and preventive role, schools bolstered and legitimated the prerogative of the police.[14]

With DARE, the police transformed schools through both educative and disciplinary functions. This approach nuances the school-to-prison pipeline model's emphasis on enforcing zero-tolerance disciplinary policy, which misses how the basic role of schools—education—became entwined in what Erica Meiners has called the school-prison nexus.[15] Building on Carla Shedd's and Damien Sojoyner's respective work on schools as sites of enclosure and carceral continuum, I use the framing of a *school-police nexus* to explain the reciprocal and cooperative relationship that developed between the police and schools.[16] DARE's use of police officers as teachers co-opted the educative purpose of schools to advance the police mission by other means. Yet, for all the effort to humanize the police, DARE officers did not shed their law-and-order message or the threat of arrest and punishment when they entered the classroom. In the process, DARE blurred the line between the state's social welfare and social control functions, which made schools into spaces of police power under the guise of drug prevention. As a police-led drug education program, DARE normalized the belief that solving youth drug use was best left to law enforcement.

Drug education literature has, not incorrectly, approached DARE primarily as a drug education program and focused on questions of its effectiveness at preventing youth drug use. Such studies have shown how DARE was part of a larger ecosystem of drug prevention programs active in the 1980s and 1990s based on social influence and affective approaches to drug prevention, methods that departed from past models based on imparting basic knowledge of drugs or scare tactics. Instead, these new programs aimed to help kids develop social skills, enhance self-esteem, and resist peer pressure.[17] But, as these studies found, DARE did not prevent youth drug use.[18] As such, this book does not revolve around that question. Instead of thinking about DARE's significance solely in relation to drug prevention, it focuses on DARE as a police program, which suggests that its historical significance has less to do with preventing drug use and more to do with the ways an ostensibly educative program expanded the power of the police into new institutions and enshrined the police with new expertise, authority, and cultural visibility. While DARE was promoted as a nonpunitive and preventive program, it employed cops as teachers and stressed a zero-tolerance-for-drugs message that bound it within a carceral frame.

As DARE gained national stature, it also intersected with a range of political and cultural developments. As scholars have shown, the reinvention of the American family became a focal point of concern in the 1970s amidst sectoral shifts in the economy, the unmaking of the Fordist family wage, and changing sexual and cultural norms.[19] Within this context, the Reagan administration saw DARE as an opportunity to promote its moralizing messages of personal responsibility, respect for law and order, and the value of morally strengthened families by providing federal funding and rhetorical support. By presenting drug use as a matter of individual choice and calling on parents to rededicate themselves to family values, DARE's proponents inserted the program into the broader culture war and punitive logics of the Reagan era.[20] For all the political-cultural work DARE accomplished, it divorced drug use from social and economic conditions and structural inequalities, which ultimately bolstered the state's carceral approach to the drug problem.

DARE grew rapidly because it seemed to offer an alternative to the enforcement side of the war on drugs. As evidence of the failure of supply reduction mounted, members of Congress pushed for greater resources and attention to prevention to combat the demand for drugs. While scholars have pointed to the role of the 1986 and 1988 Anti-Drug Abuse Acts in ratcheting up sentencing and bolstering law enforcement, those acts also earmarked funds for antidrug education under the Drug Free Schools and Communities Act (DFSCA).[21] DFSCA funds facilitated DARE's growth and tied antidrug education programs to the carceral orientation of the drug war by emphasizing partnerships between schools and the police. Amendments to the DFSCA passed in 1989 referenced the use of police officers as instructors of antidrug education, and another in 1990 explicitly named DARE as a model program and required school districts to implement drug education programming to receive federal education funds. Within such a favorable context, DARE became a national leader in drug education. More than any other program, DARE had captured political support and visibility that enabled administrators to capitalize on federal funding for drug prevention and education.[22]

DARE's funding scheme was devolutionary and based on local government support, despite claims from DARE America, the nonprofit established as a 501(c)(3) in 1987 to oversee the program, that it was essentially a private program. Proponents routinely pointed to DARE as a cheap program costing about $12 per child. Yet the real economic costs were much higher, relying on "donated services and in-kind contributions" from local police departments amounting to more than $200 million annually at its peak.[23] Additionally, administrators often pointed to DARE America's private funding sources, notably corporate sponsorship, as evidence that it was not dependent on public support or resources, something that appealed to policymakers across the political spectrum amidst the neoliberal turn toward market logics and privatization. The mix of local funding, federal grants, private donations, and corporate largesse made DARE America an instrumental part of the shifting nature of governance and reliance on public-private partnerships in the late twentieth century, a trend that scholars of American political history have shown was central to neoliberal logics.[24] DARE America's reliance on private and public funding reflected broader changes in the state's role to address social problems while corporate sponsorship built on the desire to ensure a disciplined, drug-free workforce in the future. Yet, as the history of DARE reveals, the state never got out of the business of policing. DARE, in other words, was indicative of the shifting expectations of the state to provide little more than police services while relying on the family, the private sector, and entrepreneurialism to fill in for government action in a neoliberal age.

DARE's Rise and Fall

The first chapter recounts the origins of DARE. It shows how the idea for the program derived from calls by law enforcement and policymakers to focus on drug demand reduction, which led to a new school-police partnership. Beginning in the 1970s, the LAPD engaged in an all-out battle against drugs in the city's schools. Concerned about youth drug use, the LAPD implemented an undercover officer program aimed at arresting drug dealers on school campuses. After a decade of operation, however, the program had failed to reduce youth drug use. In response, LAPD chief of police Daryl Gates proposed a new program aimed at reducing demand in conjunction with the Los Angeles Unified School District (LAUSD), what would become project DARE. The most important innovation of the new program, the second chapter demonstrates, was the use of police officers as teachers. By putting police officers on the classroom beat, DARE intended to promote positive images of the police among youth, especially those who had historically had little reason to trust law enforcement. The DARE officer was, in short, meant to become a friend and mentor to students.

Within a matter of years DARE expanded to school districts across the country and dozens of countries around the world. As chapter 3 argues, it did so through a concerted campaign by DARE officials to promote the program and bring it to every classroom in the country. Support from Bureau of Justice Assistance grants enabled DARE officials to develop a network of regional training centers to dramatically expand DARE office training and program adoption. DARE also took advantage of federal antidrug education funds. Within such a favorable context, DARE became a national leader and political winner. Politicians used every opportunity to fawn over the program and highlight their support, none more so than presidents Reagan, Bush, and Clinton, who all recognized National DARE Day as part of an annual tradition.

Yet DARE's national stature did not derive solely from federal funding and political support. As chapter 4 shows, administrators formed the nonprofit organization DARE America to oversee fundraising, marketing, and program expansion. DARE America developed partnerships with a wide range of corporate sponsors, celebrities, and athletes to raise DARE's profile and visibility. Relying on public-private partnership and the neoliberal emphasis on entrepreneurialism over state action, DARE America aggressively marketed and sold merchandise ranging from T-shirts to Matchbox cars, a tactic that enhanced the program's cultural cachet and made the DARE logo a universal part of American culture in the 1990s.

Drug education was a key battleground in the burgeoning culture wars of the 1980s and 1990s. Chapter 5 shows how DARE's proponents weighed in on those battles, often promoting the program's ability to shore up so-called traditional morals, family values, and personal responsibility. Capitalizing on the moral panic surrounding violence in inner cities and the breakdown of the nuclear family in Black communities, DARE also reinforced racialized definitions of the middle-class nuclear family. DARE officials, in turn, used federal resources to create a parent curriculum in which police officers taught proper parenting techniques to discover and prevent drug use by their children.

Although taught in every state and in dozens of countries around the world, in the mid-1990s DARE came under fire as ineffective at preventing drug use. Social scientists demonstrated that DARE was ineffective and, in some cases, led to increased drug use, especially among suburban youth. At the same time, journalists uncovered stories of DARE students turning in their own parents for drug use, which produced national controversy and contributed to a growing anti-DARE parent movement. The sixth chapter centers the debates and controversies surrounding DARE during the Clinton administration. Although DARE's lack of effectiveness did not have an immediate impact on the program's popularity, the accumulation of negative evidence and critiques forced the program to reinvent itself by the end of the decade.

DARE did not disappear after the controversies of the 1990s and early 2000s. In fact, DARE continues to develop and provide drug education in schools across the country and internationally through its current program called "keepin' it REAL." The epilogue follows DARE into the twenty-first century and shows how it remains the subject of parody aimed at pointing out the ineffectiveness of drug education in both the past and present. As the persistence of DARE suggests, the carceral state extends well beyond the boundaries of the formal criminal punishment system, and law enforcement routinely and strategically positions itself to co-opt and control seemingly nonpolice programs.

A Note on Memory, DARE Officers, and the Politics of Parody

As many readers are likely thinking, they remember their DARE officer and recall fond, if now comical, memories of going through the DARE program. My memory of the program, which I had as a fifth grader in Salt Lake City, is much less detailed. The only things I remember of my DARE officer are that they wore their firearm to the classroom, which was supposedly not allowed, and that they scared me into thinking I would be forced to join a gang, racialized as Black or Latinx in my memory, if I did not listen to the police. In my mind, DARE thereby reinforced assumptions about race and criminalization and often preexisting commitments to personal responsibility and respect for law and order among middle-class white children.

Yet as many people of my generation have told me, how they think about and remember DARE is much different from my memory. The most common remark people make is some combination of DARE being a "joke," that it "didn't work," or that they smoked pot while wearing their DARE T-shirt. While I have no intention of challenging people's memories, these stories do not always align with the archival record (interviews and discussions with former DARE students tell a more nuanced story).[25] Children, in the evidence available from fifth graders at the time, often expressed reverence for their DARE officer, especially in their DARE essays, letters to DARE officers, and end-of-semester graduation ceremonies. While anecdotal and proscribed, much of the evidence from students who went through the program in the 1980s and 1990s is devoid of the cynicism that informs many people's memories and current views of the program. Part of what explains this dissonance, I think, is that DARE was taught primarily to fifth and sixth graders, an age well before many (but by no means all) children experimented with drugs, something that many of the program's evaluations conducted in the 1990s noted as a reason why DARE failed to prevent high schoolers from using drugs. When students grew older and entered high school, many likely looked back on DARE and their DARE T-shirt with a much different opinion and perspective. By that point, I imagine, many students would have been more willing to ask questions and understood that the consequences of trying drugs was not as dire as the DARE officer had implied. For others, especially students of color, the skepticism of DARE is rooted in a larger, and often justified, skepticism of the police due to the overpolicing and underprotection of their communities.

This is not to say that DARE has not been the subject of a wide range of parody and critique. One only has to search for DARE on Twitter or read the semiregular opinion piece about DARE that is published when someone mentions the program in public, such as when former attorney general Jeff Sessions praised DARE in 2017, to find the ways DARE continues to be ridiculed in public debate.[26] There have also been repeated instances of celebrities wearing DARE T-shirts, most notably when Serena Williams's husband Alexis Ohanian wore one to the US Open in 2019 to troll Williams's opponent, Maria Sharapova, who was returning to tennis after a suspension for doping violations.[27] I have also heard many stories from friends or acquaintances who recount how they or people they know still smoke pot in their DARE T-shirt to, in the words of one such person, "stick it to the man." While these episodes provide the opportunity for ridicule, such parody also operates as a strategic political critique about the program's approach to drug education and the need for a more holistic approach. We must, in other words, take the parody of DARE seriously as a form of political critique.[28]

While DARE officers may be the brunt of jokes, speaking to former DARE officers provides a different viewpoint. From my discussions with a handful of former DARE officers and DARE America officials, they believed wholeheartedly in the program and saw their role as a positive in children's lives. The cynicism of the broader public is entirely absent from these former officers' views. They were, and are, committed to helping prevent youth drug use. And, admittedly in contrast to my perspective, they believe police officers are the best teachers to help students learn to avoid drugs, be responsible, be law abiding, and relate to the police.

As readers will gather, this is not a book that seeks to reevaluate whether DARE worked to prevent drug use. That debate was largely settled in the 1990s by researchers and prevention experts who are much more qualified to assess drug prevention programs than I am. While most studies of DARE showed it was ineffective at preventing drug use, especially over the long term, other programs showed more promise. Programs that focused on social influence, refusal, and competency skills and took an instructional approach that was interactive, including student participation and engagement, were more effective than noninteractive programs, such as DARE.[29] In short, criticism of DARE does not mean that all drug prevention programs are necessarily bad or ineffective. More recently, educators and prevention experts have promoted a wide range of other programs, including many using harm reduction methods. For instance, the Drug Policy Alliance has developed an "accurate, honest, compassionate drug education" curriculum called "Safety First: Real Drug Education for Teens." These approaches reject the zero-tolerance and abstinence model of drug education that DARE was part of. In contrast, they focus on honest conversations about drugs and the development of skills to help students navigate the various risks of drug use in an informed and knowledgeable way.[30]

However, DARE was successful by a variety of other metrics, namely the perceived benefits of having police officers enter schools as teachers, facilitating a humane and friendly relationship with children, and bolstering the image of the police among a generation of youth. While many observers may see DARE as preferable to arrest or incarceration, normalizing police in schools by turning instruction over to the police reinforced the idea that drug use was a criminal issue rather than one of public health. Just because it was educative rather than overtly punitive did not mean that DARE was immune from the adverse consequences or implications of the broader drug war, which fueled criminalization and punitive policies in the late twentieth century. If we want to understand how the police worked to position themselves as powerful entities in American social, political, and cultural life, we must reckon with DARE.

This is hardly an uncritical view of the DARE program. As a historian of American policing and race who has written critically of police power, I am highly skeptical of a police-led educational project. After the establishment of DARE and the deployment of the DARE officer as the solution to youth drug use, there was almost no approach to preventing drug use that did not involve police. Even drug education programs would rely on uniformed law enforcement officers as teachers. DARE, quite simply, defined drug use, and related social issues, as a problem to be solved solely by the police. Nowhere was this development more prevalent than in Los Angeles, the city where DARE got its start and where this book begins.

CHAPTER ONE

DARE to Keep Kids off Drugs

DARE was a product of failure.

After nearly a decade, the Los Angeles Police Department's (LAPD) campaign to reduce the supply of drugs on the city's streets through an all-out attack on drug pushers had, by the early 1980s, been largely unsuccessful. As chief of police Daryl Gates explained in the 1983 LAPD Annual Report, "Drug use has become so commonplace and traffic in drugs so enormously profitable, that all efforts of law enforcement have failed to bring the problem under anything approaching adequate control."[1] Though Gates still believed in the importance of asserting aggressive police power through antidrug raids and gang sweeps to winning the so-called war on drugs, at one point even telling a congressional committee, "The casual user ought to be taken out and shot," he admitted that such tactics were not enough to stop the perceived explosion in drug use.[2] It was time for something new.

As of 1983, what Gates had in mind was a shift in targets. As he wrote, "It became obvious to the Department that conduct of the war locally against narcotics called for a new approach, one aimed directly at a new generation of potential users in the sound belief that once the market for controlled substances diminished, so would their availability." After all, Gates reasoned, "Demand always governs supply."[3]

Instead of attempting to take drugs off the street and away from users, targeting demand flipped the script by aiming to take the users away from drugs. While this could mean increasing penalties and arrests for drug use in hopes of encouraging people to avoid using or experimenting with drugs, it also meant expanding the police mission to the realm of prevention and into places, such as schools, where they had not always been warmly welcomed.[4] This facet of law enforcement's demand reduction mission often focused on intervening in the lives of children before they had ever contemplated trying drugs, let alone using or committing drug-related crime. It was proactive and meant the police were trying to influence children at earlier ages before they would have ever previously had contact with the police.

When Gates's program arrived in the fall of 1983, it went by the name Project DARE (Drug Abuse Resistance Education). Developed with the Los

Angeles Unified School District (LAUSD), its goal was to reduce demand for drugs by teaching the city's youth how to just say no. In short order, DARE became the primary means by which law enforcement hoped to solve the problem of youth drug use.

This chapter traces the establishment of the most visible and well-known demand reduction program of the 1980s and 1990s. After years of dealer arrests did little to reduce the demand for drugs, police leadership all but admitted the impossibility of curtailing drug use through enforcement alone. But instead of relinquishing the task to another agency, LAPD officials expanded the remit of police to include working directly with kids, creating an educational program that required the presence of officers in schools as teachers.[5] By focusing on the demand side of the drug equation and turning to prevention rather than enforcement, law enforcement officials and policymakers suggested they were shifting the drug war's targets from sellers to users.[6] However, in practice, emphasizing drug prevention did not mean an end to drug enforcement or the targeting of users for arrest and incarceration. Demand reduction operated within the Reagan-era political context favoring the eradication of all drug use by the nation's youth, which enabled the carceral state to expand from within schools under the guise of prevention.

DARE was forged into a cooperative program that helped build a school-police nexus in which police ideas and personnel flowed into schools through education rather than discipline, and, in turn, schools influenced policing by helping to soften the image of the police as responsive to community concerns. The police became a regular presence in the lives of all kids but especially so for Black and Latinx youth who also experienced overpolicing in their neighborhoods when they left school.

A Product of Failed Drug Policy

Since the apex of the war on drugs in the 1980s, the LAPD had already spent decades fighting drug sales on school campuses. While the department engaged in rudimentary drug education and eradication efforts in schools during the 1940s and 1950s, department brass turned attention to the drug problem more directly in the late 1960s and 1970s following fears of a gang crisis and drug-fueled rise in youth crime and truancy. In response, the department created a program in which undercover officers were placed in high schools to catch and arrest drug sellers during a panic over a perceived growth in youth crime.[7]

Starting in September 1974, eleven undercover officers were placed in twenty-four Los Angeles–area high schools. "It appeared that, contrary to general opinion, the use of drugs among students was a present and growing problem," according to an LAPD report to the LAUSD. "More to the point, the schools in our community were becoming sanctuaries for drug distribution." The program aimed to reduce drug use through enforcing drug laws in and around schools. It was decidedly not a prevention program; it rested on a firm distinction of responsibilities between schools and law enforcement. "The schools are responsible for education," the LAPD's Juvenile Division reported on the program's first year. "The police are responsible for identifying and repressing crime wherever it occurs. Accepting this responsibility, the Los Angeles Police Department initiated a pilot program by placing one undercover officer, posing as a student, in Wilson High School."[8] With the placement of undercover officers in schools, the School Buy Program was born.

Crucially, the initiative originated from a belief that all efforts to curtail the "drug culture" on school campuses during the 1950s and 1960s, including education and prevention programs focused on providing students with information about how to identify drugs and lessons aimed at scaring kids with stories about the harm of drugs, had failed. As an LAPD report on the progress made by the School Buy Program in its first year explained, "Law enforcement and the schools tried every other means to curtail the drug culture on our campuses—education, persuasion, and peer pressure, to name only a few. All failed."[9] For the police, rampant "criminality" and drug use on school campuses required them to intervene by targeting the supply of drugs by focusing on arresting dealers. Four years before he became chief of police, then assistant chief Daryl Gates explained in a 1974 defense of undercover policemen in schools, "In the case of narcotics and drugs, we the police had no alternative but to use undercover officers in schools to fulfill our obligation to the community."[10]

As Gates suggested in his description of the police department's responsibility to aid the community by enforcing drug laws, the School Buy Program did not alter the distinct roles police and teachers played in schools, a line DARE later blurred by using police officers as instructors. During the 1970s, educators were not expected to wage the drug war in their classrooms through enforcement. Only the police, acting as police, had the ability and authority to curtail drug trafficking in the city's schools. "Teachers cannot be expected to function as cops on campus. Teachers can only be expected to teach," Gates reasoned. The same went for parents. "Parents cannot

Undercover School Buy LAPD officers Dwane White (left) and Yolanda Gonzales (middle) at a press conference with Chief Daryl Gates. Anne Knudsen, May 21, 1986, Herald Examiner Collection, Los Angeles Public Library, Los Angeles, California.

function as cops on campus," Gates continued. "Parents can only be expected to raise their children with the best values possible." Waging the drug war was therefore best left to the police. "Who is expected to provide protection from criminality on the campus?" Gates asked rhetorically. "The police. The police are hired by our community, which certainly includes our students, parents and teachers, to protect their community, which certainly includes school campuses."[11] According to Gates, the police had only one function that neither teachers nor parents could fill: drug enforcement.

Viewed in terms of arrests and confiscations, the School Buy Program was deemed wildly successful by law enforcement officials. During its first year of operation, undercover officers arrested 211 drug dealers, roughly 180 (over 85 percent) of whom were juveniles, and confiscated $20,650 worth of narcotics.[12] Arrests and seizures only increased through the 1970s and into the 1980s. High-profile drug busts on school campuses often made news in the *Los Angeles Times*, and undercover officers praised the program. "There's no question that the program is still the most effective method to combat drug dealing at high schools," Gates reported at a press conference after a bust of 105 drug suspects in December 1982.[13] Undercover operations, arrests, and publicity, it seemed, would only continue.

Undercover officers not only conducted busts at schools but also followed potential dealers to houses near schools where drug transactions occurred. Between February 9, 1988, and May 18, 1988, for instance, officers working in the buy program made more than 230 drug purchases on high school campuses and surrounding neighborhoods. In the program's first fourteen years of operation, according to LAPD data, 4,670 suspects had been arrested in 251 schools, leading to an estimated 90 percent conviction rate and seizure of narcotics valued at over $854,000. The LAPD lauded the program as "so successful" that they had trained personnel from other Southern California law enforcement agencies to carry out similar school buy procedures.[14] LAPD officials touted the program as a successful strategy to reduce the supply of drugs on school campuses by targeting drug sales and dealers. They continued to promote the program's effectiveness at combating drug trafficking in and around schools throughout the 1980s. As the department reported in a 1988 press release, "The Los Angeles Police Department will continue to assist and cooperate with school administrators toward the goal of providing our youth with a learning environment that is safe and drug free. Hopefully with increased public awareness, parental and student support, that goal will become a reality." Yet in an indication of the limits of the program's efficacy, the LAPD admitted, "the use of illicit drugs by high school age children remains high."[15]

Local activists and residents grew vocal as evidence accumulated showing student rights violations and the program's inability to actually reduce drug use. Civil liberties groups and representatives of the LAUSD's Black and Mexican American students criticized the program. The Mexican American Education Commission, for instance, opposed the program due to its disproportionate impact on students of color and because it made the school an extension of the police department rather than the home.[16] Similarly, the ACLU filed lawsuits out of concern for due process and civil liberties violations.[17] As the ACLU mocked the program: "When other adults try to get young people involved with drugs, we call it contributing to the delinquency of a minor. When the LAPD does it, we call it the school-buy program."[18] Perhaps the most notable controversy emerged when one of the undercover female officers was found to have engaged in an "improper" romantic relationship with a football player at Granada Hills High School. Despite such legal challenges, courts legitimated the program as constitutional, and it persisted through the 1980s.[19]

The LAPD undoubtedly knew its program was not reducing youth drug use. During the years the School Buy Program was operational, drug use among school-age youth actually increased. One undercover officer involved in the program reported in 1983 that 75 to 80 percent of Los Angeles high school students had used some form of narcotics at least once. More alarming for local officials, they believed 40 to 50 percent used narcotics two to three times a week, and 15 to 20 percent were under the influence of drugs "most of the time." Drug use had also filtered down to junior high and elementary schools, and some experts argued that kids as young as twelve years old used marijuana on a regular basis. Yet arresting drug dealers had done little to address the reasons why the city's youth turned toward drugs in the first place.[20]

Evidence of youth drug use, particularly marijuana and alcohol in suburban schools and PCP in urban schools, led to fears of a drug crisis that the LAPD's School Buy Program had failed to prevent. "Los Angeles has a staggering drug-abuse problem and it, unfortunately, is descending the age ladder," the LAPD and LAUSD warned. "We are now seeing chronic marijuana use by 12 year olds and even younger. It must be noted that PCP is frequently used by juveniles in the Los Angeles area and its epidemic proportions give serious cause for alarm."[21] Indeed, Daryl Gates described drugs as an existential threat to the city and its children. "By far the greatest common danger threatening the safety of the people of Los Angeles is narcotics and dangerous drugs," Gates wrote in the 1983 LAPD Annual Report. "That present peril exceeds even the threat of future nuclear annihilation because the danger no longer is simply a threat, but a fact of life and death. No more deadly plague ever invaded our shores. . . . If our children are to survive, steps must be taken to turn them away from narcotics and dangerous drugs before they reap the whirlwind which their elders so recklessly are sowing."[22] Something more, and different, had to be done.

Alarmed by the belief that kids had easy access to drugs and alcohol, Gates and other law enforcement officials began to rethink the overwhelming focus on supply reduction activities. As LAPD Lt. Patrick Froehle and future deputy director of DARE America, the nonprofit organization formed in 1987 to manage DARE as it expanded nationwide, recalled in the early 1990s, "We were arresting more people than ever. We were confiscating more drugs than ever, and the problem wasn't going away."[23] Clearly, arrest, incarceration, and forfeiture had done little to solve the demand for drugs on the streets of

Los Angeles. Nor had it done much to reduce the supply of drugs. "L.A. is knee-deep in drugs," deputy chief Glenn Levant admitted in 1988. "When all is over and done with, it's the demand for drugs that is killing this nation."[24] Supply reduction had not only failed to reduce the availability of drugs but had also done little to prevent use, especially among the city's youth. "Enforcement of narcotic violations," LAPD officials readily admitted, "has proven to be ineffective in combating substance abuse by our children."[25]

Many educators, policymakers, and law enforcement officials agreed that a shift in focus would be essential for saving America's youth. Carlton Turner, Reagan's first director of the Drug Abuse Policy Office, told a congressional committee in 1983 that there needed to be "a broad effort directed at all links in the chain from producer to user. Stated simply, we must take the drugs away from the user through supply reduction efforts and take the user away from the drugs through prevention, education, and treatment." Drug policy experts emphasized the need to address the demand side through education programs aimed at the nation's youth. As Turner told the same congressional committee, "Our No. 1 priority overall has to be to reduce the drug abuse habits of young Americans and of Americans in general. That is the priority. . . . So I think the No. 1 priority, if you have to identify one, is to have a long-term education prevention program."[26] Antidrug education was the consensus means for dealing with the demand for drugs among the nation's children.

But the focus on demand did not have the same meaning for all kids. The parent movement, a grassroots movement of largely suburban white parents who had become concerned with youth drug use in the late 1970s, focused the Reagan administration's attention on marijuana use by white suburban teenagers. Indeed, antimarijuana parent organizations, such as the National Parents' Resource Institute for Drug Education (PRIDE), which joined with parent groups from across the country to form the National Federation of Parents for Drug Free Youth (NFP) in 1980, drove the Reagan administration's domestic drug policies through the mid-1980s. These policies shielded white youth from criminal prosecution by emphasizing preventing marijuana use while enhancing policing and punishment for drug traffickers who lured suburban youth into drug addiction.[27]

Calls for demand-side programs by parents continued to grow, especially after 1985 when news of crack cocaine's spread from inner cities to suburbs further alarmed many white parents and policymakers. As *Newsweek* noted in 1986, "In part, the change in the public mood has a racist tinge: drugs simply have moved from the black and Hispanic underclass to the middle-class mainstream and are being felt as a problem there."[28] Reagan's focus on addressing the concerns of the middle-class parent movement had some success, as the National Institute on Drug Abuse (NIDA) found that drug use had dropped 37 percent between 1985 and 1989. Much of this decline came from "casual users" defined largely as middle-class whites.[29] Arrest and incarceration, in other words, were viable strategies when the drug problem was perceived to most directly impact communities of color. When suburban white children were threatened by drug use, in contrast, prevention and demand reduction gained adherents in the Reagan administration.

Within this broader context of discussions related to demand reduction, the police, rather than allowing other institutions and actors to take up the effort, looked to take control of preventing the nation's children from seeking drugs. The comprehensive approach LAPD chief Gates had in mind would entail deploying police into schools directly, not to enact discipline but to take part in children's education. As Gates recalled in 1993, "We kept buying more and more [drugs on school campuses]. It was appalling, depressing. I finally said: 'This is crazy. We've got to do something.'"[30]

Project DARE

Fear of a generation lost to drugs required a new solution aimed at ensuring kids never used drugs. Building on Glenn Levant's effort in the early 1980s to develop crime prevention programs in the city, Gates approached the Los Angeles Board of Education in January 1983 to discuss the problem of drug use in the city's schools. Gates came to those meetings armed with data and an idea. He described the perpetual problem of drug use among the city's youth and asked the board members to work with the police to develop a new program to teach elementary school children and their parents about the harmful effects of drugs before students became habitual drug users in high school. Antidrug education, Gates would later claim, was the "only answer . . . the ultimate answer" to solving the demand-side problem of the drug crisis.[31] Convinced by Gates's presentation, the LAUSD board agreed to form a joint task force to develop a new demand reduction program to reach kids before they became involved with drugs.[32]

The idea for a drug-use prevention program taught in schools was not new. Los Angeles schools had drug education programs going back to at least the 1930s.[33] The LAUSD had also developed a comprehensive strategy and procedures for dealing with student drug use, possession, and sale in the

1970s. As outlined, the procedures required notifying law enforcement agencies but framed the problem of drug use in schools as one to be handled through an internal process of deliberation, notification of parents, and cooperation with law enforcement only when absolutely necessary. These procedures emphasized the importance of local control at the school level.[34] Meanwhile, police had long been involved with young people through Police Athletic Leagues, community relations programming, and Officer Friendly presentations. The LAPD, for instance, had even piloted a program called Police Role in Government in the late 1960s and early 1970s where police officers would serve as teachers in predominantly Black and Latinx schools.[35] None of these police-led programs, however, were particularly long-lasting nor did they integrate the police into the daily life of the schools through education as DARE would.

By 1983 the LAUSD was also already testing an experimental early intervention program called Project SMART (Self-Management and Resistance Training). Part of a new type of social influence approach to prevention programming which aimed to help students develop social skills and resistance training, Project SMART was developed by prevention researchers affiliated with the Health Behavior Research Institute at the University of Southern California, including Dr. Andy Johnson, Bill Hansen, and doctoral candidate Luanne Rohrbach.[36] After meeting with LAUSD board members, Gates approached Project SMART researchers and offered the services of police officers to deliver the SMART curriculum. But the USC researchers, according to Johnson, were wary of police officers bearing antidrug lesson plans, due in part to concern about the LAPD's us-versus-them attitude toward communities of color, and bowed out of the proposed collaboration. Undeterred, Gates pushed ahead anyway.[37]

Over the summer of 1983, the LAPD worked with the LAUSD's curriculum and health education specialist Dr. Ruth Rich to develop a blueprint for a comprehensive plan for substance abuse education for Los Angeles city schools.[38] With permission from SMART researchers, Rich adopted various elements of the Project SMART curriculum—including a non-SMART comparison program based on "affective" education (such as promoting self-esteem and decision-making skills) that SMART researchers found led to increased drug use and, having removed it from SMART, did not recommend adopting—into a drug prevention curriculum to be taught by police officers in a pilot program during the fall of 1983.[39] The "new" program, which combined elements of the resistance-training model and, though unclear why, the ineffective "affective" education component,[40] became part of the LAPD and LAUSD's plan to, in the words of Gates and Handler, "*institutionalize* substance abuse prevention efforts" using police officers as instructors.[41]

The developers named it Project DARE, and it marked a departure from earlier police-led youth programs for at least two reasons. First, DARE deployed uniformed officers as teachers to instruct students in a standardized curriculum on a regular and ongoing basis. Cops were, ostensibly, not in schools to enforce disciplinary policies or drug laws as they had with the School Buy Program. They were there to teach and to expand police power through the educative function of schools. Second, the DARE curriculum shifted drug education from warning students about the dangers of drugs to teaching decision-making skills, resistance to peer pressure, and techniques to enhance self-esteem. Focusing on schools as sites to intervene in youth behavior, DARE deployed police officers to promote a message about personal responsibility and respect for law and order that rooted the cause of drug use in individual decision-making and choice.

With Project DARE, then, school and police officials built on the belief that a cooperative approach to reducing demand was a necessary component of the drug war. School superintendent Harry Handler promoted the program and curriculum as a sea change in the school district's war on drugs, explaining, "This will be a more intensive program than what we were able to provide in health classes in the past. It also means a new approach by the police toward preventive action rather than just the enforcement of drug laws."[42] More than solely focused on prevention, DARE was designed, according to DARE America, "to build trust between the schools and law enforcement."[43] To do so, the LAPD and LAUSD entered into formal agreements outlining this new cooperative strategy, implicitly blurring prevention and enforcement efforts. The first joint agreement between the LAPD and LAUSD stated simply, "The program's objectives are to prevent and/or reduce substance abuse among school age children and youth."[44] The key to reducing demand, organizers believed, was effective education that helped students learn "how" to say no when offered or pressured to use drugs. "DARE," the LAPD explained in its 1988 Annual Report, "would fill this demand reduction role by ensuring that youth would say 'no' to drug use."[45]

Teaching kids how to say no was a means to solve what law enforcement believed was the underlying cause of drug use among youth, namely poor self-esteem and peer pressure. "Most strategies in the war against drugs attack the symptoms not the underlying causes of substance abuse," suggested DARE program directors. "Peer pressure and the desire to 'fit in' are the primary reasons young people try drugs and alcohol. More attention must be placed on bolstering a sense of self-worth in our children in an attempt to make them 'drug proof'—resistant to pressure from friends and the impact of advertising."[46] Elementary students, officers believed, were also at risk of peer pressure from older students. "Older children will contaminate youngsters in terrible numbers unless we build an immunity to that contamination," stated LAPD commander William Booth.[47] Setting aside the social and economic conditions that led to drug use, law enforcement and school officials focused on individual behavior. DARE would "attack the problem of drug-abuse through early educational intervention stressing value decisions, self-concept improvement and peer pressure resistance training."[48]

Educators and health experts intended for DARE to be different from previous drug education programs that operated largely on scare tactics and knowledge about drugs. Much of the focus of these programs centered on showing kids different types of drugs—using display boards of drugs or "*candid photographs* from the drug scene"—to scare students straight.[49] Fear-based drug prevention had clearly not worked, and education and health specialists had begun to develop new programs based on psychosocial approaches.[50] Officers involved in DARE envisioned the program as a departure from the "reefer-madness" style of scare films characteristic of antidrug education in the 1950s. As one officer explained, "It was clear to us during that research phase that for far too long, we in law enforcement and in education for that matter, had dealt with education on a scare-tactic approach; that is to say, we would teach young children the pharmacology and symptomology of various illicit substances, and we told them marijuana is cannibis [*sic*] sativa. . . . We had to come up with a comprehensive positive program, teach children how to say no."[51]

As DARE's curriculum materialized, it dispensed with the traditional scare tactics and focus on the harm of drugs (at least in theory), opting instead for the mix of affective and social influence approaches, which included efforts to enhance self-esteem, personal responsibility, and resistance to peer pressure. "Because the goal of prevention requires an attitudinal change in students, the traditional approach of teaching substance identification and emphasizing the dangers of abuse was abandoned," reported Ruth Rich, the LAUSD specialist who helped design the original DARE curriculum. "A curriculum which addresses value decisions, self-concept improvement, respect for the law, and peer resistance training was developed instead."[52] In these ways DARE reinforced a get-tough logic through an emphasis on behavior, personal responsibility, and the consequences of poor choices.

Initially, the program consisted of fifteen lessons presented every other week to fifth- and sixth-grade students. The curriculum was later expanded to seventeen lessons, including anti-gang and social support system lessons that replaced an officer-planned lesson and alternative activities lesson (see Appendix: Table 1). Between the first- and second-year implementation, the LAPD's DARE administrators also replaced the lesson on "Vandalism" with an expanded session on "Consequences," reflecting the focus on individual decisions and choice.[53] DARE lessons, which lasted forty-five to sixty minutes, focused on building student self-esteem, based on the belief that students with a positive self-image would be better able to say no when offered drugs. DARE officers taught kids a variety of "Ways to Say No" when offered drugs, such as "Saying 'No thanks,'" "Giving a reason or excuse," "Broken record or saying no as many times as necessary," "Walking away," "Changing the subject," "Avoid the situation," "Cold shoulder," in which students learned to turn their back on drug dealers, and "Strength in Numbers," which promoted hanging out with nonusers and one officer later described as being "like the power of a gang, but in a positive way. Nobody's going to mess with you."[54] These lessons were imparted by the DARE officer with supplemental materials, such as the DARE student workbook, which included worksheets, advice for the DARE question box, the DARE word list, and a series of activities students would complete over the course of the program.[55]

Administrators designed the DARE program to reach kids before they experimented with alcohol and drugs. Because students were more likely to experiment with drugs during the high school years, DARE targeted fifth and sixth graders, an age when experts believed kids became aware of drugs and before junior high school, when educators and law enforcement officials believed "experimentation" with drugs occurred.[56] "You still have this whole generation and a half of people who are into drugs, and into drugs deeply—a lot more than people realize," Gates said, explaining the theory behind DARE's focus on elementary-age students. "They're going to move on. Then you bring the new generation on, which is not drug-oriented, not involved to the extent this generation and a half are, and hopefully that will reduce the problem."[57]

Educators and law enforcement officers readily admitted that elementary school children were not the primary users of drugs or the cause of drug-related crime. They were far younger than the high schoolers who accounted for most of the juvenile drug arrests for narcotics violations. "Most juvenile felony crimes are not committed by the elementary or junior high school age children which DARE targets," DARE officials explained. "It is anticipated that a significant reduction in the percentage of these types of crises will be realized when DARE students reach high school age."[58]

Focusing on elementary school students was part of the growing concern for the future of the nation's children. "Without effective intervention, society may be rearing a generation dependent on substance abuse," the LAPD and LAUSD warned in a joint grant proposal to fund DARE after its first-year pilot program. "This trend must be reversed to insure [*sic*] a future of generationally mature men and women able to keep society strong and healthy."[59] In the process, DARE positioned itself as a protector of both childhood innocence and future success, which made it extremely popular and politically attractive. After all, who could be against a program meant to prevent childhood drug use, even if it involved the police as teachers?[60]

In DARE's first year in Los Angeles schools, ten LAPD officers were assigned to a full-time classroom "beat"—notably adopting the parlance of a police officer's street "beat"—with each officer responsible for instructing fifth- and sixth-grade classes in five schools. Officers visited a different school each day of the week throughout the entire school year. Administrators chose fifty elementary schools to receive DARE instruction in its pilot year (see Appendix: Table 2). They included schools from across the school district and at least one school from every city council district, suggesting that the program was meant to be universal.[61]

By the mid-1980s, however, the district was overwhelmingly Latinx with Black students making up the second-largest student group. In 1970, for example, the LAUSD was nearly 50 percent white, 24 percent Black, and 22 percent Hispanic. In 1977, however, the district had become 34 percent white, 35 percent Hispanic, and nearly 25 percent Black.[62] In short, DARE was implemented in a predominantly Latinx school district with Black students as the second-largest student group. White students had declined to a mere 18 percent of the district.[63] These demographic realities ensured that students of color came into near-daily contact with police both in their neighborhoods and in their classrooms. As one early program evaluation reported, Latinx and Black students were overrepresented in the sample while white students surveyed were below the city average, suggesting that DARE disproportionately targeted Black and Latinx schools and students.[64] While never explicitly described as a program targeting kids of color, due to the LAUSD demographics, DARE disproportionately impacted children whom both the police and many educators viewed as lacking moral values, prone to criminality, and products of broken families.[65]

In its first year, DARE significantly expanded police contact with teachers, students, and parents. DARE officers taught 87,762 elementary students in some part of the DARE curriculum, 311 teachers participated in in-service drug awareness training led by DARE officers, and officers held nearly 200 parent meetings attended by 16,698 people. All told, 105,071 people had "at least one formal session with a DARE officer."[66] The program, which many officers initially dismissed as an updated form of the "kiddie cops" community relations programs of the 1950s and 1960s, would gain widespread acceptance, respect, and status by the late 1980s. As one officer summarized the pride of becoming a DARE officer, "Yep—a 6'8", 280 lb. street cop who went off to D.A.R.E. land to become a 'kiddie cop.' That was ten years ago, and now, after all those years of being a D.A.R.E. cop, I'm at the top of my game. I became one of ten state D.A.R.E. trainers and just recently attended classes in Los Angeles for the D.A.R.E. Mentor Program."[67] While DARE officers would face ridicule and critique, for some, DARE provided a route to status and promotion in which they saw their actions having a positive impact on children.

By emphasizing weekly contact between elementary school students and police officers serving as teachers, administrators designed DARE to intervene in the lives of potential young drug users. It also marked a departure from prior approaches to antidrug education. In the process, DARE normalized the presence of police in schools and bridged the divide between supply and demand approaches to the drug war.

The Threatening Inner City: Gangs, Drugs, and Race

If the LAPD used the argument of drug use's universality to promote DARE, the program disproportionately impacted Black and Latinx youth in Los Angeles. Though rarely, if ever, mentioning race, DARE administrators deployed coded language and messages to promote the program that Angelenos would have understood as inherently racialized. With the introduction of crack cocaine during the early 1980s, the LAPD further fueled the racialized panic of African American drug gangs ravaging the streets of Los Angeles. Notably, in 1981 the *Los Angeles Times* fueled fears of young African Americans from South Central who "prey upon the suburban middle and upper classes. Sometimes with senseless savagery." In the front-page story, headlined "Marauders from Inner City Prey on L.A.'s Suburbs," reporters described the city's ghettos and barrios as "staging grounds" for robbers and thieves, described as marauders, who used the region's extensive freeway network to infiltrate white suburbs. While violence was certainly a serious social problem in Los Angeles, such stories relied on the uncritical acceptance of the words of police and prosecutors and fueled stereotypes about race and criminality among white residents.[68] Meanwhile, exposés on crack and gang violence in Los Angeles were routinely splashed on national newsmagazines such as *Newsweek* and *Time*.[69] These stories fed growing fears of inner-city drug use and violence spreading to suburban neighborhoods and the inability of aggressive law enforcement measures to prevent white kids from becoming victims of the drug war and its violence.

Police strategies associated with the drug war, in turn, disproportionately targeted inner-city Black and Latinx neighborhoods despite estimates that roughly 70 percent of monthly drug users were white. Drug arrests reflected this racially disproportionate policing. African Americans accounted for 21 percent of arrests for drug possession in 1980 though only constituting 13 percent of the U.S. population. Punitive approaches also produced vast racial disparities in sentencing. Most notably, the 1986 Anti-Drug Abuse Act established harsh mandatory minimum sentences for distribution of crack cocaine, which disproportionately fell on African Americans, with less severe punishments for powder cocaine, often associated with whites. Incarceration rates, in turn, reflected these racial disparities. Between 1983 and 2000, for instance, prison admission rates for African American drug offenders grew twenty-six times while the rate for whites increased by only eight.[70]

When describing the program's necessity for all classrooms in the city, DARE boosters often referred to gang violence and drug trafficking that the media outlets, local policymakers, and the police had long associated with Black communities in South Central. DARE was no exception in the deployment of coded language and references to the perceived violent, inner-city Black communities in need of help. "Street gangs," the LAPD reported in a 1989 grant application to expand DARE into high schools, "involving some 30,000 youths, have become involved in the estimated $130 billion dollar a year drug trade." The "escalation of trafficking and abuse of cocaine in Southern California" by street gang members led to a dramatic increase in drug seizures and the arrest of more than 12,000 residents for the sale of cocaine. According to the LAPD, crack sales by street gangs, implicitly understood as African American due to racialized portrayals of "drug gangs" by media and law enforcement, represented the greatest threat to the city's youth.[71] Due to the widespread media attention to the Bloods and Crips, the African American gangs that originated in South Central, few funding agencies, policymakers, and residents would have mistaken such references to "drug-trafficking gangs" for anything but a not-so-subtle reference to the department's war on gangs and association of crack cocaine with Black communities.[72]

Focusing attention on crack cocaine, however, did not align with the reality of drug use among the city's youth. Labeled a "generation at risk" by the California attorney general, many kids and teenagers, according to the LAPD's own data, had experimented with alcohol or marijuana, not crack cocaine. Emphasizing the dangers of crack cocaine and the relationship to gang violence while describing a color-blind antidrug education program legitimized the LAPD's racialized war on drugs on city streets. While LAPD brass were concerned about the conditions faced by children in neighborhoods with high rates of gang violence and drug crime, such feelings and the promotion of DARE as a means to prevent these problems did not exist outside the LAPD's punitive war on drugs and gangs, which added to the violence in many neighborhoods.[73]

DARE operated in lockstep with the LAPD's broader war on drugs and the media's framing of the crack cocaine crisis as a problem of the so-called inner city that had come to be associated with Black communities. Assistant Chief Robert Vernon, for instance, singled out "inner cities" as the root of the problem that DARE attempted to redress. In a speech to the National Association of Evangelicals in 1985 he explained, "There's a lot of bloodshed occurring in our inner cities. Once again, remember, as goes the cities so goes the nation. We can't isolate ourselves and say, well that's a problem of the inner city, let's don't worry, let's just contain it there. Folks, this is our country, the inner cities are our country, it's our heartbeat, it's our neighborhood. We should be concerned."[74] In turn, Vernon singled out "powerful drug trafficking organizations" in "inner cities" for special attention by police and policymakers. While acknowledging that the drug abuse problem was beginning to infiltrate the suburbs and expressing legitimate concern for "inner-city" neighborhoods, Vernon and other officials capitalized on the politically and media-constructed fears of the racialized, dangerous inner city to expand both policing and prevention projects in all schools. Even as school districts across the country used DARE, it contributed to the moral panic and political construction of inner-city crack use, drug gangs, and the breakdown of the Black family.[75] The introduction of DARE, in short, did not mean an end to the aggressive police presence in Black communities and should be understood as a component of the larger war on drugs, not a replacement for the expression of punitive police power.

DARE representatives also played on racialized tropes of crack-addicted mothers who gave birth to "crack babies" when defining the scope of the problem that DARE addressed. LAPD commander Walter Mitchell, for instance, implied as much in testimony about DARE and drug education programs to a congressional committee in 1990. "There is no question that the magnitude of drug abuse and gang violence in our society is high and spills over to the schools, especially with the increase in the use of crack cocaine in the last few years," Mitchell outlined. "The most innocent victims are babies born to cocaine-addicted mothers, the so-called crack babies. The babies are usually underweight and sometimes are mentally or physically deformed and addicted to drugs for life."[76] DARE presented the solution to this purported problem as a matter of teaching children to say no and to take personal responsibility for their actions. In the process, DARE contributed to the stigmatization of Black women while ignoring the cuts in social services and economic devastation fueling drug trafficking and use in many communities of color.[77]

Despite the overpolicing in Black communities, DARE relied on colorblind rhetoric of the drug problem as one that crossed neighborhood, race, and class. Indeed, when submitting grant proposals for DARE to the California Office of Criminal Justice Planning (OCJP) and to the Bureau of Justice Assistance, the LAPD repeatedly discussed the problem of drug abuse as universal. "All children, regardless of social-economic status or geographic location, have a high risk of developing drug-abuse behavior patterns. LAUSD and LAPD data have proven beyond any doubt that this potential is not unique to any single school or segment of the population, nor is it restricted to any particular locale."[78] Such pronouncements enabled the LAPD and LAUSD to promote their efforts as colorblind and universal while also deploying fears of gang violence that many would have understood to be targeted at the city's Black communities who were most in need of intervention.

Though rarely overtly mentioning race, DARE boosters in Los Angeles often referenced gang violence to justify the drug prevention program. The oft-used reference by DARE grant writers to "distribution of drugs by gang members," for instance, played on media and policymaker-constructed stereotypes of the dangerous inner-city and African American youth gang members involved in the organized drug trade. While these issues were certainly real for many communities, they were also part of a broader, media-fueled moral panic related to drugs.[79] In relying on these ideas, the program's proponents conveyed the message that DARE was especially necessary for kids of color. "I thought I was tough," DARE's Glenn Levant explained. "But the stories we hear from kids makes you cry. . . . Kids fall asleep in class because the gunfire keeps them up all night."[80] In upper-middle-class suburbs, such stories of gun violence and gang activity likely were something only heard on the nightly news.

As deployed by DARE officials, the fear of violence and crime associated with gangs and drug trafficking built on racialized fears of the inner city threatening to inundate innocent white suburbs. Indeed, fears of Black people moving to predominantly white neighborhoods, such as from Chicago or Milwaukee to Wausau, Wisconsin, bringing with them drugs and gang violence animated the desire to bring DARE to these communities. As one former DARE student recalled, DARE was likely welcomed in Wausau because of such perceived infiltration of racialized threats from outside the community.[81]

Although not originally intended to address gang activity, DARE administrators recognized as early as the fall of 1984 that the program and its prevention framework could be used for an anti-gang message. Many DARE instructors, according to a fact sheet on DARE's gang prevention content, were already talking "about gangs in their classes." As a result, personnel in the LAPD's DARE unit began to work with LAUSD curriculum experts to develop a specific anti-gang lesson to replace an officer-planned lesson in the fall of 1985.[82] The following year, the anti-gang lesson became an established part of the curriculum.[83] The development of the DARE gang lesson belied the rhetoric that the program was aimed at a universal problem of drug use. As one LAPD and DARE representative told Congress in 1986, "We have instituted a gang pressure lesson in the city of Los Angeles because many of our areas in our city are quite infiltrated with the gang influence, and while we are not going to solve the gang problem in Los Angeles with this lesson, we are going to teach those youngsters what the pressures are, and how gang members recruit other gang members."[84] Police and school officials in Los Angeles and across the country built on the panic about gangs to integrate anti-gang training into the DARE curriculum.

When administrators designed the DARE high school program in 1989, they further mobilized racialized fears of gang violence to expand the program. More than merely including an anti-gang lesson as part of drug prevention education, the DARE unit actively coordinated with the LAPD's gang prevention and suppression units, which linked drug enforcement with prevention. "DARE staff," administrators reported to funding agencies, "will network with LAPD Detective Support Division Gangs to monitor the suppression of gang activity in and around targeted schools."[85] Expanding DARE beyond drug abuse education to anti-gang education further blurred the distinction between reducing supply and arresting demand.

Oftentimes, educators and police relied on racialized descriptions of drugs and violence to bolster their claims for more funding. LAPD and LAUSD officials routinely used the image of the "inner-city" and "dangerous" Black neighborhoods as examples to bolster their claim for more funding and resources. As DARE developer and LAUSD official Ruth Rich told Congress in 1990, continued Drug Free Schools and Communities Act funding would allow the district "to develop and expand programs and activities which will serve those student populations attending elementary, junior, and senior high schools located in areas of high crime, high density drug trafficking, and increased gang activity." Focusing on the perceived relationship between drug use with gang violence, which the LAPD's own data suggested was not entirely connected, Rich made the case to policymakers about the need for DARE. "Law enforcement estimates that in Los Angeles County there are more than 500 gangs with some 80,000 known members," Ruth continued. "Violence and increased drug-related gang activity are impacting the schools with greater frequency. School/community related violence ranging from taunts and slurs to assaults, vandalism, drug-deals gone 'sour,' and even gang-style murders have become common place [*sic*] in Los Angeles."[86] The threat of drugs and gangs operated as a strategy to smooth community relations and expand the war on drugs into schools within the context of the drug war that was wreaking havoc in many communities of color. Policymakers were, in short, gearing up to expand the war on drugs by targeting students in schools.

Claims that DARE relied on a standardized curriculum did not mean that implementing the program was the same across metropolitan space. DARE officers often engaged more directly with students in "urban" and "inner-city" schools—labels that enabled proponents of DARE to describe the program as race-neutral while relying on the implicit racialized understandings of those terms. "At urban schools," one study found, "D.A.R.E. officers tended to spend more time on the school grounds and typically interacted more with students outside the classroom, including the playground setting. In contrast, D.A.R.E. officers in suburban schools were quick to move on to another school." As a result, students in "urban schools" had a greater "opportunity to 'connect' or 'bond' with the D.A.R.E. officer than did their suburban counterparts and to see them as part of the school environment."[87] Although suburban parents likely approved of the DARE program out of concern for drugs, the police did not need to readily convince suburban students to see them as friends or mentors because those students likely did not have a preexisting adversarial relationship with the police. The different approach reinforced the message that communities of color required greater attitudinal shifts toward the police. Such efforts to present police officers as people rather than "robots or some untouchable force," in the words of one DARE officer, were necessary because of the aggressive approach to the drug war, especially in low-income neighborhoods of color.[88]

Evidence is scarce about how exactly DARE officers explained to schoolchildren the violence of policing, as are stories about students' family members who may have been harassed or abused by the police. But DARE's emphasis on zero tolerance for drugs, and its framing of drug use as an individual choice that came with consequences including arrest, imprisonment, and even death, was an attempt to resolve the contradiction between the aggressive drug warrior on the streets and the friendly DARE officer in the classroom. DARE's message likely suggested to students in heavily policed neighborhoods that people who used or pushed drugs, including their peers and family members, deserved the consequences of their choices.[89]

If police brass and educators saw DARE as an avenue to improve relations between police and youth of color, they were battling a problem of their own making. Some Black leaders recognized this dichotomy. Testifying before the Christopher Commission, which Mayor Tom Bradley established to investigate the LAPD after the beating of Rodney King, vice president of the San Fernando National Association for the Advancement of Colored People (NAACP) Tom Montgomery explained the discrepancy between LAPD's drug war in Black and white communities. The LAPD, he said, used a battering ram to knock in suspected drug houses in the Black community, but "we also know that there's a drug problem in Bel Aire, Brentwood, and Beverly Hills. And I told him [press], I said, 'But you don't use a battering ram.' I said, 'All you do [is] ask Betty Ford, go name the building after her. . . . In my community you say they're drug addicts—in her community she's over-indulged.'" He continued by stating that Gates used DARE to go "from school to school and have police officers going to the school teaching the kids about drugs."[90] In addition to highlighting the actual treatment of communities of color, Montgomery suggested DARE did not address the fundamental issues of educational inequality and lack of opportunity in the city's Black communities that contributed to the outpouring of protest in 1992. Instead of addressing the structural problems facing many communities of color in the early 1990s, DARE attempted to give the police a human face while simultaneously expanding the scorched-earth policing of those same communities to root out drugs and gangs.

A New Partnership in the Drug War

Though an explicit admission of the LAPD's failures triggered the search for demand-side approaches, it never led to alternatives as imaginative as abandoning failed enforcement tactics or reimagining the drug war itself. Instead, the LAPD expanded the portfolio of police officers in schools, shifting from undercover officers to educators.

Well into the 1990s, DARE administrators touted DARE as part of a multifaceted drug war. LAPD chief of police Bernard Parks continued to link DARE to enforcement and interdiction abroad as part of a deep continuum in the fight against drugs. "Other prevention programs, intervention projects, and enforcement efforts by law enforcement must interact with interdiction programs and treatment efforts," Parks stated in 1999. "The reduction of the drug problem in America is a complicated issue requiring a multifaceted solution. However, D.A.R.E. is an essential component of that solution."[91] Yet DARE expanded the role of the police, an approach that did not challenge but complemented the willingness of policymakers to fund aggressive, law enforcement–based drug policy. As a result, while demand-side solutions were often described as alternatives to supply reduction activities and framed as preventive and, oftentimes, nonpunitive, DARE exposed how, in practice, the two sides of the drug war mutually reinforced one another. The police-school partnership was central to expanding police power, authority, and expertise into the nation's classrooms.

As the next chapter will detail, the use of police officers as teachers ended up giving police new means of combating challenges to their legitimacy. More significantly, by bringing police officers into schools as teachers, DARE produced a new partnership in the drug war and anticipated and facilitated a broader shift in the reach of the state's police power during the 1980s and 1990s. The DARE officer became the face of the program, the symbol of its success, and the means by which the police could reshape their image from aggressive drug warriors to friends, role models, mentors, and educators.

CHAPTER TWO

Cops as Teachers

Greg Boles, in a neatly pressed LAPD uniform, entered a sixth-grade classroom in Los Angeles to teach his weekly DARE lesson during the program's third year. A multiracial group of students sat with their name tags on tables, watching intently as Officer Boles began the weekly DARE lesson. "Everyone has their DARE notebooks out? How about your name tags?" Boles asked. "The Question Box" he announced, as he shook the notorious box where students could submit questions, concerns, and tips about people they knew who used drugs. He reached in and pulled out an anonymous note and read it: "Have you ever convinced a drug user to stop?" Boles responded out loud so the students could hear him: "I like to say that I have. I hope that I have." Boles followed with a lesson about peer pressure. In a didactic manner, Boles questioned the students about peer pressure and the different ways to say no to their friends. The students enthusiastically raised their hands, answered questions, and kept their eyes trained on Boles. Other activities included skits and role-playing, such as when one student approached a classmate at the front of the class and enthusiastically asked, "Hey, Monica! Wanna smoke a joint?" To which Monica, with arms crossed and a skeptical look, responded, "Oh, no thanks," then turned around and quickly walked the other way. Boles praised the students and the technique of saying "no thanks" to refuse offers of drugs.[1] For many students, these opportunities to role-play as drug dealers and buyers in which they sought to make their friends laugh—not the antidrug content or message—were the highlight of the DARE classroom experience.[2]

Officer Boles had been an undercover officer in Los Angeles high schools before moving to the DARE program. His desire to be a DARE officer stemmed from the perceived ineffectiveness of prior drug prevention programming, recounting his own experience with drug education and the knowledge-based drug chart and scare tactics, such as being shown pictures of dead people. But when he found out that such lessons were not entirely true, that drug use did not inevitably lead to death, he began to reconsider such tactics. Instead, he believed, the chart of drugs became a menu for kids to choose what they would like to try. DARE offered an alternative. At the end of the lesson, Boles told the students, "You've learned the words. You've learned about what the pressures are, don't ya? . . . You know how to identify 'em. You know the words. You guys did great today. I'm real proud of you. You're really learning. Practice what you've learned. But then you're going to learn more to go along with it to give you some confidence, to feel good about yourself, to be able to stand up and say 'no.' OK?" But the DARE officer's involvement did not end there. Following the lesson, Boles, still in uniform, walked on the playground with kids surrounding him before a game of kickball. When he told the kids, "I'll be in the field, OK?" they screamed with joy, chasing Boles around the playground, all vying for his attention. As with so many other DARE officers, Boles, not the students, was the star of the show.[3]

Through DARE, cops became part of schools' daily operation as nominal educators. They were explicitly trained not to act in a law enforcement role while on campus, even though that directive was implicitly undermined by the requirement to teach classes in uniform. To legitimize the use of uniformed police officers as teachers, DARE officers would not enforce drug laws in schools but teach kids self-esteem, resistance to peer pressure, and how to say no to drugs. In their minds, defining police as teachers tempered the drug war by helping kids learn to avoid drugs rather than targeting them for arrest. Yet as law enforcement representatives who taught in their police uniforms and were invested in a zero-tolerance approach to drugs, DARE officers implicitly connected the drug war's soft side of prevention with its hard side of aggressive enforcement of drug laws. More explicitly, DARE officers relayed information to police narcotics units about drug use and other so-called criminal activities that often came from students who put notes in the classroom's DARE Question Box.[4]

At the heart of this chapter is the DARE officer. It explains the reciprocal and cooperative relationship that developed between schools and the police in Los Angeles and after DARE's expansion to other school districts across the country. It shows how DARE's use of police officers as teachers co-opted the educative function of schools to advance the police mission by other means.

For all the effort to humanize the police, DARE officers did not shed their law-and-order message or the threat of arrest and punishment when they entered the classroom. Still, the program proved an effective public relations move for the police, especially during a historical moment when police came under scrutiny for aggressive tactics and violence, perhaps nowhere more visible than with the beating of Rodney King and the subsequent 1992 Los Angeles rebellion.[5] And there was no turning back from here: future programs aimed at reducing drug use through education would continue to rely on uniformed law enforcement officers as teachers.[6] In so doing, DARE was part of the attempt to legitimize and accept police in all areas of social life. With the program's adoption beyond Los Angeles, DARE officers became a ubiquitous part of children's lives, preparing the ground for the expansion of police power and authority in following years.

Police-School Partnerships and Making Cops into Teachers

DARE enabled officers to assume a new role in children's lives. Rather than representatives of law enforcement, police officers would become teachers, mentors, and role models. Positioning police as teachers allowed educators to more willingly accept cops not only in schools generally but also in classrooms than they had in the past, especially during the late 1960s when many educators opposed the growing police presence on campuses in response to student protest. For the police, DARE represented crime prevention "at its best" because it intended to reposition the police officer away from enforcement and, in turn, aimed to eliminate drug use before it started. As Gates told Board of Police Commissioner Stanley Sheinbaum in 1992, "The D.A.R.E. program places police officers in a non-traditional but no less necessary law enforcement role as we attempt to turn a generation away from involvement with drugs and gangs."[7] Yet as Gates's phrasing suggested, relying on police as teachers was defined squarely within the purview of law enforcement.

Partnering educators and law enforcement marked a departure from how the drug war in schools had been waged in the past. Beginning with the pilot program in 1983, the LAPD and LAUSD established a memorandum of understanding to govern this new partnership. These agreements, which became a requirement for adopting DARE in other school districts, mapped out the different roles for schools and the police, including resource allocation, setting aside classroom space and time for the program, and the use of DARE material in schools.[8] Although defined as a cooperative project, DARE was largely controlled by the police and housed under the broad umbrella of the LAPD's Bureau of Special Investigation, a unit that also included Narcotics Enforcement, Vice Enforcement, Labor Relations, Public Relations, and Asian Community Task Force.[9] Organizationally, the project director was an LAPD officer from the juvenile division who oversaw DARE's operations, administration and curriculum, and police supervisors and teachers at the school level. The LAUSD, in contrast, provided a project coordinator who oversaw clerical operations, ensured space at schools, and managed substance abuse counselors in schools.[10]

These agreements integrated the police into schools through their educative function. Along with considering the DARE officer a full-time faculty member, schools often agreed to provide bulletin board space for displaying DARE materials. An even greater encroachment of DARE into the school curriculum, however, was illustrated by asking whether the potential school was willing to "reinforce the D.A.R.E. curriculum throughout the week by such activities as incorporating 'D.A.R.E. Words' into the weekly spelling test, assigning D.A.R.E.-related topics for themes, etc."[11] Such agreements, in other words, helped incorporate DARE into the life of the school. DARE represented a deep connection between education and police power. As James Stewart of the National Institute of Justice commented, there were no programs where the police were "as well-integrated (into the educational curriculum) as this one."[12]

Above all, the joint agreements set the parameters for the most foundational aspect of the DARE program and the element that would make DARE the darling of law enforcement, policymakers, and educators nationwide: the use of cops as teachers. Although framed as an alternative to aggressive tactics to reduce the supply of drugs, the police officer as teacher enabled law enforcement to control all facets of the drug war, from enforcement on the streets to education in the classroom. As both teacher and law enforcement officer, the DARE officer, quite literally, embodied the reciprocity of the school-police nexus.

Because the DARE officer was the most important aspect of the program, selecting the right officers was key to DARE's success. Alongside attributes that would make an officer a good teacher, the ability to present a positive image of the police was a key part of the selection process. Program officials looked for veterans of the force who had street experience, a personality suitable to teaching, and "the ability to project a good police image."[13] Administrators routinely pointed to the rigorous selection process and training each officer received. As Daryl Gates wrote in *School Safety* about the caliber of officer chosen for DARE, "All of the officers selected are talented in human relations and communication skills."[14]

Fifty officers tried out for the program, of which ten were selected as the first cohort of DARE teachers. Selected by a group of LAUSD and LAPD administrators overseeing the program, the first cohort went through an intensive training process. Those officers received 200 hours of training and California State Vocational Teaching certificates. Future cohorts attended an

DARE session led by LAPD officer Gary Guevara. Dean Musgrove, September 15, 1988, Herald Examiner Collection, Los Angeles Public Library, Los Angeles, California.

eighty-hour training that was easily replicated and that facilitated program expansion. Training focused on imparting rudimentary teaching skills and knowledge of the curriculum.[15] But Ruth Rich and LAPD administrators also designed the training to transform the police officer from a street warrior into a classroom teacher. "We assist them to remove the macho image and become teachers," explained Harreld D. Webster, a DARE officer mentor.[16] Such efforts went beyond transforming the individual officer. As DARE officer training developed, it became a means to transform the very philosophy of the police in order to ensure the new DARE officer would be viewed as legitimate. "More importantly," a training manual explained, "the DOT [DARE Officer Training] is an instrument of socialization which initiates the trainee into the DARE philosophy, a philosophy in which success is measured by community acceptance and support rather than number of crimes and arrests."[17]

According to law enforcement administrators, choosing police officers who could present the police in a humane light and relate to kids in positive ways was central to the program's success. Selection of DARE officers focused on veterans of the force who had experience on the streets, a personality suitable to teaching, and a willingness to see prevention programs as a valuable tool in the war on drugs. The ideal DARE officer had an "AA degree or higher, 3 years policing experience, prior speaking/teaching skills, positive attitude towards drug abuse education, positive attitude towards children, good organizational skills, social and community involvement." Such qualifications aimed to reorient views of the DARE officer as a qualified instructor who could relate to children, teachers, and parents alike.[18]

As the program was adopted by police and schools outside of Los Angeles, finding the right officers for the job took on added importance. Law enforcement agencies participating in DARE, an FBI Law Enforcement Bulletin advertising the program in 1990 outlined, needed to ensure officers chosen were the best possible candidates "because of their high visibility" in schools and communities, as well as their role as a representative of the entire police department. Officers, the bulletin continued, should "reflect the department's total commitment to the program." Indeed, a qualified DARE officer was the linchpin not only for reducing drug use but also for transforming public perceptions of the police and reshaping the relationship between the police and communities. "In fact, D.A.R.E. is already changing the public's perception of law enforcement officers," the bulletin concluded. "With this in mind, each department must ensure that this key to a drug-free future is turned by the best qualified D.A.R.E. officers possible."[19]

An instructor from the Twelfth Security Police Squadron instructs a group of young people during the seventeen-week DARE program. O. J. Sanchez, August 24, 1996, Combined Military Service Digital Photographic Files, Record Group 330: Records of the Office of the Secretary of Defense, National Archives and Records Administration, College Park, Maryland.

Police were not the only law enforcement personnel trained to be DARE officers. Over time, DARE training expanded to include sheriffs, state police officers, and military personnel, including U.S. Army Military Police and Air Force representatives. Broadening officer training beyond municipal police departments blurred the boundaries between the police and military missions, and DARE's use in Department of Defense schools on military bases around the world reflected the intersection of counterinsurgency and policing at home.[20] The training apparatus was effective due to the extensive law enforcement network that DARE built upon and was a key component enabling DARE to expand nationwide.[21] And the ranks of DARE officers grew exponentially, blurring the already thin line between the police and military.[22] Indeed, DARE's placement in Department of Defense schools on military bases around the world reflected a long history of police counterinsurgency campaigns to win hearts and minds. As late as 2015, for instance, the State Department's Bureau of International Narcotics and Law Enforcement

Children from Sterling Heights Elementary recite the Pledge of Allegiance at the DARE graduation on Kadena Air Base, Okinawa, Japan. SSGT C. E. Lewis, USAF, February 28, 2003, Combined Military Service Digital Photographic Files, Record Group 330: Records of the Office of the Secretary of Defense, National Archives and Records Administration, College Park, Maryland.

Affairs offered to help at-risk youth in Central America by providing DARE officer training and programming.[23]

Proponents of DARE viewed police officers' street experience with the consequences of drug use as an asset in fighting the drug war in schools. DARE officers were described as "patrol-hardened, veteran police officers" who would command respect from youth and "effectively shore up the classroom teacher's antidrug education."[24] Police officers, many proponents of the program believed, had more credibility as teachers about drugs and drug abuse because of their ability to recall real-world stories and examples of drug use and crime.[25] Street experience was perceived to be invaluable in making an effective DARE officer. "The police officers assigned to D.A.R.E. have come straight from the streets," DARE America's promotional material explained. "Their years of direct experience with the ruined lives and street crimes caused by substance abuse gives them unmatched credibility."[26] As Lieutenant Pat Froehle, head of the LAPD's Project DARE unit, stated, "We believe police officers can be good instructors because they can provide credibility based on their firsthand experience with drug abuse victims."[27] Indeed, police officers believed that elementary school students were so aware of and used to seeing drugs that police officers were the only option for changing student attitudes toward drug use. "Fifth- and sixth-graders in our society today, they know more about this whole (drug) issue than the vast majority of the teachers do," Gates argued. "So the teachers are not in a position to do it. It's the police officers who are."[28] Such perceived student attitudes and in-depth knowledge of drugs and drug culture necessitated the use of police officers as educators.[29] For law enforcement officials bent on waging a war on drugs, there was, quite simply, no other option but to make police officers into teachers.

Educators and the DARE Officer

Educators involved with DARE backed the notion that patrol-hardened, veteran police officers would make ideal teachers. The LAUSD's Ruth Rich reaffirmed the importance of the police role. "There's a gap between the street and the classroom," Rich explained. "Police officers are believable on this subject. When it comes to drugs, they're more credible than a teacher."[30] As DARE expanded to schools throughout Los Angeles and, eventually, the nation, educators and school administrators stressed the value of police officers who had knowledge of the detrimental impact of drugs on people's lives as a key component of antidrug education to shore up the drug prevention message. In doing so, school administrators, classroom teachers, and policymakers reinforced the implicit message that officers' primary role as enforcers of drug laws and practices of mass arrests that developed in the 1980s undergirded the softer image of law enforcement presented to students in classrooms.[31]

Humanizing the police officer was not only a strategy directed at winning over the hearts and minds of students. Educators, both teachers and principals, were also a key component of DARE. Tension between educators and police, DARE administrators recognized, might arise because of the different orientation between officers and teachers. "Schools and police agencies often have different philosophies and administrative style and may not be accustomed to working together," the LAPD reported in an application nominating DARE for Innovations in State and Local Government awards. "Communities find, however, that a structured program and a mutual commitment to preventing substance abuse among young people provide strong motivation for pursuing this cooperative effort." But DARE officers, according to the LAPD, won them over. “Police officers are usually viewed as law enforcers, not as teachers,” the LAPD continued in its award application. “However, D.A.R.E. officers are well-trained, committed individuals, who quickly prove their effectiveness in the classroom. When teachers and administrators observe individual officers teaching the D.A.R.E. curriculum, their former resistance changes into a receptive attitude.”[32]

Teachers and principals, in turn, became some of the lustiest proponents for using uniformed officers as instructors. In the program’s first few years, educators in Los Angeles often wrote directly to Chief of Police Gates or other DARE administrators praising the program and asking for it to continue. Phyllis Q. Marquardt, principal of Balboa Boulevard Elementary School in Los Angeles, for instance, was effusive in her praise of DARE and its impact on her students in a 1986 letter to Gates. “Officer Tom Lendzion was the officer on our campus,” she wrote. “Words fail me to describe the impact he had on our entire student body. He became part of the school—supervising, helping, playing, and on and on and on. As a role model, he was invaluable. The D.A.R.E. program is fabulous!” Fearing that her school might lose the DARE program, she pleaded with Gates to ensure it continued. “We would like to have it every year from now on,” she concluded.[33] Marquadt was not alone in her praise.

Educators, in both their voluntary assessments and DARE’s promotional material, often confirmed that the DARE officer was a valued addition to the school environment and that they were well equipped to teach about drugs. One of the first evaluations of the program conducted by Dr. Glenn G. Nyre in Los Angeles found that over 80 percent of teachers surveyed “considered the officers themselves the best feature of the project.”[34] A more in-depth evaluation after DARE’s second year, also conducted by Nyre as part of an ongoing evaluation contract with the LAPD and LAUSD, found that 83 percent of principals and 71 percent of teachers listed the positive contact between students and DARE officers as the best element of the program. Although often parroting the official DARE line about the expertise of police officers as teachers, principals and teachers pointed to things such as the positive role model presented by uniformed officers, the “trusting relationships they developed with students,” and the “friendly, open and non-threatening manner in which the officers dealt with students’ concerns and problems.”[35] Or as one teacher believed, “Students are very positive toward police in general, which has never been the case in twenty years of teaching.” Perhaps one of the more dramatic examples of the impact of the DARE officer came from a teacher in one of DARE’s pilot schools. “These are the exact words of one of my students whose father was killed by a police officer and who had a very negative attitude toward police at the beginning of the year," the teacher recounted. "'All policemen aren't good, but then neither are all teachers. All policemen aren't bad, but neither are all teachers.'"[36] DARE officers became welcomed members of the school environment and played a key role in socializing kids into a law-and-order mission that demanded adherence to and respect for authority in the form of the police.[37]

DARE's promotional material often pointed to the overwhelming support from school administrators. Beginning in 1988, LAUSD began a "D.A.R.E. to Read" newsletter for students in which DARE students contributed articles and interviewed their DARE officers, principals, and teachers about the program. Students found a very positive response from all involved. Principal Melba Coleman of the 102nd Street School commented, "I feel very good about the D.A.R.E. Program because at the elementary level it is especially critical for young people to learn to say 'No' to drugs. I feel very grateful to the Los Angeles Police Department and the school district for having this program funded so that it could be in our school."[38] Similarly, Principal Dore Wong of Bushnell Way School praised the program and officers alike. Commenting on Officer Boles, she explained to her student interviewers, "He's a fine example and role-model for our students, and he is an excellent representative of the Los Angeles Police Department." If principals had a negative view of the DARE officer, it certainly did not come through in the material DARE used to promote the use of cops in the classroom.[39]

Teachers also valued the officers who came into their classrooms. As Mrs. Whitman, a Los Angeles elementary school teacher, explained in an interview for the drug education episode of *Crime File* produced by the National Institute of Justice and Police Foundation, DARE was especially important for sixth graders who were moving from elementary to junior high. "If you talk to sixth graders, the greatest fear that they have is being approached in junior high school and not knowing what to say. Now what we saw today was Greg, Officer Boles, giving us techniques of how to say no. . . . That's their worry, 'How am I going to say no?' That's why he has them practice it." But the DARE program was more than just a means to prepare students for the next step in their educational journey. Instead, it shaped student attitudes in the classroom and about drugs in general, sometimes with unintended consequences. "There's a noticeable change with the children. They're more freer [*sic*] about speaking about drugs. They're aware of the harms, the harmful effects of drugs. And they even remind adults that they shouldn't have caffeine in their coffee." Whitman's response revealed the positive view of DARE but also the potential for students to become part of the police enforcement apparatus. If kids were willing to criticize their parents for having caffeine, what if they found their parents engaged in more illicit substances?[40]

Not all teachers supported the program, however. Some saw the program taking time away from class time and instructional opportunities. Others saw the use of a minimally trained police officer as an affront to the professional role of lifelong educators.[41] As one study found, "Older teachers were more critical in their views about the appropriateness of prevention education at the fifth and sixth grade levels, and the presence of a police officer as an educator addressing the subject of drug use."[42] One former DARE student's parents who were public school teachers in Wisconsin, for instance, opposed the program because of the reliance on cops as teachers (especially with their gun in the classroom), taking away from class time, and promoting a moralizing message to young students. Such concerns led these parents to remove their child from the DARE program altogether.[43]

While DARE officers had the support of many teachers and school administrators, the use of cops as teachers required continual shoring up. DARE administrators were clearly aware of educators' possible reticence about cops in the classroom and worked hard to sell the officer as teacher.[44]

Selling the Officer as Teacher

Promoting the use of police officers as instructors rested on the requirement that they teach in their uniforms but do so unarmed. While DARE administrators claimed it ensured that officers would not be mistaken for other school personnel, it explicitly reinforced the presence of police on campus and the message of law and order. Uniformed officers represented a symbol of authority for students but were also identifiable and distinguishable from classroom teachers. "The identification with local law enforcement," a DARE advisory committee remarked when the program began expanding to other communities, "is one of the key elements of DARE." Identifying DARE with the police and distinguishing officers from "regular" teachers became so emblematic of the program that when the FBI requested DARE officer training, DARE advisors were skeptical due to FBI agents' lack of law enforcement uniforms. "The consensus of the group was to require a uniform," the committee stated. "The blazer would not make a significant distinction from the other staff."[45] DARE administrators, in short, wanted to ensure students knew the DARE officer was a representative of law enforcement. As DARE expanded regionally and nationally, it required local agencies to adopt the philosophy that "a school-based drug abuse program, taught by uniformed officers/deputies, can be effective with children," and "a belief in the partnership of law enforcement agencies and school districts to deliver the DARE curriculum."[46] Even as DARE was presented as an alternative to the enforcement of drug laws, it continued to promote the police message and emphasized the uniformed police officer as a figure to be respected.

Some city policymakers were initially wary of the use of police officers as teachers. Rita Walters, a member of the Board of Education who had criticized the School Buy Program, questioned the diversion of police to the classroom just before DARE's launch, stating, "I feel the police could be better used elsewhere" and "there are better agencies" to teach drug education than the police. Indeed, Walters suggested, uniformed officers in classrooms was "a little heavy-handed."[47] Following the program's first two years of operation, some on the Board of Police Commissioners continued to question whether DARE officers were really teaching about drug prevention. Commissioner Barbara Schlei, for instance, questioned both the effectiveness of the program and its reliance on police officers. "Do we want our military and paramilitary teaching moral values in our schools in a democracy?" Schlei asked even while praising police officers as a valuable resource to teach kids about drugs. "But once you start teaching attitudes, what about attitudes that aren't as clear cut? Is it a step we're really ready to take?" Pointing to leading questions on an early evaluation of the program, Schlei asked, "Is [DARE] teaching about drugs, or is that teaching about attitudes toward the police?"[48] Schlei, a critic of Gates, was by and large a lone voice of dissent on the police board. Yet such questions went to the heart of DARE's implicit message. It aimed not only to teach students how to say no to drugs but also to educate them about respecting and obeying law enforcement.

Los Angeles City Council members also debated whether using officers as teachers was worth the trade-off of removing officers from patrolling the streets. When Gates proposed adding ten more officers to the DARE program beginning in January of 1986 using private funding from the Crime Prevention Advisory Council (CPAC), a fundraising group for DARE set up to support the city's crime prevention programs, some city council members questioned further reducing the number of officers on the street. One such opponent included Robert Farrell, an African American council member who suggested that the streets were where the officers were needed most and that regular teachers should receive the additional funding to expand the DARE program in 1986. Officers should be devoted to the department's anti-gang unit (Community Resources against Street Hoodlums, known as CRASH), homicide, or crime suppression instead. While the Police, Fire and Public Safety Committee and Mayor Tom Bradley supported accepting the donation and upgrading the officers for DARE service, Farrell's opposition revealed tension within the Black community about the need for more police on the streets to address a growth in gang violence and drug-related crimes.[49] Some law enforcement officials also raised questions about using officers as teachers, something they viewed as outside the purview of police responsibilities. While supportive of DARE, Severin Sorenson of the National Association of Chiefs of Police suggested that "teachers should teach, and law enforcement officers should apply the law."[50] Yet such questioning was often the exception.

As other law enforcement agencies began to adopt the program, administrators attempted to preempt criticism of the use of officers as teachers by downplaying the threat of arrest or drug enforcement in schools. As a DARE implementation guide published by the Bureau of Justice Assistance (BJA) advised, officials who were implementing a new program should emphasize the cooperative relationship between schools and the police. The BJA advised, "Because some parents may be suspicious of a police presence in the schools, it is important for the officer to emphasize that schools have been selected as the site for the program not because of a great substance use problem but because of the high level of cooperation between the police and the schools in preventing substance use. The officers must stress that they are there to serve as role models, not to collect undercover information or otherwise serve in a law enforcement capacity."[51] Indeed, the BJA promoted DARE as a "unique opportunity for law enforcement and the schools to work together to reduce drug abuse." This cooperative venture was marketed as a potentially new role for law enforcement officers because it offered them "an effective means for positive influence on the lives of our youth."[52]

Even in 1992 when budget concerns in Los Angeles led to questions about whether drug education needed to be taught by uniformed, sworn police officers, the uniformed officer was held up as a necessary and nonnegotiable component of the program. "From its inception, an integral criterion of the DARE and other similar programs has been that instruction should be provided by uniformed police officers with peace officer status," the city administrative officer (CAO) summarized in a report on "Uniformed vs. Non-uniformed Staff." "It is believed that police field experience is very valuable for the program." But there had been no research showing whether teachers could be as effective instructors of the DARE curriculum as police officers. Yet effectiveness was not forefront on policymakers' minds. "It is also believed," the CAO admitted, "using officers helps to build better long term positive relations with our citizens." Despite that using a civilian staff could save more than $2 million, support for senior police officers taking on the role of DARE instructors went largely unchallenged.[53] Following the CAO report, Marvin Braude, chairperson of the city council's Public Safety Committee, raised questions about the cost of using uniformed officers in comparison to civilian instructors and called for further study of the issue. While the city council approved the motion, using police officers as DARE instructors not only continued unabated but was celebrated as the program's crowning achievement and purpose.[54]

More than any other part of DARE, including the antidrug message, the very success of the program centered on the DARE officer. As DARE's police officer project managers self-assessed in an assuredly congratulatory manner, "There is now little doubt that the use of police officers as instructors was truly a stroke of genius. . . . The officers have been able to develop a rapport with the students and the children enthusiastically look forward to the weekly visits by their DARE officer/instructors. There is no doubt that DARE would not be nearly as successful without the police officer/instructors."[55] The DARE officer became the star of the show, and educators, law enforcement, and politicians highlighted them as the nation's frontline agents preventing youth drug use.

DARE officers had bipartisan appeal, receiving praise from presidents Ronald Reagan, George H. W. Bush, and Bill Clinton, as well as a range of officials in their respective administrations. Although William Bennett, secretary of education and future inaugural director—otherwise known as the "drug czar"—of the Office of National Drug Control Policy often lauded DARE, perhaps the greatest example and summary of the political support for the DARE officer came in 1999 from Barry McCaffrey, Bill Clinton's director of the Office of National Drug Control Policy, four-star general, and supporter of America's security personnel:

> The most important living example of the D.A.R.E. program, however, is the unflagging dedication and commitment of the men and women of law enforcement. After "walking the beat" to keep our streets safe the D.A.R.E. officers unflinchingly give their time to help this nation's youth. D.A.R.E. officers command respect because they are community leaders who care. All of us who work to reduce drug use in America are deeply impressed with their work. D.A.R.E.

officers are a unique group of dedicated, bright and enthusiastic individuals who connect strongly with this country's youth. The success of the D.A.R.E. program is founded upon officers who love to work with kids.[56]

As McCaffrey suggested, DARE officers were to be celebrated for their willingness and ability to connect with kids. As Glenn Levant forthrightly explained in DARE America's internationally distributed newsletter, *DareLine International*, "The heart and soul of D.A.R.E. is the officer who delivers the message to the children of the world. Let there be no mistake if it's good for the kids then that's what D.A.R.E. is going to do — no matter what it takes."[57] But viewed within the context of an aggressive and punitive drug war, the DARE officer took on a different meaning, which aimed to shore up the image of law enforcement. DARE, in other words, was a campaign by the police to enhance their public image, incorporate kids into their law-and-order mission, and bolster the legitimacy of the police.

Reimagining Law and Order: The Police Officer as Friend and Mentor

DARE's police-school partnership intended to reimagine the role of the police officer far more than it prevented drug use. While health and education specialists actually had expertise in substance use prevention, both LAPD and LAUSD officials believed that using officers as teachers would "provide many essential components" of the program, including "a staff which is recognized by the students as experts in the field of substance abuse; opportunity for officers to relate with students, parents and teachers in a non-enforcement role . . . and most importantly, trust between the school community and the officers based on familiarity."[58] They envisioned the DARE officer would change youth perception of the police by creating a nonpunitive relationship between officers and kids. "DARE officers give a different face of law enforcement," DARE America executive director and former LAPD deputy chief Glenn Levant explained. "A child's first experience with a uniformed police officer is in a friendly, helpful way. . . . You have to have programs like DARE in place so police aren't viewed as an occupying army."[59] Such references to the police as an occupying army likely had little resonance in predominantly white schools, but they would have played into the deep roots of overpolicing in communities of color that had produced distrust and antagonism toward the police.[60]

Officer Charles Ravenell plays ball with children of Solley Elementary in Ann Arundel County, Maryland, between his DARE classes. Senior Airman Diane S. Robinson, January 1, 1997, Combined Military Service Digital Photographic Files, Record Group 330: Records of the Office of the Secretary of Defense, National Archives and Records Administration, College Park, Maryland.

From the vantage point of the DARE officer, DARE was a not-so-subtle propaganda campaign to reshape the image of the police. While police departments had long attempted to use community relations and youth programs to push kids to identify with the police, DARE represented a shift from earlier community-oriented policing strategies. It attempted to burnish the image of the police within the context of an aggressive drug and gang war that actively undermined trust in the police, particularly among youth of color. Indeed, the LAPD's undercover School Buy program actively created distrust of the police among many students of color. It also produced racial tensions on school campuses. As one Black student commented after undercover busts disproportionately led to arrests of Black students, "Word got out and a lot of white parents didn't want their kids hanging out with blacks." In other words, DARE's effort to increase community support and trust in the police was a solution to a problem created by the department's own policies on the enforcement side of the drug war in schools.[61]

Students in the program were also implicitly taught to identify with and respect police officers through DARE officers' participation in a wide range of extracurricular activities. When not teaching their DARE class, according

Daryl Gates pins medals on the winners of DARE's run against drugs. Paul Chinn, November 20, 1985, Herald Examiner Collection, Los Angeles Public Library, Los Angeles, California.

to an LAPD grant application for state Suppression of Drug Abuse in Schools funding, "officers would remain on campus for the balance of the school day, available to students and parents, and participate in school activities."[62] During the pilot year, for instance, one officer coached a DARE Track Club while another coached a football team. Several others were even involved in holiday activities at the school, including playing Santa Claus and Rudolf, "clearly not roles in which young people are used to seeing law enforcement officers." Crucially, the officers believed that this sort of activity was a central part of DARE's mission. "The officers feel that these extra activities and involvements are very beneficial to furthering the goals of Project DARE," an interim evaluation report concluded. The most useful part of the program, according to officers, was how students shifted their attitudes and perceptions of the police as someone to be trusted, not feared. "However, the aspect of the project which brought the most satisfaction to the officers was working with the children and having the children come to accept and confide in them."[63]

The implicit goal of changing the image of police officers was part of the program's origins. When the LAPD and LAUSD submitted a grant proposal for second-year funding, for example, they allocated resources to buy officers athletic uniforms. "Part of the DARE method is to involve the officers in the total school program," the LAPD and LAUSD grant writers emphasized. "Naturally, this includes school athletic events. The officers wear their uniforms for all other school events, but they cannot be worn for athletics. Athletic uniforms serve to remind students, spectators and parents of the officer's purpose and provide inexpensive, yet effective, program identity."[64] Such an orientation was meant to create a more positive image of police officers than aggressive crime fighters, which became a selling point of the program. "In addition to their formal classroom teaching," a 1988 Department of Justice DARE manual explained, "DARE officers spend time on the playground, in the cafeteria, and at student assemblies to interact with students informally. . . . In this way students have an opportunity to become acquainted with the officer as a trusted friend who is interested in their happiness and welfare."[65] Adding to this effort, law enforcement agencies created collectible trading cards of DARE officers to both promote the program and further humanize the police.[66]

Pro-police messaging appeared to be working, at least according to DARE's own evaluations and public relations material. A true-false question in one of DARE's early self-evaluations conducted by Glenn Nyre of the Evaluation Training Institute (ETI), for instance, highlighted the underlying goal of reshaping youth views of the police by asking students whether "police officers would rather catch you doing something wrong than try to help you." The study found that 96 percent of the experimental group of fifth graders responded in the "preferred manner"—false—while only 38 percent of the control group provided the preferred response. For sixth graders surveyed, the gap was even greater as 100 percent of the experimental group responded correctly compared to 32 percent of the control.[67] In a follow-up evaluation for 1985, Nyre concluded, "[Initial findings] show that the program has far exceeded its goal of helping students combat peer pressure to use drugs and alcohol. It also has contributed to improved study habits and grades, decreased vandalism and gang activity, and has generated greater respect for police officers."[68] While independent evaluations of DARE would raise significant questions about the ETI's overwhelmingly positive evaluations, anecdotal evidence from law enforcement officers and teachers reiterated such findings about student respect for the police. "Police officers," one report stated, "have experienced a better rapport with students both on and off campus."[69] Or as one teacher observed in a questionnaire for ETI, "Students are very positive toward police in general, which has never been the case in twenty years of teaching."[70] Indeed, teachers often made comments that students had stopped referring to the police in negative or disrespectful ways, "not even as 'cops.'"[71]

Students themselves seemed to reinforce this positive perception of the DARE officer. "I'm sad, because we can't see our officer again," DARE graduate Ruth Ramos stated when the program was over, "and happy because we know we don't have to take drugs."[72] Other students wrote to Chief of Police Gates directly about the benefits of DARE and officers as teachers. "I have learned to say no to drugs and never take drugs. It messes your life up and the people who take drugs are stupid. . . . I thought about Officer Sumpter and how he said to say no."[73] When a bilingual teacher at Cheremoya Avenue Elementary School read that the DARE program may not continue to receive funding in 1985, the teacher worked with students to write a collective letter of support, which they sent to the Los Angeles City Council. In the letter students proclaimed, "We are writing to ask you to not stop the D.A.R.E. program at our school. . . . We believe this program is very important. We also like and respect Officer Boles. . . . Officer Boles also talks to us about lots of things, not just drugs. We can talk to him about good and bad things in our lives. He is a friend to us."[74] Promoting a pro-police, antidrug message deputized students to identify with the police, to prevent negative attitudes toward law enforcement, and to see them as friends and mentors. DARE, quite simply, was working.

Many students seemed to adore their DARE officers. Photographs showed smiling students with their DARE officers both inside and outside the classroom. Oftentimes, they wrote about their experiences with officers in their "DARE Essays," which were sometimes published in newspapers across the country. As one Ohio student wrote after completing DARE in 2000, "D.A.R.E. means a lot to me. I like seeing my D.A.R.E. officer's happy smiling face every Wednesday. . . . I think D.A.R.E. is a really good program. It has taught me what to do and what not to do to protect myself from danger. I think D.A.R.E. has helped provide a good clear image in my mind if I do something bad. I have learned not to do drugs, get into gangs, or smoke. Thank you Capt. Stanley!"[75] Students in Sioux City, Iowa, variously wrote, "I believe D.A.R.E. helps people think of themselves as special"; "Whenever I see my plaque or wear my T-shirt, I'll think of all the great and fun times I had in D.A.R.E."; and "This year when I was told that we would be having D.A.R.E., I figured that it would be some officer coming into our classroom and just saying don't do drugs over and over again. Actually, it was GREAT."[76] Student perceptions of DARE usually expressed a standard essay form about the program and praise for the DARE officer. And they were all positive, of course.

Other students took the messaging to heart and elevated their DARE enthusiasm to another level. Five students from San Bernardino, for example, performed a skit for their DARE graduation based on antidrug lyrics and popular music. The San Bernardino Police Department, after learning about the group, asked the students to perform their skit at a DARE convention in August 1987. The group became known as the "D.A.R.E. Squad," a group of five kids who sang songs against drugs. The students also wrote and produced a monthly student newsletter called "D.A.R.E. Squad Speaks" with mini articles about DARE, the DARE Bear, and other antidrug initiatives, such as Red Ribbon Week.[77] For other students, the DARE experience did not end when they left elementary school. In some instances, high school students who had completed DARE came back as "DARE role models." As one Kentucky DARE officer noted, "As part of the DARE curriculum, we have a 'role model' class, using drug- and alcohol-free students from our high schools. The students talk to the elementary kids, telling them that they can be drug-free and accepted—even admired—by their peers because of their choice." The DARE role models talked to kids about not using drugs or alcohol and the high school experience. For DARE officers, the program was another metric of success. "The students chosen did an excellent job for me," the Kentucky DARE officer continued, "and the kids really enjoyed having them in the classroom."[78]

Sometimes, however, the message students took away from DARE had less to do with avoiding drugs and more to do with critiques of the program. Many students enjoyed the role-playing activities and skits not because they were invested in the antidrug messaging or content but because they enjoyed getting in front of the class and acting as a drug dealer or buyer. One student from Columbus, Ohio, recalled how they tried to make their friends laugh during skits in which they would sag their pants, wear bandanas, and act like drug dealers they had seen in movies or on television.[79] Or, more explicitly, some saw DARE as an escape from academic work. One student in Kentucky wrote, "Our DARE officer is officer Holt. In DARE, we do lots of fun things, and we never have any tests. Near the end of DARE, when we were getting ready for graduation, we missed almost two weeks of school."[80] Many children enjoyed DARE because it let them connect with fellow students, make friends laugh, or avoid regular classwork, not for its antidrug messaging or content.

Some of the students who questioned the program were slightly more biting in their critiques. Students in Wausau, Wisconsin, for instance, debated in the editorial pages of the *Rib Mountain Gazette*, a student newspaper. While the DARE proponents reiterated similar arguments about the importance of learning how to say no to drugs and resisting peer pressure, Charlie Hughes and Erik Rajek had a different take, to put it mildly. "[DARE] is useless," they argued, because "drugs are not a major problem in this area. In Los Angeles—yes. Rib. Mt.—no." They also pointed out that DARE "took away 50 minutes of our Social Studies time, which in total adds up to 900 minutes a semester." But in a more direct challenge to DARE's entire philosophy, they summed up their argument stating, "Finally, we believe that if this has to be taught, it should be taught by a teacher, not a police officer."[81]

If some students found the program absurd and openly mocked it, most officers learned a different lesson from their interactions with students. In fact, most officers recounted their time in the classroom as an overwhelmingly positive experience, one that shaped their and their department's views of law enforcement. In Cape Girardeau, Missouri, for instance, DARE officer Luther Bonds, notably with his service weapon on his hip, would "come in very enthusiastic" and ask students the time, to which they shouted, "DARE time!" Indeed, Bonds explained, "The kids get really excited when they see me come in the building with Daren [the DARE Lion mascot] because they know it's DARE time. . . . learning starts early so we want to be involved in trying to get these kids, you know, comfortable with police officers, that all police officers aren't, you know, bullies or bad guys, we're here to help, we're here for a service, and developing a rapport with the kids at a young age it helps us in the long run."[82] DARE officer Ken Rosenberg in Arlington, Virginia, expressed similar sentiment of the positive classroom environment and impact on kids. "Kids know that we know what we're talking about," Rosenberg explained. "I've been out there. I've arrested drug dealers and pushers and . . . kids who are strung out on drugs and picked up dead bodies. The rapport you build with the kids is just fantastic."[83] Whether the stories of picking "up dead bodies" animated student engagement or scared them—likely the latter—the classroom experience seemed to be enthusiastic. Officers often described the students' energy, their relationships with students, and the feeling of doing something positive about drug use rather than arresting kids on the street. One Wyoming officer recalled the positive impact he believed DARE had on kids while also lamenting those kids who resisted the DARE message. "And you hoped that, at that age, that would continue on. I've talked to a lot of the kids that I graduated and they said that what I taught them—and every kid that you talk, I won't say every kid, but a lot of the children that you talk to said that that's a positive influence and the kids, that it's changed their lives. But you can see the ones you couldn't touch."[84]

Humanizing the police officer became a selling point as the program expanded across the country. As DARE spread to schools outside Los Angeles, law enforcement quickly saw the program's value in reorienting views of the police. Lieutenant Lew Archer of San Antonio School Police defended the use of the DARE officer as an educator. "If we think of ourselves as peace officers instead of police officers, then maybe we can see that a peace officer uses a wide variety of tasks and skills to keep peace in the community," Archer explained. "If we had been involved in teaching all along, our communities may not have had the societal problems we now have."[85] DARE, it seemed, could solve all societal problems. Put another way, if only all kids had learned to trust, respect, and follow the police, America's social and economic tensions would have been alleviated. When New York City adopted the program in the mid-1990s, officials laid bare the centrality of DARE to what amounted to a public relations campaign. "That [community relations] seemed to me to be one of the major benefits of the program," admitted Robert Strange, a former Drug Enforcement Administration (DEA) agent who worked on antidrug initiatives for New York City. "*Forget about the drug education*. . . . We saw a relationship that could be built between the students and the police officers. There's no other vehicle for that that we're aware of. . . . For critics who say it's good PR for the police department, they're absolutely right and we should do more of it."[86] Community policing components of DARE and other police-led drug education programs intended to transform attitudes toward the police. And DARE was popular, especially with the police. "The idea of getting a police officer in the classroom who's a good role model is a very positive thing," stated Chuck Wexler, head of the Police Executive Research Forum. "There's a lot of support among police chiefs for that."[87] There certainly was, especially as many departments would go on to adopt the program in the years following its establishment in Los Angeles.

If DARE's founders and early boosters worked diligently to promote the program, the officers who taught DARE also supported the program by founding the National DARE Officers Association and accompanying state-level associations.[88] As the association's bylaws outlined, "The purpose of the N.D.O.A. is to provide a means to disseminate, share, advise, and coordinate information which is beneficial and noteworthy to the operation of DARE on a nationwide basis. The object of the N.D.O.A. is to promote continuity of materials and teaching techniques; to promote harmony and good will among its members; and to develop a means to disseminate information which is valuable to DARE Officers nationwide."[89] The association's officers and executive committee brought together representatives from law enforcement agencies across the country, including Arizona, Illinois, North Carolina, Ohio, and Virginia, all in the service of advancing the DARE project.[90] It held its first conference in Los Angeles as early as 1988 to facilitate DARE's programmatic development and exchange ideas about drug education. "The purpose of the National DARE Officers Association Annual Conference shall be to share techniques and developments within the Organization's field of mutual interest, and to conduct necessary national Association business," the association announced. "Emphasis should be on trends and new technology in drug prevention education." It continued to meet annually, which helped expand the DARE program and reinforced DARE's cultural significance.[91] The conferences brought DARE officers together to discuss topics ranging from recognizing drug use to the impact of "gangs and cults" on students and updates on the newest types of street drugs gaining popularity. "What we need to do is make sure that these people . . . take it back to their own communities and take it to the other DARE officers," the 1992 conference organizer Danny Glidewell commented.[92] By 1994, every state and eighteen countries had a DARE Officers Association that looked to the national association for guidance.[93] The NDOA provided an institutional network and messaging to reinforce the claim of police expertise in drug education.

Over time, DARE officers became a force unto themselves. Whether they had volunteered or been assigned to the DARE beat, DARE officers quickly became staunch advocates of the program. As researchers found in a study of what made a DARE officer, "regardless of whether their participation had been voluntary, after getting involved, most officers indicate that they became highly committed to the DARE program." For many officers, DARE was no longer an assignment but "a way of life."[94]

On its twenty-fifth anniversary, DARE officer Anthony Piergallini cogently outlined the DARE mission as one that was less about drug prevention and more about reimagining the role and perception of the police officer. "A big plus to this in my eyes was that if you put an officer in an elementary school classroom talking to kids at their level, not talking down to them, if you communicate with them, now you are not the frightening men in the blue uniforms with badges who are going to put you away. . . . Now, you are human beings. You are friendly guys. A lot of people still don't understand the concept of how important this is."[95] More than anything, DARE enabled the reimagining the police officer as a friend and mentor.

Such public relations campaigns were often necessary precisely because of the aggressive approach police took to waging the drug war, particularly in low-income neighborhoods and neighborhoods of color. As President George H. W. Bush's drug czar William Bennett explained when announcing the National Drug Control Strategy, there was a need to "take back the streets" in inner-city neighborhoods by facilitating the cooperation between residents and the police through neighborhood involvement. Notably, Bennett pointed to DARE as one of the examples of successful community policing and cooperation where police work "closely with at-risk youth."[96] In reimagining the police officer as friend and mentor, in short, DARE became a model of community policing.

DARE as Community Policing

DARE enabled police officers to take on work that was viewed as "positive" compared to aggressive law enforcement practices, or what Gates called the "long-standing principle of 'people working with police.'"[97] Indeed, DARE was at the forefront of community-oriented policing initiatives and was the subject of a *BJA Bulletin* by criminologist David Carter extolling the program's community policing bona fides, which laid the groundwork for the broader turn to community policing in the 1990s.[98]

Early adopters of the program outside of Los Angeles recognized that it enabled police to shift the narrative about police work to one based on proactive policing and community involvement. As Jeremy D. Margolis, director of the Illinois State Police, suggested upon adopting the program in December 1986, "It's easy for us to forget that there is much more to law enforcement than responding to calls, arresting people or engaging in gun battles. Police officers can also distinguish themselves in quiet, yet equally important ways, by preventing problems, heartaches and tragedies in our society before they occur."[99] Such thinking spread rapidly with DARE's expansion across the country. DARE seemed to offer a new approach by law enforcement to the drug problem. "DARE provides, I think, a focal point for total community involvement, a rallying symbol to do something positive about the drug abuse problem," a DARE coordinator from Washington state explained in congressional hearings held in 1990. "[DARE] is really law enforcement taking a proactive role, not responding to a drug abuse problem in a traditional role, but in a proactive role."[100]

Local officers praised the program for its proactive approach and because it allowed them to see their work in a positive light rather than the traditional focus on arrest and punishment. Other law enforcement officers had similar feelings. "DARE provides a number of benefits secondary to drug abuse prevention," Sergeant Roger Kessell of Washington state's Clark County Sheriff's Office testified. "DARE returns the law enforcement officer to the community as the most visible, approachable representative of our government. The local police officer is seen as a caring human being concerned with the welfare and quality of life of the people he or she serves."[101] Other officers saw DARE as a key building block of the broadly defined war on drugs and as a complement to drug enforcement. "From my perspective and my 18 years in law enforcement, [DARE is] the most positive, effective program that I have ever been involved with in saving our communities," one DARE officer from Washington state testified. "If this program would not have come along, or its equivalent, the strategy of the drug war, of enforcement, would not have succeeded. We would have failed. We would have an internal Vietnam within our society, without this educational component."[102]

In response to David Carter's *BJA Bulletin* extolling the virtues of DARE as a model of community policing for the 1990s, DARE America's executive director Glenn Levant doubled down on the community policing message by suggesting that the program had always been envisioned in such a way even if it had not been explicitly described as such. "The bulletin really confirms what those of us directly involved with D.A.R.E. have known for some time: If you want to see a model community policing program, visit a D.A.R.E. school."[103] DARE leaned into its community policing role following the controversy over its effectiveness as a drug prevention program. "D.A.R.E. is community policing," one of DARE America's early websites proclaimed. "D.A.R.E. is universally viewed as an internationally recognized model of community policing." DARE America went on to describe the ways that the United States Department of Justice identified how DARE benefited local communities beyond drug prevention, including humanizing the police, enabling students to see "officers in a helping role, not just an enforcement role," opening lines of communication between youth and officers serving as "conduits to provide information beyond drug-related topics," and "open[ing] dialogue between the school, police, and parents to deal with other issues."[104]

Such sentiments about DARE as an exemplary model of community policing were widespread in the 1990s. In many instances DARE represented the opening wedge of a broader community policing effort because it provided the necessary foundation for kids and teenagers to relate to police officers in new ways. "Being a D.A.R.E. officer gives us the opportunity to help our community and its most valuable members, the children," explained the Idaho DARE Officer Association. "There is nothing as important as the children we teach." But the importance of supporting children required a reorientation of police priorities and the training that officers received to fight crime aggressively. "It forces officers to be more involved and unlearn everything they have been taught," an Idaho DARE representative pointed out. "They can't be hard and cold anymore like they have been taught. They have to show they are a little more human and warm."[105] Or, as one Massachusetts educator said of the program, "I like this marriage of the police department and the school department because it presents a whole new relationship with law enforcement. Every week on television, children see police shooting people, cuffing people, arresting people. This doesn't give a child a sense of confidence and trust in the man in the blue suit. But through the program they learn that they are not just police officers. They are husbands, fathers. They have children and most importantly they care."[106]

Local DARE programs developed a Cops for Kids component aimed at improving relations between youth and police officers through fundraising and programming. In Garden Grove, California, the Cops for Kids component of DARE donated funds from the Southern California Chevrolet Dealers Association for a billboard featuring the slogan "Drugs and Alcohol Are a Grave Mistake" designed by a ten-year-old student. In some cases, DARE officers built on their classroom experience to extend the community policing mission on their own initiative. According to the California Office of Criminal Justice Planning report, one DARE officer involved in the Inglewood Unified School District's Drug Suppression Program recognized a "need for summer activities for Inglewood youth" after teaching DARE. In response, they created a Kops for Kids program in which "police officers, school personnel and community members volunteer in existing facility resources of several local churches." Using private funds from local businesses, the officer extended DARE's reach beyond school grounds to summer and afterschool activities the following school year. "A DARE officer's insight," the California Office of Criminal Justice Planning report continued, "gleaned from his on campus activities, resulted in creating a partnership between the schools, churches, private industry and law enforcement that is effectively providing alternative activities to drugs and gang involvement to approximately 1,000 Inglewood youth." Just as important to observers of the innovative leap this DARE officer made to facilitate community partnerships was DARE's impact. Inglewood Unified School District's DSP Project tracked approximately 2,000 graduates for seven months finding that "to date they have arrested no DARE graduates for substance violations, or any other reasons." Never mind that DARE was taught to fifth and sixth graders who were rarely arrested for substance abuse in or around schools.[107]

By the 1990s, DARE had become a preeminent symbol of community policing. Nationally recognized proponent of community policing Lee P. Brown praised DARE for its role in promoting community policing. Brown had been chief of police in Houston in the 1980s where he worked to establish neighborhood-based policing and other community-oriented programs. Brown served as drug czar under President Clinton, returning to Houston where he ran successfully for mayor.[108] As mayor, he continued to praise DARE for its community policing initiative. "I look back on my tenure as chief of police in Houston with special pride in the DARE program," Brown told the DARE Board of Directors in 2000. "It was a natural outgrowth of my neighborhood oriented policing philosophy, and I thought then—and have been proven right—that the police officers involved in DARE would become more than police officers in their communities. They have become mentors and trusted friends to go to in times of trouble." The real praise was for the officers themselves. "The DARE officers are known to pick up kids and take them to meetings if transportation isn't available," Brown continued. "Officers have been known to take money out of their own pockets for an emergency. With this kind of dedication DARE will continue to be successful."[109]

With the passage of the 1994 Violent Crime Control and Law Enforcement Act, otherwise known as the 1994 Crime Bill, community policing became mainstream.[110] DARE officers and programs capitalized on this trend. One of the most visible examples of DARE's work outside the classroom came in Columbus, Ohio, where police officers formed a rock band called Hot Pursuit in 1986. The band quickly became the "musical complement" to the local DARE program. As one band member described the important work Hot Pursuit accomplished in changing how kids would relate to the police, "For them [kids], to see a policeman on the guitar or playing a drum solo, it said: 'They're human; I can talk to them??'" Hot Pursuit had become such a central part of the city's community relations programming that it was sustained by $300,000 in municipal wages and benefits when it disbanded in 2001.[111] Hot Pursuit held citywide concerts in Columbus to packed auditoriums of DARE students, the first concert ever attended by some students.[112] The band even produced a music video, singing songs with lyrics such as, "DARE to keep a kid off drugs," "DARE to keep a kid off dope," "DARE to give a kid some help," and "DARE to give a kid some hope," with interspersed clips of the band, stereotypical portrayals of older students pressuring younger students

Officer Rick Gillilan (left) and Officer Mike Wilson (right) perform Monday at Hyatt on Capitol Square, Columbus, Ohio. Fred Squillante, December 15, 1986, The Columbus Dispatch–USA Today Network.

to try drugs, and depictions of Black gang members peddling drugs and engaging in violence.[113] The band gained a national reputation after appearing in a 1987 story on *CBS Sunday Morning*, leading to performance requests from cities across the country, the U.S. Embassy in Beijing, and the White House Conference for a Drug Free America by the uniform-wearing, guitars-shaped-as-automatic-weapons-toting police DARE band.[114]

By the late 1990s, the sense that DARE was more of a community policing program than a drug prevention program dominated public perceptions. One study even suggested that DARE should revise how it marketed itself to reflect this reality. "It seems prudent to more accurately describe the goals of D.A.R.E. in terms of its power to impact student perceptions of police, police understanding of students, and improved relationships between police and the community."[115] DARE programs fit this mold well, continuing to be promoted as a model of community policing well into the twenty-first century.[116] As one officer recalled in 2002, "My biggest reward has been in bridging the gap between the kids and the cops; the kids don't run away from the cops anymore in our town. They come to officers to get help. Part of making a program work effectively is establishing great relations with the community."[117]

As with other forms of community policing and police-community relations programming, however, DARE did not always live up to its claim of being truly responsive to student needs. Students often responded that DARE officers rarely listened to them and merely told them how to behave, a similar criticism raised by communities when the police came to community policing meetings to impose their views on residents. "It's like nobody cares what we think," one student told researchers in Kokomo, Indiana. "The DARE cops just wanted us to do what they told us and our teachers never talked about DARE. . . . It seems like a lot of adults and teachers can't bring themselves down to talk to students . . . so you don't care what they think either."[118] As with other components of the program, DARE did not live up to all its promises.

Nonetheless, DARE's ability to alter student perceptions of the police through community policing methods held wide appeal for the nation's drug warriors. Assistant Attorney General Gerald Regier wrote to then acting attorney general William Barr of the crucial role DARE played in shaping the perception of police: "A very important part of this program is to provide an environment in which children will develop a positive attitude toward law enforcement and, subsequently, will have a greater respect for our laws."[119] While the program aimed to influence kids' attitude toward the police as a legitimate authority, it did so through a law enforcement frame that emphasized respect for law and order.

Respect for Law and Order

Employing police officers reinforced the program's emphasis on enhancing student respect for the rule of law. Improving respect for and adherence to the law reinforced the effort at behavioral change and creating disciplined citizens. As one section of the DARE workbook explained, "law" was a word all students should know and understand. The lesson went on to define law as "rules of conduct that are made by people elected to the government. Laws help people respect rights of others. Laws are made to protect people and to keep them safe."[120] Respect for law aimed at creating obedience and acceptance of the laws against drug use, and implicitly suggested that breaking the law came with consequences. Antidrug education, as a result, focused as much on enhancing respect for the law and the police as it did with solving the problem of drug use among the nation's youth. Bringing police into schools thereby intended to reorient students to accept and support the law-and-order mission of law enforcement.[121]

DARE's influence on some students' desire to become police officers also underscored its success at using the drug prevention space to burnish the image of policing. As one DARE graduate wrote to Daryl Gates after describing the "fun" activities the DARE officer participated in with students, such as kickball, handball, and four square, "I want to be a policeman and teach DARE to kids, too."[122] Teachers, for example, reported on year-end evaluations that students who completed the program not only demonstrated an increased respect for law enforcement but also reported "that they want to be police officers."[123] In Whatcom County, Washington, for instance, DARE officer Dori Bowhay recounted how at recess one first grader with a family history of arrest "held [Bowhay's] hand and said, 'My mom and dad don't like cops, but I think I want to be like you.'"[124] Whether such sentiment was representative of all kids who went through DARE or how many actually went on to become police officers is unknown, but such anecdotes enabled DARE administrators to showcase the program as a means to reorient student attitudes toward the police.

Developing rapport with students was meant to encourage kids to cooperate with police officers as legitimate symbols of authority. Students would occasionally tell officers about problems ranging from abuse to relatives who used drugs. Gaining students' trust even led to "students coming forth with information requiring intervention."[125] Indeed, Glenn Levant reported that students told DARE officers and school officials about parental cocaine use on a weekly basis.[126] To deal with such information, DARE officers and school administrators developed a communication network to "ensure that enforcement is taken when necessary without direct involvement of the classroom officer." This network connected the DARE officer to the School Police Department, LAPD's Juvenile Division, and LAPD's Juvenile Narcotics Section to carry out the enforcement measures. In 1984, information acquired from students in DARE classrooms to non-DARE officers resulted in twenty-seven investigations for crimes ranging from drug abuse to child abuse as well as two arrests for the use of alcohol, twelve arrests for possession of marijuana, and five arrests for use of marijuana.[127] Despite administrators' presentation of DARE as a demand reduction program divorced from the supply side of the drug war, it blurred the lines between drug enforcement and prevention.

DARE also enabled police to continue undercover drug work in schools by another means. The combination of DARE officers with the continuation of the School Buy program enabled the police to surveil schools and monitor youth drug use. Levant, for instance, credited DARE with reducing drug dealing and drug-related arrests on school campuses in 1992. How did Levant know? "Because the officers, undercover, on campus, are talking to kids about where they get drugs on campus. They're getting the DARE message from high school kids," Levant explained. "So does DARE work? You're darned right it does." While Levant did not specify whether the cops he was talking about were DARE officers acting as undercover drug officers or undercover School Buy officers, the insinuation was that the police had effectively infiltrated schools through both prevention and enforcement measures.[128] Not only did DARE promote adherence to law and order, it also implied a message that respect for law and the police was part of model citizenship.

But not all students agreed with DARE's hardline stance or followed the prescribed law-and-order messaging. One student, Chantee Charles, made national news when, instead of reading her DARE pledge to not use drugs at a Rose Garden antidrug ceremony, she lectured President George H. W. Bush about the inhumanity of the death penalty and lack of attention to homelessness. "To me, killing someone that has committed a very serious crime is wrong," Charles emphatically announced to the surprise of Bush and other attendees. "It does not solve anything. All it does is take someone else's life." But she was not done there. She discussed the failure to address homelessness, commenting, "People in prison get better care than homeless people on the streets." She also took on Bush's push for capital punishment, explaining, "Probably thousands of prisoners get killed for a crime that they didn't even commit," and death penalty advocates "miss the point that the prisoner has a family, too."[129]

From the outset, as Charles so clearly and forthrightly pointed out, LAUSD and DARE administrators believed the program augmented the mission of the drug war to arrest, incarcerate, and punish drug traffickers and users. The program operated as a soft form of social control aimed at imbuing kids with the law-and-order message of the police. Despite repeated exhortations from law enforcement and DARE administrators, DARE officers were never solely a preventive force divorced from the punitive element of the drug war.

Humanizing Police

Deploying cops as teachers served to humanize the police officer. In doing so, DARE integrated the police into the lives of kids, their schools, and their families through the educative function of schools, solidifying a school-police

Thirteen-year-old Chantee Charles from the Thomas Jefferson Intermediate School, Arlington, Virginia, participates in DARE Day with President Bush at the White House Rose Garden, September 13, 1989. Bettmann via Getty Images.

nexus. Evaluating DARE from the metric of the DARE officer, in other words, demonstrates the program achieved a great deal for the police. Researchers who interviewed DARE officers as part of the curriculum redesign in the late 1990s concluded, "The DARE program is more than a police officer going into a school and lecturing the kids. It is a set of relationships between officers, children, parents, teachers, schools, and communities."[130] That set of relationships, a police-school-parent triad, characterized the way DARE marketed itself to the country. But as the central player in producing the school-police nexus in the 1980s and 1990s, DARE ensured that the police officer was the authority in all facets of the drug war.

Indeed, the DARE officer was the star of the show and would be held up by educators, law enforcement, and politicians as the nation's frontline against youth drug abuse. DARE was imagined as a way to counteract the negative impact of the aggressive policing associated with the war on drugs. "Traditional law enforcement efforts to control the sale and distribution of illicit drugs on school campuses, primarily through periodic 'drug busts,' have little impact on students' drug use and alienate both students and school personnel from police," one early study of DARE found. "An important byproduct of this new approach to drug prevention education is an increased trust between the schools and law enforcement officials."[131] Shifting the police officer's role from a punitive to a social welfare one was always a central part of the program. As Reagan's drug war ramped up through the mid-1980s, partnership between law enforcement and schools became a central element of nearly all drug education and prevention proposals, such as those coming out of the White House Conference for a Drug Free America.[132] It also created the context within which police departments and school districts quickly adopted the program following its establishment in Los Angeles.

If DARE represented a new approach to drug abuse prevention, it also made Los Angeles and California a model for the rest of the nation in how such cooperation would solve the drug problem. And the school-police nexus that DARE represented was also what made the program attractive to police across the country, as DARE did not stay contained to Los Angeles for long. Savvy marketing, federal political and financial support, and corporate sponsorship and funding enabled DARE to become a household name among policymakers, law enforcement, and educators by the early 1990s.

CHAPTER THREE

Spreading the DARE Message

DARE began with ten LAPD officers in fifty elementary schools. All told, administrators estimated DARE reached 87,762 students in that first year. It would only go up from there. Exponentially. The following year, 110 elementary schools and nine junior high schools participated in the program.[1] Within three years of its founding, DARE operated citywide in Los Angeles and deployed 58 uniformed officers to teach the DARE curriculum.[2] With the help of a promotional machine spearheaded by Daryl Gates and Glenn Levant, law enforcement agencies from across the country learned about the program and clamored to send officers to Los Angeles to be trained as DARE officers. In its first three years of operation, forty-eight police departments had sent officers to be trained in Los Angeles, and by 1987, 398 police departments from thirty-three states had sent cops to DARE training, making DARE the nation's leading drug education program.[3] At the start of the 1990s, DARE was ubiquitous, with more than 5,000 officers trained to teach DARE and a presence in 2,200 communities in forty-nine states. By its ten-year anniversary, DARE would be in all fifty states and reach 4.5 million students in more than 70 percent of the nation's school districts.[4]

But that was only domestically. By its sixth year of operation, DARE had gained an international footprint with programs in Australia, New Zealand, American Samoa, Canada, and U.S. Department of Defense schools.[5] Over the 1990s DARE's international presence grew dramatically. At the turn of the new millennium, at least 40,000 officers worldwide were teaching some form of DARE to more than thirty-six million students in 300,000 classrooms in all fifty states, with an additional ten million students in more than fifty countries taking the program.[6] Such rapid and widespread growth brought praise from politicians the world over. "D.A.R.E. is not only the premier drug prevention program in America, you have established worldwide prominence," the director of the Office of National Drug Control Policy, General Barry McCaffrey, crowed in 2000. "You are present in 51 countries. In Southeast Asia alone, the stage is set for over 10,000 D.A.R.E. officers to join your ranks. The tremendous expansion in Canada and Mexico, along with the huge growth in countries like the Philippines and Brazil, are examples of your success."[7] Relying on extensive global law enforcement networks combined with savvy public relations campaigns enabled DARE to spread its message and fulfill its founders' goal of bringing cops into every classroom in the country.

But before DARE went global, it had to go national. And in some ways, DARE's rapid rise to the nation's preeminent drug prevention program was fortuitous, a result of being in the right place at the right time. The Reagan and Bush administrations saw the program as an opportunity to promote moralizing messages about drug abuse and the simplistic solution promoted by Nancy Reagan—Just Say No—and followed through with ample funding. An outpouring of political attention, media, stories, and moral panic made for fertile ground for programs like DARE. Parents, educators, and policymakers across the country demanded something be done to prevent drug use by children.[8] And the legions of police officers and strong law enforcement networks were ready to step in and spread the DARE message.

DARE was primed to capitalize on the growing calls and support for drug prevention. Because it was built on a foundation of community partnership and involvement of police officers, DARE was particularly appealing to policymakers, ensuring it had long staying power. Ultimately, DARE expanded rapidly and remained popular because nearly all the stakeholders involved—from police officers to teachers to policymakers to corporate sponsors—valued the program, and it made them "feel good" regardless of actual results.[9] As researchers Rick Aniskiewicz and Earl Wysong explained in a 1990 evaluation, "Insofar as the program represents a form of symbolic action in response to the 'drug crisis,' its very existence defines it as a success from the perspectives of its political, corporate, and organizational stakeholders."[10] As local communities across the country and globe adopted DARE, the program's extensive reach became a sign of success in itself, no matter that studies would find it was ineffective at reducing drug use. Ultimately, DARE's phenomenal growth ensured that the nation's drug problem would be understood as a problem to be solved primarily by the police.[11]

Police Public Relations and Promoting DARE

From the outset, LAPD and LAUSD administrators envisioned DARE's rapid expansion. In their 1983 proposal outlining the framework for DARE, Gates and Handler laid out a five-phase implementation plan to ensure the program would be taught in all grades from kindergarten through twelfth grade in the city. This was to be no mere pilot project, but one that ensured DARE officers would be teaching the curriculum to students citywide. And they recognized that the program would not grow on its own; they needed to promote and market it to ensure its widespread adoption. "The success of this program is vital to the City of Los Angeles and the promotion and fund raising campaign is key to that success," Gates and Handler summarized before the launch of the program. "Second best should not be an alternative."[12]

With this prophetic pronouncement, Daryl Gates revealed his ambitions for police-led drug education. He envisioned DARE leading the way. Upon receiving funding from the state of California's Suppression of Drug Abuse in Schools Program for the 1984 school year, Gates wrote to state funders, "I assure you that the Drug Abuse Resistance Education (DARE) Program is the finest of its kind in this nation and I am confident that the people of California will be proud to hear that there [*sic*] tax dollars will be used for this effort. We believe that DARE will serve as the model for educators and law enforcement to unite and fight the serious epidemic of substance abuse within their communities. We in Los Angeles are truly proud that the great State of California will once again set the standard for the entire nation."[13] As the program grew, DARE administrators openly admitted having an interest in "promulgating DARE as the national model drug prevention education program."[14] Savvy public relations, law enforcement networks, and political support would ensure successful dissemination.

Gates looked first to the Reagan administration for political backing. A mere four months after the program launched, Gates wrote to First Lady Nancy Reagan to express his "appreciation for your untiring effort in combatting drug abuse by our nation's youth." Assuring her that "you are not alone in the fight," Gates pitched the first lady on the virtues of DARE and extended an open-ended invitation for her to attend a DARE class session.[15] A few months later, just prior to DARE graduates receiving their certificates and T-shirts, Gates promoted the program with other members of the Reagan administration. On April 4, 1984, he wrote to Vice President Bush's chief of staff, "It is my belief that this program is perhaps the ultimate answer to the drug problem in this country and is a model that could be implemented throughout the United States."[16] Other LAPD brass, such as Assistant Chief Robert L. Vernon, continued the pressure on the Reagan administration to support DARE in the following year with letters to First Lady Nancy Reagan, Attorney General Edwin Meese III, and Vice President George H.W. Bush.[17]

Police administrators recognized that marketing DARE was central to producing public and political support. When they launched the program, administrators outlined promotion and fundraising goals that included obtaining access to free television and radio spots, enlisting professional athletes and entertainment figures, using billboards and bus benches for advertising, and presentations before service clubs and parent teacher associations.[18] Well before DARE gained a national following or reputation, organizers recommended retaining a professional advertising and public relations firm and developing a revenue stream from both public and private sources. As the LAUSD/LAPD proposal for DARE outlined, "The ability to generate awareness by the community and media will be essential in promoting public acceptance of the educational program, obtaining funding and, most importantly, involving them in solutions to this problem." Public relations specialists saw DARE's potential for growth. "It is significant," project planners reported, "that the specialists already contacted see the concept of a joint police/educator effort to be a 'sure winner' and an ideal cause for fund raising."[19]

While some observers, such as board of education member Rita Walters, viewed the promotion as "an effort [to] raise Gates' profile, if he decided to run for mayor," the Los Angeles City Council was more readily convinced of DARE's utility.[20] Indeed, city councilwoman Joy Picus wrote to Vernon in March 1984 stating, "I am personally familiar with the DARE program . . . and can attest to the positive effect the program has had on the participating schools. . . . I commend you and the other LAPD personnel who have been involved in developing and implementing DARE. . . . I look forward to continuing to work together on programs such as DARE to improve the quality of life in our community."[21] Other council members had similar feelings. When Gates and DARE staff, for instance, asked the council to pass an ordinance amending city policy regarding bumper stickers on city vehicles so DARE bumper stickers could be attached to LAPD patrol cars, the council quickly approved the change. "Many police patrol cars have had affixed to their rear bumpers special stickers which refer to Project DARE, and which have helped spread public awareness of this exceptional effort," a council motion stated. "This public information effort could be greatly augmented by the placing of these bumper stickers, which the police department can supply, on the approximately 1,000 city fleet and assigned cars. Such an action would significantly increase public curiosity about, awareness of and support for Project DARE specifically and drug aversion instruction for children generally."[22] The council also approved funding for DARE billboards to promote antidrug and anti-gang messages across the city and passed a resolution encouraging "government, industry and private contributions in order to expand the D.A.R.E. Program throughout the city, state and nation."[23] With the council's overwhelming support, DARE became a fundamental part

Daryl Gates shows off a DARE campaign billboard. Javier Mendoza, January 1987, Herald Examiner Collection, Los Angeles Public Library, Los Angeles, California.

of the school experience for Angeleno youth and a centerpiece of the LAPD's prevention programming.

With Gates proselytizing every chance he got, DARE took off. Gates highlighted DARE in nearly every LAPD Annual Report following its introduction in 1983, wrote articles about it in educational and law enforcement magazines, including *School Safety*, *The Police Chief*, and the *FBI Law Enforcement Bulletin*, and routinely spoke about DARE at International Association of Chiefs of Police annual meetings. His aim? To encourage other law enforcement agencies to adopt the program.[24] And it worked. Building on this use of law enforcement networks, Gates also partnered with local community and nonprofit organizations to develop materials to publicize the program. In 1985, for instance, the Los Angeles Rotary International arranged funds and "technical expertise" to produce a thirty-minute documentary on DARE with the LAPD and LAUSD.[25] The following year, Gates embarked on a media campaign to "create a high profile image" for DARE using billboards, radio, and television to promote the message: "Say No to Drugs."[26] Such promotional activities led other departments to look to DARE as a possible model for drug education in their cities and states.

Gates and LAUSD representatives also marketed DARE using slogans—"DARE to Keep Kids off Drugs"—and, more overtly, with a DARE mascot. In 1985, they created a DARE mascot, the "DARE Bear," "as a symbol of the efforts of two agencies [LAPD and LAUSD] working together in the development and implementation of DARE." More than an expression of collaboration between schools and the police, the DARE Bear was intended to become a national cultural symbol of DARE and its drug resistance message. "It is hoped," Gates reported to Mayor Tom Bradley, "that the DARE Bear becomes a national symbol of drug prevention similar to McGruff the Crime Dog."[27] Like McGruff, the DARE Bear would signal positive messages about drug prevention and the acceptance of police as trustworthy partners in the war on drugs and crime. With the help of such savvy marketing and the DARE Bear mascot—later changed to the DARE Lion (named Daren), which was also made into a stuffed toy and passed to students as they answered questions correctly in class—DARE was becoming a nationally known commodity. When local communities adopted the program, they would "acquire the logo and the look" of DARE.[28]

Police vehicles with DARE logos also became a promotional tool of local law enforcement agencies to make the program visible in communities across the country. Law enforcement agencies often held contests for the best DARE vehicles, the winners of which were publicized in police magazines. In 1991, for instance, *Law and Order* highlighted a converted truck with DARE messaging seized from a drug dealer, asserting that the DARE vehicle "shows students that the consequences of using/selling drugs is very costly." While some vehicles were donated by dealerships to help promote DARE, many DARE vehicles had been seized using asset forfeiture and intended to "emphasize the association between D.A.R.E. instruction and law enforcement."[29]

From an experimental program taught in fifty elementary schools, by the end of the 1980s DARE boosters had put DARE on the map.[30] It also elevated Los Angeles as a crucial site of innovation in the so-called war on drugs. As the Los Angeles City Council reported in 1986, "The implementation of the DARE Program has placed the City of Los Angeles at the forefront of drug abuse prevention education. It has been recognized by both local and national agencies around the United States as the most comprehensive officer/instructor drug education program in the country."[31] Public relations and marketing was surely key to DARE's visibility and cultural status. But when it came to actually bringing the program to new schools, DARE benefited from state-sponsored support. As policymakers looked to demand reduction strategies, DARE's school-police partnership model fit just right.

A military police officer from the Provost Marshal's Office poses with McGruff the Crime Dog and Daren the DARE Lion, October 16, 2009. McGruff and Daren met with children and promoted safety and drug resistance. Courtesy of Wikimedia Commons.

A 1995 Ford Falcon DARE vehicle. New Zealand Police, May 17, 2004, Creative Commons Attribution 2.0 Generic, https://creativecommons.org/licenses/by/2.0/deed.en.

DARE Goes National

Because DARE relied on the police officer as teacher, the project was well suited to be a model for the state's promotion of joint law enforcement and education programming in the realm of drug education and prevention. In 1983, somewhat coincidentally, state legislators passed Assembly Bill 1983 to facilitate partnerships between law enforcement and school officials to combat the problem in the state's schools. The legislation aimed to facilitate "increased efforts of local law enforcement agencies working in conjunction with school districts and county drug offices . . . to . . . suppress drug trafficking and prevent drug abuse among school-age children on and around school campuses."[32] Under the law, to be eligible to receive state funding, law enforcement agencies and school districts had to submit a co-application outlining the various ways they would cooperate in a joint program to fight drug abuse in schools, something that was built into the DARE model.[33] By promoting the connection between prevention and apprehension and tying state antidrug funding to law enforcement involvement, DARE was primed to expand.

Although state officials resisted DARE officials' pressure to mandate the program be taught in all California schools, they supported it by funneling state drug abuse and criminal justice funds into the program.[34] Within a matter of years, DARE became a model program held up by the state's

Suppression of Drug Abuse in Schools Program.[35] Beginning with the 1984–1985 school year, DARE received grant funding totaling $478,443 from the California Suppression of Drug Abuse in Schools Program, which explicitly aimed to connect schools and law enforcement through innovative antidrug programming.[36] Grant funding enabled the LAPD to expand the program in its second year from a budget of $812,000 to roughly $1.29 million, which allowed the LAPD to increase the number of officers teaching the curriculum from ten to fifteen.[37] The grant-funded expansion allowed more schools in the San Fernando Valley to receive the DARE curriculum, suggesting that in its first year, and as envisioned by Gates and LAUSD, the program focused more directly on schools in the predominantly Latinx and Black neighborhoods of East Los Angeles and South Central.[38]

Federal and state grant funding facilitated the goals of DARE administrators who looked to aggressively expand the program. During the pilot year program, the LAPD recommended that one of the changes to the program as it moved into its second year was to begin the planned expansion into junior high schools.[39] The program seemed so successful that after its second year, the Los Angeles Board of Education passed a resolution that DARE should be expanded to "*all* elementary and junior high schools" in the city, which it did by 1988, as well as introducing a private school program in 1988 and a high school program in 1989.[40] DARE was well on its way to becoming omnipresent in LA schools, and kids would have weekly, if not daily, contact with a DARE officer.

Word was also getting out among law enforcement professionals that something was happening in Los Angeles. Before DARE's second year began, the LAPD DARE Unit and LAUSD instructional specialists received numerous requests for information from school districts and police departments across the nation. To fulfill such requests and to expand the DARE program, the LAPD developed a two-week DARE Training Seminar to introduce outside agencies to the DARE program and curriculum.[41] The training provided an overview of all components of the DARE project, ranging from panels with educators and classroom visits to discussions of funding and administration. Expanding DARE was a key part of the seminar. Leaders of the training hoped that "all agencies who participate hopefully will be committed to joining with their school districts in successful implementation of the DARE concept."[42] Within DARE's first year of operation, LAPD and LAUSD representatives provided training for twenty-four officers from police departments in several California communities as well as Washington and Hawaii.[43] In following years, numerous law enforcement agencies nationwide sent officers to Los

Angeles to attend DARE training. Crucially, the agencies trained were not local school districts but law enforcement agencies. Alongside representatives from law enforcement agencies coming to Los Angeles for training, DARE staff also traveled across California and eventually the country to give presentations on DARE at law enforcement and educational professional associations.[44] DARE was well on its way to becoming not only a nationally recognized symbol of the drug war but also the primary law enforcement–led drug prevention program used by schools nationwide.

DARE capitalized on law enforcement officials across the country openly admitting the failure of source country eradication and border interdiction and calling for demand reduction strategies. "I started off by saying this frustration that I share with a lot of my colleagues, that this frustration has finally turned to saying why are we even bothering in Mexico and Colombia," explained Colonel Ralph Milstead, the director of the Arizona Department of Public Safety during hearings on drug abuse and trafficking along the Southwest border. "Let's bring our people back and let's go ahead and work on the problem here and let's work on the demand side rather than keep pouring dollars on the supply side. I liken it to killing a snake tail first. We ought to start at the head and the head, of course, is the demand."[45] From border agents to local police officers, attention to the demand problem increasingly gained a foothold. As Frances Mullen, former administrator of the DEA and deputy director of the FBI, told Congress in 1983, "For too long, we have expected law enforcement to eliminate the nation's drug problem. While it obviously has an important role to play, we won't have any lasting success until we start working on reducing the huge demand for drugs."[46] Support from law enforcement for demand reduction had become so widespread that Republican California senator Pete Wilson remarked in 1989, "The most eloquent arguments for engaging on the demand-reduction front come from police officers."[47] Such sentiment enabled stakeholders to promote DARE as a ready-made demand reduction solution.[48]

One of the first places DARE was implemented on a widespread basis beyond Los Angeles was in Virginia.[49] After contacting the LAPD in November 1984, Virginia officials began planning to adopt DARE in 1985 with the Virginia State Police and Department of Education proposing to implement DARE in fifteen school divisions starting in the fall of 1986, forty in 1987, and 140 in 1989. The Virginia program reinforced the partnership between schools, police, and parents as a joint effort in combating drug use. Using similar rhetoric as the Los Angeles program, the Virginia DARE project envisioned the approach as "an effective long term solution to reduce the 'demand' for drugs."[50] Implementing DARE in new areas relied on adapting the program to local conditions. "Some localities in Virginia also felt the lesson on gang activities was not necessary." As a result, the Virginia program revised the curriculum to suit its needs, most significantly by removing the anti-gang education component.[51] Such changes indicated the extent to which the Los Angeles program sought to address the intersection of drugs and gangs unique to its locale. With the establishment of the Virginia DARE program, the foundation was set for growth. While the LAPD spearheaded the expansion of DARE training and promotion, the Virginia assistant director of the Bureau of Criminal Investigation reported that he had been approached by law enforcement officials from states across the country to visit the Virginia State Police DARE program.[52]

Federal law enforcement and Department of Justice officials began to take notice of DARE. James Stewart, executive director of the National Institute of Justice (NIJ), observed DARE in operation and came away "very impressed," calling the program the only one of its kind in the country. Such praise led Stewart to send DARE brochures to police departments and school districts across the country, which encouraged other police departments to visit Los Angeles to learn about the program, receive training, and implement the curriculum in their local schools.[53] The NIJ also highlighted DARE in its first episode of *Crime File,* a series of informational episodes on criminal justice issues and solutions, in which they interviewed Daryl Gates, teachers, and a DARE officer, followed by political scientist and self-described father of Broken Windows Policing James Q. Wilson moderating a discussion of the program.[54] The NIJ was, quite simply, lining up behind DARE and providing a platform to make other law enforcement agencies aware of its existence.

Meanwhile, the NIJ supported an initial evaluation of the program conducted by William DeJong. DeJong's initial findings, published in a series of NIJ reports and in the *Journal of Drug Education,* positively reviewed DARE and its ability to prevent drug use.[55] While DeJong notes that the results of these studies were preliminary and he called for more structured research and evaluation of the program, the LAPD's Gates took the results and ran with them.[56] With the help of the NIJ's financial support and its positive evaluation, DARE took off.

Stemming from this national recognition, the LAPD received federal financial support when the Department of Justice awarded the department a $140,000 grant in 1986 to "share its unique DARE Program with other communities throughout the United States."[57] Under the title Technical Assistance

Program (DARE-TAP), DARE trainers in Los Angeles used Bureau of Justice Assistance funds to create a reproducible model of drug education and to train partner agencies across the country, such as the Arizona Department of Public Safety, Illinois State Police, and the Commonwealth of Massachusetts Committee on Criminal Justice.[58] When proposing the grant, they argued the DARE-TAP program would lead to "positive networking between law enforcement representatives and educators."[59] DARE-TAP extended not only the reach of the DARE curriculum but also the importance of the DARE officer. As one grant report concluded, "Visitations gave an added dimension to the overall effort to promulgate drug abuse prevention education to our youth across the nation. News media response and coverage evidenced the positive community response to students receiving DARE instruction in the classroom."[60]

Policymakers in Los Angeles believed that expanding DARE through DARE-TAP would help combat interstate and international drug trafficking. "If illicit drug use among our youth is curtailed through DARE implementation in other cities, the interstate trafficking of drugs via the City of Los Angeles will be reduced," the City Council Grants, Housing and Community Development Committee explained in a quarterly progress report on DARE-TAP. "The resulting reduction in local drug-related crime would be a direct benefit to the city."[61] Developing a nationwide network of DARE programs would also facilitate communication and knowledge about drug abuse and trafficking patterns that law enforcement could use to wage a more efficient war on drugs. "In the short term, participation in this federal assistance program will foster better working relationships between the city and other localities and organizations concerned with the effects of drug abuse," explained Rose Ochi, director of the Mayor's Office of Criminal Justice Planning. "This relationship would enhance the city's ability to obtain information about drug-related violence and corruption experienced by other communities and would be of great assistance in developing anticipatory strategies oriented toward meeting local challenges which might arise in these drug-related areas."[62]

Following the initial adoption by individual police departments and the creation of a replicable training model through DARE-TAP, the LAPD became overwhelmed by the interest in DARE. In response, the LAPD and LAUSD collaborated with the BJA to establish a series of regional training centers (RTC) to train officers across the country in the DARE curriculum. Building out of the DARE-TAP program, the LAPD used the contact with law enforcement agencies to create the groundwork for a robust network of RTCs.

Planners identified five locations for RTCs, including the Los Angeles Police Department, Illinois State Police, Arizona Department of Public Safety, Virginia State Police, and North Carolina State Bureau of Investigation. The RTCs became instrumental in expanding and replicating DARE nationwide. Guided by a DARE Training Center Policy Advisory Board, which was responsible for overseeing DARE officer training, the RTCs provided officers with the eighty-hour DARE training, a forty-hour training for officers who would lead the trainings (labeled the "Trainer of Trainers" curriculum), in-service training to ensure DARE officers stayed up to date, accreditation of state-level training, and monitoring of implementation to ensure program fidelity.[63] Federal investment institutionalized the DARE program, made it easily adopted by local law enforcement officials, and, notably, would make DARE difficult to criticize.

As DARE expanded to schools nationwide, the school-police partnership was a prerequisite for adopting the program. Requirements set by the DARE Regional Training Center Advisory Committee, a group established to help standardize DARE curriculum and training across all the regional training centers in 1988, made such partnerships part of the training policy. Each regional training center had a written policy including a philosophy that "reflects a belief that a school-based drug abuse program, taught by uniformed officers/deputies, can be effective with children" and "demonstrates a belief in the partnership of law enforcement agencies and school districts to deliver the DARE curriculum."[64] Such thinking became self-reinforcing. An early study of DARE implementation by law enforcement agencies across the country conducted for Los Angeles officials by Kathleen M. Wulf found that the most successful programs allocated most of the assigned officer's time to DARE, established strong partnerships between the law enforcement agency and school district, spent most of their DARE funding on student materials, and "the officer spends more time in visitation to kindergarten through fourth grade classrooms at the school site." Programs tended to founder, Wulf concluded, if the DARE officer did not feel welcome in the school or devote more than 50 percent of an officer's time to DARE. In turn, the evaluation recommended LAPD training emphasize the importance of the school-police partnership and the DARE officer's commitment to being in schools on a "full-day basis."[65] Adopting DARE meant police officers would be a regular presence in local schools. If there was some flexibility in local implementation of DARE programming, in short, the fundamental precept of the role of law enforcement officers as teachers and the school-police partnership was nonnegotiable.

DARE celebration with students holding signs of the names of states and countries with DARE programs. Dean Musgrove, September 15, 1988, Herald Examiner Collection, Los Angeles Public Library, Los Angeles, California.

As DARE grew, it benefited from federal funding dedicated to law enforcement programs. One funding stream came from DARE's eligibility for the Edward Byrne Memorial State and Local Law Enforcement Assistance Program, which was named for an NYPD officer killed in 1986. These Byrne grants, according to the BJA, were earmarked for law enforcement programs and provided "federal assistance in a national campaign against drug abuse and other serious crime." Because DARE was led by law enforcement agencies partnered with schools, it was eligible for Byrne grants, an indication of DARE's fundamental law enforcement—rather than educative—orientation.[66] This funding enabled DARE RTCs to provide training seminars and curriculum material to officers nationally and, in time, internationally.[67] At the core of the RTC and DARE-TAP model was the belief that the DARE curriculum had to replicate the Los Angeles model, what evaluators called fidelity. The RTC concept was intended to standardize DARE programs in hopes that all DARE officers would teach the same thing in the same way in classrooms around the world.[68] Although there was evidence that the diffusion of DARE was much more flexible and prone to reinvention based on local needs, the claim to have a standardized, and successful, program that was easily replicable went a long way to convincing policymakers to support the program.[69]

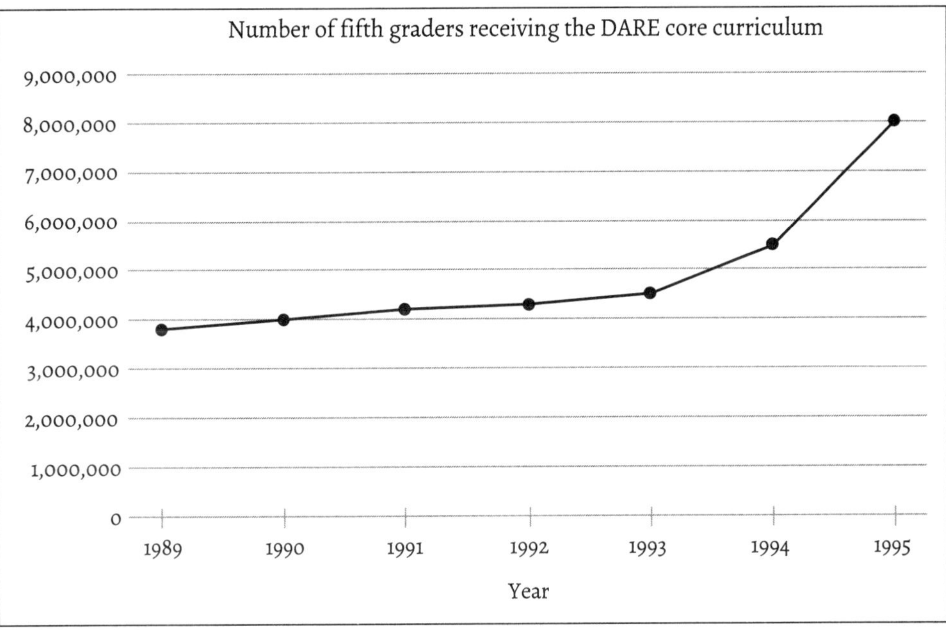

These data are only for the core fifth-grade curriculum and do not reflect the various other DARE programs taught to middle and high school students or one-day presentations to children in younger grades. Source: Bureau of Justice Assistance, *Drug Abuse Resistance Education (DARE)—Fact Sheet*, Department of Justice, Office of Justice Programs, Bureau of Justice Assistance, NCJ FS000039 (Washington, DC, September 1995).

By emphasizing program integrity, training standardization, and replication, the RTC system facilitated the program's rapid growth across the country. DARE America envisioned the training centers as part of a network that "collectively assist[s] BJA and D.A.R.E. America in their efforts to reduce gang violence, the demand for drugs, and drug related crimes."[70] On the program's fifth anniversary, DARE held a celebration at Gates Elementary School in Los Angeles where kids held up signs of the states and countries that had adopted the program. By 1989, the Los Angeles Regional Training Center alone operated trainings for ten states and had trained 904 officers from 315 agencies who operated in 13,588 schools and 2,928 school districts.[71] And the growth did not stop there. By its ten-year anniversary, the program operated in 5,200 communities in all fifty states and dozens of countries, and the Department of Defense had adopted the program for its schools in bases around the world.[72] As of 1995, more than 8 million children in fifth- and sixth-grade classrooms learned how to say no to drugs and resist peer pressure through

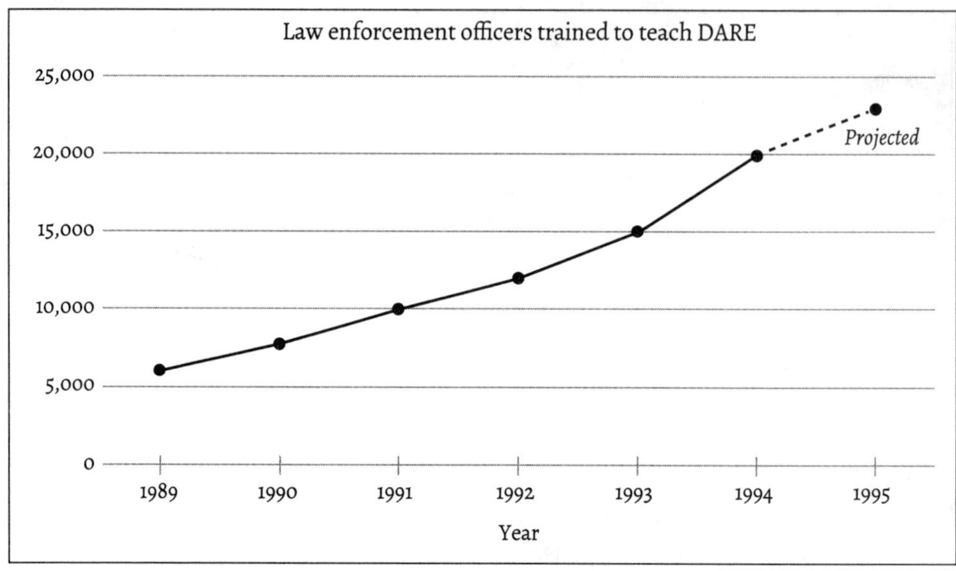

Data for 1995 were projected. Source: Bureau of Justice Assistance, *Drug Abuse Resistance Education (DARE)—Fact Sheet,* Department of Justice, Office of Justice Programs, Bureau of Justice Assistance, NCJ FS000039 (Washington, DC, September 1995).

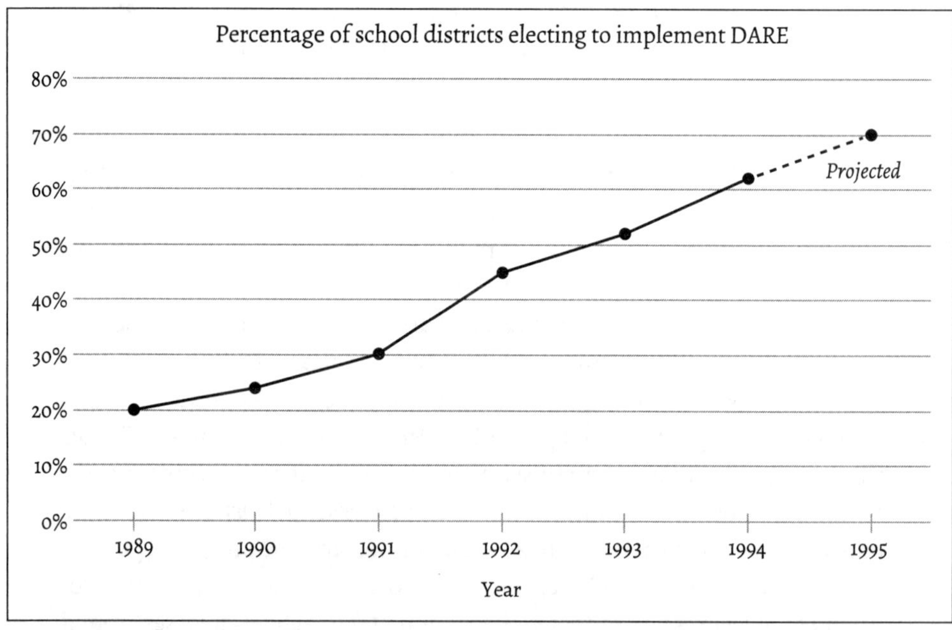

Data for 1995 were projected at 65–70 percent. Source: Bureau of Justice Assistance, *Drug Abuse Resistance Education (DARE)—Fact Sheet,* Department of Justice, Office of Justice Programs, Bureau of Justice Assistance, NCJ FS000039 (Washington, DC, September 1995).

DARE.[73] Daryl Gates was not wrong when he stated in 1990, "The D.A.R.E. program has become a model that can be exported to other cities."[74]

Expanding DARE broadened law enforcement control over the drug problem while also becoming a goal unto itself. "We're not really going to be happy until we've got the program everywhere," stated Levant. "There is no place in the United States where substance abuse is not a deadly epidemic." The curriculum became so popular that it would be taught in over 80 percent of the nation's school districts in all fifty states and dozens of countries around the world, reaching more than thirty-six million children domestically and more than ten million internationally.[75] As DARE grew, it also became the primary beneficiary of federal funding for drug-free schools and received widespread support from across the political spectrum.

Mandating Drug Education: The Drug Free Schools and Communities Act

Political support for drug prevention and education programming gained even more traction following the death of Len Bias, the star University of Maryland basketball player and number one pick of the Boston Celtics, from a cocaine overdose in 1986. Alongside renewed calls for greater punishment for drug dealers and users, Bias's death created opportunities for policymakers to propose alternatives aimed at demand reduction, particularly for children. Media attention to crack in national newsmagazines and television news, as well as Gallup polling showing that Americans saw drugs as the country's most important problem, created the conditions for legislative action in what would become the 1986 and 1988 Anti-Drug Abuse Acts.[76]

A key component of this legislation was the Drug Free Schools and Communities Act (DFSCA). Initially proposed by Los Angeles Congressman Augustus Hawkins as the Drug Abuse Education and Prevention Act of 1986 "to help attack the nation's growing drug epidemic by reducing demand," the amended DFSCA facilitated the complementary nature of enforcement and prevention—the soft and hard power of the developing carceral state. As Hawkins commented during debate over and revisions to the DFSCA, the legislation "reflects the consensus that enhanced interdiction and law enforcement—however desirable—must be accompanied by drug abuse education and prevention. We need to turn the heavy pressure to experiment with drugs around into an attitude that says the cool thing to do is not do drugs."[77] Just as many law enforcement officials had concluded, congressional representatives began to see the need for additional measures beyond punitive policy to attack the nation's drug crisis.

Focusing on demand attracted Congressman Charles Rangel (D-NY), the African American representative from Harlem who cofounded the Congressional Black Caucus and led the criticism of what he saw as the Reagan administration's tepid response to the drug crisis. Rangel had long championed expanding law enforcement's capacity to wage the war on drugs and to increase penalties for drug dealing and possession.[78] While Rangel pushed for more arrests and longer jail and prison sentences for dealers, he also saw the need for education and prevention. He highlighted law enforcement's support for demand reduction and prevention programming in hearings on drug abuse education in 1986. "Most of the law enforcement agencies in the United States," Rangel stated, "have now come to an agreement that the emphasis has to be placed on reducing demand through education and prevention."[79] With Rangel's backing, drug education and prevention would be integrated into the broader legislative effort to ramp up the war on drugs.

Support from a wide range of policymakers ensured drug prevention education became a crucial weapon in the war on drugs. "No entity has a more important role than our schools and our children's dedicated teachers who are frequently the most influential factor in a child's life," one Congress member stated.[80] Or as Rangel described in more depth during congressional hearings on the drug education component of the 1986 Anti-Drug Abuse Act, "I believe this committee has before it proposals dealing with one of the most important parts of the package—drug abuse education. . . . I say this not because I feel that international narcotics control and drug enforcement do not have crucial roles to play in addressing our nation's drug problem. I say this because when one considers the serious levels of drug use and trafficking in our nation, we must take immediate steps to defend our children and families against the massive onslaught of illegal drugs engulfing our communities."[81] The DFSCA provision of the 1986 Omnibus Anti-Drug Abuse Act played a significant role in elevating prevention programs and providing federal funds that would go a long way in helping DARE expand nationwide, especially because it became the model program on which much of the DFSCA and subsequent amendments would be based.[82]

The DFSCA put the federal government firmly in the business of funding drug prevention programming. Federal funding for drug prevention and education grew accordingly. From $189 million in 1987 to $463 million in 1990 to $613 million in 1993 and a request for $660 million in 1995, spending on drug education increased, though never as rapidly or to the same extent as support for building more prisons and equipping police officers with new tools to wage the drug war.[83] Regardless, such federal backing provided a strong foundation on which DARE and other drug education programs could grow. DARE, as many observers pointed out, was not only the most popular of such antidrug programs but also one of the programs well positioned to take advantage of the federal largesse.[84]

An amendment to the DFSCA in 1989 went even further, mandating that schools have drug prevention programs to receive federal education funding. The amendment made it clear that "no local educational agency shall be eligible to receive funds or any other form of financial assistance under any federal program unless it certifies to the state educational agency that it has adopted and has implemented a program to prevent the use of illicit drugs and alcohol by students or employees." To fulfill this requirement, programs had, at a minimum, to include a message that drug use was "wrong and harmful," adopt standards of conduct that prohibited "possession, use, or distribution of illicit drugs and alcohol by students and employees," and an explicit statement of the consequences "up to and including expulsion or termination of employment" for violating the school's standards of conduct. More significantly for DARE, the legislation stressed using uniformed law enforcement personnel as an accepted—and desirable—form of prevention education for federal funds. While it did not mention DARE by name, the amendment encouraged adopting programs that "may bring law enforcement officers into the classroom to provide antidrug information and positive alternatives to drug use, including decision making and assertiveness skills," which was almost certainly a direct reference to DARE.[85]

Mandating that schools implement drug prevention programming to receive federal funding and mentioning the use of police officers as instructors put DARE in a prime position to use the DFSCA to build on its established national visibility and prominence. In short order, various members of Congress singled out DARE in proposed legislation to allocate federal funding to the program. California senator Pete Wilson, during his 1989 run for governor, sponsored legislation allocating $10 million in federal funds directly to DARE.[86] The following year, other members of Congress, including Dale Kildee (D-MI) and Jolene Unsoeld (D-WA), who earned the nickname "Ms. DARE" from Kildee, proposed the Drug Abuse Resistance Education Act of 1990. That act would have allocated $15 million from the DFSCA to local communities to develop DARE programs. "Part of what you all are doing today is to help us build that momentum, establish the record," Unsoeld outlined in hearings held in Vancouver, Washington, "so that we can go back to Congress to give that extra push to promote this very worthwhile program." Allocating federal funds to DARE explicitly aimed to expand the program. As a report on the legislation summarized, "A federal commitment will help

US senator Pete Wilson sponsors legislation allocating $10 million for DARE. He joined Daryl Gates at Betty Plasencia Elementary School in Los Angeles. Javier Mendoza, 1989, Herald Examiner Collection, Los Angeles Public Library, Los Angeles, California.

extend the program to more schools and commit more law enforcement officers to DARE duty without sacrificing patrol strength." While the Drug Abuse Resistance Education Act did not pass, the program had become a clear political winner for many. As Unsoeld summarized, "In a nation that is desperately seeking solutions to our drug problems, I believe DARE stands out as a proven weapon." Supporting DARE was a win-win for policymakers—they could be both antidrug and pro-police.[87]

Advocates were not deterred by the failure to pass the Drug Abuse Resistance Education Act. Many prominent supporters, including Daryl Gates, members of Congress, and former president H. W. Bush, ensured that it would be singled out when Congress amended the DFSCA in 1990. The amendment intended to provide resources for replicating "successful drug education programs" by requiring that 10 percent of "governor's funds" (discretionary funds made up roughly 30 percent of the funding available to states under the DFSCA) be used for grants to local school districts for programs to help students "recognize and resist pressures that influence such students to use controlled substances . . . such as Project Drug Abuse Resistance Education."[88] Earmarked funds for DARE allowed governors to support the establishment, growth, and continuation of the DARE program in local school districts across their states. In Georgia, for example, Governor Zell Miller approved the "transfer of $10,000 from my discretionary fund to assist with operating expenses for the DARE program" in Macon.[89] Meanwhile, in Wisconsin, law enforcement officials wrote to Governor Tommy Thompson asking for his support in funding the DARE program, which had returned "respect to the police officer."[90] But the legislation went a step further. It not only singled out DARE but also highlighted the program's foundational idea: the partnership between schools and police. Local school districts would not be eligible for such federal grants if they did not include "classroom instruction by uniformed law enforcement officials."[91] As the only prevention program specifically named in the DFSCA, DARE was given pride of place in the growing funding available for prevention education. Between 1989 and 1995, the BJA discretionary funding level for DARE increased accordingly from $625,000 to $1.75 million.[92]

Federal support did not stop there. When Congress amended the DFSCA as part of the Violent Crime Control and Law Enforcement Act of 1994, it continued the 20 percent set aside for governor's funds, of which 10 percent was required to be spent on DARE or similar law enforcement and school-based partnership programs.[93] Indeed, as researchers summarized the deep investment policymakers had in appearing to support DARE, "The popularity of DARE among national political leaders was clearly evident in the House debate on the reauthorization bill during which many House members repeatedly praised DARE and worked to include provisions that would ensure continued federal funding for the program."[94] While DARE was no longer the sole program eligible for such funds, the police-school partnership remained foundational in the federal government's education and prevention efforts. Reauthorizing the DFSCA in 1994 as part of the Improving America's Schools Act revisions to the Elementary and Secondary Education Act expanded the program's scope under the Safe and Drug Free Schools and Communities Act of 1994 (SDFSCA).[95] As the Improving America's Schools Act laid out, "A chief executive officer shall use not less than 10 percent of the 20 percent of the total amount . . . for law enforcement education partnerships." Under the acceptable Law Enforcement Partnerships section, the legislation named DARE as one of the exemplary programs that qualified for the 10 percent requirement.[96] Federal funding for education became conditional on local educational agencies submitting "certifications that they have comprehensive drug prevention programs and anti-drug policies in place."[97] Support for drug prevention programs by the DFSCA often meant adoption of DARE by local school districts. In a longitudinal study of the DFSCA, researchers found that roughly 65 percent of the students surveyed over a five-year period had participated in DARE, far outpacing other drug education programs.[98]

Alongside prevention funding, DARE also benefited from resources that derived from the supply side of the drug war. Police departments supported DARE through asset stripping of communities targeted by law enforcement's use of forfeiture laws, practices which tend to exacerbate racially discriminatory policing.[99] Gates, for instance, advocated for the use of asset forfeiture to fund DARE—and lobbied for the California legislature to pass new laws that would directly allocate seized funds for drug education and prevention—as early as 1984. While unclear if the California legislature passed the specific law requested by Gates, by the late 1980s revenue generated by seizures of property was often allocated to DARE in Los Angeles and other cities nationwide.[100] Shared asset forfeiture funds were commonly used for purchases ranging from vehicles and computers to drug education programs, including salaries for DARE officers.[101] The LAPD saw the potential in using drug war forfeiture monies as a near-limitless source of future funding. LAPD and LAUSD administrators suggested "monies obtained through the forfeiture process in conjunction with 'equitable sharing' provisions of the United States Code will provide a valuable new source of DARE funding for years to come." DARE administrators anticipated that of $2.8 million earmarked for department use in the city's Forfeited Assets Trust Fund (FATF), the fund used to collect and disburse seized drug assets, "at least part of the aforementioned fund will be used to finance the DARE regional training. It is anticipated that one-third of the Forfeited Assets Trust Fund may be set aside for the DARE financing." They also reported that the "United States Attorney General's Asset Forfeiture Office has indicated that such monies may be used to fund drug prevention programs such as DARE."[102] Even as police and school officials repeatedly suggested that DARE offered an alternative to the get-tough strategy of supply reduction, they relied on police practices that extracted value from the communities most directly impacted by the drug war.

Relying on asset forfeiture as a means for local law enforcement to fund DARE produced a double effect. First, it meant that DARE and prevention programs relied on funding from the punitive side of the drug war, thereby encouraging the continuation of aggressive policing, drug busts, joint task forces, and interdiction, which had devastating effects on communities of color in particular. Second, as attitudes about the drug war shifted, a source of funding dried up. In Santa Cruz, California, for instance, the sheriff's office had sent deputies into classrooms to teach the DARE program for over a decade when, in 2004, the department had to cancel the program. Sheriff Mark Tracy reported that the decision to end the program was "purely a financial decision. I had no choice because there was no money." Although DARE had also been burdened by "over expectation about what this program could accomplish," the budget crisis rested on reductions in county funding and asset seizure funds.[103] If DARE came to rely on a myriad of public and private funding sources, the program's deep roots and reliance on asset forfeiture in many communities belied its presumed innocence as nonpunitive. Rather, if local police required asset forfeiture funds to fund their DARE programs, the framework *encouraged* an ongoing commitment to punitive and aggressive policing.

A New Tradition: National DARE Day

Alongside its phenomenal growth, DARE garnered national recognition from politicians and policymakers. President Reagan declared September 15, 1988, the first National DARE Day, a tradition that would continue every year through Barack Obama's presidency.[104] State governors also declared "DARE Day" to coincide with the federal day of recognition. If politicians saw opportunity in supporting DARE, DARE America officials also actively encouraged politicians to hold the program up as a model of drug education. DARE America director Nathan Shapell, for instance, wrote to Reagan congratulating him on recognizing the DARE program and asking for a public ceremony to celebrate National DARE Day. "I would like to add my voice encouraging your consideration of a White House signing ceremony," Shapell wrote.

Fourth grader Maribel Andrade holds one of the hundreds of cards to be released in gas-filled balloons during DARE's fifth anniversary celebration at Gates Elementary. Dean Musgrove, September 15, 1988, Herald Examiner Collection, Los Angeles Public Library, Los Angeles, California.

"Such ceremony would help to honor children everywhere who are learning the skills to stay off drugs and are making a commitment to live drug-free lives. While schools and communities across the nation will be planning special events and ceremonies in honor of their local students who 'D.A.R.E. to keep off drugs,' all would be rewarded by your taking a few minutes of National D.A.R.E. Day to commend their efforts and recognize the commitment these children are making to live drug-free lives."[105]

The Reagan administration was instrumental in helping DARE expand, which aligned with Nancy Reagan's Just Say No campaign. Indeed, Nancy Reagan even attended a DARE class at Rosewood Elementary School, a racially diverse school in West Hollywood, in 1987.[106] Directly following Reagan's signing of the 1988 Omnibus Anti-Drug Abuse Act, Chief of Police

Nancy Reagan speaks to a DARE class at Rosewood Elementary School in Los Angeles. Paul Chinn, February 11, 1987, Herald Examiner Collection, Los Angeles Public Library, Los Angeles, California.

Gates named the Reagans honorary DARE graduates on the first National DARE Day in 1988 in recognition of President Reagan and the First Lady's support of the program. "The Reagans have been the only First Family in memory to bring a crime related issue to the forefront of national attention," Gates commented during the first National DARE Day. "Their efforts have contributed immensely to creating a national concern for this country's drug problem and a recognition that the only real solution, the long-term solution, is to eliminate the demand for drugs—and that means teaching kids how to stay off drugs before they ever get started. . . . Both the president and the First Lady have been very supportive of D.A.R.E. . . . We're proud to name them honorary D.A.R.E. graduates."[107]

With the establishment of National DARE Day, congressional representatives clamored to demonstrate their support for DARE. As Southern California congressman Mel Levine (D-CA) stated in 1990, "D.A.R.E. has become one of our most effective weapons in combating the war on drugs. It has set the national standard for drug education programs because it is innovative, cost-effective, and it works. For parents and students on the front lines of our drug crisis, D.A.R.E. sends a beacon of hope."[108] The role of law enforcement in the program and the perception that the program was "cheap," something that would be debated when DARE came under scrutiny for being ineffective in the 1990s, was a particularly notable reason for DARE's ascendance to national political attention. Politically, DARE continued to gain support as Congress members across the country touted the program and their support for it, often in the weeks surrounding National DARE Day. Some even attempted to increase DARE funding through targeted legislation, such as when Senator Robert Kasten (R-WI) proposed funding for DARE be increased by $50 million in 1992. Kasten called DARE "the most valuable tool we have to educate our young people about the dangers of drug abuse."[109]

DARE was, if nothing else, a political winner. On the program's tenth anniversary, DARE America, the nonprofit set up to oversee DARE's growth, held an awards ceremony for one of its board members, Greg Penske. Politicians from across California and across the country sent in congratulatory messages for Penske and DARE. The most prominent included former president George G. W. Bush and President Bill Clinton, who praised the program for its role on the front line of the drug war, stating, "The D.A.R.E. program is invaluable in the fight to free our children from the dangers of drug abuse." Others expressing their gratitude included California governor Pete Wilson, Senator Barbara Boxer (D-CA), former First Lady Nancy Reagan, and a wide range of DARE officers and educators from around the country. As Gray Davis, controller of the state of California and future governor, summarized the central role DARE played in the drug war and shaping the attitude of the nation's youth: "For a decade now, D.A.R.E. has spearheaded the war on drugs, teaching millions of our children that the best possible life is a drug-free one. Perhaps this is the most valuable lesson we can teach them."[110]

Accolades from members of Congress and presidents were only one sign of DARE's symbolic value to politicians. Beginning in the mid-1980s, the program received high-profile visits in Los Angeles from First Lady Nancy Reagan, President George H. W. Bush, director of the Office of National Drug Control Policy William Bennett, and Princess Alexandra, the first cousin of Queen Elizabeth.[111] President Bush was a particularly strong booster. "I've been out there and witnessed the program in action," he recounted. "D.A.R.E. sends these police officers into the classroom to work with kids, build their self-esteem, teach them that they can refuse when they're pressured to try drugs."[112] Bush also highlighted the importance of the school-police partnership. "And the program is teaching youngsters something else," the president told kids and parents at an event in Lancaster, Pennsylvania, "that the police and their schools are united in a common effort to stop drug abuse."[113]

Redefining drugs as a police problem and the capture of the drug war by law enforcement was reflected in the celebration of DARE as a successful program. On the second annual DARE Day held on September 13, 1989, President Bush used the moment to recommit the nation to fighting the drug war. "So let us finish the job DARE has started and create an America we can all be proud of—an America free from drugs."[114] In a sign of how the program was viewed, those invited to the Rose Garden ceremony were law enforcement personnel; the education and public health specialists who had helped design the program were notoriously absent. As presidential staffers told Bush, "On Wednesday, September 13, at 10 A.M., in the Rose Garden, you will address a group of law enforcement officials and students who have conducted and participated in the Drug Abuse Resistance Education (DARE) program."[115] In doing so, Bush sent the message that drug abuse was a police problem, not a school or health problem. His remarks reaffirmed the central role of law enforcement officers:

> To Officers Morales from California and his counterpart, Officer Chapman from the East Coast, this "Hands across the Continent" that we saw here today says something about DARE and its national nature. To Chief Gates, my respected friend, the Deputy Chief, Mr. Levant and, of course, Mr. Shapell [*sic*]. . . . Barbara is a late starter for this event, but when I told her that Daryl was here for the DARE program, she changed her schedule to be with us, and I am delighted she is because she feels so strongly about what you're doing. So let me welcome you to America's House, where today we reaffirm our commitment to stop the scourge which threatens every American.[116]

To the ire of some Los Angeles teachers who sent telegrams complaining to the White House, the Bush administration had not invited any of the LAUSD education and health experts who developed the DARE curriculum, most notably Ruth Rich. As one intervention advisor to the LAUSD's Drug Free Schools Program wrote, "WE ARE AGHAST THAT YOU HONORED OFFICERS OF THE LOS ANGELES POLICE DEPARTMENT WITHOUT HONORING THE WOMAN WHO WROTE THE CURRICULUM. THERE WOULD BE NO PROGRAM WITHOUT HER . . . PLEASE RECTIFY THIS NEGLIENCE."[117] If the absence of educators from the White House's Rose Garden event honoring DARE officers and kids was an oversight and unintentional, it was an implicit acknowledgment about DARE's original aim and source of the program's popularity to highlight the police in an educative and prevention role.

Overly simplistic messages and symbolic commitments became a centerpiece of DARE Day celebrations, not increased funding for education and rehabilitation. On DARE's sixth anniversary, for instance, there was a national bell ringing to "ring in national Drug Abuse Resistance Education Day" across the country. Schoolchildren in cities across the country rang bells coinciding with Nancy Reagan ringing a bell in Los Angeles. Students in Philadelphia rang the Liberty Bell, leading Lieutenant Larry Goebel, assistant commanding officer of the LAPD's DARE Division, to comment, "We believe it was hundreds of communities throughout the nation. Everywhere from Florida to the upper Eastern Seaboard, all the way to the West Coast." The bell ringing was meant to impress upon students the continued commitment to lead drug-free lives. "The thing it was meant to do for the kids, of course," Goebel explained, "was to reaffirm their commitment to what the program is all about and to help raise the level of awareness throughout the country that it is keeping kids off drugs." Local DARE officers doubled down on the symbolic meaning of the event. "I feel lucky and honored that we can do this," Harlow Elementary School DARE officer Harold Driskell told his pupils in Harrodsburg, Kentucky. "It's all for you, all for you kids. That's our main concern."[118]

National DARE Day became an annual tradition. Politicians from both sides of the aisle made it a point to laud the program and put their weight behind it. As one journalist summarized, "For politicians, standing with DARE became akin to standing against drugs and crime: mayors, members of Congress and the president relished having their pictures taken with DARE kids and officers."[119] Indeed, National DARE Day became a moment when politicians could demonstrate their commitment to the drug war and claim they had taken positive action against youth drug use. In addition, DARE was often singled out in the ONDCP's annual "National Drug Control Strategy" as a model program.[120] "By linking themselves to DARE, national political candidates clearly stood to gain in terms of boosting their own popularity," researchers noted in a 1994 evaluation of DARE. "At the same time, their political support helped to further legitimize the DARE program and increase its funding prospects benefiting individuals and organizations directly involved with its operation and/or expansion."[121] Every year when National DARE Day rolled around, Congress members routinely made statements lauding DARE and its contributions to the drug war on the Congress floor and entered them into the congressional record.[122]

DARE became a potent political symbol that attracted praise of policymakers looking to reinforce their law-and-order bona fides and show support for the police. Politicians across the country lined up to speak to DARE officers and conventions. Wyoming governor Mike Sullivan, for instance, spoke to the Wyoming DARE Officers Association Conference after returning from a visit to Southern California in 1990. He called DARE "one of the best examples" of drug education at work and emphasized that "substance abuse isn't just an urban problem." Sullivan went on to praise the officers, commenting, "Through your work on the streets and in the schools, you are making a valuable contribution to our efforts to combat this scourge of our society."[123] DARE's reliance on police officers had undoubtedly been the element that made the program politically appealing. This was especially so for George H. W. Bush, who saw DARE as not only Daryl Gates's most lasting legacy but also as an influence on the development of the National Drug Policy. As Bush commended Daryl Gates on his fortieth anniversary of service to the LAPD just weeks after the Rose Garden event, "I've watched the DARE Program in action. I was there in a school classroom where an officer reached out to the kids. I was terribly impressed and it made a lasting impression on me as we formulated national drug policy here in Washington."[124] DARE, in other words, was not only a reflection of drug war priorities, it had actively shaped those policies' direction.

To anyone paying attention, policymakers overwhelmingly understood DARE to be a law enforcement program first and education program second. This law enforcement orientation was especially appealing amid the national panic about drugs, and support and praise from policymakers made DARE into the national symbol of drug prevention programming.[125] Yet the backing from policymakers was no accident. By the end of the 1990s, DARE was as much a promotional machine for the police as it was an antidrug education program. "What DARE has excelled in is promotion for their program," observed Lloyd Johnson, director of the annual Monitoring the Future study at the University of Michigan, in 2001. "They get testimonials from just about everybody."[126]

A Marketing Coup

Through aggressive marketing and public relations, DARE became a household name. Given DARE's rapid growth and diffusion across the country, it is no wonder that stakeholders ranging from law enforcement to politicians to corporate boards to athletes praised the program. As one article in the *FBI Law Enforcement Bulletin* claimed, albeit hyperbolically, "The Drug Abuse Resistance Education Program, D.A.R.E., may be one of the most successful undertakings in the history of modern law enforcement."[127] But such success had less to do with DARE's ability to prevent drug use than its political timing. "DARE was at the right place at the right time," evaluators observed, "with just the right types of political support to become what the Justice Department called the 'long term solution to the drug problem.'"[128] Quite simply, DARE had become popular and, for a moment, untouchable. In the process, it was becoming a cultural icon as well.

While political support was a significant driver in making DARE a national and international commodity, DARE also benefited from nonprofit status and private sector investment. Support from the Reagan, Bush, and Clinton presidential administrations and a swath of Congress members ensured DARE was elevated as a model program in federal Safe and Drug Free Schools funding, but the role of DARE's own marketing and private sector support was, arguably, just as or more important to making the program's widespread presence and growing cultural cachet. Indeed, the aggressive marketing by DARE officials, the establishment of a nonprofit corporation to oversee the program's national and international operations, corporate sector support and sponsorship, and political appeal combined to make DARE into the nation's preeminent drug education program. It is to the nonprofit DARE America, aggressive marketing, and support of the private sector that we now turn.

CHAPTER FOUR

DARE America, Inc. and Public-Private Partnerships

On April 20, 1993, a who's who of Los Angeles business leaders, law enforcement officials, and policymakers attended DARE America's Future of America Award Gala at the Beverly Hilton Hotel. The gala honored Greg Penske, a DARE America board member and president of Longo Toyota/Lexus, and the 25 million students enrolled in DARE programs in schools across the country. The gala was a crowning moment for DARE America, the 501(c)(3) nonprofit that DARE administrators established in 1987 to help the program expand beyond Los Angeles, raise funds through corporate partnerships, and manage the operations and distribute materials to schools across the country. Accompanying the award ceremony was a combined silent and live auction held by DARE America, entitled "DARE to Make Your Dreams Come True—Auction Book." The auction's sponsors reflected the broad support and partnership with the private sector, which supplied the prizes. Prizes ranged from a "Raider Road Trip—The Perfect Touchdown" during which the winner would accompany the Los Angeles Raiders on a trip, to "Luxury Items" such as a new Lexus or speedboat. There were also getaways, such as trips to Club Med in Martinique and Las Hadas Resort in Manzanillo, Mexico, and a Palm Springs Sports package. Such corporate sponsorship brought in funding and added to the program's cultural cachet. As DARE America encouraged attendees in the award ceremony program, "Let's D.A.R.E. to win. With your support, we will."[1]

While DARE America was instrumental in the program's rapid growth across the country, it also reflected an era in which public-private partnerships were becoming a preferred approach to addressing the country's social problems. Reagan's antipathy to publicly funded social welfare programs and the New Democrats' turn to entrepreneurialism and public-private partnership created a ripe political and cultural context for DARE America. Administrators worked with business leaders to establish DARE America as a tax-exempt nonprofit corporation in 1987. It was a deliberate response to budget austerity in the 1980s and, according to officials, needed to facilitate fundraising and program expansion.[2] Following the creation of DARE America, DARE's growth certainly relied on generous public support, but it also turned to private donations, corporate sponsorship, and sales of DARE paraphernalia. DARE's use of private and public funding reflected broader changes in the state's role to address social problems while corporate sponsorship built on the hope of promoting a disciplined, drug-free workforce.[3]

DARE encompassed not only local school districts but also political clout, corporate sponsorship, media attention, and celebrity status. The marketing and sale of DARE merchandise combined with support from entertainers and athletes enhanced the program's cultural star power and visibility. In the process, DARE became a cultural icon as much as an antidrug education program. If nothing else, DARE America was a marketing machine. Viewed in this light, DARE was wildly successful at positioning itself as a staple of American culture.

DARE America and the Nonprofit Approach

If federal funding and political attention aided DARE's expansion, it belied a broader shift in state formation based on a reduced role for government through an assault on state services for social programs and education. Throughout President Reagan's first term, law enforcement received the bulk of drug war funding while support for treatment and research declined.[4] In 1986, nearly 85 percent of the federal drug budget went to enforcement while education programs received roughly 1 percent. Over the Reagan administration's first five years, enforcement budgets increased 70 percent while education and prevention programming decreased by 5 percent.[5] The massive disparity in funding reflected Reagan's effort to reassert American martial authority and dismantle social programs.

Reagan recognized the need to reduce the demand for drugs, even if his administration refused to provide anywhere near comparable funding as it did to attacking the supply. As early as 1981, the president pointed to the demand-side problem. "It is my belief, firm belief," Reagan told reporters in a news conference, "that the answer to the drug problem comes through winning over the users to the point that we take the customers away from the drugs, not take the drugs, necessarily—try that, of course—you don't let up on that. But it's far more effective if you take the customers away than if you try to take the drugs away from those who want to be customers." In fact, after declaring a war on drugs in 1982, the administration outlined a five-point plan to prevent and control drug abuse that linked law enforcement, international cooperation, education and prevention, treatment, and research.[6]

Yet focusing on demand produced a problem for Reagan. It would require building up state resources for social programs and policies that Reagan's New Right constituency of evangelicals and social conservatives had been battling to eliminate. As a result, officials in the Reagan administration proposed turning over those roles to private social institutions and the family in order to avoid spending on social policy and programs and devolution of governing responsibility. As Carlton Turner put it, comprehensive educational programs against drugs "can be best accomplished by the private sector" with rhetorical, but not financial, support from the administration.[7] There was, in short, little role for the federal government on the demand side of the drug war aside from moral support.

Blaming government programs for a decline in traditional character-building social institutions, in effect, created an opening for a relatively low-investment program like DARE to fill the void. It provided a solution to drug abuse that was rooted in morality and choice rather than building up social programs, providing a means to avoid critics who had been calling for more treatment, rehabilitation, and jobs programs. It also enabled the Reagan administration and other policymakers around the country to show they were doing something on the drug front to combat demand among the nation's youth without having to back it by expanding funds for prevention or social programs.

While congressional representatives saw the allocation of federal funding to schools as a key component of the drug war, Secretary of Education William Bennett, a conservative culture warrior who promoted moral education and tough-love policies in schools, and President Reagan were not as convinced. Mere months after the passage of the DFSCA, which allocated $200 million for antidrug education programs in 1987 and $250 million in both 1988 and 1989, Reagan's budget proposed reducing the funding for 1988 to a mere $100 million. Bennett and other Department of Education officials defended this approach in front of Congress by saying that government funding alone was not going to solve drug use by the nation's youth. Rather, local school districts, nonprofits, businesses, and parents needed to take greater responsibility.[8]

While the Reagan administration was more than happy to promote government intervention for policing and drug interdiction, when it came to antidrug education, the solution focused on developing business investment, philanthropic involvement, and private donations. In line with this approach, local DARE projects often relied on fundraising and donations from local business and civic leaders.

In Los Angeles, DARE administrators dove headlong into fundraising efforts. Program administrators worked with United Way to create a development strategy and private sector development plan to facilitate public-private partnership in the program's first year.[9] Assistant Chief Robert Vernon also approached potential funders. Writing to the Rotary Club of Los Angeles in March 1984, for instance, Vernon explained, "The continued success of the DARE Program is dependent not only on the involvement of public agencies, but also upon the support of the various service clubs and civic groups. Because of limited municipal and school district funds, attempts are being made to involve all facets of the community in the program's funding." If the DARE program was going to expand to one hundred schools in the fall of 1984, Vernon suggested, they would need Rotary support. Although unstated, Vernon implied that many of the new schools would be located in impoverished neighborhoods, writing, "Because many of these sites are located in neighborhoods which cannot provide the necessary financial assistance, I would suggest that our Rotary Club of Los Angeles assist in the purchasing of these items through our Community Service Fund."[10] The Rotary Club obliged, sending the LAPD $3,000 to support the DARE program.[11] The philanthropic, nonprofit grant-making Weingart Foundation also provided the LAPD with a $500,000 grant to support DARE in 1985.[12]

Fundraising efforts accelerated with the formation of the Los Angeles Crime Prevention Advisory Council (CPAC). The CPAC was founded in 1985 by business leaders and law enforcement members, including future DARE proponent and administrator Glenn Levant, to support the city's war on crime. It funneled donations from the private sector to police-related programs. DARE was the primary recipient of the CPAC's largesse. The program benefitted from a 1986 advertising campaign organized by the CPAC in support of DARE and received funds from a wide range of Los Angeles–area businesses through CPAC channels.[13] For instance, Peter O'Malley, president of the Los Angeles Dodgers, donated $25,000 in the fall of 1984. The CPAC and DARE also received donations from Lew Wasserman of MCA, Inc., the John and Beverly Stauffer Foundation, the Southern California Gas Company, and Lloyds Bank California.[14] Gates, noting that "a program such as DARE is costly," reached out to the Xerox Corporation and the Northrop Corporation to provide additional support.[15] Without the CPAC, which continued to direct money into DARE, including a $50,000 contribution in 1988 to help offset the cost of ten officers, DARE would not have grown to become the nation's leading drug prevention program.[16]

Ultimately, the CPAC fit within the broader push by the Reagan administration to pursue privatization and nonprofit funding to create new revenue streams for the police. Reduced budgets and mayor Tom Bradley's refusal to include DARE in the proposed 1984 city budget especially irked Gates and other DARE proponents. So they looked elsewhere for support.[17] As Gates suggested in a letter to Lew Wasserman, "Prevention programs such as DARE could not survive without the fervent support of community leaders and their commitment to the war on drugs."[18] The CPAC was at the crux of this growing public-private partnership and offered an alternative means of funding public services in an era of austerity. As Gates recognized, "The Crime Prevention Advisory Council is one example of how managers can do more with less now and in the future."[19] Its mission was to support the LAPD's crime prevention programs "by purchasing crime prevention materials not otherwise obtainable through the City of Los Angeles' normal budgetary process."[20] The CPAC also facilitated donations of vehicles and other equipment from local foundations and organizations to be used by DARE officers.[21] In effect, the CPAC was a fundraising arm of DARE that worked to make the program a compelling place for business and people to put both their resources and goodwill.

Local DARE projects developed similar public-private funding coalitions. In Las Vegas, for instance, the Junior League of Las Vegas (JLLV), a nonprofit organization led by women to promote voluntarism, partnered with the Las Vegas Metropolitan Police Department and Clark County School District to bring DARE to the city in 1986–1987. Like the CPAC, the JLLV was a nonprofit corporation that aimed to "coordinate the efforts of all agencies involved to seek funds from the community to support Project D.A.R.E."[22] The JLLV, for instance, agreed to supply DARE with volunteers to support the project and provided between $5,700 and $8,000 in funds in 1986 and more than $10,000 in 1989.[23] The JLLV also helped form DARE, Inc. of Las Vegas as a nonprofit focused on "the procurement and extension of financial aid toward the operation, management and expansion, and the actual management and day-to-day operation of an educational program [DARE] to be provided to school age children in Clark County, Nevada, aimed at the prevention of and deterrence to drug and alcohol abuse."[24] As in Los Angeles, the JLLV produced public service announcements, distributed materials in participating schools, sponsored billboards, wrote articles, and facilitated appearances of DARE boosters to raise awareness of the program, solicit funds and sponsorships from local residents and businesses, and develop political alliances and support from state legislators.[25] Such efforts led to local businesses sponsoring golf tournaments and other fundraisers, including individual donations, with proceeds going to the local DARE program.[26] As DARE promoted these sorts of public-private partnerships and funding models, it reinforced the message that the state should take a backseat to private action, voluntarism, and business sponsorship rather than support robust social welfare programs.

Given such reliance on fundraising, voluntarism, and corporate sponsorship, DARE administrators suggested that the turn to private investment was a result of both the lack of public funding available for drug education and the importance of mobilizing the business community. "We have motivated the private sector in our city, and they have been overwhelmingly responsive to donating to this project and have really kept us afloat," LAPD officer Van Velzer told a congressional committee in 1986. "The only public moneys we have received is a grant from the State of California, and that is a seed grant. We have had to rely on the private sector, and without question we must mobilize the communities."[27] DARE, in other words, fit neatly within the Reagan and Bush White House's approach to governance because it was devolutionary and inexpensive for the federal government.[28]

Perhaps no other example reflected the possibility of public-private partnership in the drug war better than when DARE America incorporated in 1987 as a 501(c)(3) nonprofit corporation. DARE America grew out of Levant's work with the CPAC and, after DARE took off in Los Angeles, the transformation of the CPAC first into DARE California and then into DARE America. Although DARE had always been envisioned as a public-private partnership in its funding scheme, establishing DARE America as a tax-exempt organization was a major step for the organization and the DARE program. This status enabled DARE America to manage the program's operation and become the fundraising arm for DARE across the country and around the world.[29] DARE America would go on to hold award ceremonies and fundraising events, such as a silent auction, in which the list of corporate sponsors included banks, car rental companies, and advertising firms, among others.[30]

DARE America operated as a national clearinghouse for DARE programming, instructor training, curriculum development and copyright, and fundraising and sponsorship opportunities. "The formation of DARE America is the first step toward making the DARE Program a part of every school's curriculum nationwide," Levant told Congress in 1988.[31] DARE America, according to Levant, would be led by "nationally prominent business and community leaders," such as Nathan Shapell, who served as president, and philanthropist Armand Hammer, who administered DARE America's goals, to, in part, "coordinate fund-raising and sponsorship opportunities on the national level."[32] Shapell, who was head of California's independent state oversight agency known as the "Little Hoover" Commission, organized DARE America's fundraising efforts. "This program's continued growth depends on the financial support of individuals, government and businesses across the country." Shapell spearheaded a national fundraising effort with a "coin container campaign" in which DARE America coin containers were installed in Arco AM/PM Mini Marts in Los Angeles.[33] Following the Reagan administration's emphasis on defunding social services and the prevention side of the drug war, DARE America along with other nonprofits rose to fill the gap left by state abandonment to address social problems.

DARE America operated as an umbrella organization that managed DARE's development. For all intents and purposes, DARE America was DARE. As one DARE America pamphlet outlined, "The specific functions of D.A.R.E. America are: financial support for instructor training, coordinating fund raising and sponsorship opportunities, and regularly monitoring instruction standards and program results. It also helps provide participating communities with educational materials, program outlines, student workbooks, drug awareness information for parents, information pamphlets for citizens and community groups . . . everything needed to put D.A.R.E. to work. And work it has."[34] Within the context of declining support for public services, DARE America provided an alternative route to provide antidrug education. In the spring of 1987, lieutenant Rodger K. Coombs, the LAPD officer in charge of the DARE unit within the LAPD, for instance, recommended that DARE America budget $10 million per year "to provide financial assistance to other agencies who wish to replicate DARE in their communities."[35] In the minds of DARE America's leadership, notably Glenn Levant, it would not be the government that provided the resources and support for DARE but a committed group of private citizens, law enforcement officials, and corporate donors who would ensure the program's viability. And it would all be organized by DARE America.

Another impetus for DARE America was to create a funding scheme that was not subject to the whims of politicians, city budgets, or election cycles. "Yet it had to be sustained so it wouldn't die from a lack of funds like so many other promising drug prevention programs," Levant explained. "Because it needed a nongovernmental source of financial support, I founded D.A.R.E. America as a nonprofit organization that would pay for all educational materials and training."[36] DARE America looked to coordinate a three-way partnership between law enforcement, schools, and corporations. "This program's continued growth depends on the financial support of individuals, government and businesses across the country," Shapell explained.[37] While based on a partnership, DARE America touted its support from fund-raising and corporate sponsorship over government funding. "Less than 1 percent of D.A.R.E. America's operating budget comes from the federal government," Levant claimed; "99 percent comes from grass roots sources at the community level, plus corporate sponsorships. This breaks the funding cycle dilemma and ensures the program will continue operating for generations."[38]

DARE America facilitated program expansion through national training seminars and conferences. "DARE America belongs to all of us," Captain Michael Bostic told attendees at a regional training center conference in 1989. "Officers trained should be made aware that DARE America exists. The organization will be a national fund-raising program at the corporate level to try to raise funds for DARE, for national conferences, and national and state DARE officers associations."[39] The first DARE America conference was held in July 1988 in Los Angeles. Chief Gates outlined the importance of the conference: "I view this conference as a giant advance in our war against an enemy that has ravaged our adult population and is now seeking to enslave our youngsters. This nation's future rests in the hands of today's children. DARE America can save those hands from being shackled with drugs. That's why your participation in this, our first DARE America Conference, is so essential. Together, we can anticipate a tomorrow free from the narcotics plague."[40] Bringing DARE officers together in this way deepened the DARE network and bound them to the DARE America universe.

Ownership and protection of the copyright to the DARE name, logo, and associated slogans was key to DARE America's influence. Originally developed and owned by the CPAC, the CPAC transferred the DARE trademark to DARE California, which gave it to DARE America in turn. The DARE logo trademark was a valuable asset for the program as it became a nationally known and, for a time, beloved part of the war on drugs. DARE America explained the importance of the DARE logo and trademark at a 1989 regional training center conference held in Rockville, Maryland: "The DARE logo is a registered trademark belonging to DARE America, a national organization. DARE is a local program but still must enforce copyright and trademark laws." As DARE America suggested to conference participants, DARE America would work with local DARE programs for the use of DARE material.

"DARE America wants to license states to use the trademark and further DARE in their state."[41]

The DARE logo and trademark not only provided monetary value to DARE America but also allowed the nonprofit to control the DARE message, shape the spread of the program, and attempt to ensure fidelity in how the program was taught. As evaluators recognized, "The D.A.R.E.® name is considered a valuable intellectual property." The organization used the control over all things DARE to frame the debate about how to wage the drug war and the role of prevention education in local communities. "D.A.R.E.® America approves all materials (e.g., bumper stickers) and celebrities used to promote the D.A.R.E.® program." It also monitored implementation of DARE in local communities and reserved the right to withdraw permission to use DARE "if a local school district has improperly modified the curriculum." In addition, the organization used its growing influence to screen sponsors and refused to allow alcohol or tobacco companies to donate to fundraising events.[42]

DARE's expansion dovetailed with the organization's efforts to increase the influence of law enforcement in developing prevention and addiction policy nationally. In 1994, for example, DARE opened an office in Washington, D.C. If law enforcement had traditionally operated outside the "social services–based prevention field," the establishment of the D.C. office marked a departure. Bill Alden, DARE America deputy director and former head of demand reduction programs for the Drug Enforcement Administration, explained that the goal was to "make DARE a full partner in the prevention field." Law enforcement "has a real role to play" in prevention, according to Alden.[43] Alongside DARE's entrance into the prevention field, the D.C. office raised DARE's national profile and positioned the organization to further influence policymakers. Lobbying was also an important component of DARE America's positioning. In DARE America's 2008 tax return, the nonprofit recorded $50,400 in lobbying expenses.[44]

Alongside DARE America's fundraising efforts, an entire private industry and merchandise campaign developed around the program. In 1996, for example, DARE America "created a wholly owned 'for profit' subsidiary known as D.A.R.E., Inc. D.A.R.E., Inc. was created to sell sponsor-related items with the D.A.R.E. logo on the package. The profits from these sales will be used to fund D.A.R.E. America programs."[45] The founding of DARE, Inc. led to the sale of the now notorious T-shirts, bumper stickers, textbooks, license plates, fashion twill sport jackets, backpacks, duffel bags, watches, slap bracelets, ballpoint pens, pencils, and affinity credit cards.[46] Mattel, Inc. also got in the game, producing a model DARE van as part of its Matchbox Collectibles series.[47] In the process, DARE became a generational cultural icon known by the slogan emblazoned on bumper stickers across America, "DARE: To Keep Kids off Drugs" and, after the addition of anti-violence curriculum, "DARE: To Resist Drugs and Violence."[48] While merchandise sales amounted to roughly $104,261 in 2000 but only $23,725 in profits for DARE, Inc., hardly a windfall profit, it was a key element in making DARE a household name.[49] Indeed, such merchandise was not merely a gimmick as officers used it to incentivize the no-drug-use pledge. "Make a promise in your heart and mind, then write the essay," DARE officer Thomas Shaw told a class before they turned in their final no-use personal essay. "If people write and orally present a pledge, usually they will keep it. That's how you'll get that great D.A.R.E. T-shirt you've all been asking about."[50]

DARE America's efforts did not stop at America's borders. As part of DARE's international presence, DARE America also spun off DARE International (later changed to DARE Worldwide) to disseminate the curriculum and organize training of law enforcement personnel around the world. New Zealand had adopted the DARE program as early as 1988, with England and Australia exploring the program as well.[51] In the following years, more than fifty countries adopted DARE, and DARE America published *DareLine International*, a quarterly newsletter published between 1997 and 2004, "to keep the international D.A.R.E. community abreast of information affecting the D.A.R.E. program and united in its efforts to eradicate the twin scourges of drug abuse and violence around the world." By the late 1990s, DARE International was active around the world with training teams helping bring new officers into the fold in numerous countries.[52]

DARE America and DARE International had created a marketing machine aimed at raising DARE's place in American society, politics, and culture. And it had largely succeeded. To facilitate an even greater extension into American life under the guise that the program was not a mere example of government largess but a privately supported initiative, DARE America cultivated corporate partnerships and sponsorship.

Corporate Sponsors and Public-Private Partnerships

As DARE went national, its expansion reflected the Reagan era's turn toward the privatization of government services and promotion of market logics. The LAPD's DARE Unit recognized the limitations of relying on government funds, stating, "In a time of fiscal austerity for municipal governments, it becomes necessary for the police department and the school district to look to the community and private sector for this type of support."[53] DARE's promotional material placed investment from the business community as vital. "A pledge in support of Project DARE is a sound investment in the future of our children," one pamphlet noted. "The private sector is an important part of a team effort to help children say 'NO!' to alcohol and drugs." Such promotional material was aimed at increasing the investment from businesses by claiming that "DARE needs *you*." Corporate sponsorship would not only help kids stay off drugs but also ensure quality workers and model citizens in the future. Sponsoring DARE was, according to DARE promotional material, "an investment in protecting the health and potential of half a million students . . . an investment in the future of our next employees, neighbors and citizens . . . an investment in our own future." While DARE stressed kids should adhere to the "DARE to Say No" message, they simultaneously told business leaders and corporations that DARE was a "blue chip investment" and asked them to "DARE to Say Yes!"[54]

By 1987, the DARE program reflected and reinforced broader shifts in the privatization of public policy. Nancy Reagan's Just Say No campaign had been developing corporate sponsors for years, most notably Procter and Gamble, and DARE similarly hoped to attract corporate backers.[55] And they did. DARE quickly brought on a number of corporate sponsors, including Arco, Bayliner, Coca-Cola Bottling Company, Herbalife, Kentucky Fried Chicken, Kimberly-Clark, McDonald's, Packard Bell, Shell Oil Company, and Warner Brothers. Pacific Security, for example, donated $1 million to DARE in 1989, including a $500,000, one-time cash contribution to support DARE America's efforts. Corporate sponsorship became a key component of DARE in states across the country. Lockheed Martin sponsored Idaho's 1996 DARE Day while KFC franchises supported local DARE programs, including one in Downey outside of Los Angeles that raised $1,000 to help buy T-shirts for DARE graduates in 1989.[56]

When KFC partnered with DARE America, it became the organization's first major corporate sponsor. KFC enlisted actor Michael Warren, who played an African American police officer in the television series *Hill Street Blues*, as national chairman and established a toll-free hotline to help DARE children achieve a drug-free future.[57] The corporation promoted DARE's achievements, such as in 1994 when KFC and DARE celebrated the graduation of the forty-millionth DARE graduate. "We recognized right away the importance of supporting D.A.R.E. and providing America's kids with the opportunity for a drug-free future," Darlene Pfeiffer, chairperson of the KFC National Cooperative Advertising Program, reflected on the corporation's half-decade-long relationship with the program. "We developed a partnership that has grown to save the lives of millions of kids and given them the self-confidence they need to resist drugs and alcohol and succeed in life." Corporate sponsorship facilitated and accelerated DARE's expansion. During KFC's first full year of support, for instance, DARE America reached 3 million children in classrooms in every state.[58]

Corporate sponsorship was a key element in the turn toward public-private partnerships. As former president George H. W. Bush wrote to congratulate DARE and Penske at the Future of America gala, "D.A.R.E. provides an outstanding example of cooperation among parents, educators, law enforcement personnel, business owners and civic and religious leaders. Through innovative public-private partnerships such as D.A.R.E., our nation has made significant progress in reducing the demand for drugs."[59] A DARE pamphlet funded by the Coca-Cola Bottling Company of Los Angeles summarized, "The private sector is an important part of a team effort to help children say 'NO!' to alcohol and drugs."[60] Corporate donations and sponsorship, in sum, created a "three-way partnership among law enforcement, education and the corporate community" that was vital to the program's growth in Los Angeles and expansion across the country.[61]

DARE America also partnered with media firms to influence student attitudes through advertising, television, and cultural productions. One partner they brought on was Hanna-Barbera Productions, creator of the Yogi Bear cartoon. Hanna-Barbera worked with the LAPD and LAUSD to make Yogi Bear, known as "DARE Bear Yogi," the program's official mascot and "spokesbear." Cooperation with the production firm also led to the creation of educational comic books for DARE students, with a new character, Dr. Bearfacts, who served as "the resident authority on drug education at Yogi's home of Jellystone Park." DARE America employed DARE Bear Yogi in hopes of raising enthusiasm for the program among students and parents. LAUSD superintendent Britton commented that "with Yogi as spokesbear, D.A.R.E. and its antidrug messages will help reach even more children, teachers and parents. We expect D.A.R.E. Bear Yogi to add a lot of enthusiasm to the program, for adults as well as children. With Yogi celebrating his 30th year this year, a lot of us grew up with Yogi. He has universal appeal." In a joint comic book designed by DARE and Hanna-Barbera, for instance, Yogi graduated from a seventeen-week DARE course taught by Ranger Smith, who also provided

Chief Daryl Gates and Yogi Bear press event. Chris Gulker, no date, Herald Examiner Collection, Los Angeles Public Library, Los Angeles, California.

tips for parents on how to identify and promote antidrug messages and resistance techniques to their kids. Working with Hanna-Barbera went beyond supporting DARE's educational mission. It was meant to shore up future corporate sponsorship. "With Hanna-Barbera behind us," Gates stated, "we'll be more visible to civic leaders and potential corporate sponsors whose support is crucial to the continued growth of the D.A.R.E. program. Yogi and other Hanna-Barbera characters will be featured in D.A.R.E.'s promotional and fund-raising literature, TV public service announcements and they'll make live costumed appearances at student graduations or other D.A.R.E. events."[62] DARE Bear Yogi appeared most prominently in a 1989 animated public service announcement produced by Hanna-Barbera Productions with cooperation from Gates and DARE America that reinforced the DARE message and aimed to promote the adoption of the program in every school in the United States.[63] In addition to the animated short, DARE Bear Yogi attended fundraising and promotional events, such as a celebration at a KFC restaurant in Downey, California, on the second National DARE Day where Yogi met and distributed prizes to children.[64]

Corporate funding insinuated that DARE was not a government program. DARE reportedly received three times as much corporate funding and twice as many individual donations as other drug prevention programs in 1995. As the Republican agenda in the 1990s doubled down on budget cuts and President Clinton decimated social welfare, DARE seemed designed to withstand the onslaught.[65] "If federal funding were entirely eliminated tomorrow," Levant claimed, "the program would survive." Such assertions belied the large-scale government investment in the program, namely in supporting local police departments that oftentimes used public funds to divert officers to become part of the program. As Officer Janice Strauss in Mesa, Arizona, for instance, recalled, "In reality, the police department funded the entire program. I can't tell you right now what it was but it's extremely expensive."[66] In fact, DARE America estimated on its 2001 tax form "that organizations [law enforcement and related agencies] participating in the D.A.R.E. program donated services approximating $212,500,000.00." As one journalist concluded, DARE was "fundamentally a government program."[67] However, the image of DARE as entrepreneurial and corporate funded benefited not only DARE America during an era of assault on government services but also the corporate sponsors themselves.

Investment in drug education was advantageous for corporations in a number of ways. In particular, investing in DARE was part of promoting an image of corporate social responsibility and community improvement in an era of austerity. As Tom Adams and Barbara West suggested, corporate America could fill in for the public sector, especially in the field of drug and alcohol prevention. "During the past six years, the field of drug and alcohol prevention has benefitted from unprecedented support from the private sector; largely the local business community and corporate America. As public funds have dwindled the private sector has assumed an increasingly active role in prevention." Corporations ranging from Coca-Cola to NBC to Standard Oil and Chevron had invested in a variety of antidrug programs in schools, communities, and workplaces. As the language of "social corporate responsibility" suggested, however, these investments were not entirely out of their own goodwill to give back to communities. Donations to DARE and other antidrug programming, in essence, allowed corporations to say they were doing their part in helping the nation wage the war on drugs. In the process, corporations generated an image of responsible corporate citizenship that could "win good will and support," leading to improved business.[68]

Beyond a public image of corporate responsibility and citizenship, investment in drug education would most directly help form children into productive future workers and shore up the corporate bottom line. Drug abuse, policymakers and executives routinely commented, threatened worker safety and corporate profits. As a Coca-Cola-funded DARE pamphlet warned, "Drug and alcohol abuse within the American workplace is common and widespread, taking its toll in lost productivity, medical expenses and related crime costs."[69] Combined with the broader Reagan-era effort to "ensure a drug-free workplace," support for drug education would help safeguard future corporate earnings by ensuring that idle workers or drug-related costs did not threaten productivity.[70] As Glenn Levant, then president of DARE America, described DARE's role around the world in 1998, "D.A.R.E. offers hope in the international effort to reduce the level of violence brought about by drugs. Drug abuse destroys individual potential and the well-being of the world community. D.A.R.E. helps bring drug-free and productive citizens into the workplace, which will ensure a stronger nation and world for all of us." Investing in DARE, in short, was an investment in future corporate profits and disciplined workers.[71]

Corporate interest in creating an obedient workforce was a key component of support for DARE. As California attorney general John Van de Kamp's Commission on the Prevention of Drug and Alcohol Abuse explained in a report on the need for drug prevention programming in the state, "The private sector and public employers also have a vested interest in healthy children: for the short run, parents are more productive workers if their children are growing up healthy; for the long run, these children will enter the work force one day."[72] For many proponents, DARE's goal of "teaching students decision-making skills" and respect for authority provided a model for following directions.[73] Enhancing respect for authority was often cited as a central sign of DARE's effectiveness. Arizona's director of public safety, for example, told Congress, "Fortunately the school administrators and teachers report that there's a higher degree of respect for authority in general among the students that have received D.A.R.E."[74] Evaluations of DARE in Los Angeles also found that DARE students had fewer defiance or discipline incidents at school and exhibited better behavior than non-DARE students.[75] While the goal of ensuring a drug-free workforce was certainly desirable, corporate sponsorship of DARE also provided an implicit curriculum to shape America's youth into a disciplined labor force that respected corporate authority.

CPAC members promoted DARE for its ability to ensure "economic vitality" and productive workers. Michael Wagman, executive vice president of the advertising firm Foote, Cone & Belding, was on the board of the CPAC and promoted the DARE program as part of a broader effort to ensure productive workers and profits in the future. As he wrote in an article for *Advertising Age* highlighting the importance of DARE:

> With the great influence we in advertising have, with the kinds of clients we represent, clients who need healthy, productive work forces and a healthy population so they can continue to prosper, with the media accessibility we have, we can be a major force in making our country a place free of drugs and despair. . . . For economic vitality to continue requires a healthy and dynamic work force and population. But if we have a work force and population that is weakened by drug abuse and all its ramifications, then corporate America might begin to see a permanent decline in productivity and consumption, resulting in a decline of profits. In turn, that will result in advertising budgets being slashed by millions of dollars. Then what will we do for a living?

For business owners, the benefit of DARE centered on the loss of profits from on-the-job drug use, which, according to the CPAC, cost California businesses $3 billion in lowered productivity, employee injuries, and theft. DARE provided a hedge for corporate interests seeking to ensure a productive, disciplined, drug-free workforce.[76]

Grants from private foundations and corporate sponsorship became a central means of funding the drug war through antidrug education programs. Privatizing prevention made corporations into a key partner with police and schools. In the process, DARE America facilitated a shift in the relationship between citizens and the state to one between citizens and the corporate partners of the drug war. Programs such as DARE received praise from Reagan and other policymakers at the federal and local levels because it offered a preventive alternative to the punitive drug war.[77] But it also offered something else. Most notably, DARE was a prime candidate for the Reagan administration's efforts to "deglamorize" drugs through a media and public relations campaign enlisting actors, entertainers, and athletes.

Deglamorizing Drug Use

Drug warriors enlisted athletes and celebrities to promote the DARE and just say no message as part of a broader effort to deglamorize drug use. The 1982 federal drug strategy outlined how "private business, labor organizations, and the 'influencers of youth'—mass media, the entertainment industry, and the sports establishment—must use their unique abilities to deglamorize the drug scene and raise concern about drug and alcohol abuse."[78] What followed was a range of efforts by companies to capitalize on the drug prevention message. DC Comics in collaboration with the IBM Corporation and the National Federation of Parents for Drug Free Youth, for instance, published a version of *The New Teen Titans* comic book for the President's Drug Awareness Campaign in 1985.[79] The comic included a message from Nancy Reagan advising children they were "right in the center of combat" in "one of the most important battles our nation has ever fought." The comic, as with DARE, enlisted children as warriors in the fight against drugs and included Just Say No slogans and messaging.[80] Copies of the comic were distributed to all DARE students in Los Angeles during its inaugural year.[81]

Efforts to enlist celebrities began when DARE officials met with Hollywood producers and screenwriters to reshape the messaging about drug use in television shows. "We feel the youngsters must recognize what the media is trying to do in commercial television, and we have met with screenwriters and so forth in Los Angeles, to try to write out some of the unnecessary drinking scenarios that we see in some of the TV shows," DARE officer Van Velzer told Congress. According to Velzer, they had been successful in getting television shows to revise their plots to promote an antidrug message.[82] DARE America also looked to television and entertainment stars to promote the program. DARE America recruited celebrities such as comedian Arsenio Hall and singer Ted Nugent to serve as DARE spokespersons. Over the years, the board of directors included a wide range of celebrities, business owners, and politicians, such as philanthropist Armand Hammer, singer Michael Jackson, Diane Disney Miller, and former Virginia governor Gerald L. Baliles (see Appendix: Table 3).[83] DARE America's board of directors from 1993 included real estate magnate and philanthropist Eli Broad, Brian J. Strum, chairman of the Prudential Property Company, Arsenio Hall, and Michael Jackson. The diversity and high profile of DARE America's boosters was a mere signal of the prominent place that the organization and program had gained in national consciousness. The irony was that even as celebrities and athletes would promote the program, the DARE officer was always the star of the show, even outshining the Los Angeles Lakers in the heart of Inglewood.

Athletes were prime figures to promote DARE's no-use message, especially in the wake of the death of Len Bias. In Los Angeles, for example, Capitol Records partnered with the Los Angeles Lakers in 1987 to produce an antidrug rap single, including a music video of individual Laker players rapping, entitled "Just Say No." Laker players and coaches such as Pat Riley, Magic Johnson, and Kareem Abdul-Jabbar became foot soldiers in the war on drugs by promoting the just say no message in the song. The Lakers' just say no single merged celebrity with a zero-tolerance message and support for law enforcement. As Kareem Abdul-Jabbar rapped, "I'm Kareem, the captain of the team, I don't need drugs, I got a higher thing. My skyhook makes the team look good, but there's a hook we've got to shake from the neighborhood." Proceeds from the song benefited the Forum Community Services, which was formed by the wives of the Lakers in 1984 to reach the children of Inglewood with educational and antidrug programs. Forum Community Services donated all the revenue from the song to help implement the DARE program in Inglewood schools.[84] Laker players also participated in annual rallies and antidrug walks, often organized by the Laker wives, to raise funds for DARE.[85]

Laker players also appeared as role models at an April 1988 Say No to Drugs rally that 10,000 students attended wearing DARE T-shirts. The Lakers reinforced the message that "drug free is 'in,' or 'rad' as the students would say." Whether indicative of the actual response of the attending DARE students, officials reporting on the event suggested that the Lakers were not the stars of the show. "Perhaps the best indicator at the rally of the impact of the Inglewood DSP Program [Suppression of Drug Abuse in Schools Program] was the fact that the most applause from the students was for the 3 DARE officers that implemented the program."[86]

Athletes became a key component of DARE America's marketing campaign. Los Angeles Raider running back Marcus Allen, for instance, worked with the CPAC to promote DARE in Los Angeles.[87] Boxer Sugar Ray Leonard was another proponent of DARE. For Leonard, DARE officers served as role models for kids at risk of entering the drug life. Leonard told a congressional committee about the influences kids faced on the streets and, absent the DARE officer, the lack of moral guidance:

> But instead, what they see is the guy on the street corner who says, "You want to get high?" "You want to make some fast money, a nice ride, be a part of something?" Which, when translated, it really means, "Do you want to take a fast ride down a short, dangerous street?" . . . What might happen on that same street corner, stood some body else—a mentor—and that mentor walked to that same kid and said, "Hey, want to take advantage of life?" "You want to be somebody that counts?" "Do you want to make a difference? I can't get you fast money, but hang with me and I'll teach you how money works. Let's take a long walk down a longer, but safer street." That mentor standing on that same street corner, that is D.A.R.E. . . . D.A.R.E. can, quite

DARE Campaign with, from left to right, LAUSD official William Anton, L.A. Raider Marcus Allen, and Daryl Gates at the kickoff of a DARE campaign. Unknown photographer, April 3, 1986, Herald Examiner Collection, Los Angeles Public Library, Los Angeles, California.

> literally, change the face of that puzzle known as America's future. A mentor for every needy kid—wouldn't that be great? Think of the possibilities.[88]

Leonard reinforced DARE's messaging about the importance of police officers as mentors. "And let's not forgot that all of D.A.R.E.'s officers are police officers," he continued in his testimony. "So, for every relationship forged now, that's one less that might one day, end up in the rear seat of a patrol car."[89] In doing so, he also implicitly linked DARE officers in schools to the potential future of arrest and incarceration. If not for DARE, the thought process went, there would be more kids lost to drugs and arrested in the future.

Employing athletes as spokespersons for DARE was central to the program's effort to deglamorize drugs. Leonard, along with boxer Evander Holyfield, who was touted as "D.A.R.E.'s Children's Champion" on the cover of *DareLine International,* supported the program by attending the first DARE carnival at Parkman Middle School in Los Angeles. Leonard commented on the importance of using his celebrity to promote the antidrug message. "Events like this have a major influence on the star because we're doing something positive for the kids," Leonard summarized. "Telling children not to use drugs is one of the most important things we can do." The kids, apparently, got the message. Sixth-grader Diana Dunn commented, "I think kids will stay off drugs because the stars were here and told us not to. If stars don't do drugs, then kids won't do drugs."[90]

DARE America also used Black celebrities to enhance the program's appeal with Black students. The organization, for instance, appointed comedian and actor Arsenio Hall as DARE's first national ambassador to promote the program in Black communities. For Hall, DARE could address the perception among many in the city's Black community that the police were the "enemy." "One of the things I wanted to do with DARE was expose it more to the Black community because in cities like L.A., cops and the Black community are not a marriage made in heaven," Hall told *Jet* magazine in 1991. "When I sit down and talk to rappers like Easy E [*sic*] and some of the boys, those guys will say 'All my life all the cops ever done to me was cuss at me, mistreated me for the way I'm dressed, screamed at my mother when they were harassing me.' And they run that stuff down to you. So, the cops and the Black community have never been good friends. Here is a situation where I see law enforcement officers doing something positive with the community. It is education from the time when you can first comprehend. That's what DARE does."[91] With the help of Black celebrities, DARE sought to address the perception of the police as a violent, occupying army in Black communities rather than changing how they policed those same communities.

A wide range of other celebrities also got in on the DARE action. In 1994, for instance, fashion designer Richard Tyler, Vogue editor Anna Wintour, and Neiman Marcus hosted a $100-a-ticket party to raise money for DARE at Culver City's Smashbox Studios. A who's who of celebrities attended, including Cher, Heather Locklear, Kate Moss, Leonardo DiCaprio, Sarah Jessica Parker, William Baldwin, Chynna Phillips, Linda Evangelista, Tatjana Patitz, Jeanne Tripplehorn, and three actors who played the Mighty Morphin Power Rangers. Ironically, especially in hindsight, the event featured Johnny Depp, who presented a short antidrug film he directed, which, according to

Wintour, made that point that "you have a choice in life. Don't choose drugs."[92]

With the help of high-profile athletes and actors, DARE positioned itself not only in the halls of political power but in the nation's cultural milieu. By the mid-1990s, DARE had become a cultural icon of its own, with enough cultural capital to attract the plaudits and endorsement from a who's who of athletes and celebrities.

DARE's Cultural Cachet

As DARE came to be a part of the lives of students around the world, the program's rise to becoming a national and international cultural icon reveals how the program operated on ideological foundations that ignored the structural roots of the drug crisis. Rather than addressing social or economic conditions that led to drug use, DARE America focused its message on encouraging a change in behavior. It also, proudly and incorrectly, suggested it was primarily a self-funded program supported by corporate donors, not a recipient of public handouts from the federal government. Although DARE America's tax returns often showed hundreds of millions of dollars of "donated services" from local law enforcement agencies, schools, and volunteers, effectively making it a publicly supported program, DARE's image benefited from perceptions that it was built on a public-private partnership between the not-for-profit DARE America, corporate sponsors, and local police. It was a perfect fit with both the GOP's effort to dismantle the social safety net and the New Democrats' emphasis on entrepreneurialism and corporate social responsibility.[93]

However, DARE was much more than a marketing and fundraising machine. It played an important role in the cultural politics of the Reagan era. Most directly, DARE America complemented the Reagan administration's culture war, with its focus on family values, personal responsibility, and moral education. Indeed, DARE's orientation, as discussed in the next chapter, reinforced the turn toward blaming the problem on drug users themselves and framing solutions rooted in individual behavior, family values, and morality. Such an orientation combined with DARE's omnipresence would reinforce and define governing logics focused on getting tough, and extended the police into every facet of daily life.

CHAPTER FIVE

DARE's Culture War

Perhaps no one was more influential in shaping the cultural battles surrounding drug and education policy than William Bennett, who served as secretary of education during the Reagan administration and later became President George H. W. Bush's first director of the Office of National Drug Control Policy (ONDCP), otherwise known as the drug "czar." Bennett was an ardent culture warrior. He believed schooling should impart two things: basic education and, despite later revelations of his own proclivity for high-stakes gambling, moral character.[1] The problem of poverty, drug use, and crime, Bennett believed, was a result of the decline of "traditional values" and "traditional culture" in America. Emphasizing traditional values, the nuclear family structure, and personal responsibility followed the Christian Right's growing political influence during the 1980s.[2] It also informed the belief that the drug problem was a result of permissiveness and failed government social programs of the 1960s. "But we need to remember that families, churches, schools, and individuals are the primary agents in the development of a people's moral disposition. Government is an auxiliary," Bennett reflected in his memoir. Bennett's approach placed the family, personal responsibility, and morality at the crux of the drug war and blamed drug users for the effects of government cutbacks and economic devastation.[3]

Bennett's centrality to the drug war reflected the renewed attention to the culture of poverty and the "underclass" by conservative intellectuals such as Charles Murray. For culture warriors, the explanation for the rise of social pathology, especially in so-called inner-city communities of color, was quite simple. Social programs meant to help the poor and disadvantaged were at fault, not racism, poverty, and structural economic changes in America's cities.[4] Bennett reinforced such thinking in the first National Drug Control Strategy, stating, "We must avoid the easy temptation to blame our troubles first on those chronic problems of social environment—like poverty and racism—which help to breed and spread the contagion of drug use." While Bennett acknowledged the need to continue to fight "such social ills," he located the primary solution to drug use elsewhere.[5] To Bennett, government social programs destroyed the work ethic, values of right and wrong, and stable family life that led to drug use, crime, and "moral poverty."[6] What was needed, according to Bennett, was a get-tough policy rooted in simplistic messages of right and wrong.

From the perspective of culture warriors, the "drug crisis" was about much more than drug use. Many, for instance, saw a country being morally undermined by hip-hop culture and rap songs with sexually explicit lyrics and expressions of discontent with law enforcement, most notably N.W.A's anti-police brutality song "Fuck tha Police," which became a symbol of resistance to the policing of the drug war in particular.[7] Others mocked the Reagan administration's drug war messaging. In "Gangsta Gangsta," for instance, Ice Cube took a direct jab at the Reagans' moralizing, rapping, "And then you realize we don't care; We don't 'just say no'; We're too busy saying, 'Yeah!'"[8] In response to such cultural and political resistance, many policymakers and law enforcement officials mobilized fears about drug use to advance other political agendas promoting morality and family values.[9] Within this context, DARE's culture warriors hoped the program would accomplish much more than teaching kids to resist drugs. It devolved the responsibility of preventing drug use from federal social or public health policy to a local, police-led, educative project that sought to teach kids personal responsibility, the value of morally strengthened families, and respect for authority. Indeed, the battle waged by police officers in the DARE classroom accomplished important political-cultural work during the Reagan era beyond the purported goal of drug prevention. Using police officers to deliver the DARE curriculum and its message of personal responsibility, family values, and self-esteem, however, ignored the ways the drug crisis was one of material conditions and structural inequality, which ultimately bolstered the state's carceral approach to the drug problem.

DARE officials and policymakers' use of the term "drug abuse" to describe any substance use whatsoever rejected alternative approaches to drug education, such as responsible use, and was part of the effort of drug warriors to shape public perceptions that the only correct decision was to avoid drugs at all costs or take responsibility for poor choices and face the consequences. By simultaneously stressing the consequences of poor behavior and zero-tolerance policies, DARE attempted to solidify popular consent among kids, parents, educators, and policymakers for the police to advance the carceral project that divorced drug use from social and economic conditions, including rising unemployment, reductions in social welfare spending, and the growth in incarceration during the 1980s and 1990s.[10]

DARE seemed to be a color-blind approach to reducing drug use. Policymakers at the local, state, and federal levels routinely emphasized the ways drug abuse was a problem that impacted youth across race, ethnicity, and class, as well as the urban-rural divide. Much of the program's focus on self-esteem, resisting peer pressure, and values, however, reflected the message promoted by the predominantly white, middle-class parent movement concerned with marijuana use by suburban kids and teenagers.[11] While Black parents and policymakers undoubtedly also supported messages of family values, self-esteem, and personal responsibility, they were also the very issues often used by culture warriors to blame African Americans for continued inequality. Within the context of the "underclass debates" and criticism of the Black family—Black motherhood in particular—DARE reinforced racialized definitions of the middle-class nuclear family with its calls for parents to take greater responsibility for enforcing the zero-tolerance, pro-police message outside the classroom.[12]

DARE and drug education's popularity was never entirely about drugs but part of broader debates about social, cultural, and political issues of personal responsibility, family values, and zero tolerance in the late twentieth century. Employing the DARE officer to deliver color-blind values lessons to both students in the classroom and parents in targeted parenting sessions established the police as the means to shore up the nuclear family, morality, and discipline and, hopefully, prevent youth drug use.

Schools without Drugs

William Bennett emphasized the need for a return to lessons based in morality, values, and personal responsibility as a solution to the drug crisis. Yet Bennett's emphasis on values education was directly tied to certain and swift punishment for drug use.[13] Supply and demand reduction strategies were not mutually exclusive; they worked hand in hand. The guarantee of punishment on the supply side would send a message to users and would-be users to not use drugs. "In the final analysis, the distinction often drawn between the 'supply reduction' and 'demand reduction' sides of the drug equation is a false one," Bennett explained in his first speech as the inaugural director of the ONDCP. "Many things to be done on the 'supply' side have remarkable ramifications on the 'demand' side." Citing James Q. Wilson's book, *Drugs and Crime*, Bennett suggested that get-tough law enforcement measures were not meant "merely to apprehend and punish the guilty, though both are worthy goals. . . . Rather, we do so because we believe the message effective law enforcement sends will have a real impact on those who use drugs." The get-tough approach would teach the lesson of the punitive consequences of drug use to both pushers and users. Linking supply to demand strategies was "an ethic of personal responsibility." Promoting such an ethic among the nation's youth would "reverberate from the inner city to the marijuana fields in California and the coca fields in South America."[14] Stressing the swift sentencing of the pusher alongside a belief that the "ultimate deterrent has to be education," federal, state, and local policymakers inherently linked punitive solutions with preventive ones. Such policies enabled martial rhetoric and law enforcement to infiltrate public education.[15]

Nowhere did Bennett lay out his vision of the intersection between education and enforcement more explicitly than in the 1986 Department of Education report *What Works: Schools without Drugs*. The report framed the solution to drug use as a combination of values education, get-tough policies, and personal responsibility. Working alongside Nancy Reagan's Just Say No campaign, Bennett brought the complementary threat of punishment to the table. "We must work to see that drug use is not tolerated in our homes, in our schools, or in our communities," the report summarized. "Because of drugs, children are failing, suffering, and dying. We have to get tough and we have to do it now." Teachers, parents, and law enforcement had to deliver the same message that drug use of any kind was unacceptable and that if students did decide to use drugs, they would be punished swiftly and harshly. "They all must transmit a single consistent message that drug use is wrong, dangerous, and will not be tolerated," Bennett continued. "This message must be reinforced through strong, consistent law enforcement and disciplinary measures."[16]

Bennett's zero-tolerance message advocated for suspension of students for first-time offenses of drug use and expulsion for second-time offenders. But he also went further in the effort to combat drugs, "the enemy within."[17] He also encouraged children to turn in their friends for using drugs. "Let's be absolutely clear about this point," Bennett told Latinx students at W. R. Thomas Middle School in Miami. "It isn't snitching or betrayal to tell an adult that a friend of yours is using drugs and needs some help. It's an act of true loyalty—of true friendship. It's the right thing to do."[18] Such encouragement meshed well with DARE's message to say no to drugs, and for kids to put their trust in the police officer. Indeed, DARE was highlighted in *What Works* as an exemplary program that fit the emphasis on no use and zero tolerance.[19]

"Zero-tolerance" became the watchword of the Bush and Bennett drug war. In his remarks after the swearing-in of Bill Bennett as drug czar, Bush reminded listeners that the nation was on a crusade to eliminate drug use. "Drugs threaten what we are as a nation and as a family, and they chain the human soul and they destroy the lives of our children." Just as Bennett had done during his time as secretary of education under Reagan, Bush described the drug problem as a moral one that threatened the values Americans held dear. Alongside funding for education and prevention, in "urban schools where the emergency seems to be the greatest," Bush doubled down on the get-tough rhetoric and commitment of the drug war. "You know, I've talked a lot about 'zero tolerance.' Well, 'zero tolerance' is not a catchword. It means, quite simply: if you do crime, you do time."[20]

While Bennett and Bush routinely talked about zero tolerance for drug pushers, the message was meant to become the norm for students and youth as well. As outlined in antidrug abuse efforts talking points prepared by Bush's staff, "We must establish 'zero tolerance' as an attitude and a way of life by educating our children at home and at school on the dangers of experimenting with drugs. All schools should develop antidrug programs for the classroom, and adopt tough 'no use' disciplinary policies to show that drug use will not be tolerated."[21] It was a vision of a past America that was held not only by Bush and those in his administration. As Terry Johnson of the DARE Officers' Association praised Bush in an invitation to speak at the 1992 conference, "Thank you for your leadership in helping America return to some of those old fashioned moral values that we need so badly in our nation." For Johnson, DARE officers the world over, and members of the Reagan and Bush administrations, a return to "traditional" values and morality was something DARE, with its commitment to personal responsibility and zero tolerance, fulfilled in spades.[22]

Drug prevention programs thereby operated within a larger punitive framework of zero tolerance. Within this context, DARE and other drug prevention programs complemented and legitimized the emphasis on getting tough. If young drug users failed to change their behavior, adhere to so-called traditional values and morality, and dare to say no to drug use, they would face the consequences: policing and punishment. In doing so, DARE and other antidrug education programs legitimized the accompanying intensified policing and punishment as the solution to drug use among the nation's youth.

Choices and Consequences

If Bennett and culture warriors believed the nation's children needed DARE's message, they downplayed structural forces and inequalities shaping drug markets and use. In 1988, for instance, Los Angeles detectives arrested a twelve-year-old boy for selling PCP-laced cigarettes on the street. The child was wearing a DARE T-shirt with the slogan "DARE to keep kids off drugs." As Detective George Sumpter noted, "The kid didn't seem tough at all. There was a degree of innocence. He knew not to take drugs himself. Period." Following the advice of what he may have learned in his DARE class, the child told the officer, "If someone tries to force you to take drugs, just say 'no' and walk away." Yet as Los Angeles detectives noted, "Selling drugs was part of his community. He was making money." As this episode suggests, DARE may have succeeded in its focus on the individual with the message of personal responsibility to say no to drugs.[23] However, as the detective unwittingly admitted, the ability of children to say no to drugs missed the larger social and economic context that led to drug use and dealing. For children of color in particular, DARE's message missed the reality of their daily experience.

DARE administrators operated on the assumption that youth merely needed to be taught—and could be in a seventeen-week program—how to make correct moral choices to avoid experimenting with drugs and their potentially harmful consequences. But the idea behind preventive education went a step further. It assumed that children also needed to be told what the correct choice was: saying no. The DARE approach centered on individual behavior, self-esteem, and resistance to peer pressure as the means to solve the drug crisis using strategies that stressed moral values and choices. The focus, in other words, was on ensuring "attitudinal change" in individual students.[24] "The program will stress value decisions, self-concept improvement and peer pressure resistance training for elementary school youth," the LAPD and LAUSD explained in a grant application.[25] Those "value decisions" did not allow for any form of drug or alcohol use. "Its purpose," Chief Gates explained, was "to teach youngsters how to remain free of drug contamination; how to create a decent future for themselves and, in so doing, awaken our city and country from its narcotics nightmare."[26] Within the structure of zero tolerance for drug use and the use of police officers as educators, prevention programs such as DARE focused on ensuring students chose to never use drugs. One version of the DARE student workbook from Las Vegas promoted this message in a word game in which students had to uncover a "hidden message," which, when completed, read, "say no to drugs."[27] DARE, in other words, targeted youth to alter behavior, not structures or conditions in cities that led to drug use or sales.

The DARE curriculum encouraged students to take personal responsibility for their choices and to understand the potential punitive consequences for drug use. As LAUSD's Ruth Rich explained, "We try to establish with these children that drug abuse by anybody is not responsible."[28] If young drug users failed to say no to drugs, they would in turn face the consequences. In fact, the DARE curriculum foregrounded the consequences and risks of drug use as the second lesson. The session was meant to help "students understand that there are many consequences, both positive and negative, that result from using and choosing not to use drugs." The lesson on consequences, for instance, stressed the repercussions of using and not using alcohol and marijuana.[29] The goal of the lesson was to shape behavior and promote a no-use message. In the classroom, DARE officers led students through a series of questions in their DARE workbooks where students listed three consequences for using alcohol and marijuana and three consequences of choosing not to use alcohol and marijuana.[30] "If students are aware of those consequences," a Bureau of Justice overview report of DARE suggested, "they can make better informed decisions regarding their own behavior."[31]

The lesson suggested the negative effects of drug use for health and future success. For instance, a student in New York responded in their DARE workbook that the consequences of using marijuana included "you could die."[32] Another student from Presque Isle County, Michigan, learned a similar lesson from their DARE education. The student submitted a poster entitled, "The Grave Truth about Drugs," with a drawing of an open grave and headstone reading "RIP" to a DARE poster contest.[33] Although not explicitly stated, the program's framework of zero tolerance rested on the assumption that drug use could lead not only to significant health risks but also to legal consequences. In comments on the value of DARE, educators expressed support for how the program implicitly reinforced the lesson that arrest or incarceration was a potential consequence for drug use. As one educator in Nashville, Tennessee, praised DARE, "Yes, it gives the students a sense of awareness. Such as: what goes on if you are arrested for some type of disorderly behavior." Or as another wrote, police were appropriate teachers "since it is a criminal offense to use illegal drugs."[34]

Within this context, antidrug education complemented the free market orthodoxy of choice, which assumed that all students had the ability to make independent decisions without recognizing how opportunity was structured by discriminatory housing policy, economic devastation, and policing. The January 1991 revision to the DARE student workbook, for instance, included a new introduction emphasizing choices and their consequences. "As you grow up, you will need to make many choices. Some choices are more difficult to make than others. One of the most important choices you make will be about the use of alcohol and drugs. Your decision about the use of alcohol and drugs can have either good or bad effects on you and your family." Luckily, for students, the DARE program and officer were there to help them make the best choices. "The D.A.R.E. program includes activities to help you learn to make wise choices," the student workbook continued. "The D.A.R.E. officer will provide help and assistance to you as you complete each activity in your D.A.R.E. notebook."[35] The emphasis on decisions and choices continued even as DARE came under scrutiny for ineffectiveness at preventing youth drug use, most notably after a 1993 cartoon video called "Land of Decisions and Choices" was shown to students. By providing students with the information to make the correct choice—to never use drugs—DARE reinforced the cultural assumptions made by the likes of William Bennett about the importance of personal responsibility, values, and morality.[36]

DARE's message fit neatly within the Reagan administration's framing of drug use as both a moral and law enforcement issue. If students made the wrong choice—to use drugs—the police were there to ensure they understood the potential consequences. Focusing on personal responsibility meant students had to learn to recognize and accept that drug use was the individual's choice and could not be solved through social spending. The first step to address drug use, Reagan explained in the summer of 1986, "is making certain that individual drug users and everyone else understand that in a free society we're all accountable for our actions. If this problem is to be solved, drug users can no longer excuse themselves by blaming society. As individuals, they're responsible."[37] Because drug use was a moral problem, it required kids to change their behavior to align with the law-and-order mission of the drug war. As one group of police scholars suggested in 1990, "DARE is the thin blue line operating at a moral level." Along with DARE, schools implemented a variety of antidrug activities aimed at changing attitudes and creating a culture of no use, such as the Red Ribbon campaigns where students pledged to not use drugs and participated in a Red Ribbon Run. In doing so, the multipronged antidrug education programming not only denied the structural roots of the drug crisis but also threatened punishment for stepping out of line and *choosing* to use drugs. Crucially, it also sent the message that the blame for irresponsible behavior was entirely the individual's and thus the consequences justly deserved.[38]

Making any drug use whatsoever unacceptable complemented zero-tolerance policies. In turn, DARE organizers drew explicitly on Bennett's connection—articulated in *What Works*—between moral education and zero tolerance. Referring to the "poignant commentary made by William Bennett," DARE administrators noted that such "get tough" rhetoric echoes the sentiments of parents, educators, and law enforcement professionals in conveying the urgency of the drug abuse problem, including distribution of drugs by gang members."[39] LAPD officials often echoed such themes of personal responsibility, morality, and getting tough when describing DARE's utility. Assistant Chief Robert Vernon, an evangelical Christian, described the importance of DARE's values education to the National Association of Evangelicals Convention in 1985 after a long introduction on the problem of gang violence and drug trafficking in Los Angeles. "We have young people today that don't understand why certain things are wrong," Vernon explained. "They just don't understand. . . . We need to have values education. . . . We have a program in Los Angeles we call DARE. . . . And part of the program is educating them as to why they should not use drugs. . . . You know, the thing about values, and the concept of right and wrong, the issue is here, it takes a lot of time. It doesn't take one class, we have to be in that school all semester in order to get across the point.[40] DARE proponents reinforced these messages by having students sign no-use pledges in DARE classrooms and write personal essays upon completing DARE in which students pledged to remain drug-free for life. The message was also meant to be carried into the future, as DARE administrators sealed antidrug messages from students across the country in a time capsule to celebrate the first National DARE Day in 1988.[41]

Relying on the police to disseminate messages of zero tolerance and personal responsibility also promoted a vision of producing disciplined citizens. "Moral strength," "choice," and "individual responsibility" were the watchwords of the definition of a good citizen, and one that was uttered by DARE officers in classrooms across the nation and all the way to the Oval Office.[42] As DARE America director Glenn Levant made clear, DARE's success was evident during the 1992 Los Angeles rebellion, when "we saw kids in DARE shirts walking the streets with their parents, hand-in-hand, as if to say 'I'm a good citizen, I'm not going to participate in the looting.'"[43] Levant's definition of citizenship, coming within the context of the LAPD's war on drugs and gangs that rested on an us-versus-them mentality, would not have included those who expressed discontent with the police in the days following the acquittal of the officers involved in the beating of Rodney King that sparked the 1992 rebellion.[44]

Emphasizing moral choices, as Levant suggested, contributed to a broader effort to produce model citizens who respected authority. Implicit messages within the DARE curriculum aimed at socializing youth to accept law and order as a prerequisite of citizenship. "D.A.R.E.® opens the door to young people to lay the foundation of responsible citizenship," criminologist David Carter noted in an analysis of DARE and community policing. Contact with law enforcement was key to developing not only positive views of the police but also the characteristics of good citizens, namely obedience to the law and the police, respect for parents and community, and a moral sense of right and wrong. "Constant positive exposure to a police officer over a sustained period of time can shape a positive attitude toward the community, its values, and the police," Carter suggested. "Consequently, D.A.R.E.® can help develop good citizenship in the students who participate."[45] DARE officers reinforced this message in the classroom, suggesting that America's future was at stake. "If we are going to save our country, and I sincerely believe we are, DARE is but a start of getting communities and parents back together with our most vital element, our children," one DARE officer told a congressional committee. "Forming them into positive, responsible citizens for our future."[46] The values and character-building lessons embedded in DARE's curriculum would lead to better and more disciplined citizenship, law enforcement officers believed. "Most kids want to do what is right, but the peer pressure to conform is unbelievably strong," a Florida DARE officer commented. "What they learn in D.A.R.E.® discussion sessions is that there are lots of other kids who share their values to do 'what's right.' That lesson goes far beyond drug resistance and gets to the heart of being a good citizen."[47]

Oftentimes, these lessons had negative and unintended results. The program's just say no message was highly effective even if not in the intended purpose. The Honolulu Police Department adopted DARE in 1985 and an evaluation on the program's effectiveness was conducted in 1986. One teacher responded that the "Saying No" lesson was highly effective but also had an unintended detrimental effect. "The lesson was taught and immediately the teacher noticed the students using the skill of saying 'no' when they were confronted with a request to which they did not wish to respond. Unfortunately, as the teacher noted, the students were saying 'no' to HER requests."[48] Refusal skills could not only lead to saying no not only to drugs but also to teachers and authority figures.

With the passage of the 1986 Drug Free Schools and Communities Act (DFSCA), a part of the 1986 Anti-Drug Abuse Act, federal officials facilitated a connection between prevention and aggressive enforcement of school disciplinary policies through funding incentives. The Drug Free Schools Act provided funds for prevention programming but connected the granting of funds to the establishment of punitive school discipline codes. Federal funding thereby supported a multipronged approach of both substance use education curriculum, such as DARE, and the "promotion of established policies to eliminate drug abuse on school campuses and to enforce school discipline codes relating to use, possession, and sale of substances."[49] Programs that received federal and state funding were required to fulfill these standards of multipronged curriculum and disciplinary policies. The DFSCA, in short, made zero-tolerance federal policy. In doing so, preventive programs legitimated and widened the punitive side of the drug war. As Melody Lark explained in a study of the DFSCA and National Drug Control Strategy, state and federal drug education policies "fuel the war on drugs and perpetuate it in schools throughout the nation."[50]

DARE's prevention message—to say no when offered drugs and to "never" use drugs—relied on an overly simplistic zero-tolerance policy toward drug use that treated all drugs as equally dangerous. Indeed, DARE's message of taking personal responsibility for the consequences of drug use worked hand in hand with the school district's zero-tolerance drug policy. LAUSD policy related to drug use and sale on school campuses had become increasingly punitive over the 1980s. Alongside the federal establishment of the Drug-Free School Zones Demonstration Program in 1988,[51] which enhanced sentencing for drug trafficking near schools, LAUSD adopted ever-more punitive zero-tolerance policies for the sale and possession of drugs on campuses. "Any student who possesses, furnishes, uses, or sells narcotics, drugs, or intoxicants on school premises or during school activities," the LAUSD's 1991 Drug-Free Schools policy stated, "shall be subject to arrest, suspension, expulsion, or other disciplinary action."[52] In fact, five years after DARE's founding, expulsions for drug-related offenses reached over 200, up from double digits in the 1970s.[53] Rather than an alternative to enforcement of drug laws, DARE produced the image of a humane LAPD while schools ratcheted up disciplinary policies and officers continued to arrest students for drug use and dealing. The LAPD and LAUSD's mutual diagnosis of the drug crisis as a problem rooted in poor behavior and a lack of personal responsibility, with all the related racialized assumptions, rather than one of social and economic structures and inequities enabled DARE's prevention message and zero-tolerance policies to develop concurrently.

Proponents sold DARE as an alternative to the supply-side solutions that emphasized aggressive enforcement of drug laws. The belief was that as more students were exposed to DARE, "the acceleration of the program [would] help meet the objectives of limiting the demand for drugs and, in turn, reduce the need for arrests on and off campus."[54] Yet enforcement of zero-tolerance drug laws on school campuses did not disappear. When the LAPD proposed expanding the DARE program to high schools, for example, the LAPD and LAUSD believed that it would effectively link the hard and soft side of enforcement and prevention. Crucially, the high school program was envisioned as an explicit addition, rather than alternative, to the department's enforcement efforts around school campuses. "Initiation of the DARE High School Program and advancement of drug resistance education to the tenth through twelfth grade levels is expected to reduce the demand for drugs," the Mayor's Office of Criminal Justice Planning explained in the DARE high school project overview and grant proposal. "This cumulative effect will complement enforcement efforts on or near high school campuses."[55] More pointedly, in 1989 some DARE "officers received training during their squad meetings in the areas of foot pursuits and K9 searches."[56] Such training belied the notion that DARE officers offered an alternative role or responsibility of the police. Rather, DARE presented a means to bring the drug war into the nation's classrooms under the guise of preventive education.

Alongside zero-tolerance policies and lessons, DARE reinforced the strict enforcement of truancy violations. While LAUSD administrators estimated that the reported number of truants represented only one-tenth of the district's actual truancy rate, between September 24, 1985, and March 31, 1986, LAPD officers detained 14,927 truants and took them to one of eight LAUSD Truancy Centers. DARE program facilitators routinely linked drug abuse, truancy, and juvenile crime in their funding proposals. "To the community, truancy represents a substantial loss through crimes against property committed by truant students," one grant application explained. "Strict enforcement of truancy laws, combined with the positive reinforcement provided in the DARE program, will reduce this problem."[57] Connecting truancy, crime, and drugs fed into the broader punitive framework of the drug war and reinforced DARE's dual emphasis on prevention and punishment.

Perhaps nowhere did the complementary nature of prevention and punishment culminate more than at a DARE graduation held in Miami in 1999. Governor Jeb Bush presided over the graduation of 20,000 DARE students decked out in DARE T-shirts in what was dubbed the largest DARE graduation ever and included an appearance by Dwayne "The Rock" Johnson. When Bush took the stage, however, he did more than present a drug-free message. He also signed three punitive drug-related bills into law, including the establishment of a state drug czar, a three-strikes law, and a law designating ketamine (Special K) an illegal substance. Bush stated that the three-strikes law "creates a greater certainty of punishment."[58] There was no mistaking DARE's integral role in supporting the drug war's punitive, zero-tolerance message and police practices. In doing so, it also contributed to the racialization of crime given the ways drug enforcement targeted predominantly Black and Latinx neighborhoods and schools.

Appealing to "Disadvantaged" Youth

Perceptions of drug use and criminality among youth of color had been particularly influential in federal policymakers' thinking and get-tough approaches to not only drug enforcement but also antidrug education. Secretary Bennett was forthright in his views that the central problem of drug abuse rested on youth of color. "Unless we do something about drugs," Bennett testified at a congressional hearing on Drug Abuse Prevention in America's Schools in 1987, "we're never going to do very much about the 50 percent of black and Hispanic kids who drop out of our schools. So many of them are into the business of drugs."[59] Together with addressing drug use among youth of color, changing the attitudes of these students toward the police became an important goal for policymakers, law enforcement, and educators.

Many proponents of DARE believe that the pro-police message would be especially beneficial in neighborhoods and schools with a historically antagonistic relationship to law enforcement. As one DARE teacher in San Francisco observed, "In the schools where I teach, I see kids who are already predisposed to getting in trouble. They have numerous contacts with police at home and on the street. But in my classes, they see that cops have a more human side, that we care about helping them stay away from crime and drugs."[60] While not overtly mentioning race, some observers suggested that DARE would help alleviate the tension between African American communities and the police. "The police instructors themselves do not question for a moment the value of what they are doing. After years of being the anonymous, uniformed 'enemy,' viewed with suspicion in some neighborhoods," reported James Stewart of the National Institute of Justice, "it is gratifying and energizing for these officers that the children come to see them as positive role models who want to help them protect their future."[61] Others were more explicit. Charles Gruber, chief of police in Elgin, Illinois, commented that "a dialogue is opened that leads to less discontented attitudes between police and young adults. DARE programs can also be especially helpful in bridging the cultural diversity gap between children from minority communities and the police department."[62]

Better relations with African American communities were only the beginning. The DARE officer, proponents believed, would also have a significant positive impact on the relationship between police and immigrant communities. Testifying to the Los Angeles City Task Force on Immigration, the LAPD's Vernon provided an overview of DARE and indicated that "the program had a positive effect on cultural interaction and awareness among the student participants."[63] By making officers an integral part of the school's antidrug curriculum, DARE built on long-standing police-community relations programs in Black and Latinx neighborhoods that intended to normalize the presence of police not only in schools but in every aspect of American life.

If police brass saw DARE as a means to improve relations between kids and the police in communities of color in particular, they were battling a problem of their own making. As Los Angeles County officials advocated for more funding to be pushed to police-led school prevention programs, such as DARE, they reinforced sentiments among many residents of color and activists that their communities had been abandoned of all services except for the police. As the Coalition Against Police Abuse's (CAPA) Michael Zinzun explained, "They (the police) shouldn't be leading the community. People here don't trust the police as a leader. And why should they? Not very much has been done to improve relations. There is a 'police-against-us' attitude throughout the community. If you live here you are immediately a suspect. When those kids are picked up during those sweeps, scars are left. It's not only degrading at the moment, but it puts a stamp on their lives."[64] The adversarial relationship between the police and communities of color was an issue not only in Los Angeles. Children in other cities and states reinforced such beliefs that DARE officers did little to alleviate the tension between police and residents of color. "I think it depends on where you come from—some people don't trust the police . . . living in the area that I did and seeing the police, I never trusted the police," one student in Minnesota told evaluators of the state's DARE program, "and I don't necessarily think a police officer was right for a school like that. It was a bad neighborhood."[65] Some studies found that the use of police officers actually increased animosity toward the police among students of color. One 1989 study of 400 "inner-city youth" conducted in Nashville, Tennessee, for instance, found that "the attitudes of students became more negative toward the police as a consequence of the program."[66]

Principals and teachers held similar assumptions about race and criminality as Bennett and other culture warriors. They welcomed DARE officers as credible experts on drugs and antidrug education but also for the way the program socialized students to respect the police. And in predominantly

Black and Latinx schools, the program had an added function for principals because DARE officers were representatives of law enforcement. The principal of McKinley Avenue School in South Central commented, "Great public relations were fostered between the school children and the officer. And with our location in the (high-crime) inner city, it was great having the officer on the school grounds for all-around purposes."[67] In facilitating the entrance of police officers into schools, DARE complemented and reinforced the broader structure of the war on drugs that was underpinned by enhanced sentencing and policing on the one hand, and education and personal responsibility on the other.

Despite widespread criticism of the LAPD's racist policing in communities of color following the beating of Rodney King and the 1992 Los Angeles rebellion, or perhaps as a means of image control in response to it, DARE America focused on a new after-school program to intervene in the lives of students from "disadvantaged," "inner-city," and "high-crime" neighborhoods. Such targeted attention on kids of color using such color-blind and race-neutral language expanded with the development DARE Plus—Play and Learn Under Supervision—in 1993.[68] The mission of DARE Plus, which received support from the post-rebellion Rebuild L.A. (RLA) economic development initiative focused on facilitating private investment in South Central Los Angeles in particular, was "to offer a safe, enjoyable and educational alternative to the local streets after completion of the school day."[69] In contrast to DARE, which was often described as a "universal program designed to reach the general population," DARE Plus explicitly targeted "at-risk" kids with all its racialized connotations.[70]

The program began in Los Angeles middle schools in "disadvantaged" neighborhoods before expanding to at least 350 schools around the country. Marina del Rey Middle School was the school chosen to launch DARE Plus. "D.A.R.E.+P.L.U.S. will officially start here in September with a year-long pilot program at the inner-city Marina del Rey Middle School, located approximately 10 miles from downtown Los Angeles," DARE America summarized in its press release introducing the new program. "All students enrolled in this school next year will be able to participate in a wide range of educational, vocational and recreational clubs and classes after school, in a safe and well-supervised campus setting."[71] More crucially, Marina del Rey Middle School was targeted due to its demographic profile. According to DARE America, the school "was selected as the site for the pilot program because of its inner-city location and the high rate of crime and gang activity in the neighborhood surrounding the school. The school has an ethnically diverse student body, many of whom do not participate in supervised after-school activities, and an extensive physical plant that can easily accommodate an after-school program."[72]

As the press release suggested, DARE Plus was much more than an after-school program. DARE America and RLA appear to have been informed by material from the American Enterprise Institute (AEI), a conservative think tank, on out-of-wedlock births, teenage pregnancies, and rising Aid for Families with Dependent Children (AFDC) rolls.[73] In turn, DARE Plus targeted kids from communities perceived to be especially "at risk," which fit within racialized conceptions of poverty, the "underclass," and "welfare queens" of the Reagan era that portrayed poor Black communities—Black women in particular—as the cause of poverty, crime, and violence.[74] While it is not entirely clear how DARE America and RLA used the data on "Out-of-Wedlock Births and Poverty" from the AEI, the after-school program fit the racial and cultural assumptions about the "culture of poverty" perceived to be plaguing "inner-city" Black communities. DARE Plus focused on "disadvantaged" students who, according to Levant, needed vocational training and "productive, constructive after-school activities that will allow them to develop their skills and interests. Personal safety is also a vital concern."[75] While underserved children certainly faced serious social problems, including violence, that needed a response, DARE Plus did not address deeper social or economic conditions or structures that produced those problems.

DARE Plus brought police and corporate sponsors together to connect kids from so-called disadvantaged neighborhoods with future job opportunities. The program recruited business executives to teach classes. For example, the CEO of California Pizza Kitchen had managers volunteer to teach enrichment classes at the after-school program. DARE America provided materials, and the manager's job was to teach kids about their future opportunities. Organized around the idea that children living in the inner city did not have many opportunities, DARE Plus intended to broaden their horizons and show them alternatives to drugs and violence. As Glenn Levant reflected, the program's goal was to improve relations between the police and youth in disadvantaged neighborhoods.[76]

The program was another example of DARE's reliance on public-private partnership and donations from corporations to expand its reach both in Los Angeles and across the nation. "The benefit of a program like this to students in our district is incalculable," said LAUSD superintendent Sid Thompson in explaining the benefit of receiving private funding for a public school district amid fiscal constraints. "Given the funding constraints the school district faces, D.A.R.E.+P.L.U.S. is vital in bringing educational and recreational enrichment program[s] back into our schools for the first time in years."[77] Many of the corporate donations for DARE Plus, including support from Kodak, Fujifilm, and the Great Western Forum, were facilitated by RLA's focus on privatization and capital investment after the 1992 Los Angeles rebellion.[78] "D.A.R.E. PLUS is an RLA project accepted and referred to the Community Development Team at the start of 1993," one official with RLA summarized. "Since that time RLA has been instrumental in the program's success." Indeed, RLA funded some of the equipment for DARE Plus as well as volunteers to run the after-school programs.[79]

Some of DARE Plus's partnership choices were, especially in retrospect, questionable at best. Corporate sponsorship and involvement also led to the program receiving substantial attention from national press because junk bond investor Michael Milken worked with the program as part of his prison sentence's community service obligations. Milken's responsibilities included "meeting with businesspeople, teachers, parents and other community members to encourage their participation in DARE Plus; teaching students math and other academic subjects; [and] assisting volunteers in learning how to teach the program and developing similar programs for other schools." Organizers asked Milken to "please advise" when it came to "potential candidates" who were ready to volunteer for the program. What expertise the former junk bond king had in after-school programs went unexplained.[80] Alongside Milken, DARE Plus invited Michael Jackson, described in the program as "Guest Mega Star,"[81] to participate in the launch at Marina del Rey Middle School along with a slew of other actors and athletes, including Tom Selleck, Rosey Greer, Jamaal Wilkes, James Worthy, Florence Griffith Joyner, Al Joyner, and Sherri Howard.[82] In doing so, DARE Plus doubled down on DARE America's efforts to deglamorize drug use through partnerships with athletes and celebrities while doing little to address social and economic realities.

The focus on the "inner city," "high-crime" areas, and "at-risk" children ultimately meant that these students faced even greater police presence in their daily lives. Indeed, one suggestion from volunteers with the program advised to "increase police patrol" around the Marina del Rey Middle School, where the program was established.[83] DARE Plus reinforced the DARE program's larger focus on changing the relationship between police and under-resourced communities where the drug war took its most devastating toll.[84] Indeed, DARE and DARE Plus aimed at burnishing the image of the police within the context of an aggressive drug and gang war that actively undermined trust in the police. In other words, DARE's effort to increase community support and trust in the police by using officers as teachers was a solution to a problem created by the department's own enforcement policies. Such efforts to soften the image of the police blurred the line between supply and demand reduction and defined prevention programs within a punitive framework.

Family Values and the DARE Parent Program

Speaking at a DARE Officers Association conference in Louisville, Kentucky, in 1992, Vice President Dan Quayle emphasized the importance of personal responsibility, family values, and respect for the police in the crusade against drugs. "The ultimate weapon against drug and alcohol abuse is the commitment to values . . . values like faith, hard work, integrity, and personal responsibility," he told the officers. Evil forces promoting drug use, such as pushers, media outlets glamorizing drugs, and rappers such as Ice T, whose mere mention elicited boos from the audience and whom Quayle vilified for lyrics that "say it's OK to kill cops," were undermining traditional morality, a belief in family values, and trust in police officers. And the nation's youth were most at risk of succumbing to such threats. But, Quayle stated, "that is where DARE comes in. By teaching children how to recognize and resist peer pressure, by informing them about positive alternatives to drug use, by building their self-esteem, yes, DARE reinforces the importance of family values." The vice president commended the DARE officers for their vital contribution to the drug war, telling them that "together we will keep America great."[85]

Policymakers at the local, state, and federal level routinely emphasized the ways drug use was a problem of lost morality and the crisis in family values that impacted all youth regardless of race, ethnicity, or class. When he envisioned DARE, Daryl Gates believed that the threat of drugs in Los Angeles resulted from what scholars described as his belief in "the failure of family and other social institutions to teach the young proper values."[86] Strengthening the nuclear family was a central goal of the program, as administrators sought to deputize parents to take responsibility for helping their children say no to drugs when not in school. In the process, however, DARE administrators relied on and reinforced racialized assumptions of the crisis in family values produced and disseminated by media outlets, sociological studies of the urban "underclass," and the coded language of the "inner city" that pointed to the broken Black family as the source of the drug crisis.[87]

Schools and the police thereby provided two prongs in what was a three-pronged approach to drug prevention. The third element was parents. DARE incorporated implicit messages about family responsibility not only in the classroom but also through police officer meetings with parents and community groups. DARE leaders placed the program at the center of a school-police-parents triad to help students say no to drugs.[88] "The Los Angeles Police Department and the Los Angeles Unified School District are but two members of the partnership needed to help D.A.R.E. achieve its promise," Gates explained in the DARE America Parents Guidebook introduction. "The other, *and most important partners in this effort are the children's parents*. All of us, working together, can save this nation's most vital resource, our children."[89] Every DARE officer, for example, conducted at least one parent education session each semester for every DARE school. While the sessions focused on prevention strategies and encouraged family communication, they also stressed "parenting skills." "Parent education sessions, as presented by DARE instructors, provide parents with information regarding drug recognition, physical symptoms of drug usage, and behavioral changes from drug usage," one DARE grant application summarized. "Additionally, parenting skills to increase awareness of strategies for improving family communications are provided." By 1986, DARE officers had reached nearly 50,000 parents in Los Angeles, where officers taught them ways to get "involved in their child's life."[90]

The emphasis on parental involvement and responsibility expanded over time. With support from the Bureau of Justice Assistance, law enforcement officials in Illinois and North Carolina created the DARE Parent Program (DPP). The DPP was organized to bring parents more directly into the DARE program by having police officers teach parents about how to tell if their kids were using drugs and proper parenting skills.[91] The parent program quickly became an institutionalized part of DARE. Throughout the 1980s and 1990s, DARE staff produced a variety of parent program materials meant to engage parents in DARE and the antidrug message. Beginning in 1989, for instance, DARE partnered with the University of Southern California School of Cinematography to create a parent video, which "will illustrate positive parenting skills and demonstrate their application in vignettes showing 'how to' and 'how not to' deal with the child at various stages of development."[92]

Such messaging expanded when DARE America's executive director Glenn Levant wrote a book for parents entitled *Keeping Kids Drug Free: D.A.R.E. Official*

Parent's Guide in 1998. "The goal of D.A.R.E.—the mission of this book—is to create a generation of young people who choose not to smoke, drink, or take drugs during their childhood and adolescence," Levant summarized. "As adults, they will make decisions and live with the consequences. As children, they need your time, your guidance, your understanding and your love—now. Good luck." Parents had to reinforce messages of personal responsibility by teaching their kids correct morals and values. But the message of responsibility also extended to parents themselves. As Levant instructed, "You must take responsibility for learning to recognize the signs and symptoms that your child may be abusing drugs and alcohol, involved with gangs, or participating in other illegal activities, and you must deal with these problems as soon as possible."[93]

While some parents opposed DARE due to its potential to turn kids into spies for the police and turn their own parents in for drug use, others responded positively.[94] Many studies found that parents were supportive of the DARE program, responded to calls for them to take responsibility, and wanted to learn what they could do to help their children avoid drugs. Annual evaluations of the program found that parents who attended DARE Parent Meetings learned about the problem of youth drug use and what they could do about it. As the ETI found in 1985, parents "thought it [was] a good idea to have uniformed police officers teaching about drugs."[95] Such parental support was crucial to the larger political-cultural work the program accomplished for those law enforcement officials and policymakers who, in DARE, saw the opportunity to shore up the nuclear family and values.

Law enforcement officials also deployed DARE to promote the vision of the nuclear family and played on racialized descriptions of family breakdown. For instance, after an introductory description of gang violence in Los Angeles focused entirely on African American neighborhoods, a *MacNeil/Lehrer NewsHour* report turned to LAPD assistant chief Robert Vernon to describe how police in Los Angeles were dealing with such problems. Vernon placed DARE and its lessons about family values at the center of the solution to gangs and drugs. "I think the root cause here is the emphasis of the important role of parenting," Vernon suggested. "I really think we need to get back to that. . . . However, the police department here in Los Angeles under my boss's direction have instituted a program called DARE. . . . This year all of our elementary schools in Los Angeles have police officers in there teaching these important values."[96] Political constructions of the drug and gang crisis as the product of disorganized, immoral Black families was deployed to justify the need for DARE. Describing the need for kids to learn "clear concepts of right and wrong" based on biblical principles, Vernon in another speech pointed to the department's DARE program as a means by which the police taught kids "values" and that drug use was "wrong."[97] Even as DARE was used by school districts across the country, it played on panic about the connection between the inner city, crack use, and the breakdown of the Black family to garner more resources.[98]

Framing the potential for drug use to spread from inner cities and ghettos to poison suburban families reinforced the politically constructed dichotomy of the violent drug dealer and innocent suburban youth. DARE officials often employed the description of an innocent white suburban family who had no reason to believe their kids would use drugs to promote the benefits of the DARE message. "This does not just happen in ghettos or inner cities. It does not just happen to poor kids or kids from broken homes," Levant wrote in *Keeping Kids Drug Free*. "It happens everywhere in America to families in circumstances exactly like your own and to kids of every age, gender, race, and social class." But for Levant, the coded message was that white suburban parents had more to fear, and lose, than those kids "in ghettos or inner cities." "Discovering that your preteen uses drugs is a tremendous jolt to any parent," Levant continued, "but particularly to a mom and dad who had no reason to believe they might have to face this problem." Levant followed this assertion with a story of "Patti and Al," a typical suburban couple who were shocked to learn their nine-year-old daughter, Meredith, had a friend who proposed trying her mother's marijuana. Luckily, Levant noted, their eleven-year-old son, Lee, had received a visit from a DARE officer in school and imparted some of DARE's lessons to his younger sister. "They never considered that drugs existed in their community because they lived in a nice neighborhood in the suburbs and all the children went to a 'good school.'"[99]

DARE's defenders used the conditions in inner cities not to demand greater investment in social and economic programs to address the root causes of the drug crisis but to defend DARE's lack of success in preventing drug use. As Lieutenant Lew Archer of San Antonio School Police commented, "It is unrealistic to expect a child to be 'inoculated' against drugs, gangs, or violence by exposure to a 45–50 minute class, given twice weekly, when the child lives in an environment where those things are a daily occurrence. . . . Every police officer who has visited a school and talked with students can tell of the student(s) who tell about a brother, cousin, uncle or father who was arrested or is in jail."[100] Building on race-neutral language, DARE's objectives embraced and reinforced racialized assumptions of the drug war promoted by media outlets and policymakers.[101] Mobilizing the fear of suburban preteen drug use provided entry for DARE into suburban schools, but without the accompanying heavy-handed policing that Black kids faced.

DARE's emphasis on parental responsibility and family values connected squarely with both the Reagan and Bush administrations' race-based attacks on the Black family and welfare recipients. No one reflected on the ways that policymakers deployed coded language about the problem of a breakdown in family and moral values more than former secretary of education and drug czar William Bennett. Speaking to the Houston Area Urban League in 1989, Bennett described the problem of drug use not as one related to poverty, joblessness, or racism but rooted in family, values, and personal responsibility, the very things often used to browbeat Black people for continued inequality. "At the very time when we need to affirm things like individual responsibility, civic duty, and obligations to parents and to God, too many segments of society are equivocating and sending mixed messages," Bennett exhorted the League. "This sort of moral enervation must be renounced in the strongest terms."[102]

The DARE officer was on the front line combating the breakdown in morality and family values. As President George H. W. Bush told DARE representatives upon signing the National DARE Day proclamation in 1989, "Because perhaps no one has manned more front lines than the hundreds of dedicated Americans who form the ranks of D.A.R.E.—Drug Abuse Resistance Education. You talk of values and we heard that here today—of right and wrong, and teach kids to do good and reject evil, by avoiding drugs and by, then, opposing drugs."[103] Such messaging about the crucial role of both the DARE officer and parents to shoring up family values and morality was a key component of Bush's drug war. Indeed, Secretary of Education Lauro F. Cavazos, who succeeded William Bennett, continued to focus attention on cities and the need for parental involvement. "I believe we can reclaim our cities and our children from the worst ravages of drug abuse," Cavazos stated in a speech at the Department of Education's third annual conference on drug-free schools and communities. "We cannot expect our schools to succeed at teaching respect for laws and human dignity if we as parents have not done our jobs."[104]

After Bush's lone term, Bill Clinton continued to praise the DARE officer for showing parents the way to combat drugs. "Parents have to recognize that the real war on crime begins at home," Clinton emphasized in a speech to the International Association of the Chiefs of Police (IACP) in 1994. "If the first responsibility of the government is to provide law and order, then the first responsibility of parents is to teach right from wrong. . . . We've got to have more folks helping them, like those wonderful police officers in the DARE programs all across America."[105] First Lady Hillary Clinton reinforced the president's message. Speaking at a DARE event at Mott Elementary School in Flint, Michigan, on October 8, 1996, Hillary Clinton lauded the program. "The battle against drugs is going to be fought in the family rooms and the classrooms of America," Clinton told the audience. "We need D.A.R.E. and other community-based drug prevention programs like it to win this battle."[106] In such ways, police officers were granted the expertise that brought them not only into schools but also into the home as experts on parenting and family life.

The key point was that both conservative culture warriors and third way Democrats like Clinton proposed devolving the social costs of the drug problem to families. As a draft of Clinton's speech to the IACP in 1994 stated, "The most important tool in the fight against crime—the most essential resource we have—is the moral education of our children. And that is the responsibility of parents, not of our government, our courts, or our police. It doesn't cost money and it doesn't require a new bureaucracy, it requires parental attention."[107] And DARE would help promote containing the costs to families and communities. "You know, the old saying that has become current from African communities is it takes a community to educate a child," Deputy Secretary of Education Kunin told Congress in 1993. "I think we are recognizing that as our families very often are troubled, the whole community has to pitch in and provide that kind of guidance and love and sense of ethics that sometimes just slips between the cracks and DARE is one of those vehicles to provide that."[108]

Lessons about family values and parental responsibility played into the racist tropes of the broken Black family and attacks on social welfare during the Clinton era. Congressmen routinely brought up the problem of absent fathers as a root of child misbehavior and drug use. In a not-so-veiled statement about the Black family, congressman Mark Souder (R-IN) explained while questioning boxer Sugar Ray Leonard, a DARE ambassador, in hearings about drugs and DARE in 1998, "The point of D.A.R.E. and a lot of these programs and school teachers and coaches is that without a dad there, particularly, young boys which is increasingly a focal problem that we have in our society are young boys who don't have dad impacting in their lives, they are more likely to be looking for some other role model because they don't see a male model in front of them. . . . If it's a drug dealer who has a big car, that's the danger and we're trying to counter-balance that."[109] DARE, as

Souder implied, aimed to address this problem by reinforcing the nuclear family and family values, especially in communities of color, while Clinton vowed to "end welfare as we know it" and signed the 1996 Personal Responsibility and Work Opportunity Reconciliation Act into law, which imposed severe limits on welfare and further devastated communities most directly impacted by the drug war and economic disinvestment.[110]

Combined with the zero-tolerance orthodoxy of drug warriors, DARE's moralizing messages legitimized punishment for those kids who did not live up to the standards of responsible citizenship and for their parents, implicitly from inner-city communities of color, who threatened the sanctity of the imagined nuclear family. George W. Bush continued the rhetoric of family values when he announced April 10, 2003, as National DARE Day. "The most effective way to reduce the supply of drugs is to reduce the demand, and I am confident that we can help accomplish this goal through a focus on effective, family-centered education and prevention."[111] Touting the DARE officer as a means to teach and promote family values allowed the program's proponents and drug war policymakers to double down on the growing consensus that the drug war would be won not through government investment in positive social policy but by youth altering their behavior, backed, as always, by the threat of arrest and incarceration.

Cops and the Culture War

DARE's widespread adoption and popularity pointed to the significant political and cultural work the program accomplished for the police across the country. For many, DARE represented a positive element in their community because it affirmed traditional values and reinforced the nuclear family structure. One study of Wisconsin's program asserted, "DARE affirms traditional values and is widely accepted in communities that adopt it,"[112] while a community representative in Minnesota summarized, "I think D.A.R.E. is like religious teaching . . . if we teach faith and values when they're young, they might experiment, but they'll come back to it. What would it be like without D.A.R.E.?"[113]

Relying on the police to teach messages of zero tolerance, personal responsibility, family values, and respect for law and order accomplished political-cultural work for policymakers and law enforcement in at least two major ways. First, it diverted attention from the reality of the drug war. While the police may have softened their image and worked to improve perceptions of the police among kids and teenagers, their major emphasis in the war on drugs centered on mass arrest and punishment, especially in and around predominantly Black and Latinx schools. Second, praise for programs like DARE and the broader message of drug prevention education belied a lack of evidence that such programs prevented drug use. While evaluations of DARE conducted in the early 1990s suggested that the program had not proven to be the panacea to youth drug use that officials had hoped it would, as the next chapter explores, viewed through a different lens, the program was a success. By bringing police into schools to teach morality, family values, personal responsibility, and respect for law and order, DARE produced the social and cultural context within which get-tough policies and an expanded police presence in schools were accepted as legitimate.

CHAPTER SIX

Just Say No to DARE

By its tenth anniversary, DARE had become "a darling of America's drug war." Parents held garage sales to fundraise for the program and slapped DARE bumper stickers on their cars in demonstrations of support. Politicians also routinely referenced DARE in speeches and appeared at DARE-related events to great applause. Not to be outdone, police departments affixed the DARE logo to squad cars and held DARE vehicle decoration contests in what had effectively become a "public-relations bonanza with the program."[1] The program was a fixture in many American schools, communities, and, in some cases, homes. As evidence of the program's popularity and public relations chops, DARE America held the first "Kids' Convention" in Los Angeles in 1994. When asked if they would ever do drugs, join gangs, or use guns, the 6,000 kids in attendance screamed, "No, no, no!" at the top of their lungs. Deploying a giant video screen, fireworks, a massive sound system, an appearance by DARE ambassador comedian Arsenio Hall, and a performance by the Mighty Morphin Power Rangers, the convention presented a fifteen-point "Students Bill of Rights" based on suggestions submitted by DARE students from across the country. Alongside the public relations machine, the convention also coincided with the introduction of a revised curriculum focusing on anti-violence lessons, which aligned with new federal funding requirements established by the Violent Crime Control and Law Enforcement Act of 1994, popularly referred to as the 1994 Crime Bill.[2] By all accounts, DARE was immensely popular and well positioned to continue its reign as the drug war darling.

But this DARE celebration obscured a growing discontent with the program. Although taught in every state and in dozens of countries worldwide, DARE was coming under intense pressure for failing to achieve its stated purpose of preventing youth drug use. Over the decade, dozens of evaluations conducted by social scientists and prevention experts repeatedly demonstrated that DARE was not only ineffective at reducing or preventing youth drug use but, in some cases, led to increased drug use, especially among suburban youth. Despite DARE America executives' vehement defense of the program, it could not avoid being at the center of a fierce debate about how to prevent drug use. The revised curriculum rolled out at the 1994 Kids' Convention, in fact, was part of DARE America's effort to respond to criticism from the research community. For the time being, however, DARE remained immensely popular despite findings of ineffectiveness, and the defense of the program exposed DARE's fundamental purpose: bolstering police legitimacy, giving cops a human face, and integrating the police into the daily lives of youth.

Policymakers in the Bush and Clinton administrations promoted DARE as a model drug education program regardless of the critical evaluations from the research community. The Violent Crime Control and Law Enforcement Act of 1994 included funding for DARE and linked drug prevention with the growing attention to addressing youth violence.[3] DARE's continued popularity despite evidence of its ineffectiveness was a function of what political scientists refer to as "symbolic politics." As Rick Aniskiewicz and Earl Wysong explained in a 1990 study of DARE's multiple meanings of success, "When drug education programs are viewed as symbolic actions that have political utility for various sponsoring groups, the continuation of such programs is likely to be only loosely coupled to their actual efficacy."[4] More than reducing drug use, DARE maintained its popularity because it represented positive action to combat the "drug crisis," which appealed to parents, politicians, and educators. It was, in other words, a palliative approach to the drug crisis that went a long way in making people feel better without addressing the root causes of drug use.

The debate over DARE pointed to the symbolic value of a police-led educational project for stakeholders. DARE, in short, was popular not because it prevented drug use but because policymakers, corporate sponsors, law enforcement, and educators saw the relationship between kids and cops as a primary benefit of the program unto itself. Few, if any, critics of the program seriously questioned the aspect of DARE that made it the darling of the drug war—the use of cops as teachers. If DARE failed to reduce drug use, it had effectively reshaped the image of the police officer during a crisis of police legitimacy following the beating of Rodney King. The DARE officer was, quite simply, untouchable.

Yet the research community continued to hold DARE's feet to the fire. As evidence mounted pointing to DARE's inability to accomplish its stated goal of preventing drug use, combined with high-profile stories of kids turning in their parents for drug use, budget constraints at the local level, and requirements from policymakers that federal funds be used to support scientifically proven programs, many started to just say no to DARE. Indeed,

DARE's days as the most popular and widespread drug prevention program would be numbered if it did not evolve. But DARE did not disappear. It introduced a completely revised curriculum in 2003 (along with subsequent revisions in following years) and ensured the continued presence of police in schools as teachers; it also lived on as a cultural icon and parody. While it came under ridicule and became the target of irony, especially surrounding its notorious T-shirt, the continued attention DARE received, whether praise or mocking, demonstrated the deep impact the program had on American society, politics, and culture in the 1990s.

Truth and DARE: Evaluation and the Failure to Prevent Drug Use

DARE had a long history of evaluation and assessment. The LAPD and LAUSD built in mechanisms to evaluate the program from its establishment in 1983. They contracted with the Evaluation Training Institute (ETI) to conduct yearly evaluations, which overwhelmingly expressed favorable responses from students and statistical effectiveness of DARE.[5] In the annual evaluation conducted in 1988, for instance, ETI reported statistical significance in reduction of drug use between DARE and non-DARE students. As Daryl Gates relayed to the Board of Police Commissioners, "Analysis of the student survey data showed statistically significant differences between DARE and non-DARE students in reported use of all categories of alcohol, tobacco, heroin and inhalants." In addition, ETI found that teachers and principals had nothing negative to say about the program except for wishing DARE officers would come to their schools even more frequently.[6] DARE continued to work with ETI through the 1980s, using its positive evaluations as evidence of DARE's unqualified success. Bolstered by additional studies funded by the National Institute of Justice finding initial positive results, DARE seemed to be an effective program.

By the early 1990s, public health researchers and criminologists not associated with DARE turned their attention to evaluating the program. It was, after all, receiving upwards of $700 million in taxpayer funds, and researchers wanted to know if it was effective. Initial studies found a lot of support for the program from the police, educators, and parents but little evidence that DARE helped reduce youth drug use.[7] One of the first studies conducted in North Carolina, for instance, found that DARE had little effect on student drug use but that it was successful in changing student attitudes and assertiveness toward drugs. Such results were not surprising, researchers suggested, because "generally speaking, drug education programs have revealed somewhat more success with changing attitudes than behaviors."[8] Many of the first independent evaluations similarly found that the program had a positive impact on student knowledge and attitude about drugs and suggested it was an effective way to deliver information to kids who saw police as authority figures, but it did not have a strong impact on behavior when it came to drug use. Indeed, a 1991 study based in Kentucky found "no statistically significant differences between experimental groups and control groups in the percentage of new users of . . . cigarettes, smokeless tobacco, alcohol, [or] marijuana."[9] In an effort to confirm such findings and to justify the growing amount of public money the program received from the Drug Free Schools and Communities Act, DARE became the subject of a bevy of social scientists, at times with federal grant funding, interested in evaluating the program.

Rising pressure led DARE America officials and officials from the National Institute of Justice (NIJ) to attempt to confirm what they believed to be DARE's unbridled positive impact on kids. In turn, the NIJ solicited proposals for a nationwide study of DARE. They awarded the grant to a group of researchers at the Research Triangle Institute "to conduct an extensive review of the D.A.R.E.® program and to assess its place within the context of the broad spectrum of school-based drug use prevention efforts."[10] DARE America, thinking that the evaluation would prove DARE's effectiveness at preventing drug use, supported the study. In fact, DARE America sent a letter to state DARE coordinators in 1992 urging cooperation with the study. "The review of the D.A.R.E. evaluation literature will give us ammunition to respond to critics who charge that D.A.R.E. has not proven its effectiveness," DARE America representatives stated.[11] As designed, the study would be a meta-analysis of prior evaluations of DARE, which meant the researchers did not collect new primary data.[12] While DARE America urged collaboration at the beginning, the organization's tone changed when researchers presented the initial findings from the RTI at a drug education conference held at the University of California San Diego during the spring of 1993.

The RTI study results were front and center at the conference, which was attended by researchers, DARE state coordinators, and DARE America representatives. An entire section of the conference, including three panels, a response panel, and a question-and-answer session, was devoted to the RTI study, entitled "Drug Abuse Resistance Education (DARE): Past, Present and Future." Study authors, including Susan T. Ennett and Christopher Ringwalt, reported that DARE was immensely popular and broadly disseminated but ineffective at preventing drug use, especially as students moved through their school years after taking the program. Any initial effect, in short, faded with time.[13] Even as researchers questioned DARE's effectiveness at reducing drug use, they highlighted several areas of strength, including its widespread implementation, emphasis on relations between schools and the police, and the deep commitment of those involved with the program. Researchers also pointed to the role of marketing strategies in making the program popular and its infrastructure in making the program and its message easy to implement, especially with DARE-branded items to serve as reminders—what scholars called "gimmicks." However, as researchers recognized, none of these areas of strength actually prevented drug use. As Bill Hansen, who had been involved with Project SMART at USC but was not part of the RTI team and had been invited to attend the conference, commented about the praise for DARE's community relations success, "Goodwill does not prevent substance abuse."[14] DARE, it seemed, was a successful program for a variety of reasons but not for its stated one of keeping kids off drugs.

Scholars also questioned DARE boosters' suggestion that it could address breakdown in family values and community cohesion, the moral and values education touted by the likes of William Bennett and Robert Vernon. As Ringwalt explained in extended comments after the conference, "First, many people look to school-based drug prevention programs in general—and to DARE, because of its popularity, in particular—as panaceas that should correct deficits within the family and community. To the extent this is true, expectations for such programs may be substantially inflated."[15] Addressing problems of family and community breakdown were important, but as researchers observed, programs such as DARE missed the mark.

DARE America's executive director, Glenn Levant, attended the conference and was in the audience for the presentation of the RTI findings. And he did not like what he heard. What conference attendees heard, Levant claimed, is "a bunch of $200,000 and $300,000 superficial evaluations," none of which were conclusive, he argued. "I would hate to see a program that is as widespread and as productive as the DARE program be disparaged by the mediocrity of the studies that have been the basis of the evaluation today. So I would urge, as the finding of this panel, that somebody fund an appropriate national evaluation of the DARE program. Only then will we know if the program lives up to all the anecdotal information (from) principals, teachers, parents and others who attest to its effectiveness."[16] As Levant and other DARE defenders had often done in the face of such critical reports, they continued to suggest that evaluations of the program were all flawed for one reason or another. Whether it was studies becoming outdated after a curriculum revision, the lack of effective control groups, or the need for long-term longitudinal studies, Levant and his allies had a ready-made response to critical studies. With the initial presentation of findings, the battle lines were drawn between researchers and DARE.

When the full RTI was disseminated in draft form following the conference, the results were damning. It concluded that although DARE "has been extremely successful at placing drug education in our nation's schools," the program "has not been as successful in accomplishing its mission to prevent drug use among fifth and sixth graders as have interactive programs."[17] Evaluators raised questions about the fundamental assumptions of the DARE curriculum and model. DARE did increase student knowledge about drugs and enhanced their social skills, researcher Susan Ennett reported, "but we also know that knowledge has very little to do with behavior."[18] Crucially, the findings suggested that DARE did not have lasting effects and that a booster program was likely needed to ensure that kids would resist drugs as they entered their middle and high school years. "Unless there's some sort of booster session that reinforces the original curriculum, the effects of most drug-use-prevention programs decay rather than increase with time," Ennett explained. Because DARE was primarily an elementary school program, in other words, it did not have an impact on the age group of students most likely to experiment with drugs. As one eighteen-year-old who had gone through the DARE program in Los Angeles admitted, he smoked pot. "Mostly everyone I know who was in DARE back with me are doing the same thing I'm doing and more," he explained. "Everybody I know gets high. I don't think it worked. Not for me."[19]

To the surprise of the study authors, the NIJ refused to publish the findings. Some of the researchers involved in the RTI study recalled substantial pressure from DARE America to quash the study and ensure it was never published, raising questions about the NIJ's commitment to rigorous social science research and its cozy political relationship to DARE America.[20] The NIJ ultimately released a two-page research update on the study highlighting the positive results from the study, such as raising kids' self-esteem, enhancing their social skills, and improving their attitudes toward police, while downplaying the lack of drug prevention.[21] And a version of the RTI study was eventually published, after peer review and in abbreviated form, in the *American Journal of Public Health*. But it had not been easy. "D.A.R.E. has tried to interfere with the publication of this," one of the journal's editors reported. "They tried to intimidate us."[22]

The *American Journal of Public Health* article highlighted the disparity between DARE's effectiveness and popularity. "DARE's limited influence on adolescent drug use behavior contrasts with the program's popularity and prevalence," the authors wrote in the *AJPH* article. "An important implication is that DARE could be taking the place of other, more beneficial drug use curricula that adolescents could be receiving."[23] It also raised questions about DARE's signature element, the use of police officers as teachers. Although they recognized that DARE led to improved relations between cops and kids, researchers found that interactive programs taught by regular classroom teachers were more effective at achieving the desired behavioral change among students. The study singled out the nature of classroom instruction provided by police officers for critique. "The curriculum relies heavily on the officer as expert and makes frequent use of lectures and question-and-answer sessions between the officer and pupils," the team suggested. "In fact, it is in teaching style, not curriculum content, that DARE most differs" from other interactive programs studied.[24] Perhaps police officers did not make for the most effective teachers or a valuable learning environment for drug prevention. As one of the study authors summarized, "The kids learn to have respect for police: fine and dandy. But if it's sold for the prevention of drug use, it's not working."[25]

Unsurprisingly, DARE spokespeople criticized the publication, saying that it was excerpted from the larger study and taken out of context. They called out the study for what they saw as a flawed research design (the meta-analysis) and its focus on an older model of the curriculum that was no longer in use. Findings of ineffectiveness, according to Roberta Silverman, a DARE spokeswoman, relied on "old students and old curricula that are no longer being taught."[26] The Justice Department, which oversaw the NIJ, defended its decision to oppose publishing the full report in ways that suggested the problem was less the research methods of the study than the actual results. "We don't publish things when we don't agree with the results or don't think the research is good," said Justice Department spokeswoman Anne Voigt.[27] To researchers, the NIJ's opposition was political, not scientific. "I'm really not surprised NIJ refused to publish it," stated Richard Clayton, who was conducting a five-year longitudinal study in Kentucky at the time and later became an advisor to DARE America, "but I'm disappointed. DARE has a leadership role to play because it's in half the schools. An organization that receives that much public funding has an obligation to be honest with the public."[28]

DARE America executives responded with the tried-and-true us-versus-them attitude of the police. But instead of seeing the public as the enemy, they now targeted the research community. Mocking scientific research, DARE America's Levant quipped, "Scientists will tell you bumble bees can't fly, but we know they can."[29] In contrast to rigorous evaluative studies, Levant pointed to a Gallup poll conducted in 1993 in which 93 percent of DARE students surveyed said they had never tried marijuana, cocaine, heroin, crack, or inhalants. "The Gallup survey confirms that DARE works," Levant claimed.[30] Levant also responded to the criticism with open contempt and mockery at the seeming inability of researchers to see DARE as an unbridled good, stating, "I don't get it. It's like kicking Santa Claus to me. We're pure as the driven snow."[31] In a similar defense to another reporter, Levant claimed, "Knocking D.A.R.E. is like kicking your mother, or saying that apple pie doesn't taste good."[32] Quite simply, Levant suggested DARE was a target for criticism merely because it was popular and widespread.[33] And it was certainly popular. When journalist Dennis Cauchon wrote a series of articles for *USA Today* in 1993 questioning the program's effectiveness, for instance, he received letters from across the country addressed to "Dear DARE basher."[34] DARE America and its supporters also chalked up criticism of the program to drug legalization advocates. Levant, once again, suggested, "Parents love it [DARE], kids love it, administrators love it. The only people who don't like D.A.R.E. are the [drug] legalization people."[35] And, apparently, nearly every independent academic researcher and evaluator. Because DARE was born of the police, the response to criticism and demand for reform reflected the ways the police dealt with its critics—by closing ranks—reinforcing the program's law enforcement bona fides more than its role as an educational program.

If DARE was mired in controversy, it continued to operate and receive praise from politicians who saw the program as a political winner. Indeed, DARE's defenders lined up behind the program. "My experience has been positive," stated Clinton's director of the Office of National Drug Control Policy Lee P. Brown, who implemented the program during his time as chief of police in Houston. "The research has pointed in many different directions, but my conclusion is it's better to have it than not have it. I know firsthand that young people are impressed by it and look up to the D.A.R.E. officer as a role model."[36] Others in the Clinton administration's Department of Education understood that DARE's drug prevention efforts had been ineffective, but it had been "effective in developing better relationships with students," leading them to suggest that DARE officers should continue their work and could even be used for other "violence prevention efforts."[37]

Local officials also routinely defended the program, especially the relationship between children and cops. "There's something magical in the rapport between officer and student," Joanna Goldberg, a key liaison between the LAPD and LAUSD when DARE was introduced in 1983, noted in 1992.[38] Similarly, a local official in Kokomo, Indiana, responded to a study of DARE's ineffectiveness at changing student behavior in that city by criticizing the researchers. "They must not know how to measure things . . . if they could just see the kids' faces they'd know how much good its [*sic*] doing."[39] Indeed, DARE officers emphasized the special relationship between officers and kids as the true value of the program. "I may not have the statistics, but when I look at those faces . . . no one can tell me that something positive isn't happening there," stated Sgt. J. J. Gustin, a DARE coordinator in the Chicago area. "If we last year educated approximately 1,000 students in DARE, if we encouraged one child not to engage in drug or alcohol activity, we have done our job." From this vantage point, the value of DARE was in the rapport developed between officer and student.[40] As one *Los Angeles Times* journalist summed up the argument of DARE's defenders, "DARE backers say the real proof is not in studies or surveys but in the grateful responses of parents, teachers and children nationwide."[41]

Amid the controversy, DARE America established a scientific advisory board chaired by Dr. Herb Kleber, a psychiatry professor and director of the Center on Addiction and Substance Abuse at Columbia University, to consult on program revisions.[42] Under the board's guidance, DARE introduced its first substantially revised curriculum since the program's inception, supposedly incorporating changes in response to the growing evaluation literature on the program. Between 1992 and 1994, DARE America developed new lessons to include a greater emphasis on preventing tobacco use and a new emphasis on violence prevention. Alongside new content, the curriculum was revamped to be more "interactive," including more role-playing activities, "rather than one-directional from officer to student."[43] Despite such revisions, some researchers believed the curriculum changes were a politically motivated effort by DARE America to silence criticism and enhance the program's legitimacy.[44] As the curriculum evolved through repeated revisions, studying the program was like trying to hit a moving target, making evaluations lack credibility as outdated and based on older models of the curriculum. As an National Institute of Justice Update on the RTI study concluded, "The effects of the new curriculum on learning and behavior may in turn call for a new evaluation."[45] Yet the criticism did not stop, especially since some observers estimated that by 1997, the program received upwards of $750 million in taxpayer money.[46] To pile on, the program received public attention from journalists who found stories of DARE students who turned in their own parents for drug use.

Surveillance State

For some students, DARE worked, perhaps too well. As early as 1986, stories surfaced of students telling their parents to not use alcohol or the impact of caffeine in their morning coffee after receiving DARE lessons. They also became the eyes and ears of the police, turning in their own parents for drug use after completing the DARE curriculum. In 1986, for instance, an eleven-year-old girl reported to her principal that her parents had a marijuana plant in the backyard following her DARE graduation the year before at Normandie Avenue Elementary School in the heart of South Central Los Angeles. While the parents were not immediately arrested, the child was removed from their home and placed in a foster home.[47] While not advertised as a benefit of DARE, the program clearly had an added utility for the police. As DARE administrators reported to the Office of Criminal Justice Planning, "Officers in the classroom have developed rapport with the students, which has resulted in students coming forth with information requiring intervention."[48] Drug prevention, in short, bolstered police power on the streets with all its collateral consequences for families and communities.[49]

The DARE curriculum implicitly suggested the DARE instructor was a trusted confidant who could be told when a student found drugs or knew of someone using drugs. As the DARE curriculum evolved, it came to focus around the "Three R's: "Recognize, Resist, and Report" as the primary lesson for students to take with them. Exercises in the *DARE Officers' Guide for Grades K-4* workbook, for instance, asked students to identify who they should tell if they found drugs. The possible answers included "police" alongside "mother or father," "teacher," and "friend."[50] And there was the notorious DARE Question Box placed in every classroom, which students could use to submit information, anonymously, to the DARE officer. While the Question Box was not advertised as a place for students to report on parental drug use, it often functioned in that capacity.[51] As one aide to Wisconsin congressman Gerald D. Kleczka (D-WI) observed, "Officers have found that children will use this box to talk about physical or sexual abuse, or their parents' (or their own) drug or alcohol abuse."[52] Providing children with an avenue to report abuse and violence was laudable, but the line between ensuring child safety and police surveillance was an especially blurry one that led to significant concerns for many parents and critics.[53]

DARE spokeswoman Roberta Silverman defended DARE from accusations that the program taught children to spy on their parents. When faced with stories of kids alerting their DARE officers to their parents' drug use, she told reporters that "when students begin the DARE program they are specifically advised not [to] talk about their parents or friends. We are very clear that when DARE instructors are in the classroom, they are there as teachers, not as law enforcement officers." However, in stating that "any time a child makes a disclosure [of parental drug use] to an officer, the DARE officer would be required like any other teacher to report that to the proper authorities or agencies," Silverman reaffirmed the program's inherent investment in and contribution to the school as a disciplinary space.[54]

The most prominent example of students acting as the eyes and ears of the police came in 1991 when eleven-year-old Crystal Grendell was asked by her Searsport, Maine, elementary school counselor if her parents used drugs. Assured that "nothing would happen," Crystal reported that her parents smoked marijuana. A few days later, three DARE officers interrogated Crystal about her parents' drug habits and asked her to report back on the number of marijuana plants in her home. One of the officers, Sergeant James Gillway, told her that "if [she] 'cooperated' and told him about [her] parents' use of marijuana, nothing would happen to [her] parents, but that, if [she] did not 'cooperate,' [her] parents would be arrested." Gillway continued with a hardly veiled threat, telling Crystal that "if [she] did not tell him about [her] parents' use of marijuana, [her] parents and [she] would be 'in a lot of trouble.'" Finally, Gillway warned Crystal not to tell her parents about their meeting because "often parents beat their children after the children talk to police."[55] After Crystal complied, police raided her home, arrested her parents, and took Crystal and her younger sister to a distant relative's house because the police had failed to find arrangements for the girls prior to the raid. Crystal's case led to a civil suit against the officers. The court ruled in favor of Grendell, finding "that the officer's coercive extraction of indicting information from an eleven-year-old girl about her parents was shocking to the conscience and unworthy of constitutional protection."[56]

Yet law enforcement officials did not see much wrong with the practices of using DARE officers to find information about parental drug use. Sgt. Robert Gates, an administrative officer with DARE America, suggested that arresting drug-using parents was a positive outcome. "In such environments, there are usually no morals, values or training for the child," Gates stated. "My personal opinion is that an arrest is the best thing that could ever happen to that parent. Marijuana could lead to harder drugs, which, in turn, could ultimately lead to death. What may turn out to be negative for the parent is positive for society." While other evidence is sporadic about kids providing information to DARE officers about drug use requiring law enforcement intervention, such as parental or peer drug use, Crystal's case is instructive for what it reveals about the political-cultural work the DARE officer accomplished for the LAPD and other law enforcement agencies.[57]

DARE America representatives were especially cutthroat when it came to its critics' suggestions that it turned children into informants. "Our detractors like to characterize DARE as an 'Orwellian reality' or 'Big Brother' at work," Levant stated. "These bush-league tactics are transparent for what they are: attempts to support various individual personal agendas at the expense of our children."[58] Yet the lessons and messaging of DARE led to students telling DARE officers about parents or friends who used drugs more than Levant let on. In Caroline County, Maryland, for instance, a mother and father spent thirty days in jail after their daughter informed her DARE officer they had marijuana plants in their home. In Boston, two students tipped off the police and walked out of their homes with their DARE diplomas in hand when the police arrived to apprehend their parents. In another instance, a student in Englewood, Colorado, called 911 when he found marijuana in a bookshelf at his home. The child had proudly announced to the 911 operator, "I'm a DARE kid." While these incidents were certainly few when compared to the more than 25 million kids who had received some form of DARE programming, many were getting the message that drug use was wrong and, unexpectedly, acting as informants. One nine-year-old in Douglasville, Georgia, for instance, told a reporter after calling 911 on his parents' drug habit, "At school, they told us that if we ever see drugs, call 911 because people who use drugs need help. . . . I thought the police would come get the drugs and tell [my parents] that drugs are wrong. They never said they would arrest them. . . . But in court, I heard them tell the judge that I wanted my mom and dad arrested. That is a lie. I did not tell them that." Silverman defended DARE, stating these cases were "making a mountain out of a molehill," but, in doing so, missed the broader picture of DARE's long-time no-use and personal responsibility message. DARE's effort to humanize the police and make them into a trusted friend and mentor enabled cops to become part of kids' lives in ways that led to punitive consequences.[59]

DARE America took no quarter when it came to opponents. When journalist Stephen Glass, who published a series of critical stories for the *New Republic* and *Rolling Stone* about DARE and its role in students informing about parental drug use, was found to have fabricated some of the quotes for the stories, DARE America went on the offensive. Levant wrote a letter to the editor of the *New Republic* lambasting its journalistic standards and defending DARE. "It was disappointing to see the *New Republic,* which has had a history of responsible journalism, sink to the level of a tabloid in printing such an outlandish, slanted article on DARE," Levant wrote. Levant went on to challenge claims that DARE trained students to turn in their parents for drug use, which did happen on occasion. Levant reiterated his usual defense: "DARE is a tremendous force for good."[60] Glass eventually apologized to DARE America, but DARE's image and credibility had taken a hit. Charlie Parsons, who served as DARE America's executive director and chief operations officer between 1996 and 2005 and then as president and chief executive officer until 2013, explained, "We have tried to tell people it's false, but it has done damage."[61] In turn, Levant and DARE America sued *Rolling Stone* for defamation for publishing the Glass article, but the United States District Court for the Central District of California held that the magazine was not liable and dismissed the case, which was upheld on appeal. While the case ended up revolving around whether Glass was an employee of *Rolling Stone* or an independent contractor (the court decided the latter), the litigation demonstrated the deep commitment of DARE America to vehemently defend itself.[62]

With DARE's spread nationwide, episodes of students turning over parents to the police, often for marijuana use, led to growing concerns that DARE was merely a form of police surveillance. In some cases, parents responded with remorse, reaffirming the message of personal responsibility that they had failed to uphold. "We are to blame for getting Crystal into this mess," Crystal's parents told one journalist. "This would never have happened if we never smoked hemp."[63] For Crystal, however, the message was different. As she told a reporter six years after her parents' arrest, "It makes it hard for me to trust anybody. People I thought I could trust let me down."[64] So much for building trust in the police. Over the next two decades, examples of DARE students turning in their own parents to the police for drug use emerged on occasion and became national news. DARE, in effect, deputized students to alert the police of friends and family members who engaged in drug use. As Jimmie Reeves and Richard Campbell suggested in their study of media coverage of the crack epidemic, DARE put "uniformed police in the elementary classroom and encourage[d] students to not only just say 'no,' but to snitch on those who dare to say 'yes.'"[65]

Parents Against DARE

With the news of children reporting on their parents' drug use to DARE officers, some parents also began to speak out against DARE. While many parents supported DARE, others were much more wary. In 1992, Gary Peterson, a parent in Fort Collins, Colorado, formed an organization called Parents Against DARE after his son brought home instructions about DARE. Parents Against DARE chapters grew quickly, spreading to at least twenty-eight states in 1992.[66] Their opposition rested on a belief that DARE wrongly taught kids they had a choice to use drugs, undermined parental and religious authority, brought the state into the private sphere of the home, and quite simply did not work to prevent youth drug use.

Those parents who joined Parents Against DARE chapters vehemently rejected the language of choice in favor of an even more hardline position that using drugs was not a choice. Period. "I don't think the police officers who teach this program to students realize what they're doing to kids," Peterson said, explaining his opposition to the program. "They're telling children they can make their own decisions about drugs. Our research has shown a pattern of failure for this technique. I don't want my children being given that message. I've told my children that drugs are illegal, and they won't use them, period. They have no choice in the matter."[67] Peterson went so far as to pull his kid out of the school district because he "saw how they were trying to brainwash children."[68] In other words, for many parents DARE impinged on parental authority and interfered with their prerogative to teach their kids which values to live by.[69]

While Parents Against DARE began in Colorado, other parents quickly piled on. Many of these parents held strong commitments to family values, religious beliefs, and parental authority. "DARE is awash in the touchy-feely stuff of the '70s," Richard Evans of Northampton, Massachusetts, believed. "It's tricky and the kind of thing parents need to take a closer look at."[70] The perceived threat DARE posed to the prerogatives of parents was at the heart of much opposition. Another parent from Rogersville, Alabama, Judy McLemore, expressed immense concern with the program. Most notably, she believed the psychosocial approach that focused on values clarification was an assault on parental, community, and religious authority. After ridiculing DARE as a public relations stunt operated by the police, she wrote that the values clarification skills taught by DARE were harmful, "whereby [the children] are taught to clarify and distinguish their own values from those of their parents, family and church, etc. Then they are taught a step by step process on how to make decisions based upon their own values and self-interest, rather than those of their parents, etc." What was most appalling to McLemore and other Parents Against DARE advocates was the perception that DARE officers emphasized drug use as a choice, not as a moral right or wrong, something which seemed to miss DARE's avowed zero-tolerance and values-laden messaging. While such sentiment misread some of DARE's just say no and zero-tolerance origins, McLemore was incensed. She concluded that DARE was a "crime against humanity and humanity's children."[71] Loss of parental control seemed to be DARE's biggest threat, along with its supposed moral relativism about drugs. Parents Against DARE literature raised a wide range of concerns with the program. One Parents Against DARE pamphlet outlined its six central objections to the program:

- D.A.R.E. uses fear tactics and misleading generalizations when talking about drugs.
- D.A.R.E. officers have little or no information about the health risks of using drugs.
- The D.A.R.E. program uses 17 weeks of rhetoric and slogans and did not engage our children in meaningful discussion.
- D.A.R.E. is financed by assets forfeiture and property seizure.
- D.A.R.E. officers are not adequately trained as educators.
- D.A.R.E. is a public relations program for the police but not an effective drug education program.[72]

Although skeptical of DARE's effectiveness, Parents Against DARE was more concerned with the loss of parental control and the state's potential surveillance of the family via their children-as-informants.

Some of DARE's defenders, including officers, believed that the emphasis on choice and recognition of consequences was part of the program's strength. "That's what I think is the most positive thing about it," stated Karl Geib, who taught DARE in Portland, Maine. "We tell kids the positive side and negative side. I say to them, 'You can smoke dope if you like, as long as you've considered the consequences.' We downplay the high."[73] Such statements did not help, especially among those parents who wanted an even stricter zero-tolerance approach to drug use. Drugs were not a choice in these parents' minds. "Children have a choice about drug use only in the same sense that they have a choice to drive up the off-ramp of Highway 5," stated

William Coulson, a Northern California psychologist and former member of the Federal Technical Panel on Drug Education Curricula. "They can do that, but it's adult stupidity to teach them that's a legitimate choice."[74]

Parents were also wary of the use of police officers in schools and the enlisting of students as an adjunct to the police mission. Peterson dubbed DARE "the stuff of Orwellian fiction. This is Big Brother putting spies in our homes."[75] Although Peterson was not opposed to DARE because he feared being outed for his own drug use, other anti-DARE parent groups opposed the program because they viewed it as a police network aimed at rooting out drug use in their homes. "It's a statewide police network run out of the attorney general's office. . . . I don't want the police or the school eliciting information about what's happening in my house without my knowledge or my consent," said Ross Culverhouse, a White Bear Lake, Minnesota, engineer who led the local Parents Against DARE chapter.[76] Some of the parents in Parents Against DARE chapters were also proponents of drug legalization. "Three of my four children have gone through the DARE program in Hayward. Police should be out on the street, not in the position of educators in our schools," explained Bob Wilson, who founded a chapter of Parents Against Dare in Oakland, and owned the Hayward Hempery, a shop that sold books about drug legalization.[77]

Finally, some parents did not believe police were the best people to be teaching about drugs. Parents Against DARE member Andrew Seltser pushed back at the program for its use of police officers as teachers and its lack of effectiveness. "It's great PR for the police departments, but as far as getting kids to stay off drugs, it doesn't work," Seltser summarized. "The drug problem is a public health problem, so we should have public health officials teaching this. We should have doctors, drug counselors, people who are in the business of health, because that's where the concern is."[78] While Peterson and others succeeded in requiring Fort Collins schools to receive parental permission before a student went through DARE, they also hope to get DARE removed from the schools, which was rejected by the chief of the Fort Collins Police. Yet in attempting to remove DARE from the schools, Peterson and Parents Against DARE were at the forefront of a growing move by cities across the country who were dropping DARE.[79]

Dropping DARE

Following reports of DARE's ineffectiveness, concerns over student privacy, and demands to put more officers on the street, many schools planned to scrap DARE beginning in the mid-1990s. One city that planned to drop the

DARE program was Seattle, where the police chief, Norm Stamper, saw rising youth drug use as evidence of DARE's diminishing returns. "What we were discovering is I think what people know nationally, and that is teenage drug use has been up dramatically in this country," said Stamper in explaining his reasoning for dropping the program. "D.A.R.E. has been around now for a long time, and many of those graduates of the D.A.R.E. program are precisely the same kids who are choosing to take the so-called threshold drugs, the drugs that the D.A.R.E. program examines and attempts to discourage kids from taking."[80] While many schools believed using DARE had been a "commandment" of the federal government due to it being singled out in the Drug Free Schools and Communities Act (DFSCA) and related amendments in 1988, 1989, and 1990, by the mid-to-late-1990s, the director of the federal Safe and Drug Free Schools program, the office in the Department of Education providing support for state and local DFSCA programs, suggested otherwise and encouraged local school districts to "carefully evaluate [DARE's] effectiveness."[81] Many began to do just that.

But cutting the program was difficult. Its symbolic value had long legs. "The problem is that DARE is identified with everything that is good and important and desirable. It is in many ways a symbol, like the American flag," Stamper suggested.[82] Or, as Larry Austin, a spokesman for the Oregon Department of Education, explained when officials in Salem, Oregon, considered dropping the program, "It's almost sacred. Sometimes it's hard to let go."[83] Even in Los Angeles, the birthplace of DARE, the program came under pressure in 1993. Budget constraints had reduced the program from over one hundred officers to ninety-two, and the association with former chief of police Daryl Gates tarnished the program's image following the beating of Rodney King. As former LAPD deputy chief and DARE America executive director Glenn Levant lamented, "The plan is not to let DARE wither and die. But that's what's happening."[84]

Proponents of DARE could not turn the tide of criticism. Some cities, such as Oakland, Seattle, Spokane, Omaha, Rochester, and Salt Lake City, dropped the program because of budget constraints, a belief that the program was ineffective, and a desire to use classroom time for academic instruction. "I felt like it was a very expensive program with very poor results," Oakland City councilwoman Sheila Jordan stated after Oakland abandoned its program in 1994. Local officials critical of DARE and who intended to drop the program recognized that it had accomplished at least one underlying goal, that of humanizing the police officer. "What the research really shows is that the relationship that has developed between children and police officers is very important and very laudable, but the long-term effects on reducing drug and alcohol abuse is unknown and hasn't been substantiated," Nancy McPherson, director of Seattle's community policing bureau, reported. However, the promotion of DARE as a drug education program did not match the public's understanding of the program's primary goal of reducing drug use.[85] As Salt Lake City mayor Rocky Anderson explained, his reasoning for dropping DARE was because it was a "fraud on the people of America," saying, "For far too long, our drug prevention policies have been driven by mindless adherence to a wasteful, ineffective, feel good program."[86]

News of Seattle and other cities dropping the program led representatives to defend the program's integrity once again with a ramped-up public relations and media campaign. Glenn Levant responded to the Seattle chief of police: "In addition, the chief claimed that 'cops are not teachers.' It should be noted that every study on D.A.R.E. indicates that one of the key elements that separate[s] D.A.R.E. from other programs is the high quality teaching and delivery of D.A.R.E. by the uniformed officers."[87] State DARE programs and officer associations, such as the Idaho Peace Officers Standards & Training Academy's *D.A.R.E. Idaho* newsletter, ran articles offering advice about "How to Save Your D.A.R.E. Program" and defending the program from its critics.[88] Levant also doubled down on defending DARE and challenged journalists who paid more attention to a singular example of a department dropping DARE compared to the numerous cities continuing to adopt it. "Last year we added 300 cities!" he said. "Some loudmouth like Rodney [*sic*] Anderson in Salt Lake City criticizes the program and he gets national attention!"[89]

By no means did all school districts drop DARE, and in many cases, educators faced backlash if they proposed reallocating DARE resources or repurposing the DARE officer in other roles. Opposition to dropping DARE came from parents and others who saw the program as a positive way to influence kids. "The parents go crazy if anyone talks about stopping it," Chief Hegermiller said. "They like the contact between the officer and the kids, too, but when I talk about putting officers in the schools in some other capacity, they start screaming. It doesn't make sense to me because I see them as the same thing."[90] Indeed, DARE America's spokespeople touted the positive relationships between officers and students as a central element of the program that convinced parents of its value. "Parents feel good about it . . . because (DARE officers) create these sound, positive relationships with kids at a very early age," Bill Alden, DARE America's deputy director, explained.[91] Regardless of the criticism and news of municipalities dropping the program, DARE's extensive reach across the country meant that the program would continue, zombie-like, for years. Even after numerous critical studies about the program's ineffectiveness, the program persisted because of its popularity and extensive reach, not because of its effectiveness at reducing drug use.

Violence Prevention and Pressure to Change

If DARE faced criticism and questioning through the 1990s, the program continued to benefit from political support. Following a discussion of the important role of the Violent Crime Control and Law Enforcement Act of 1994 to help fight crime by "forming community partnerships with local police forces," President Bill Clinton praised DARE as an example of such partnerships at work. In fact, DARE was directly referenced as a model program for the "Ounce of Prevention Grant Program" and specifically named as a program that would qualify local governments for drug prevention funding included in the Crime Bill.[92] Clinton also singled out the program in his State of the Union address in 1996. Clinton stated, "Finally, to reduce crime and violence we have to reduce the drug problem. The challenge begins in our homes, with parents talking to their children openly and firmly. It embraces our churches and synagogues, our youth groups and our schools. I challenge Congress not to cut our support for drug-free schools. People like the D.A.R.E. officers are making a real impression on grade-school children that will give them the strength to say no when the time comes."[93] The Democratic Party also backed DARE, mentioning it by name in the 1996 Democratic Party Platform.[94] Politicians recognized that any reduction to DARE funding or support threatened to undermine their standing as ardent drug warriors in the eyes of parents. "We suspect that there are gaping holes in the program and that it may not be cost-effective, but legislators are politicians," said one legislator. "No one's going to risk their political future by doing anything other than standing up with the parents. Parents vote."[95] Appearing with DARE officers and students was a political winner.

With the passage of the 1994 Crime Bill, Congress revised the Safe and Drug Free Schools program to address violence more directly through the Improving America's Schools Act of 1994, which reauthorized the Drug-Free Schools and Communities Act (DFSCA) as the Safe and Drug-Free Schools and Communities Act (SDFSCA). The act added violence prevention as a key element of programs that would be supported by federal prevention funding.[96] DARE followed suit, promoting itself not only as an antidrug program but as an anti-violence program as well. The revised curriculum introduced in 1994 included a more specific focus on violence prevention, anger management, and conflict resolution as well as "more participatory learning activities." Although law enforcement had routinely linked drugs and violence through the 1980s, DARE did not formally incorporate anti-violence lessons into its curriculum until the 1990s. "It's very clear that substance abuse is fueling much of the violence that we see in urban America today," Herbert Kleber, a Columbia University psychiatry professor and chair of DARE's scientific advisory board, commented. DARE officials adapted to the new funding reality, asserting that the DARE approach to drug prevention could also reduce youth violence. "We found that the same kind of peer pressure that led to substance abuse was also clearly leading children into certain types of potentially violent situations," Levant stated.[97] The new curriculum and associated motto was "D.AR.E.® to Resist Drugs and Violence," a shift from the program's long-standing title and slogan, "DARE to Keep Kids off Drugs." Of central concern was gang prevention, driven by the broader fears of "super predators" and gang violence.[98]

When DARE came under fire from researchers, the Clinton administration repeatedly came to DARE's defense. Lee P. Brown, mayor and former drug czar and chief of police of the Houston Police Department, continued to tout DARE as an important component of the ongoing war on drugs during a 1998 press conference. Brown praised DARE as vital to preventing drug use and lauded DARE America because it "diligently monitors the program and makes changes based on feedback they receive from parents and educators."[99] Brown's successor, Barry McCaffrey, was an even bigger DARE booster. "One of the most important parts of the DARE curriculum is providing kids with hard facts about drug use. By dispelling many of the myths and misinformation surrounding drugs, DARE helps kids make informed decisions." As countless policymakers and drug warriors had emphasized in the years before him, McCaffrey lauded the importance of the DARE officer. "No other program provided the practical tools to help kids say no to drugs or highly-qualified officers who 'make an impact,' than DARE."[100] As he told a DARE Officers' Association conference, "As we look across the country to the people who are making a difference, D.A.R.E. stands out. You have the most comprehensive and widespread drug prevention curriculum in the world. . . . The strength of D.A.R.E.'s organization is a major reason for our declining juvenile drug use rates. D.A.R.E. knows what needs to be done to reduce drug use among children and you are doing it—successfully. Prevention in America cannot and will not ever be successful without D.A.R.E. as a key national leader."[101] For McCaffrey, DARE was a "premier prevention program" and "a key partner" in the national drug strategy.

Just as more school districts dropped DARE and the social science evidence of its ineffectiveness mounted, some in the Clinton administration also began to put pressure on DARE to respond to criticism from researchers and evaluators. "There were a lot of reservations about DARE," recalled former assistant attorney general Laurie Robinson. "[Attorney General] Janet Reno was pushing us hard" to compel DARE to change. "She was hearing grousing in the field [of effectiveness]. . . . She said we need to try to set in motion some kind of process to determine whether DARE can be responsive to some of these concerns." Robinson, along with Deputy Assistant Attorney General Reginald Robinson, held meetings with officials from the Department of Education, the Office of National Drug Control Policy, and the Department of Housing and Urban Development about how to handle DARE. Despite growing criticism, Laurie Robinson recalled, "It was our feeling that the program was here to stay." Politicians and police continued to support the program even as some began to suggest the need for reform. "The cops love the program for reasons that aren't part of the stated program goals" to reduce drug use, Reginald Robinson admitted. "The cops love the program because it gives them a chance to be Officer Friendly with the kids."[102] Crucially, DARE's extensive network of programs across the country proved invaluable. Federal officials hoped to harness that system built over a decade and a half while changing the curriculum delivered by DARE officers.

DARE Checks into Rehab

Just when the Clinton administration pushed DARE to change, the program faced a new round of critical evaluations. Pressure had been mounting on DARE since the 1993 UC San Diego conference as studies continued to show ineffectiveness and school districts publicly dropped the program.[103] But the most high-profile controversy came in 1998 following a newly released evaluation that raised alarm bells about the connection between DARE and suburban youth drug use. When University of Illinois at Chicago professor Dennis P. Rosenbaum released a 1998 study that tracked 1,798 urban, suburban, and rural sixth graders who had participated in the program and found that "the effectiveness of DARE in altering students' drug use behavior has yet to be established," the controversy over DARE elevated to a new level. Rosenbaum's study was the subject of news reports raising questions about DARE's efficacy. Most threatening to DARE's image was the finding that DARE led to increased drug use among suburban youth. "Suburban participation in D.A.R.E. is associated with an increased level of drug use of 3 to 5 percentage points on average," Rosenbaum found.[104] Unsurprisingly, evening news anchors quickly latched onto the findings that DARE exacerbated drug use among suburban youth.[105]

DARE America officials attempted to shape how the report played in national media by creating a campaign to downplay the study. They promoted studies with positive results and pointed to widespread support from police officers for the program while downplaying negative ones. DARE engaged in a media offensive with Glenn Levant, even debating one of the study's authors on the *Today Show*. The campaign was effective enough that the director of the Office of National Drug Control Policy referred to the research findings in the national media as "twaddle." DARE's campaign against critical academic studies continued off the nation's television screens and newspapers. "Behind the scenes, they had used high-powered lawyers to sue or threaten to sue people who criticized the D.A.R.E. program, arguing that reporters, producers, and researchers were making false statements," Rosenbaum claimed. "Reputations and careers were ruined."[106]

DARE spokespeople responded to Rosenbaum's study with defensiveness. Former DEA agent and then DARE spokesperson Bill Alder told *NBC Nightly News* that schools needed more DARE, not less. "It's not that DARE doesn't work. DARE does work, but it dissipates. It erodes. What has to happen, there has to be more, not less." In contrast to studies showing no statistical evidence that DARE produced long-term change, Alder and other DARE proponents pointed to anecdotal evidence of DARE's popularity as a reason for expansion in the face of mounting criticism. "We got thousands and thousands of principals, millions of parents saying, 'DARE made a difference in my child's life. I like DARE,'" Alder reported.[107] Internally, DARE America waged a campaign to answer its critics and promote positive portrayals of the program as they prepared local DARE officials for battle. "D.A.R.E. America continued to accentuate the positive in its responses to the media, D.A.R.E. officers and the general public," the organization reported in 1997. "Response packets were mailed/faxed to all D.A.R.E. agencies that requested assistance in their efforts to counter any unwarranted attacks on the D.A.R.E. program. Letters to editors (attached) in response to negative editorials were written and sent out either directly to the media or provided as ammunition for local D.A.R.E. officers to use and incorporate into their own responses." Alongside these efforts, DARE America promoted media events and fundraisers with celebrities to divert attention from the growing evidence of ineffectiveness.[108]

Law enforcement officers around the country, once again, came to the program's defense. But in their defense of the program, officers rarely pointed to DARE's impact on youth drug use. Instead, they highlighted how DARE solved the crisis of the legitimacy of the police officer, especially in the years after the Rodney King beating and national attention to police violence. As Lieutenant Dave Bales, a DARE officer in a Seattle-area elementary school, suggested, DARE's success could not be measured only in the statistics of youth drug use. "The interaction between not just the students and the law enforcement officer but the entire family, the entire community, and law enforcement is changed, and building community between law enforcement and the public they serve makes us far more effective," Bales argued. "It builds a level of trust. Those are things that aren't measured in D.A.R.E. studies."[109]

For other officers, DARE filled in where families and schools failed. Some law enforcement officials asserted that DARE worked, blaming "lazy parents" and a "corrupt political culture" for the continuation of youth drug use, especially among suburban whites.[110] Indeed, some officers suggested that parents and schools had not taught students the proper respect for authority. "In a perfect world, children would develop a positive attitude about police officers through discussions with their parents, lessons learned in school and a respect for authority instilled in them since birth," stated Charles A. Gruber of the Elgin Police Department in Illinois. "Unfortunately, we do not live in a perfect world, so police departments must take an active role in fostering positive relationships with their many constituents—especially the young." DARE was valuable in filling this role regardless of the impact on drug use. "A small bridge of trust is built during these precious hours each week," Gruber continued. "Enhanced communication occurs that can greatly influence the perception those children will have of police officers when they become young adults, and continue throughout their lives." The impact of giving a "'cop' a human face" ultimately "should never be underestimated when evaluating the success of the DARE program."[111] Indeed, DARE officers and educators often pointed to secondary effects bolstering policing legitimacy and acceptance rather than reduced drug use as their reason for continuing the program. As one Massachusetts school superintendent put it, "If you ask the question . . . 'Does it reduce the illegal use of drugs and alcohol?'

apparently D.A.R.E. can't demonstrate that for various reasons. If you ask, 'Does it help kids understand their community better? Does it produce favorable relationships between police and kids?' all of the survey results . . . [are] positive."[112] So much for drug prevention; DARE was a means to enhance the position of the police in communities across the country.

However, some officers raised concerns about the program, the use of officers as teachers, and the distribution of resources that came with it. One officer from Colorado suggested in the police magazine *Law and Order*, "Law enforcement officers are not teachers and they should not be expected to become teachers by virtue of the minimal training provided in the DARE program." The same officer took aim at DARE's symbolic value to policymakers, stating, "The program should be stripped of its politically untouchable shield and then subjected to serious objective analysis."[113] Eamon Clifford, a former patrol officer in the Washington, D.C. Metropolitan Police Department, raised other concerns. He suggested that DARE offered little to "kids in the ghetto" because they already knew the dangers of drugs. For suburban police departments, DARE merely represented the ways they copied programs from large urban forces, including SWAT teams and bicycle units. "Any time there is federal money available," Clifford wrote in an article entitled "Taking a Bite out of DARE: Why Not More Cops in Clown Suits?" for *Law and Order*, "many chiefs start rattling their cups for grant money. The DARE programs [*sic*] of sending officers into the classrooms to talk to young people certainly didn't drop the crime rate on my beat." Clifford echoed the refrain of some chiefs of police that DARE took officers off the street where they were needed most. "When chasing a 16-year-old crack dealer down streets and through backyards, the thought never entered my mind that if only a policeman dressed in a dog suit had gotten to him a little earlier in grade school, this whole thing could have been avoided. Perhaps we would be better served if we skipped the middle man and put the grant money toward more cops on the streets—and teachers in the schools—instead of cops in the schools." More importantly, Clifford raised questions about how the war on drugs had missed the mark. "Until we attack the root causes of crime, abject poverty, the violence of the welfare cycle and lack of access to affordable housing, crime and drug addiction will be problems that continue to plague us."[114]

Although DARE America continued to proclaim the program's effectiveness, the tide had begun to turn against DARE. Within the context of the attacks on government spending, Newt Gingrich's "Contract with America," and the Democratic Leadership Council's "third way" policy agenda, DARE's political appeal began to wane.[115] Congress members who had been full-throated supporters of DARE earlier in the decade, in some cases even seeking to pass a bill specifically funding DARE, began to balk at continuing federal funding for a program that failed to show effectiveness. Senator Richard Durbin (D-IL), for instance, commissioned the General Accounting Office (GAO) to undertake a study to determine DARE's effectiveness, and the White House Office of National Drug Control Policy's National Drug Control Strategy for 1999 made research-based and scientifically backed drug prevention programming for youth key objectives in winning the war on drugs.[116] Pressure from Congress, the potential loss of SDFSCA funds, and the newly publicized studies slowly convinced DARE America to change.

Policymakers voiced support for DARE while also pressing the organization to adapt. Studies showing that few schools used their SDFSCA Safe and Drug Free Schools program funds to pay for proven programs and that implementation was "variable and inconsistent, even within schools," led to calls for change.[117] Bill Modzeleski, who ran the SDFSCA's Safe and Drug Free Schools program and expressed frustration with DARE, "The report validated on a research basis everything that we thought was occurring. Lots of schools are doing a lot of things that are untested, in a hurried time frame, and without proper training. And the results are what is to be expected. No reductions in alcohol and drug use."[118] In turn, Congress pushed the Department of Education to make changes to the Safe and Drug Free Schools program by identifying a list of drug prevention programs that demonstrated evidence-based results of efficacy. Congress had directed the Office of Educational Research and Improvement of the Department of Education to establish a panel of experts to evaluate programs to be designated as exemplary or promising in 1994, but it did not get off the ground for several years. When the panel was fully established in 1998, it began a review process to identify prevention programs with proven effectiveness within two years.[119] DARE was on a deadline to revise its curriculum and ensure its program received scientific backing if it wanted to continue to receive federal funding.

Meanwhile, the Senate Committee on Appropriations called for DARE America to revise its curriculum as a condition to receiving federal funding. Indeed, the language in the appropriations committee report showed support for continuing DARE funding while pressuring the Bureau of Justice Assistance to convince DARE America to revise its curriculum. "The Committee also urges BJA to favorably consider funding for continuation of the Drug Abuse Resistance Education [DARE America] Program"; however, "recent studies indicate the need for the program to adapt to the changing culture within our schools. The Committee directs the Department to work with officials with the DARE America Program to create new and more effective course criteria aimed at reducing the use of drugs by children."[120] Federal officials had made initial moves to reduce DARE's funding but appeared to hope that DARE would provide a fix before such cuts became necessary. The program, after all, was still extremely popular among politicians, police, students, educators, and parents. As debates about federal prevention funding revealed, DARE was hard to quit even when stakeholders knew it did not work.

The Departments of Justice and Education, at DARE's request, intervened, facilitating a meeting between researchers and DARE America administrators in May 1998 to iron out their admittedly hostile relationship. The first meeting was combative as researchers, most notably Dennis Rosenbaum, criticized DARE for ignoring scientific studies and taking results out of context to spin DARE in a positive light. Yet the two sides agreed to meet again five months later to begin working out a plan to redesign DARE.[121] Coming out of the meetings, DARE America agreed to begin studying and revising its curriculum. Not only did DARE America prevent the loss of federal funding, but it also received the help of a $14 million investment from the Robert Wood Johnson Foundation (RWJF) to revamp the curriculum. RWJF had been paying attention to the meetings between DARE and researchers and was interested in improving drug prevention programs. DARE's delivery network and training of police officers was impressive to RWJF, especially given that convincing schools to switch programs was especially difficult. They worked out a plan in which the DARE network of officers and schools would be used to deliver a proven curriculum that included an older cohort of students and to make the lessons more participatory rather than didactic.[122] "We're very willing to change," Glenn Levant admitted. "If someone's got a better mousetrap, we'll use it."[123]

Federal officials seemed to see little choice but to ensure DARE's continued existence. "A decision was made in [the Department of Justice], sitting around [Attorney General] Janet Reno's conference table, that we should mend it, not end it," said former assistant attorney general Laurie Robinson. "We were realists."[124] Embedded in schools, police departments, and American culture, DARE would be difficult to abandon altogether. Compared to other more scientifically proven programs, DARE had a leg up. Its network of DARE officers and regional training centers was too integrated in the drug prevention landscape for the program to disappear. As RWJF representatives found, "D.A.R.E. continued to be the only prevention program with a sustained presence in schools, and the only vehicle for delivering a curriculum to all students."[125] DARE administrators knew that their extensive network of DARE officers and training regimen would not be easy to abandon. "Our position is that we have this great delivery system in place that will probably never be replicated," stated DARE America's Charlie Parsons. "If the researchers can tell us how to improve the message we deliver, we're open to it. Everything is on the table, and that is our position."[126] Researchers and evaluators concurred with DARE's role as a robust network that could be used to deploy a different, more effective curriculum. "DARE represents the single largest prevention effort directed at reducing the use of drugs and other harmful substances among school-age children in the United States," researchers involved in the DARE redesign stated. And the DARE officer would not be going anywhere. "Regardless of the changes taking place," researchers asserted, DARE officers "will remain the core and source of the ultimate success (or failure) of this effort."[127]

Following the series of meetings between DARE, researchers, and government officials in 1998, DARE worked with RWJF to develop a revamped curriculum that would continue to be taught by police officers. Between 1999 and 2001, the RWJF team designed a new curriculum, called "Take Charge of Your Life," that would be taught under the auspices of DARE America and with DARE officers.[128] The New DARE curriculum that came out of the Take Charge of Your Life project launched in 2003 after what was a five-year research and design project organized by RWJF. As the University of Akron's Institute for Health and Social Policy team that was evaluating the new curriculum summarized, the "new, highly interactive programming also incorporates the most up-to-date evidence and research-based youth education strategies which involve the adolescents in the learning process via small group discussions and role-play sessions around real-life authentic substance-abuse scenarios."[129] The researchers were not the only ones to praise the new curriculum. DARE officials also quickly praised it as the standard for drug education moving forward based on scientifically proven efficacy, a response to Congress requiring programs to show scientific research demonstrating program effectiveness to receive SDFSCA funds. "This IS exactly what Congress asked us to do: work with the top researchers to integrate the latest in science into the D.A.R.E. program. This is great news and we will now move forward in making this state-of-the-science program available to communities across the country in September 2003," Levant stated.[130] The curriculum revision and development had the potential to give DARE a new life.

Amid the curriculum revisions and collaboration between DARE and researchers, the GAO came out with its study of DARE commissioned by Senator Durbin in 1998. The report, which was released in 2003, confirmed many of the findings from critical studies in the 1990s that there was no evidence that DARE reduced drug use among kids and teenagers. The report found "the six long-term evaluations of the DARE elementary school curriculum that we reviewed found no significant differences in illicit drug use between students who received DARE in the fifth or sixth grade (the intervention group) and students who did not (the control group)."[131] At the same time, the Safe, Disciplined, and Drug-Free Schools Expert Panel finally came out with its list of "Exemplary and Promising: Safe, Disciplined, and Drug-Free Schools Programs" in 2001. Notably, DARE was not on the list of proven programs, further threatening its federal funding.[132] By 2002, the principles of effectiveness were incorporated into the No Child Left Behind law championed by the Bush administration.[133] DARE was left off the list, and some schools dropped the program because it did not qualify under federal guidelines.[134]

If the GAO report was another shot fired at DARE and disingenuous based on timing since it came out as the curriculum was being revised, the organization moved ahead with the launch of its new curriculum. New DARE reflected the supposed willingness of DARE America's new leadership team to work with the research community following Glenn Levant's retirement. As DARE America stated on its website in 2004, "Gleaming with the latest in prevention science and teaching techniques, D.A.R.E. is reinventing itself as part of a major national research study that promises to help teachers and administrators cope with ever-evolving federal prevention program requirements and the thorny issues of school violence, budget cuts, and terrorism."[135] Combining DARE's popularity and reach with rigorous scientific evaluation and research, proponents believed, would lead to a new era in effective drug education programming. RWJF also funded a study of the new curriculum, led by Dr. Zili Sloboda, the University of Akron's Adolescent Substance Abuse Prevention Study, which meant to bolster the curriculum's basis in scientific evaluation and was "designed to blend the latest in prevention science with the nation's largest prevention delivery network—the D.A.R.E. program."[136]

The new DARE curriculum emphasized a more interactive approach while continuing to center the antidrug message using police officers. Rather than the officer at a podium lecturing to students about drugs, as Idaho DARE administrators suggested, “New D.A.R.E. officers are trained as ‘coaches’ to support kids who are using research-based refusal strategies in high-stakes peer-pressure environments.”[137] Initial studies conducted by Sloboda and her team found that the approach was more effective than the old DARE program. “We structured the lessons so they can incorporate real situations to get the kids engaged in something that is very relevant to them,” Sloboda explained. “I think a lot of the officers really like the new curriculum for that reason—we hear that a lot from them.”[138] New DARE also provided a solution to the criticisms of DARE and the requirements for federal-funded programs to receive scientific evidence of efficacy while also not throwing out DARE America’s deeply rooted infrastructure and network. “D.A.R.E. has had the highest dissemination for decades of any school-based drug prevention program. It reaches 26 million children a year in 75 percent of all school districts and is admired by children and parents alike,” explained Kleber. “The generous support of the Robert Wood Johnson Foundation and the talent of the University of Akron group have made it possible to combine this acceptance with state-of-the-art teaching and content to make D.A.R.E. not only the most popular, but the best.”[139]

Those involved in the curriculum redesign saw a need for greater integration between DARE and communities, not less. As some of the researchers involved wrote in the *Police Chief* magazine in 2002:

> Thus, the DARE program is more than a police officer going into a school and lecturing the kids. It is a set of relationships between officers, children, parents, teachers, schools, and communities. DARE should be part of a larger prevention infrastructure needed to implement successfully the education and service programs required to help kids resist drugs and alcohol and deal with related problems. . . . If DARE is to be maximally successful, it cannot be viewed or function solely as a school-based effort. The program and the officers can only do their jobs fully when they are part of that larger system.[140]

Part of the effort to place DARE in a positive light rested on the community relations side of the program and its ability to redefine the role of the police in American society. “The program offers an important link to the community, strengthening both the role of the police and its image as a valuable and accepted contributor to that community’s safety and well-being,” the researchers continued. “DARE also makes the individual police officer a more valued representative of the police department from [a] law enforcement perspective and, perhaps more importantly, in terms of how the police are viewed in that community." The suggestion for chiefs was to not simply abandon the program but see it as an asset in their larger police mission. They concluded with a word of caution for chiefs who only looked at DARE as a drug prevention program, arguing, "In judging DARE, chiefs may want to take a fresh look at this program and the value it can provide in terms of both public safety and the image of the police in the community."[141]

New DARE expanded the police-school partnership that was at the heart of the program from its inception. Concerns surrounding school violence and terrorism after the 1999 school shooting at Columbine High School and the 9/11 attacks provided an opening for DARE America to market New DARE as a program well suited to the new reality because it relied on police officers as teachers. DARE officers would now also take on the role of "school resource officer," the euphemism for what was otherwise known as a school police officer. "New D.A.R.E. is setting the gold standard for the future," stated Charlie Parsons, president and chief executive officer of DARE America. "Prevention inside the 21st century school house will need to be effective, diverse, accountable, and mean more things to more people, particularly with the safety issues that have emerged since Columbine and terrorist alerts. That's one reason why every New D.A.R.E. officer is also being trained as a certified School Resource Officer (SRO)."[142] As new DARE integrated the position of SRO and DARE officer, it more fully integrated the DARE program as part of the school policing project, even developing a DARE SRO program. "Under the D.A.R.E. School Resources [*sic*] Officer Program, trained peace officers work with educators to support safe schools and healthy students."[143] One indicator of this integration between DARE and SRO came in Idaho, where the Idaho POST Academy merged its informational newsletter to DARE officers and school resource officers into Idaho Cops for Kids.[144] SROs and DARE officers also held joint conferences in Idaho and other states as part of professional development and training related to sharing ideas for policing in schools.[145] Certified as SROs, DARE officers in the twenty-first century would no longer be mere interlopers in the school teaching drug education in a non-law-enforcement function.[146]

Following the 9/11 terrorist attacks, DARE America mobilized to link drug trafficking and use with support of terrorism. As DARE officials had done in the past, they used the crisis to argue for more investment in programs like DARE to reduce the demand for drugs that was, in their words, fueling international terrorism. As Glenn Levant's message to the DARE community after 9/11 summarized:

> It is well documented that Afghanistan is the source country for Southwest Asian heroin and hashish. . . . Stated simply, drug money—hundreds of millions of dollars from protecting drug trafficking routes, airstrips, and laboratories—supports terrorists and ultimately the governments which harbor them. Drug-financed terrorists are called Narco-terrorists for a reason. As criminals engaged in drug trade, arms-trafficking and money-laundering, this network of criminals are partners with terrorists. Together they murder men, women, and children, and undermine our freedoms as directly as the fanatics who turn hijacked airliners into flying bombs. As our nation mourns the tragic loss of life and prepares for its long campaign against these inhuman animals, our leaders must obviously prepare for a war on many fronts . . . among them must be drug abuse, its trafficking, and organized crime. Federal, state, and local drug enforcement efforts and drug resistance education programs must not only continue, but must be expanded. As a nation, we must recognize that those who buy and consume illicit drugs are ultimately supporting acts of terror and violence.[147]

Linking terrorism and drugs to end users redeployed the language about supply and demand reduction that had been crucial to DARE's origins in the 1980s. Drug users, as they had been blamed for gang warfare and other drug-related crime, were now, at least in part in the minds of DARE administrators, responsible for fueling international drug trafficking networks that financed terrorism. To be sure, the enforcement and interdiction arm of the drug war was alive and well, but the focus on users remained central to DARE's purpose. DARE had a continued role to fill in order to prevent demand from fueling not only violence in schools but international terrorism.[148] However, as many looked back on DARE's place in American society and culture, the program did not hold the same clout as DARE America seemed to think.

Parody and the Irony of the DARE T-Shirt

For all the revisions to the DARE curriculum and the controversy surrounding evaluations of its efficacy at preventing young people from abusing drugs, DARE's legacy was the cultural reception and parody that has continued it well into the twenty-first century. Over time DARE increasingly became the subject of ridicule, especially among students. Some students, for instance, recalled that their DARE officer insisted that rock music "led to Satan worship and drug use." Such views led to derision for students, including one who recalled, "We mostly made fun of him; especially what he said about rock music." Over time, DARE's "cool" factor, if it had such a standing among students, seemed to dissipate. "Nobody cared about DARE in high school," one student reported. "They didn't care what you told them in the seventh grade. They just didn't think about it any more."[149] Even academic researchers mocked the program's marketing and self-promotion. As one researcher suggested, "It is sad to say, but an overwhelming majority of people in the United States have a rather naive view of . . . how to solve social problems such as drug use and abuse by adolescents. Drug use is not a simple phenomenon. It will not be solved by simple slogans and bumper stickers and T-shirts and a bunch of people believing DARE is 'the' answer to drug abuse in America."[150]

Many kids took the popular DARE acronym and logo—DARE to keep kids off drugs—and turned them into objects of parody and satire. The ubiquitous DARE bumper sticker, for instance, was transformed into "DARE TO KEEP COPS OFF DONUTS."[151] Marsha Rosenbaum of the Lindesmith Center suggested that kids would find easy ways to mock DARE's zero-tolerance lessons. "What happens is that the culture takes these messages and twists them around, which is what happened with the 'This is your brain. This is your brain on drugs' commercials. And now there's a whole T-shirt line that's a spoof."[152] DARE also faced ridicule and parody from drug legalization proponents, such as those in the National Organization for the Reform of Marijuana Laws (NORML). Marijuana enthusiast Mark Hornaday raised the hackles of DARE and law enforcement proponents when he made a T-shirt bearing the DARE stamp and logo with the mocking slogan "I turned in my parents and all I got was this lousy T-shirt" underneath.[153] DARE America filed a lawsuit again Hornaday for copyright infringement, but the charges were later dropped.[154]

Alongside the all-too-common anecdote about students wearing their DARE shirts ironically as they smoked marijuana, the ironic use of the DARE T-shirt continued well into the twenty-first century. Actors such as Dakota Johnson, celebrities, and fashion bloggers have been spotted wearing DARE T-shirts. In many ways, as *Vice* observed, the program's very slogan "accidentally spoke to the feeling of *daring* to experiment with drugs."[155] Perhaps the most high-profile example of the ways the DARE T-shirt continued to be used ironically occurred when Serena Williams's husband and Reddit founder Alexis Ohanian wore a DARE T-shirt to the U.S. Open in 2019 when Williams faced off against Maria Sharapova, who had previously been temporarily suspended due to doping violations. For anyone who observed the moment, Ohanian was clearly trolling Sharapova and, in the process, exhibiting another ironic use of the DARE T-shirt.[156]

The DARE T-shirt regained its popularity in the 2010s, but not for the reasons DARE America might have hoped. Social media comments about DARE's failure and high school students, a generation who may not have gone through the program, wearing the DARE T-shirt did so as a form of irony, parody, and political critique. The wave of teenagers wearing their DARE T-shirts while smoking pot or high was, as researchers from the Drug Policy Alliance described, "a witty form of protest against the poor drug education they received in high school." Parody and irony, in this sense, was a strategic political move and form of resistance to poor or irrelevant drug education. The popularity of wearing the DARE T-shirt ironically led companies, such as Urban Outfitters and Forever 21, to sell fake DARE T-shirts while others have created parody shirts reading "C.A.R.E." (care about me please) and "V.A.P.E." (very addictive piece of equipment). If DARE was proven ineffective, it has remained a cultural touchstone but not in the way that DARE America had intended. The DARE T-shirt has become a form of subtle cultural protest against the war on drugs and ineffective approaches to drug education that relied on zero-tolerance and abstinence models.[157]

DARE America did not quite get it. The DARE America website includes a page entitled "D.A.R.E. logo and shirt—one of the most recognized logos in the world." The page goes on to explain that Design Hill, a creative marketplace helping businesses, ranked the DARE T-shirt the number ten "coolest" T-shirt of all time. In addition, they touted that Stuff Ltd. named the DARE T-shirt the ninth-most iconic T-shirt of all time. The website follows with a list of celebrities who have been spotted in a DARE T-shirt, including Olivia Rodrigo, Demi Lovato, Bella Hadid, Issa Rae, and Abel Makkonen Tesfaye, among others, including the aforementioned Alex Ohanian. As the site concludes, "We did not set out to be a fashion trendsetters [*sic*]. The reason for the popularity of the D.A.R.E. T-Shirt is simple . . . the public's positive reception of the good work done by D.A.R.E." While the reasoning presented by DARE America about the T-shirt's popularity is questionable, they certainly saw the opportunity for continued marketing and revenue creation. "How often has someone approached you at an event and said they still have their D.A.R.E. T-Shirt. Or where can they get a new D.A.R.E. T-Shirt? D.A.R.E. T-Shirt [*sic*] can be purchased from D.A.R.E.'s licensed vendor, D.A.R.E. Catalog," the site shares, encouraging visitors to buy more merchandise. However, anyone who wants to buy the retro DARE shirt would be disappointed because "the classic black D.A.R.E. graduation T-Shirt cannot be purchased; it is reserved for presentation to students graduating from D.A.R.E."[158] Perhaps DARE America got it after all, using any opportunity to promote itself once again.

The Ultimate Answer to Drug Use

DARE was never solely a drug prevention program. As many law enforcement officials believed, the real value and goal of DARE was as much about integrating police into schools and as part of the broader community. Yet DARE had always touted its drug prevention focus and efficacy but operated in ways that belied such goals. As such, it opened itself up for criticism from prevention researchers. "While I appreciate these 'voices,'" Rosenbaum critiqued, "D.A.R.E. was marketed and sold exclusively for its drug prevention benefits, not for other possible outcomes."[159] As a drug prevention program, DARE had repeatedly failed to live up to its promises. While evaluations of DARE suggested that the program had not proven to be the panacea to youth drug use, viewed through a different lens, the program was a success. By bringing police into schools to teach morality, family values, personal responsibility, and respect for law and order, DARE produced the social and cultural context within which get-tough policies and an expanded police presence in schools were accepted as legitimate.

DARE's public relations campaigns, challenges to researchers, and use of freebies to promote an antidrug message reflected the larger failures of the just say no and drug education approach to the drug war. Such programming was out of touch with how to address the complexity of the drug problem. Those involved in the DARE program, including educators, policymakers, and law enforcement officials, in other words, misread the structural nature of the drug crisis in American cities as a problem of moral behavior, personal responsibility, and good choices that could be solved through catchy slogans and T-shirts. Indeed, DARE had not been the answer, or what Daryl Gates called the "ultimate answer" to youth drug use.[160] But, as suggested, that was never the goal of DARE. The long staying power of DARE in American society and culture, even if through parody and irony, spoke less to the efficacy of the program than to the ways the program had attempted to shape the image of the police and enable cops to infiltrate schools.

EPILOGUE

Keepin' It Real

For all the controversy surrounding the program in the 1990s, DARE hardly disappeared. Yet it continued to face obstacles and challenges. The closing of the DARE regional training centers (RTC) in the early twenty-first century had a major impact on DARE America's ability to continue training officers across the country, and with the requirement for evidence-based, proven, effective, and approved programs to receive Safe and Drug Free Schools and Communities Act (SDFSCA) funds, it also led to reduced resources for local DARE programs.[1] Many local school officials, in turn, shied away from, and in many cases dropped, DARE because it was not an approved program, evaluation had not shown effectiveness, and municipal budget constraints could not justify it. Such conditions meant that it became significantly more difficult to convince local stakeholders to adopt the program since they would be taking on more of the financial burden. Federal funding from the SDFSCA, in contrast to the long-standing claims of DARE America executives, was key to local buy-in for the program from law enforcement and school officials.[2] Yet many school districts that continued to use DARE were not as worried by the negative press or lack of effectiveness. They remained supporters of DARE because they saw it as a means to improve the relationship between cops and kids, something that was not measured in many evaluations.[3] Despite things changing for DARE in terms of evaluation, curriculum design, and federal funding, the fundamental importance of the police officer as teacher remained the same. DARE's staying power, in short, was rooted in that foundational decision made in 1983 to use officers as teachers.

With the closing of the RTCs, the dissolution of the National DARE Officers Associations, and the retirement of longtime DARE America executive Glenn Levant, DARE America entered a new phase in the twenty-first century, first under CEO Charlie Parsons and then Frank Pegueros.[4] A former LAPD officer, Pegueros had not been a DARE officer but had been involved with the department's DARE Division.[5] Yet critical evaluations from the research community did not disappear with these changes. In 2007, Dennis Rosenbaum authored an article entitled "Just Say No to D.A.R.E.," arguing that the program should be scrapped, public funding should be used only for programs that show effectiveness under rigorous evaluation, and the federal government should mediate ongoing conflicts between researchers and the drug prevention community.[6] Indeed, the "stigma" of the studies conducted in the 1990s continued to haunt the program as it attempted to relaunch itself and develop partnerships with police departments, including a renewed partnership and memorandum of understanding with the LAPD and LAUSD in 2013, after which it held the first LAPD DARE officer graduation in more than a decade.[7]

DARE America's new leadership continued to adapt to criticism and provide drug education in schools across the country and around the world. DARE America introduced a new version of the curriculum in 2007 called "keepin' it REAL" (kiR).[8] In contrast to previous versions of the curriculum that had been developed by DARE, kiR was developed by researchers at Pennsylvania State University and Arizona State University who were supported by the National Institute on Drug Abuse; it was a turn toward using a verified program that had scientific backing. DARE America worked with the researchers to adopt the curriculum and "initiated an intensive, extensive and lengthy process to, in essence, 'D.A.R.E.ify' the curricula," most notably by having it delivered by its nationwide network of DARE officers. The kiR model decentered the antidrug message and emphasized life skills.[9] The most recent DARE America website reflects this change as the new slogan is "Teaching Students Decision Making for Safe & Healthy Living."[10] While many proponents of the program continued to tout DARE as the best means to prevent drug use, others questioned the kiR curriculum and its effectiveness, eventually moving on to new drug prevention ventures, such as the Law Enforcement Against Drugs (LEAD) program.[11]

Although the kiR curriculum and DARE America's new orientation may have seemed a far cry from the "DARE: To Keep Kids off Drugs" or "DARE: To Resist Drugs and Violence" of the 1980s and 1990s, the heart of DARE—the DARE officer—remained at the core of the program. DARE, in short, has become largely a delivery network of police officers rather than a unique curriculum developed by DARE, something that would continue in subsequent revisions of the program.[12] As throughout DARE's history, debates continued to arise about the best and most effective curriculum for achieving the stated purpose of drug prevention. Despite all of DARE's messaging to help students resist peer pressure to use drugs, DARE was never entirely about drug prevention. It was as much about the DARE officer as anything else. And that element is what many proponents continue to point to as one of the most valuable elements of the program. The relationship between kids and cops often outweighed anything else. Regardless of the curriculum changes throughout DARE's four-decade history, one thing remained constant: the DARE officer. Those officers repeated similar lines about the importance of positive interactions between kids and the police as the main benefit of the program into the 2010s. As one Ohio DARE officer noted in 2014, "One of the biggest positive factors with DARE is that . . . the kids get to meet a police officer and see him/her as a friend and not as a person who is there to arrest someone."[13]

DARE still exists.[14] Schools continue to graduate DARE classes, others have adopted or restarted defunct DARE programs, and still others continue to drop the program in favor of alternatives. For all the ridicule that DARE continues to receive in public culture, DARE America continues to report millions of dollars in revenue and expenses.[15] It is a viable and, if not as robust, fairly widespread police-led education program in 2023. Its mission may have changed slightly to "teaching students good decision making skills to help them lead safe and healthy lives," but it continues to bring police officers into schools.[16] The DARE officer remains at the center of the program, an indication of the ways the police continue to blur the line between their supposed role ensuring public safety and prevention through education. To be sure, DARE does not have the visibility it once did. But as it just passed its fortieth anniversary, its continued operation demonstrates the significant place it created for itself in American society, culture, and politics.

And DARE is not without controversy. It continues to be the subject of ridicule on social media feeds, even becoming a parody on TikTok in which young people post niche videos about what DARE did not teach them about addiction.[17] Using parody, these TikTockers poke fun at DARE and its ineffectiveness. One TikTocker, for instance, posted a TikTok in which they wore a DARE T-shirt while rolling their eyes and shrugging their shoulders to the caption, "5th grade me who won the dare essay and pledged to never do drugs or drink alcohol" and commented, "officer pat would be so disappointed."[18] DARE America, likely in a bid to assert DARE's continued relevance by giving an interview to TMZ in 2022, also criticized the HBO show *Euphoria* over its portrayal of drug use, which did not elicit much of a reaction from the showrunners or lead actor Zendaya, who brushed off the critiques, telling *Billboard* in response to the DARE comments, "Our show is in no way a moral tale to teach people how to live their life or what they should be doing. If anything, the feeling behind *Euphoria*, or whatever we have always been trying to do with it, is to hopefully help people feel a little bit less alone in their experience and their pain. And maybe feel like they're not the only one going through or dealing with what they're dealing with."[19]

While the debates and critiques of DARE on social media are useful for understanding ways DARE has been remembered as a joke and the way parody has served as a strategic political move, other incidents at the local level are much less humorous. For instance, following the mass shooting at Robb Elementary School in Uvalde, Texas, a benefit held by the Belton Police Athletic Association (BPAA) in Belton, Missouri, decided to cancel a fundraiser in which it was raffling off a "Radical Firearms AR Rifle—.223/5.56—Semi Automatic" to benefit the local DARE program. "After recent tragic events, the Police Athletic Association decided that it would be inappropriate to continue with the raffle as planned," Lieutenant Dan Davis reported. "As a result, the golf tournament will not include a rifle in the raffle for this year." Even though the BPAA decided to cancel the gun raffle, that a local police athletic association would hold a gun raffle in support of the program is telling. It reveals the continued integration between DARE, police, and militarization of American society. Raffling off an AR-15 is merely an updated form of using asset forfeiture funds to support DARE in its early years.[20] Other evidence has come out about former DARE officers being sentenced on child pornography charges, for prescription drug thefts, and for sexually assaulting teenage boys.[21] DARE, quite simply, has never been divorced from the violence work of policing.[22]

DARE and the War on Drugs

For proponents of the program throughout its four-decade history, DARE was a win-win. As officers and boosters continue to suggest, DARE centered on legitimizing the police, bringing kids into the law-and-order mission, and, in the process, growing police power through education rather than discipline. Politicians could appear pro-police and tough on crime while simultaneously supporting kids through a supposedly nonpunitive prevention and education program. Being pro-police and pro-kids, however, rested on at least two problems. First, it diverted attention from the reality of the drug war. While the police may have softened their image and worked to improve perceptions of the police among kids and teenagers, the major emphasis of the police in the war on drugs rested on mass arrest and punishment. Second, praise for programs like DARE and the broader message of the Just Say No campaign belied a lack of evidence that such programs actually worked.

Yet the DARE program helped expand the drug war into new arenas of children's lives without addressing the social and economic circumstances in which drug use was produced. Most notably, it brought uniformed police officers into schools as teachers and symbols of the law-and-order message of the police and the enforcement side of the drug war. For law enforcement, DARE provided a means to soften the image of the police forces that had otherwise pursued policies of eradication, aggression, and scorched earth in communities of color across the country in the name of the drug war. For politicians, they could appear as both pro-police and pro-children.

Drug education policies and programs operated on a continuum of solutions to the drug crisis, ranging from source-country eradication, border interdiction, and intensified policing and punishment of selling and using in American cities. DARE and related antidrug education programs brought police into schools and reinforced the logic of the drug war's punitive arm that framed drug use as a problem of a lack of personal responsibility, moral failure, and poor behavior deserving of punishment rather than something deeply rooted in state retrenchment, the abandonment of social service provisions, and structures of social and economic inequality. The two sides of the drug war—punishment and prevention—in short, were mutually constitutive. Viewed in this light, DARE and other drug prevention curricula were not alternatives to arrest and punishment but worked hand in hand with punitive policies.

Crucially, even as LAPD officials framed DARE as a demand-reduction alternative to the militarized drug task forces engaging in scorched-earth tactics on city streets, DARE remained connected to these punitive supply-side approaches to the drug war. Despite law enforcement's best efforts to assert that the DARE officer was not on school campuses for security or safety, in practice the DARE officer blurred the line between supply and demand reduction and between prevention and punishment. Indeed, DARE administrators designed the program to reinforce and legitimate the law-and-order and zero-tolerance message in the minds of the nation's youth, especially Black and Latinx children who disproportionately witnessed or experienced the consequences of policing when they left the classroom. By attempting to humanize police officers through DARE, the LAPD meant to counteract the aggressive policing typical of the war on drugs. Yet DARE was a solution to a problem of its own making. DARE demonstrated that many so-called preventive approaches to the drug crisis still involved the police. Viewed in this light, DARE was less an alternative to the punitive policies of the war on drugs than a complementary program that reinforced racialized constructions of criminality and personal responsibility.

DARE's Legacy

"We all leave footprints in the sand. Over the years, many of those footprints are washed away by the tide, only a few remain forever. Those that remain are legacies and every great leader leaves them," President H. W. Bush wrote to chief of police Daryl Gates for his fortieth anniversary of service with the LAPD in 1989. "Yours will surely be the DARE Program. Veteran police officers with unmatched credibility, going into classrooms, teaching children the facts about drugs and alcohol. . . . My friend, thank you for not looking the other way and instead, through DARE, teaching kids how to say no, but even more to say yes to life."[23] Bush's praise for DARE was no accident or aberration. DARE was the most popular antidrug education program the world over and praised by educators, policymakers, and law enforcement officials alike.

Bush was not the only one who thought DARE was Gates's most important legacy. In the eyes of Gates himself, DARE was, perhaps, his greatest achievement. He opens his 1993 autobiography, *Chief: My Life in the LAPD*, with a story about returning to Los Angeles the day after the beating of Rodney King from Attorney General Richard Thornburgh's 1991 conference on violence, where he had been asked to speak about the DARE program.[24] As Gates goes on to recall about his efforts to establish the program in Los Angeles and the importance of DARE officers' relationship with kids:

> I had practically no support for D.A.R.E. Some politicians and libertarians questioned the wisdom of putting police officers in the classroom, fearing we might turn L.A. into a police state, and pointing out that police officers were desperately needed on the streets. I tried to get additional budget money for D.A.R.E., but Tom Bradley refused. . . . The program was a hit from day one and it was hard to tell who enjoyed it more, the officers, the kids, the teachers (who remained in the classroom), or the frightened parents. . . . The officers would spend their day at the school, getting to know the kids, joking, playing with them, showing they were regular people too. The officers, to their amazement, often discovered that they were the first people to teach values to some children whose parents had never done so.[25]

In many ways, Gates was not wrong to tout DARE as one of his—and the LAPD's—most significant legacies. As this history has shown, DARE was important less for its role in preventing drug use than in what Gates, perhaps unwittingly, described as the effort to legitimize the police and convince kids to accept the police as authority figures not to be questioned. Indeed, as DARE boosters routinely suggested in their defense of the program, DARE had everything to do with the supposedly positive relationship it created between police and kids.

DARE evolved from a program taught in ten Los Angeles elementary schools in 1983 to an internationally renowned model of drug education with significant political and cultural cachet. From such a vantage point, there was nothing like DARE. What other police program became so well known and integrated into schools the world over? Aside from the immense power and reach that police departments themselves have produced over the past half century, there is no better example of the way the police positioned themselves and advocated for law enforcement as an unfettered good than DARE. For all the parody and irony, those who view DARE as a joke—which it certainly is among many who look back on their DARE experiences and among some who believed the program was a waste of time—should also see that it created a significant and unprecedented network of law enforcement agencies and personnel who were able to enter schools as teachers with almost no opposition. It went a long way to solidifying the position and power of the police in American society.

More insidiously, DARE made messages of law and order, the friendly police officer, and support for law enforcement common sense in the minds of many children. It is no coincidence that police messages continue to inundate children's programming, perhaps nowhere more directly than Nickelodeon's *Paw Patrol,* a show in which Ryder and his six dogs effectively serve as a form of law enforcement in Adventure Bay. There is perhaps no better example of copaganda at work and the legacy of DARE's cultural labor in the lives of America's children today.[26]

If we want to understand how the police continue to receive widespread support and resources, we would do well to look at the hegemony of DARE and the hard work law enforcement officials engaged in to bring the program to every child in the United States.

The history of DARE and the nation's antidrug education arm of the drug war reveal the ways such programs operated on ideological foundations that ignored the structural roots of the drug crisis. The orientation of DARE and similar programs on morality, values, choices, and personal responsibility reinforced the turn toward blaming the problem on drug users and framing solutions rooted in individual behavior. The history of DARE and the nation's preventive arm of the drug war shows how such programs operated on intellectual foundations that ignored the structural roots of the drug crisis. Teaching kids to just say no fell squarely within the Reagan, Bush, and Clinton administrations' approach to poverty governance. Viewed in this light, DARE and drug education programs complemented the policies of punishment, policing, and incarceration that together reinforced and defined new governing logics focused on personal responsibility, privatization, racial hierarchy, and getting tough.

APPENDIX

TABLE 1 Project DARE Curriculum from 1988

Session	*Lesson*	*Description*
1	Practices for Personal Safety	Acquaints students with role of police and practices for student safety.
2	Drug Use and Misuse	Helps students understand harmful effects of drugs.
3	Consequences	Helps students understand the negative consequences of drug use and the positive consequences of saying no to drugs.
4	Resisting Pressures to Use Drugs	Makes students aware of kinds of peer pressure they may face and helps them learn to say no to offers to use drugs.
5	Resistance Techniques: Ways to Say No	Teaches students ways to say no in resisting various types of pressure.
6	Building Self-Esteem	Helps students understand that self-image results from positive and negative feelings and experiences.
7	Assertiveness: A Response Style	Teaches that assertiveness is a response style that enables a person to state his or her own rights without loss of self-esteem.
8	Managing Stress without Taking Drugs	Helps students recognize stress and suggests ways to deal with it other than by taking drugs.
9	Media Influences on Drug Use	Helps students develop the understanding and skills needed to analyze and resist media presentations about alcohol and drugs.

(*continued*)

TABLE 1 *(continued)*

Session	*Lesson*	*Description*
10	Decision Making and Risk Taking	Helps students apply the decision-making process in evaluating the results of various kinds of risk-taking behavior, including that of drugs.
11	Alternatives to Drug Abuse	Helps students find out about activities that are interesting and rewarding and are better than taking drugs.
12	Role Modeling	Older student leaders and other positive role models that do not use drugs talk to younger students to clarify the misconception that drug users are in the majority.
13	Forming a Support System	Students develop positive relationships with many different people in order to form a support system.
14	Resisting Gang Pressure	Helps students identify situations in which they may be pressured by gangs and evaluate the consequences of the choices available to them.
15	Project DARE Summary	Helps students summarize and assess what they learned from the program.
16	Taking a Stand	Students complete own commitment and present to class. Helps them respond effectively when pressured to use drugs.
17	DARE Culmination	Student graduation from the D.A.R.E. AMERICA program.

Source: DARE America, "D.A.R.E. Program Lessons," 1988, box OA18771, folder DARE to Keep Kids off Drugs [Information Kit], Office of the First Lady, Press Office, RRPL.

TABLE 2 First Fifty Elementary Schools with DARE in Los Angeles

Region A

Barton Hill
Fries Avenue
7th Street

Region B

Holmes Avenue
Nevin Avenue
102nd Street

Region C

La Salle Avenue
McKinley Avenue
75th Street
93rd Streetw
Budlong Street
Hyde Park Boulevard
59th Street

Region D

Braddock Drive
Castle Heights
Crescent Heights
Hancock Park
Pacific Palisades
Virginia Road
36th Street
Cienega
Melrose Avenue
Queen Anne Place
Van Ness Avenue

Region E

Colfax Street
Kester
Valerio Street
Canoga Park
Cantara
Gault
Nestle
Tarzana

Region F

Noble Avenue
Broadous Street (Filmore)
Germain Street
Harding Street
Plainview Avenue
Tulsa Street
Vena Avenue

Region G

Albion Street
Bridge Street
First Street
Glen Alta
Utah Street

Region H

Dorris Place
Elysian Heights
Glenfeliz Boulevard
Solano Avenue
Toland Way
Los Feliz

Source: Harry Handler to Members, Board of Education, "Drug Abuse Resistance Education (DARE)," August 22, 1983, box 1,424, folder 5, LAUSD. Other sources suggest that the Palms School was included instead of Crescent Heights in Region D. This may have been a change following Handler's initial list of selected schools. See "School Assignments 1983/84," [ca. 1983], box 40931, folder 20, AAMI.

TABLE 3 DARE America Officers and Board of Directors, 1993

Officers

Nathan Shapell—President Chairman of the Board Shapell Industries
Bram Goldsmith—Treasurer Chairman of the Board City National Bank
Glenn A. Levant—Executive Director Worldwide D.A.R.E. America

Directors

Robert Bonner—Administrator Drug Enforcement Administration
Eli Broad—Chairman of the Board Broad, Incorporated
Robert W. Buckingham—Vice President Measured Marketing Services, Inc.
Marvin Davis—Davis Company
Ted Field—Chairman Interscope Investments, Inc.
Arsenio Hall—Arsenio Hall Productions
Hubert H. Humphrey, III—The Attorney General State of Minnesota
Michael Jackson—MJJ, Incorporated
M. M. Maltz—Community Leader
Diane Disney Miller—Community Leader
John R. Neal—President JRN, Inc.
Jack Needleman—Anjac Fashion Buildings
Greg Penske—President Longo Toyota/Lexus
Michael Schwab—President Zurich Investment Company
Brian J. Strum—Chairman Prudential Property Company
Lawrence Teplin—Attorney-at-Law Cox, Castle and Nicholson
Willie Williams—Chief of Police Los Angeles Police Department

Source: DARE America, "Board of Directors," 1993, box 148, folder 681, RLA.

Acknowledgments

Writing a book is often a solitary experience. In completing this book, however, I have had the benefit of hearing from so many people who relayed their memories of and stories about DARE. At every turn, simply mentioning that I was writing a book on DARE to whomever was willing to listen led to stories and memories about the program. Nearly everyone, it seems, has had some experience with DARE. Hearing people's memories of DARE and the deep interest people have in the program was a source of motivation while researching and writing.

My interest in writing a book on DARE has its own history. The idea for a book on the history of DARE emerged from material I found in the Tom Bradley archives at UCLA while conducting research for my book *Policing Los Angeles*. I came across archival sources that referenced the DARE program and its origins in Los Angeles in 1983. Since I had DARE as a fifth grader in Salt Lake City, I wondered how and why an LAPD program had come to be taught in my elementary school in the early 1990s. Pulling on this thread led me to a wide-ranging story about the ways the police positioned themselves as teachers and spread DARE to nearly every school in the country. It began as a story of the LAPD and Los Angeles and ended in a story of the relationship between drug education, the police, culture, and education in the late-twentieth-century United States.

This book would not have been possible without the help of many archivists and librarians who provided advice and offered services to provide digital reproductions of archival material. Archivists at the George H. W. Bush Library, the Los Angeles City Records Office, Loyola Marymount Special Collections, the Ronald Reagan Presidential Library, the Southern California Library, UCLA Special Collections, and the Woodson Research Center at Rice University provided crucial support in the development of the project. Following the COVID-19 pandemic, archivists at a host of institutions, including the Idaho State Archives, National Archives and Records Administration, Mesa Public Library, New York State Archives, University of California, Santa Barbara, Department of Special Collections, University of California, Santa Cruz, Special Collections and Archives, University of Georgia, Richard B. Russell Library for Political Research and Studies, University of Nevada, Las Vegas, Special Collections, and University of Wyoming, American Heritage Center graciously provided scans of archival material that enabled me to complete this project in a timely manner. Librarians at the Los Angeles Public Library were especially helpful in providing information about images and permissions. At the last minute, Isaac Lee provided crucial research assistance that helped me complete the manuscript. He graciously offered his time and expertise with archival material at the Wisconsin Historical Society.

My understanding of DARE would have also been immeasurably less complete or nuanced without the generosity of a range of people who were willing to speak to me about their experiences with the program. Zili Sloboda responded to a random LinkedIn message and connected me to many people who had been involved with DARE. I would like to thank the social scientists and researchers who were willing to relive their experiences with DARE, including Anderson Johnson, Allan Cohen, William DeJong, Susan Ennett, Bill Hansen, Chris Ringwalt, Luanne Rohrbach, and Zili Sloboda. A number of former and current DARE administrators also spoke with me. Thanks to Nick DeMauro, Glenn Levant, John Lindsay, and Frank Pegueros. Thank you to John Carnevale, who spoke to me about his time in the Office of National Drug Control Policy during the Clinton administration. Alongside a wide range of informal conversations with friends and colleagues about their DARE experiences, Charles Hughes and William Sturkey graciously told me about their experiences as DARE students. Adam Goodman also provided me with material that provided insights into the DARE program in his elementary school.

Ball State University has been a fruitful place for research and writing. This book benefited from financial support from Ball State University travel funding and publishing support funds. The history department also provided start-up funds that contributed to this project. A number of graduate assistants at BSU also provided crucial support. Ciera Boyes, Will Connolly, Emily McGuire, and Payton Holland all provided vital research assistance for this project. My colleagues in the Ball State History Department have made for a vibrant and collegial place to research and teach. Thanks especially to Jim Connolly, Jennifer DeSilva, and Nicole Etcheson for their mentorship. Emily Johnson has been a collaborator on many projects and came in at the last minute with an important cover suggestion. In the African American Studies Program, Emily Rutter and Kiesha Warren-Gordon have been important sources of inspiration, camaraderie, and advice.

The team at the University of North Carolina Press has been a joy to work with. My editor, Brandon Proia, was behind this project from the beginning and helped make it a reality. I cannot express how thankful I am to have worked with Brandon on two books. His editorial insight, advice, and support have made me a better writer and thinker. He cannot be beat. When Brandon left UNC Press, I had the absolute pleasure to work with Dawn Durante, who jumped on board and was an immensely generous sounding board as we finalized the manuscript. Her guidance and comments have made for a better book. I cannot thank the Justice, Power, and Politics series editors Heather Thompson and Rhonda Williams enough for including this book in the series. Mark Simpson-Vos has ensured UNC Press is fully behind this project. Sonya Bonczek provided invaluable advice for marketing and positioning the book. Carol Seigler and Erin Granville made the final steps of manuscript submission a breeze. Joseph Stuart provided expert indexing support and Tessa Hauglid proofread the manuscript. Both have been a pleasure to work with. Thank you as well to the anonymous reviewers who provided constructive feedback on the manuscript.

A number of conferences and publications provided important venues for me to work out early parts of this project. I presented parts of this work at conferences including the Rethinking American Political History Conference at Purdue University, the American Historical Association, the Organization of American Historians, the Society for U.S. Intellectual History, the Urban History Association, and the History of Education Society. Sebastián Sclofsky invited me to present an early version of my research with the Critical Police Studies group. I would also like to thank Walter Stern for organizing and editing a special issue of the *Journal of Urban History* on education and the carceral state. Walter provided keen insight and editorial comments that informed not only my article for the issue but also this book. Thanks to Sarah Phillips, Brooke Blower, and the team at *Modern American History* for their work and support in publishing one of my articles for the journal.

This book would not have been possible without the support of a wide range of friends, scholars, and activists. My friends in Salt Lake City have opened their homes and provided a needed respite from academic life whenever I visit. Thanks to Jessie Berggren, Mitch Diaz, Spencer Henderson, Andy Jensen, and Dave Weissbard. My thinking on the carceral state and role of police in American society has been influenced by my comrades from IDOC Watch whom I have been struggling alongside for years. I have learned so much about the LAPD that I did not know from Kelly Lytle Hernández and the Archiving the Age of Mass Incarceration (AAMI) team. Working with them has been crucial to my thinking about DARE, the LAPD, and Los Angeles. My longtime friends and comrades Heather Ashby, Christian Paiz, and Monica Pelayo are some of my biggest fans and always help put things in perspective. Finally, I have benefited from an especially generous scholarly community. Simon Balto, Brent Cebul, Anne Gray Fischer, and Paul Renfro all read various parts of the manuscript and provided crucial comments. Their friendship and incisive critiques have made this work immeasurably better. Jonathan Zimmerman provided advice and resources at a very early stage in this project. Julilly Kohler-Hausmann was invaluable in the development and thinking about this project. She pushed me to think more deeply about the politics of DARE and its place in American society. Alyssa Ribeiro and Alex Fore were as hospitable as always, allowing me to stay with them during my research trips in Los Angeles. Lauren Acker and Eric Braun also welcomed me into their home during research trips to Los Angeles.

An especially generous group of scholars have offered support and friendship over the years. Thanks to Chris Agee, Andy Baer, Brian Behnken, Aaron Bekemeyer, Dan Berger, Katie Brownell, Katherine Bynum, Gerry Cadava, Genevieve Carpio, Mauricio Castro, Araceli Centanino, Daniel Chard, Shiau-Yun Chen, Peter Chesney, Will Cooley, Deirdre Dougherty, Emily Dufton, Garrett Felber, Lily Geismer, Julian Go, Adam Goodman, Carly Goodman, Aaron Griffith, Matt Guariglia, Ray Haberski, Andrew Hartman, Nicole Hemmer, Elizabeth Hinton, Ashley Howard, Clay Howard, Alex Hyres, Emily Johnson, Judith Kafka, Matt Kautz, Jessica Kim, Shannon King, Julilly Kohler-Hausman, Matt Lassiter, Marisol LeBrón, Tim Lombardo, Toussaint Losier, Anna Lvovsky, Gordon Mantler, Rebecca Marchiel, Sara Mayeux, Austin McCoy, Naomi Murakawa, Donna Murch, Jessica Neptune, Melanie Newport, Peter Pihos, Carie Rael, Nic Ramos, Vanessa Rapatz, Noah Remnick, Jessica Reuther, Alyssa Ribeiro, Charlotte Rosen, Dan Royles, Stuart Schrader, Micol Seigel, David Stein, Tim Stewart-Winter, Will Tchakirides, Heather Thompson, Alex Vitale, and Vesla Weaver.

A special shout-out to Simon Balto and Carl Suddler. I have been on a near-daily text thread with Simon and Carl throughout the research and writing of this book (and well beyond). Without a doubt, this book would not be what it is without their friendship, comradery, and conversation that can only be described as wide-ranging.

I would be remiss to not thank Robin D. G. Kelley. I would not be doing the work that I do without him. Although not directly involved with this project, Robin's insights and influence can be felt throughout. Thank you for the constant inspiration and support of my scholarship, Robin.

My parents, Janet Felker and Harvey Kantor, have been unwavering in their support. They provided me with inspiration and challenging questions that deepened my thinking and ideas about DARE and its place in American society. They read significant portions of the manuscript and provided insightful feedback. I cannot thank them enough for everything. My sister, Erica, and brother-in-law, Dave, have been hearing about this book for more years than they would like and have done nothing but encourage me. Their daughter, Sophie, has been a joy for us all. Sophie, "the man from the book" has another one for you to read! My partner's family, the Appels, have made Indianapolis my home and been behind me in all my work, even when it takes me back to Los Angeles. My pal Duds was literally by my side through nearly this entire project. It was one of the saddest days when we had to say goodbye to him. We miss you. While I lost my forever writing companion and loyal friend, Franklin has certainly kept us on our toes.

Mary Appel has made this book possible. She has been with me throughout the entire research and writing process, never once batting an eye when I left for weeks at a time to visit archives or to present pieces of the book at conferences. She makes every day better and keeps me grounded. I could not have completed this work without her.

Notes

Abbreviations

AAMI	Archiving the Age of Mass Incarceration Project, LAPD Records, UCLA, Los Angeles
APP	The American Presidency Project, University of California, Santa Barbara
GBPL	George H. W. Bush Presidential Library, College Station, Tex.
ISA	Idaho State Archives, Boise, Idaho
JLLV	Junior League of Las Vegas Records, 1946–2010, MS-00179, Special Collections, University Libraries, University of Nevada, Las Vegas
LACCF	City Council Files, Los Angeles City Archives, Los Angeles, Calif.
LAUSD	Los Angeles Unified School District Board of Education Records (Collection 1923), UCLA Library Special Collections, Charles E. Young Research Library, University of California, Los Angeles, Calif.
LBP	Dr. Lee P. Brown Papers, 1960–2004, MS 509, Woodson Research Center, Fondren Library, Rice University, Houston, Tex.
NYSA	Division of Criminal Justice Services Commissioner's Subject and Correspondence Files, New York State Archives, Albany, N.Y.
RG 581	Office of National Drug Control Policy Subject Files, National Archives and Records Administration, College Park, Md.
RG 60	Subject Files of the Attorney General, 1974–93, General Records of the Department of Justice, National Archives and Records Administration, College Park, Md.
RLA	Rebuild LA Collection, CSLA-6, Department of Archives and Special Collections, William H. Hannon Library, Loyola Marymount University, Los Angeles, Calif.
RRPL	Ronald Reagan Presidential Library, Simi Valley, Calif.
SSC	Stanley K. Sheinbaum Collection, MSS 217. Department of Special Collections, Davidson Library, University of California, Santa Barbara, Santa Barbara, Calif.
TBAP	Mayor Tom Bradley Administration Papers (Collection 293), UCLA Library Special Collections, Charles E. Young Research Library, University of California, Los Angeles, Calif.
WHS	Wisconsin Historical Society, Madison, Wisc.

Introduction

1. Daryl F. Gates, "Project DARE—A Challenge to Arm Our Youth," *The Police Chief*, October 1987, 100–101.

2. Gates, "Project DARE—A Challenge to Arm Our Youth."

3. Daryl F. Gates, *Chief: My Life in the LAPD* (New York: Bantam Books, 1993), 268.

4. DARE America, *DARE America Form 990—Return of Organization Exempt from Income Tax*, 2001, accessed May 15, 2020, https://projects.propublica.org/nonprofits/organizations/954242541. On DARE as the largest drug prevention program, see Jeffrey Merrill, Tracey Dilascio, and Ilana Pinsky, "Law Enforcement and Drug Prevention: A Profile of the DARE Officer," *The Police Chief*, August 2002, 81.

5. For more on the context of the police and the drug war in communities of color, see James Forman, Jr., *Locking Up Our Own: Crime and Punishment in Black America* (New York: Farrar, Straus and Giroux, 2017). See esp. chap. 5, "'The Worst Thing to Hit Us Since Slavery': Crack and the Advent of Warrior Policing, 1988–1992," 151–84; Max Felker-Kantor, *Policing Los Angeles: Race, Resistance, and the Rise of the LAPD* (Chapel Hill: University of North Carolina Press, 2018), esp. 190–216.

6. On the war on drugs, see Dan Baum, *Smoke and Mirrors: The War on Drugs and the Politics of Failure* (Boston: Back Bay Books, 1997); Steven B. Duke and Albert C. Gross, *America's Longest War: Rethinking Our Tragic Crusade against Drugs* (New York: Tarcher Perigee, 1994); David R. Farber, ed., *The War on Drugs: A History* (New York: New York University Press, 2021); David R. Farber, *Crack: Rock Cocaine, Street Capitalism, and the Decade of Greed* (New York: Cambridge University Press, 2019); Kathleen Frydl, *The Drug Wars in America, 1940–1973* (New York: Cambridge University Press, 2013); Laura E. Huggins, ed., *Drug War Deadlock: The Policy Battle Continues*, Hoover Institution Press Publication, no. 539 (Stanford, Calif.: Hoover Institution Press, Stanford University, 2005); Jill Jonnes, *Hep-Cats, Narcs, and Pipe Dreams: A History of America's Romance with Illegal Drugs* (Baltimore, Md.: Johns Hopkins University Press, 1999); Michael Massing, *The Fix* (New York: Simon & Schuster, 1998); Richard L. Miller, *Drug Warriors and Their Prey: From Police Power to Police State* (Westport, Conn: Praeger, 1996); Jimmie L. Reeves and Richard Campbell, *Cracked Coverage: Television News, The Anti-Cocaine Crusade, and the Reagan Legacy* (Durham, N.C.: Duke University Press Books, 1994); Craig Reinarman and Harry Gene Levine, eds., *Crack in America: Demon Drugs and Social Justice* (Berkeley: University of California Press, 1997); Arnold S. Trebach, *The Great Drug War, and Radical Proposals That Could Make America Safe Again* (New York: Macmillan, 1987).

7. Elizabeth Hinton, *From the War on Poverty to the War on Crime: The Making of Mass Incarceration in America* (Cambridge, Mass.: Harvard University Press, 2016); Julilly Kohler-Hausmann, *Getting Tough: Welfare and Imprisonment in 1970s America* (Princeton, N.J.: Princeton University Press, 2017); Joe Soss, Richard C. Fording, and Sanford F. Schram, *Disciplining the Poor: Neoliberal Paternalism and the Persistent Power of Race* (Chicago: University of Chicago Press, 2011).

8. A few scholars have focused on the preventive side of the drug war, the Just Say No campaign, or antidrug advertising campaigns. Emily Dufton has explored the Just Say No campaign and Joseph Moreau has explored the Partnership for a Drug-Free

America. Emily Dufton, *Grass Roots: The Rise and Fall and Rise of Marijuana in America* (New York: Basic Books, 2017); Joseph Moreau, "'I Learned It by Watching YOU!': The Partnership for a Drug-Free America and the Attack on Use Education in the 1980s," *Journal of Social History* 49, no. 3 (June 9, 2016): 710–37. Joshua Reeves has a chapter on DARE but not the program's history: Joshua Reeves, "Recognize, Resist, Report: D.A.R.E. America and the Kid Police," in *Citizen Spies: The Long Rise of America's Surveillance Society* (New York: New York University Press, 2017), 109–36. A recent master's thesis by Vaughan Shubert also includes a chapter on DARE and neoliberalism, Vaughan Shubert: "DARE (Drug Abuse Resistance Education) The Neoliberal Trojan Horse," in "Rationalizations within Neoliberalism: Public Schools, Protection, and the 1980s–1990s Culture Wars in Whatcom County, Washington" (master's thesis, Western Washington University, 2020), 71–100.

9. On the carceral state, see Michelle Alexander, *The New Jim Crow* (New York: The New Press, 2012); Katherine Beckett, *Making Crime Pay: Law and Order in Contemporary American Politics* (New York: Oxford University Press, 1997); Dan Berger, *Captive Nation: Black Prison Organizing in the Civil Rights Era* (Chapel Hill: University of North Carolina Press, 2014); Jordan T. Camp, *Incarcerating the Crisis: Freedom Struggles and the Rise of the Neoliberal State* (Oakland: University of California Press, 2016); James Forman, Jr., *Locking Up Our Own: Crime and Punishment in Black America* (New York: Farrar, Straus and Giroux, 2017); David Garland, *The Culture of Control: Crime and Social Order in Contemporary Society* (Chicago: University of Chicago Press, 2001); Ruth Wilson Gilmore, *Golden Gulag: Prisons, Surplus, Crisis, and Opposition in Globalizing California* (Berkeley: University of California Press, 2007); Marie Gottschalk, *Caught: The Prison State and the Lockdown of American Politics* (Princeton, N.J.: Princeton University Press, 2014); Marie Gottschalk, *The Prison and the Gallows: The Politics of Mass Incarceration in America* (New York: Cambridge University Press, 2006); Kelly Lytle Hernández, *City of Inmates: Conquest, Rebellion, and the Rise of Human Caging in Los Angeles, 1771–1965* (Chapel Hill: University of North Carolina Press, 2017); Kelly Lytle Hernández, Khalil Gibran Muhammad, and Heather Ann Thompson, "Introduction: Constructing the Carceral State," *Journal of American History* 102, no. 1 (June 1, 2015): 18–24; Naomi Murakawa, *The First Civil Right: How Liberals Built Prison America* (New York: Oxford University Press, 2014); Christian Parenti, *Lockdown America: Police and Prisons in the Age of Crisis* (New York: Verso, 1999); Heather Schoenfeld, *Building the Prison State: Race and the Politics of Mass Incarceration* (Chicago: University of Chicago Press, 2018); Heather Ann Thompson, "Why Mass Incarceration Matters: Rethinking Crisis, Decline, and Transformation in Postwar American History," *Journal of American History* 97, no. 3 (December 1, 2010): 703–34; Heather Ann Thompson and Donna Murch, "Rethinking Urban America through the Lens of the Carceral State," *Journal of Urban History* 41, no. 5 (July 10, 2015): 751–55; Bruce Western, *Punishment and Inequality in America* (New York: Russell Sage, 2006).

10. On the history of policing color and overpolicing and underprotection of Black communities, see Simon Balto, *Occupied Territory: Policing Black Chicago from Red Summer to Black Power* (Chapel Hill: University of North Carolina Press, 2019), Introduction.

11. As Vaughan Shubert insightfully describes this process, "Through DARE, policing became education and education became policing." Shubert, "Rationalizations within Neoliberalism," 95.

12. Tamara Gene Myers, *Youth Squad: Policing Children in the Twentieth Century* (Montreal: McGill-Queen's University Press, 2019); Elizabeth Hinton, "Juvenile Injustice," in *From the War on Poverty to the War on Crime: The Making of Mass Incarceration in America* (Cambridge, Mass.: Harvard University Press, 2016), 218–49; Carl Suddler, *Presumed Criminal: Black Youth and the Justice System in Postwar New York* (New York: New York University Press, 2019); Geoff K. Ward, *The Black Child-Savers: Racial Democracy and Juvenile Justice* (Chicago: University of Chicago Press, 2012). See also articles about police and schools in the *Journal of Urban History*'s special issue on education and the carceral state, including Max Felker-Kantor, "Arresting the Demand for Drugs: DARE and the School-Police Nexus in Los Angeles," *Journal of Urban History* (OnlineFirst, December 30, 2022); Judith Kafka, "Growing Up Together: Brooklyn's Truant School and the Carceral and Educational State, 1857–1924," *Journal of Urban History* (OnlineFirst, January 18, 2023); Matthew B. Kautz, "From Segregation to Suspension: The Solidification of the Contemporary School-Prison Nexus in Boston, 1963–1985," *Journal of Urban History* (OnlineFirst, January 2, 2023); Mahasan Offutt-Chaney, "Disciplining Our Own: Politicizing the Image of the Strict Black Principals, 1970–1985," *Journal of Urban History* (OnlineFirst, January 11, 2023); Noah Remnick, "'The Police State in Franklin K. Lane': Desegregation, Student Resistance, and the Carceral Turn at a New York City High School," *Journal of Urban History* (OnlineFirst, January 11, 2023); Walter C. Stern, "Where Protection Meets Punishment: Public Education and the Carceral State in Urban America," *Journal of Urban History* (OnlineFirst, January 12, 2023).

13. Araceli Centanino, "Chain Link and Concrete: Discipline, Surveillance, and Policing in Los Angeles Schools, 1945–1985" (PhD diss., University of California, Los Angeles, 2021); Judith Kafka, *The History of "Zero Tolerance" in American Public Schooling* (New York: Palgrave Macmillan, 2011); Damien M. Sojoyner, *First Strike: Educational Enclosures in Black Los Angeles* (Minneapolis: University of Minnesota Press, 2016).

14. Historians of education have debated questions of expertise in schools. See Jonathan Zimmerman, *Distilling Democracy: Alcohol Education in America's Public Schools, 1880–1925* (Lawrence: University Press of Kansas, 1999); Jonathan Zimmerman, "'One's Total World View Comes into Play': America's Culture War over Alcohol Education, 1945–1964," *History of Education Quarterly* 42, no. 4 (January 23, 2007): 471–92. Police made similar claims to expertise in queer life in the 1950s and '60s. See Anna Lvovsky, *Vice Patrol: Cops, Courts, and the Struggle over Urban Gay Life before Stonewall* (Chicago: University of Chicago Press, 2021). On the ways that rehabilitation programs expanded the carceral state, see Cyrus J. O'Brien, "'A Prison in Your Community': Halfway Houses and the Melding of Treatment and Control," *Journal of American History* 108, no. 1 (June 1, 2021): 93–117.

15. On the school-prison nexus, see Erica R. Meiners, *Right to Be Hostile: Schools, Prisons, and the Making of Public Enemies* (New York: Routledge, 2007). On the school-to-prison pipeline, see Annette Fuentes, *Lockdown High: When the Schoolhouse Becomes*

a Jailhouse (New York: Verso, 2013); Nancy A. Heitzeg, *The School-to-Prison Pipeline: Education, Discipline, and Racialized Double Standards* (Santa Barbara, Calif.: Praeger, 2016); Elizabeth Hinton, "The Schools," in *America on Fire: The Untold History of Police Violence and Black Rebellion Since the 1960s* (New York: Liveright, 2021), 144–69; Kathleen Nolan, *Police in the Hallways: Discipline in an Urban High School* (Minneapolis: University of Minnesota Press, 2011); Benjamin Justice, "Schools, Prisons, and Pipelines: Fixing the Toxic Relationship between Public Education and Criminal Justice," *Choice* (2018): 1169–76; Victor M. Rios, *Human Targets: Schools, Police, and the Criminalization of Latino Youth* (Chicago: University of Chicago Press, 2017); Kelly Welch and Allison Ann Payne, "Racial Threat and Punitive School Discipline," *Social Problems* 57, no. 1 (February 1, 2010): 25–48.

16. Carla Shedd, *Unequal City: Race, Schools, and Perceptions of Injustice* (New York: Russell Sage Foundation, 2015); Sojoyner, *First Strike*.

17. William B. Hansen et al., "Affective and Social Influences Approaches to the Prevention of Multiple Substance Abuse among Seventh Grade Students: Results from Project SMART," *Preventive Medicine* 17, no. 2 (March 1, 1988): 135–54. Social influence programs included a range of components, including peer pressure resistance training, correction of normative expectations, inoculation against mass media messages, information about parental and other adult influences, peer leadership, and miscellaneous other components. Affective programs included components such as enhancement of self-esteem and self-image, stress management, values clarification, decision-making, and goal setting. There were a wide variety of programs that did not fit neatly into either category but mixed components of both. Nancy S. Tobler, "Meta-Analysis of 143 Adolescent Drug Prevention Programs—Quantitative Outcome Results of Program Participants Compared to a Control or Comparison Group," *Journal of Drug Issues* 16, no. 4 (Fall 1986): 538–59. On the history of debates about responsible use of drugs and the turn to no-use, see Jerome Beck, "100 Years of 'Just Say No' versus 'Just Say Know': Reevaluating Drug Education Goals for the Coming Century," *Evaluation Review* 22, no. 1 (February 1, 1998): 15–45; Jonathan Zimmerman, "Sex, Drugs, and Right 'N' Wrong: Or, the Passion of Joycelyn Elders, M.D.," in *Civic and Moral Learning in America*, ed. Donald R. Warren and John J. Patrick (New York: Palgrave Macmillan, 2006), 191–205.

18. See chapter 6 for an overview of this literature and the debates spurred by social scientific studies finding DARE ineffective at preventing drug use.

19. Melinda Cooper, *Family Values: Between Neoliberalism and the New Social Conservatism*, Near Futures (New York: Zone Books, 2017), 7, 22–24; Matthew D. Lassiter, "Inventing Family Values," in *Rightward Bound: Making America Conservative in the 1970s*, ed. Bruce J. Schulman and Julian E. Zelizer (Cambridge, Mass.: Harvard University Press, 2008), 13–28; Natalia Mehlman Petrzela, *Classroom Wars: Language, Sex, and the Making of Modern Political Culture* (New York: Oxford University Press, 2015); Paul M. Renfro, *Stranger Danger: Family Values, Childhood, and the American Carceral State* (New York: Oxford University Press, 2020); Robert O. Self, *All in the Family: The Realignment of American Democracy Since the 1960s* (New York: Hill and Wang, 2012); Natasha Zaretsky, *No Direction Home: The American Family and the Fear of National Decline, 1968–1980* (Chapel Hill: University of North Carolina Press, 2007).

See also Aaron Griffith, *God's Law and Order: The Politics of Punishment in Evangelical America* (Cambridge, Mass.: Harvard University Press, 2020).

20. Andrew Hartman, *A War for the Soul of America: A History of the Culture Wars* (Chicago: University of Chicago Press, 2015).

21. On the 1986 and 1988 Anti-Drug Abuse Acts, see Alexander, *The New Jim Crow*; Farber, *Crack*. See also note 6.

22. As Earl Wysong, Richard Aniskiewicz, and David Wright argue, "By linking themselves to DARE, national political candidates clearly stood to gain in terms of boosting their own popularity. At the same time, their political support helped to further legitimize the DARE program and increase its funding prospects benefiting individuals and organizations directly involved with its operation and/or expansion." Earl Wysong, Richard Aniskiewicz, and David Wright, "Truth and DARE: Tracking Drug Education to Graduation and as Symbolic Politics," *Social Problems* 41, no. 3 (1994): 448–72.

23. Loeb and Troper, *DARE America Financial Statements and Auditors Reports* (New York: December 31, 2000), box 729604, folder Fund 477 DARE RTC 12th Year, Mayor Antonio R. Villaraigosa Files, Los Angeles City Archives, Los Angeles. Classifying the participation of police and schools as voluntary enabled DARE America to claim that the program did not rest on significant government funding and to report on its IRS documents that it only received $2.8 million in government contributions in 2002. DARE America, *DARE America Form 990—Return of Organization Exempt from Income Tax*, 2002, accessed May 15, 2020, https://projects.propublica.org/nonprofits/organizations/954242541.

24. Brent Cebul, *Illusions of Progress: Business, Poverty, and Liberalism in the American Century* (Philadelphia: University of Pennsylvania Press, 2023); Brent Cebul, Lily Geismer, and Mason B. Williams, eds., *Shaped by the State: Toward a New Political History of the Twentieth Century* (Chicago: University of Chicago Press, 2018); Claire Dunning, *Nonprofit Neighborhoods: An Urban History of Inequality and the American State* (Chicago: University of Chicago Press, 2022); Lily Geismer, *Left Behind: The Democrats' Failed Attempt to Solve Inequality* (New York: Public Affairs, 2022).

25. See, for instance, Charles Hughes, interview by Max Felker-Kantor, December 30, 2022; William Sturkey, interview by Max Felker-Kantor, December 29, 2022.

26. Kelly M. Hayes (@MsKellyMHayes), "I was in the D.A.R.E. program in the 5th grade. That cop was shady as hell and lied all the fucking time. Even as a fifth grader, I could tell he was just making shit up," Twitter, August 13, 2022, 9:09 A.M., https://twitter.com/MsKellyMHayes/status/1558440568673411078; Christopher Ingraham, "A Brief History of DARE, the Anti-Drug Program Jeff Sessions Wants to Revive," *Washington Post*, July 12, 2017, www.washingtonpost.com/news/wonk/wp/2017/07/12/a-brief-history-of-d-a-r-e-the-anti-drug-program-jeff-sessions-wants-to-revive/; German Lopez, "Jeff Sessions's Praise of DARE Shows He Just Can't Quit the 1980s," *Vox*, July 12, 2017, www.vox.com/policy-and-politics/2017/7/12/15957490/jeff-sessions-dare-crime.

27. Justin Kirkl, "Serena Williams' Husband Turned a Vintage T-Shirt into a Brilliant Fashion Troll," *Esquire*, August 27, 2019, www.esquire.com/style/a28820657/serena-williams-alexis-ohanian-maria-sharapova-us-open-dare-shirt/.

28. My thoughts on parody as a form of political critique have come out of my discussions with Julilly Kohler-Haussman. I am also informed by Robin D. G. Kelley's formulation of politics and culture that reaches beyond formal political participation or action. See Robin D. G. Kelley, *Race Rebels: Culture, Politics, and the Black Working Class* (New York: Free Press, 1994).

29. Nancy S. Tobler, "Meta-Analysis of 143 Adolescent Drug Prevention Programs—Quantitative Outcome Results of Program Participants Compared to a Control or Comparison Group," *Journal of Drug Issues* 16, no. 4 (Fall 1986): 538–39; Nancy S. Tobler and Howard H. Stratton, "Effectiveness of School-Based Drug Prevention Programs: A Meta-Analysis of the Research," *Journal of Primary Prevention* 18, no. 1 (September 1, 1997): 71–128; Nancy S. Tobler et al., "School-Based Adolescent Drug Prevention Programs: 1998 Meta-Analysis," *Journal of Primary Prevention* 20, no. 4 (2000): 275–336. The Life Skills Training (LST) program, for example, is often held up as one of the interactive programs that has shown effectiveness, even if it rests on neoliberal logics. See Theo Di Castri, "The Settler Colonial Roots and Neoliberal Afterlife of Problem Behavior Theory," *Journal of the History of the Behavioral Sciences* 59, no. 2 (Spring 2023): 121. The other program that emerged alongside LST and DARE was All Stars, a prevention program designed by William Hansen. See "Home Page," All Stars: Building Bright Futures, accessed January 11, 2023, www.allstarsprevention.com. As Ennett et al. found, "Despite the extensive DARE training received by law enforcement officers, they may not be as well equipped to lead the curriculum as teachers. No studies have been reported in which the DARE curriculum was offered by anyone other than a police officer; results from such a study might suggest whether teachers produce better (or worse) outcomes among pupils." Susan T. Ennett et al., "How Effective Is Drug Abuse Resistance Education? A Meta-Analysis of Project DARE Outcome Evaluations," *American Journal of Public Health* 84, no. 9 (September 1994): 1398.

30. "Safety First: Real Drug Education for Teens," Drug Policy Alliance, March 22, 2022, https://drugpolicy.org/resource/safety-first-real-drug-education-teens; Rodney Skager, *Beyond Zero Tolerance: A Reality-Based Approach to Drug Education and School Discipline* (New York: Drug Policy Alliance, 2013).

Chapter One

1. Los Angeles Police Department, *1983 Annual Report* (Los Angeles, 1983), 11.

2. U.S. Congress, Senate, Committee on the Judiciary, *One-Year Drug Strategy Review*, 101st Cong., 2nd sess., September 5 and 6, 1990, 77. Gates and other drug warriors used the language of "drug abuse," which suggested that any drug use or experimentation qualified as abuse, especially among kids and teenagers. This framing informed the ways DARE operated on the belief that all drug use was wrong and should not be tolerated. Gates's son also had a history of drug use, including at least four arrests. This personal experience may have been part of what pushed Gates to a zero-tolerance, "tough-love" approach. As Gates wrote in his autobiography, "Never before had I said no to my son and it was probably the hardest thing I've ever done. But by then, I was as desperate in my own way as he was in his. After one failed attempt at rehabilitation after another, after seeing him steal from his own family to support his

habit, I had reluctantly gone over to the 'tough love' school dealing with addicts." Daryl F. Gates, *Chief: My Life in the LAPD* (New York: Bantam Books, 1993), 144, 314.

3. Los Angeles Police Department, *1983 Annual Report*, 11.

4. The police had been involved with youth for decades through programs such as Police Athletic Leagues and Policeman Bill programs. For a discussion of the program in the 1960s and how it aimed to intervene in the lives of "ghetto" youth who drew pictures of the police as monsters with whips and badges, see "Police: The Thin Blue Line," *Time*, July 19, 1968. The LAPD had also initiated a Police Role in Government school program in which officers served as teachers, but it operated for only a few years in the late 1960s and early 1970s. See Damien M. Sojoyner, "Black Radicals Make for Bad Citizens: Undoing the Myth of the School to Prison Pipeline," *Berkeley Review of Education* 4, no. 2 (January 1, 2013).

5. Although framed as an alternative, DARE's supposed demand reduction focus was never entirely divorced from law enforcement strategies aimed at combating supply. After all, DARE was a police-led program that intended to advance the law enforcement mission of eradicating drugs, drug use, and perceived drug crime. In targeting potential future drug users—kids—for drug prevention, the LAPD found a new avenue to expand its authority in the war on drugs under the guise of prevention. Distinguishing between supply and demand measures enabled educators and law enforcement officials to justify working together to combat the drug crisis not by arresting kids but inoculating them against future drug use through education and peer resistance training. But this view of prevention as isolated from punitive enforcement of drug laws on school campuses was false. Using police as teachers and as law enforcement representatives who promoted the law-and-order message of the drug war blurred supply and demand reduction strategies.

6. On the blurriness of the user/seller dichotomy, see Julilly Kohler-Hausmann, "The Public versus the Pushers: Enacting New York's Rockefeller Drug Laws," in *Getting Tough: Welfare and Imprisonment in 1970s America* (Princeton, N.J.: Princeton University Press, 2017), 79–120.

7. Max Felker-Kantor, "'Kid Thugs Are Spreading Terror through the Streets': Youth, Crime, and the Expansion of the Juvenile Justice System in Los Angeles, 1973–1980," *Journal of Urban History* 44, no. 3 (May 1, 2018): 476–500; Araceli Centanino, "Chain Link and Concrete: Discipline, Surveillance, and Policing in Los Angeles Schools, 1945–1985" (PhD diss., UCLA, 2021).

8. Los Angeles Police Department, Juvenile Division, *Los Angeles Police Department's Report to the Board of Education: Narcotics Buy Program* (Los Angeles: Los Angeles Police Department, December 30, 1974), box 1,424, folder 2, LAUSD.

9. Los Angeles Police Department, Juvenile Division, *Los Angeles Police Department's Report to the Board of Education*.

10. Los Angeles Police Department, Juvenile Division, *Los Angeles Police Department's Report to the Board of Education*. Gates also wrote an op-ed for the *Los Angeles Times* defending the use of undercover officers. Daryl F. Gates, "In Defense of Undercover Policemen at School," *Los Angeles Times*, December 23, 1974, A5.

11. Los Angeles Police Department, Juvenile Division, *Los Angeles Police Department's Report to the Board of Education*.

12. Los Angeles Police Department, Juvenile Division, *Los Angeles Police Department's Report to the Board of Education*.

13. Phil Kerby, Undercover Narcotics Officers Are in the Schools for Good," *Los Angeles Times*, July 21, 1983, Part II, D1; Joelle Cohen, "Undercover Agent with Sense of Purpose," *Los Angeles Herald Examiner*, February 12, 1984, box 4,205, folder 3, TBAP; Lori Grange, "'Student' Officers Pinpoint 105 School Drug Suspects," *Los Angeles Times*, December 12, 1982, 3-4, folder Los Angeles Police Department (LAPD) 1981 to 1987, Los Angeles Subject Files—Clippings File, Southern California Library for Social Science Research, Los Angeles, Calif.

14. Los Angeles Police Department, "School Buy Program Operations Spring Semester—1988," 1988, in author's possession. This document will be available in AAMI.

15. Los Angeles Police Department, "School Buy Program Operations Spring Semester—1988."

16. Garcia Ramiro to Robert L. Docter, February 20, 1976, box 1,424, folder 1, LAUSD. On the racial disparities of the program and criticism from Black students, see Joelle Cohen, "Students Give Police Drug Program Poor Grades," *Los Angeles Herald Examiner*, February 12, 1984, A12, box 4,205, folder 3, TBAP.

17. Joyce S. Fiske, "The Recent Drug Arrests, Due Process and Secret Police," address to the board, January 6, 1975, box 1,424, folder 1, LAUSD.

18. James Bovard, "A Look at . . . The Child Protection Debate: Kids, Cops and Caseworkers: America's Newest Parent Traps DARE Scare: Turning Children into Informants?" *Washington Post*, January 30, 1994, a25.

19. Gabe Fuentes, "Drug Counts Dropped Because of Officer's Relationship with Pupil," *Los Angeles Times*, January 27, 1987, V6.

20. Los Angeles Police Department and Los Angeles Unified School District, "Drug Abuse Resistance Education," Office of Criminal Justice Planning, Suppression of Drug Abuse in Schools Program, Grant Award, June 29, 1984, box 116, folder 1, TBAP.

21. Los Angeles Police Department and Los Angeles Unified School District, "Drug Abuse Resistance Education."

22. Los Angeles Police Department, *1983 Annual Report*.

23. Jeff Donn, "DARE Has Grown into Biggest Anti-Drug Program, but Critics Grow Too," *AP News*, September 30, 1994, sec. Archive, accessed April 25, 2022, https://apnews.com/article/f7694c9686831e05864e9802a5b6e781.

24. Sandra Evans, "DARE Drug Program Provides Answers to Peer Pressure," *Washington Post*, April 15, 1988, D4.

25. Mayor's Office of Criminal Justice Planning, "Drug Abuse Resistance Education Grant Application," April 12, 1984, box 116, folder 1, TBAP.

26. U.S. Congress, House of Representatives, Subcommittee on Crime of the Committee on the Judiciary, *Coordination of Drug Enforcement and Drug Prevention Efforts*, 98th Cong., 1st sess., February 17 and August 4, 1983, 113, 66.

27. On views of crack as an "inner-city" drug threatening the suburbs, see David R. Farber, *Crack: Rock Cocaine, Street Capitalism, and the Decade of Greed* (New York: Cambridge University Press, 2019), 131–33. On the parent movement, see Emily Dufton,

Grass Roots: The Rise and Fall and Rise of Marijuana in America (New York: Basic Books, 2017).

28. Larry Martz et al., "Trying to Say 'No,'" *Newsweek*, August 11, 1986, 15.

29. Michael Massing, *The Fix* (New York: Simon & Schuster, 1998), 163, 201–2; Matthew D. Lassiter, "Impossible Criminals: The Suburban Imperatives of America's War on Drugs," *Journal of American History* 102, no. 1 (June 2015): 126–40. On the distinction between casual drug users and cocaine addiction, see William J. Bennett, Director, Office of National Drug Control Policy, *National Drug Control Strategy* (Washington, D.C.: The White House, September 1989); William Bennett, "Drugs: Consequences and Confrontation," May 3, 1989, folder Drug Strategy: William Bennett Speech, OA 021312, Kristen Gear Files, White House Office of Public Affairs, GBPL.

30. Bovard, "A Look at."

31. Andy Furillo, "DARE: It's Working and in Trouble: Police Anti-Drug Project at Schools Praised but Council Is Cool," *Los Angeles Times*, April 28, 1985, B1.

32. Los Angeles Board of Education, *Minutes, Regular Meeting, Board of Education, City of Los Angeles, January 17, 1983*, box 603, LAUSD; Los Angeles Board of Education, *Regular Meeting, Board of Education, City of Los Angeles, June 20, 1983*, box 605, LAUSD; Greg Braxton, "Students Learn Drug Resistance," *Los Angeles Times*, February 19, 1984, box 116, folder 2, TBAP.

33. Los Angeles City School District, *Junior High Program in Science, Alcohol, Tobacco, and Other Narcotics, Suggestive Guide for Teachers, B-8 Science*, School Publication No. 279 (Los Angeles: Los Angeles City School District, 1936), box 1,424, folder 3, LAUSD; Los Angeles City School District, Curriculum Division, *Information and Suggestions for the Teaching of Narcotics and Their Effects*, Supplement to Publication No. 279 (Los Angeles: Los Angeles City School District, October 1951), box 1,424, folder 3, LAUSD.

34. Los Angeles City Schools, Office of the Superintendent, *Drug Abuse Control: Policies and Procedures* (Los Angeles: 1973), box 1,424, folder 2, LAUSD. See also Los Angeles City Schools, Office of the Superintendent, *Drug Abuse Control: Policies and Procedures* (Los Angeles: 1970), box 1,424, folder 3, LAUSD.

35. Los Angeles Police Department, Public Affairs Division, Youth Section, "The Police Role in Government: Policy Outline" [ca. 1972], box 32, folder 7, Urban Policy Research Institute Records (UPRI), MSS 011, Southern California Library, Los Angeles. See also Centanino, "Chain Link and Concrete"; Sojoyner, "Black Radicals Make for Bad Citizens," 254.

36. William B. Hansen et al., "Affective and Social Influences Approaches to the Prevention of Multiple Substance Abuse among Seventh Grade Students: Results from Project SMART," *Preventive Medicine* 17, no. 2 (March 1, 1988): 135–54.

37. Bill Hansen, interview by Max Felker-Kantor, January 27, 2021; Luanne Rohrbach, interview by Max Felker-Kantor, December 20, 2021; Anderson C. Johnson, interview by Max Felker-Kantor, April 29, 2022.

38. Daryl F. Gates and Harry Handler, "Substance Abuse Education for Los Angeles City Schools," June 14, 1983, folder 3, box 4,205, TBAP; William DeJong, *Arresting the Demand for Drugs: Police and School Partnership to Prevent Drug Abuse*, Department of

Justice, National Institute of Justice, Office of Communication and Research Utilization, NCJ 105199 (Washington, D.C., November 1987), 23.

39. My understanding of this dynamic comes from various interviews with SMART researchers. See Bill Hansen, interview by Max Felker-Kantor, January 27, 2021; Luanne Rohrbach, interview by Max Felker-Kantor, December 20, 2021; Anderson C. Johnson, interview by Max Felker-Kantor, April 29, 2022. On the history of the SMART program and the comparison program based on affective education and increased drug use, see Hansen et al., "Affective and Social Influences Approaches."

40. DARE, in other words, took part of Project SMART that SMART researchers had abandoned because they knew it was ineffective. In all my research, I have been unable to find out why Ruth Rich and the DARE developers kept the affective education component after SMART found it to be ineffective. There was some controversy over DARE's use of the Project SMART model. One USC researcher later commented, "They ripped off our materials," and, ironically, "they took a version of the program that we had radically revamped, because it wasn't working." Patrick Boyle, "A DAREing Rescue," *Youth Today*, April 2001, 1, 16–19. See also Jeff Elliott, "Drug Prevention Placebo: How DARE Wastes Time, Money, and Police," *Reason*, March 1995, 14–21, accessed August 7, 2019, https://reason.com/1995/03/01/drug-prevention-placebo/. On the relationship between Project SMART researchers and DARE, see William DeJong, interview by Max Felker-Kantor, January 14, 2021; Bill Hansen, interview by Max Felker-Kantor, January 27, 2021; Luanne Rohrbach, interview by Max Felker-Kantor, December 20, 2021; Anderson C. Johnson, interview by Max Felker-Kantor, April 29, 2022.

41. Gates and Handler, "Substance Abuse Education for Los Angeles City Schools."

42. Los Angeles Unified School District, "Project DARE: Police-in-Classroom Anti-Drug Program Inaugurated at 50 Elementary Schools, *Spotlight*, no. 6, October 31, 1983, 2–3, folder 5, box 1,424, LAUSD.

43. DARE America, "Backgrounder: D.A.R.E.—Teaching Children How to Resist Peer Pressure," ca. 1988, box OA18771, folder DARE to Keep Kids Off Drugs [Information Kit], Office of the First Lady, Press Office, RRPL.

44. Superintendent of Schools to Los Angeles Board of Education, "Los Angeles Police Department/Los Angeles Unified School District Cooperative Substance Abuse Prevention Education Program," Communication No. 3, June 20, 1983, box 1,424, folder 5, LAUSD.

45. Los Angeles Police Department, *1988 Annual Report* (Los Angeles, 1988), 4–7.

46. DARE, *Drugs Are Everyone's Problem*, pamphlet, 1985, box 19, folder DARE [Drug Abuse Resistance Education] (1), OA18765, Office of the First Lady, Projects Office, RRPL.

47. Rich Connell, "Los Angeles Police, Schools Move Drug War into Elementary Classrooms," *Los Angeles Times*, August 28, 1983, V1.

48. Los Angeles Police Department and Los Angeles Unified School District, "Drug Abuse Resistance Education."

49. Narcotics Information Clinic (NIC) Program, "Fact Sheet" (1973), box 1,424, folder 3, LAUSD.

50. When DARE began, drug prevention had come to focus on two broad categories, the social influence approach and the affective approach, developed by social

scientists and prevention experts. Social influence programs included a range of components, such as peer pressure resistance training, correction of normative expectations, inoculation against mass media messages, information about parental and other adult influences, and peer leadership. Affective programs included components such as enhancement of self-esteem and self-image, stress management, values clarification, decision-making, and goal setting. A wide variety of programs did not fit neatly into either category but mixed components of both. Nancy S. Tobler, "Meta-Analysis of 143 Adolescent Drug Prevention Programs—Quantitative Outcome Results of Program Participants Compared to a Control or Comparison Group," *Journal of Drug Issues* 16, no. 4 (Fall 1986): 538–39. See also Richard R. Clayton, Anne Cattarello, L. Edward Day, and Katherine P. Walden, "Persuasive Communication and Drug Prevention: An Evaluation of the DARE Program," in *Persuasive Communication and Drug Abuse Prevention*, eds. Lewis Donohew, Howard E. Sypher, and William J. Bukowski (New York: Routledge, 1991), 295–313, which provides a nice review of the school-based prevention literature. Drug education and prevention has a long history, which was informed by broader theories aimed at identifying what led to deviant behavior. Understanding how and why deviant or "problem" behavior developed among youth was influenced, in varying ways, by problem-behavior theory (PBT). PBT developed out of a series of studies conducted by Lee and Richard Jessor, who were trying to understand the high rates of alcoholism among Native Americans in the 1950s, and later adapted to explain the involvement of white, middle-class youth in the counterculture and political protests of the 1960s. Influenced by logics of settler colonialism, PBT ultimately aimed "to assimilate all those who deviated from white, middle-class, settler norms and institutions back into the reigning status quo." Similar uses of deprivation theory and attitudes toward the poor influenced youth programming associated with the war on poverty, which reinforced beliefs of the need to contain and control minoritized youth assumed to be deviant. Rooted in these logics, social scientists influenced by PBT later developed a wide range of prevention programs, including drug prevention in some cases. Theo Di Castri, "The Settler Colonial Roots and Neoliberal Afterlife of Problem Behavior Theory," *Journal of the History of the Behavioral Sciences* 59, no. 2 (August 9, 2022): 107–28. For a discussion of the influence of psychiatry and pathologizing the poor and the community mental health movement in Los Angeles, see Nic John Ramos, "Pathologizing the Crisis: Psychiatry, Policing, and Racial Liberalism in the Long Community Mental Health Movement," *Journal of the History of Medicine and Allied Sciences* 74, no. 1 (January 1, 2019): 57–84. See also Dennis A. Doyle, *Psychiatry and Racial Liberalism in Harlem, 1936–1968* (Rochester, N.Y.: University of Rochester Press, 2016). Thank you to Nic Ramos for his recommendations and conversation on this topic.

51. U.S. Congress, House of Representatives, Committee on Education and Labor, *Hearing on Drug Abuse Prevention and Education*, 99th Cong., 2nd sess., August 6, 1986, 54.

52. Los Angeles Police Department, DARE Unit, "Los Angeles Police Department Training Seminar Project D.A.R.E." [ca. 1985], box 19, folder 2, OA18765, Office of the First Lady, Projects Office, RRPL.

53. While I have been unable to locate the original fifteen-session curriculum, an outline of an early version of the sessions can be found in Los Angeles Police Department, DARE Unit, "Los Angeles Police Department Training Seminar Project D.A.R.E."

and Los Angeles City Council, City Council File No. 85–1757, LACCF. On the removal of the "Vandalism" lesson and replacement with "Consequences," see Local Suppression of Drug Abuse in the Schools Advisory Committee, "Meeting Summary," September 18, 1984, box 108649, folder DARE Drug Abuse Resistance Education Program 1984, AAMI.

54. DARE, "DARE Workbook," June 20, 1983, box 2,669, folder 10, LAUSD. Quote from officer in Paul Gordon, "The Truth about DARE," *Buzz: The Talk of Los Angeles*, September 1995, 72–77, 115.

55. Harry Handler letter to Members, Board of Education, "Project DARE—1984–5 Program," August 28, 1984, box 1,424, folder 5, LAUSD. For various examples of the DARE workbook, see DARE, "DARE Workbook," June 20, 1983, box 2,669, folder 10, LAUSD; DARE America, "Workbook," January 1991, box 148, folder 681, RLA; Illinois State Police, Illinois State Board of Education, and Department of Alcoholism and Substance Abuse, "DARE: To Keep Kids off Drugs," 1987, NCJRS 109637; Houston Police Department and Houston Independent School District, "DARE to SAY NO! Workbook" [ca. 1986], box 18, folder 35, LBP; Las Vegas Metropolitan Police Department, Clark County School District, and Junior League of Las Vegas, "DARE TO SAY NO! Student Workbook" [ca. 1989], box 17, folder 3, JLLV.

56. Braxton, "Students Learn Drug Resistance."

57. Furillo, "DARE: It's Working and in Trouble."

58. Los Angeles Police Department, "Drug Abuse Resistance Education (DARE)," December 26, 1986, box 117, folder 3, TBAP.

59. Los Angeles Police Department and Los Angeles Unified School District, "Drug Abuse Resistance Education."

60. On the focus on family, children, and the future, see Lee Edelman, *No Future: Queer Theory and the Death Drive* (Durham, N.C.: Duke University Press Books, 2004).

61. Harry Handler to Members, Board of Education, "Drug Abuse Resistance Education (DARE)," August 22, 1983, folder 5, box 1,424, LAUSD.

62. United States Commission on Civil Rights, *Desegregation of the Nation's Public Schools: A Status Report* (Washington, D.C., 1979), 50–51.

63. David G. Savage, "For L.A. Schools, Double Jeopardy: Segregation, Overcrowding," *Los Angeles Times*, October 27, 1985, V_7; Elaine Woo, "The Changing Face of L.A.'s Schools," *Los Angeles Times*, March 13, 1987, V_B1.

64. Glenn F. Nyre, *Drug Abuse Resistance Education (DARE) Longitudinal Evaluation Annual Report to Board of Police Commissioners, Los Angeles*, (Los Angeles: Evaluation and Training Institute, January 1987), box C-1968, City Council File No. 87–0667, LACCF.

65. Damien M. Sojoyner, *First Strike: Educational Enclosures in Black Los Angeles* (Minneapolis: University of Minnesota Press, 2016), 85–88.

66. Glenn F. Nyre, "Drug Abuse Resistance Education (Project DARE) in Elementary Schools: Police as Teachers," in *Expanding Mental Health Interventions in Schools*, ed. Irving H. Berkovitz (Los Angeles: Kendall/Hunt, 1985), 99–104.

67. DARE America, "D.A.R.E. Officers in the News: So You Think You're a Failure," 1999, accessed June 30, 2020, https://web.archive.org/web/20011107023424fw_/http://www.dare.com/D_NEWS/D_news_Frame.htm.

68. Richard E. Meyer and Mike Goodman, "Marauders from Inner City Prey on L.A.'s Suburbs," *Los Angeles Times*, July 12, 1981, SD1; Times Editorial Board, "Our Reckoning with Racism; The Failures of This Institution, Our Apology and a Path Forward," *Los Angeles Times*, September 27, 2020, AA.2. Thank you to Mark Vestal for reminding me about this article and the *Los Angeles Times* reckoning series.

69. Tom Morganthau et al., "Kids and Cocaine," *Newsweek*, March 17, 1986; Jacob V. Lamar et al., "Kids Who Sell Crack: The Drug Trade Has Become the Nation's Newest—and Most Frightening—Job Program," *Time*, May 9, 1988; Michael Massing, "Crack's Destructive Sprint across America," *The New York Times Magazine*, October 1, 1989, Gale Academic OneFile.

70. Elizabeth Hinton, *From the War on Poverty to the War on Crime: The Making of Mass Incarceration in America* (Cambridge, Mass.: Harvard University Press, 2016), 318; Michelle Alexander, *The New Jim Crow* (New York: The New Press, 2012), 49–50, 53, 98; Marc Mauer, *Race to Incarcerate* (New York: The New Press, 2001), 160–61.

71. Los Angeles Police Department and Los Angeles Unified School District, "DARE High School," Office of Criminal Justice Planning, Project Summary, October 1, 1989, box 42, folder 7, TBAP. On media portrayals of crack, see Jimmie L. Reeves and Richard Campbell, *Cracked Coverage: Television News, The Anti-Cocaine Crusade, and the Reagan Legacy* (Durham, N.C.: Duke University Press Books, 1994).

72. On African American gangs and racialized understandings of gangs in Los Angeles, see Alex A. Alonso, "Racialized Identities and the Formation of Black Gangs in Los Angeles," *Urban Geography* 25, no. 7 (2004): 658–74. On the racialized drug and gang war, see Donna Murch, "The Color of War: Race, Neoliberalism, and Punishment in Late Twentieth-Century Los Angeles," in *Neoliberal Cities*, ed. Thomas J. Sugrue and Andrew J. Diamond (New York: New York University Press, 2020), 128–53.

73. On the LAPD's war on drugs and gangs, see Max Felker-Kantor, "The Enemy Within: Drug Gangs and Police Militarization," in *Policing Los Angeles: Race, Resistance, and the Rise of the LAPD* (Chapel Hill: University of North Carolina Press, 2018), 190–216.

74. Robert Vernon, "Salt for Chrisis Concerns," NAE Convention, 1985, box 121, item 55, tape 173, National Association of Evangelicals Records, Wheaton College Archives and Special Collections. Thank you to Aaron Griffith for this source.

75. Steve Macek, *Urban Nightmares: The Media, the Right, and the Moral Panic Over the City* (Minneapolis: University of Minnesota Press, 2006). See esp., chap. 4, "Crack Alleys and Killing Zones: News Coverage of the Postindustrial City," 139–98.

76. U.S. Congress, House of Representatives, Subcommittee on Elementary, Secondary, and Vocational Education, Committee on Education and Labor, *Oversight Hearing on Drug Abuse Education Programs*, 101st Cong., 2nd sess., September 6, 1990, 8.

77. Reeves and Campbell, *Cracked Coverage*. On "crack mothers" and media depictions of Black women during the war on drugs, see Drew Humphries, *Crack Mothers: Pregnancy, Drugs, and the Media, Women and Health* (Columbus: Ohio State University Press, 1999); Tanya Telfair Sharpe, *Behind the Eight Ball: Sex for Crack Cocaine Exchange and Poor Black Women* (New York: Haworth Press, 2005).

78. Los Angeles Police Department and Los Angeles Unified School District, "Drug Abuse Resistance Education (DARE)," Office of Criminal Justice Planning, Project Summary [ca. 1987], box C-1968, City Council File No. 87–0667, LACCF.

79. Los Angeles Police Department and Los Angeles Unified School District, "DARE High School," Office of Criminal Justice Planning, Project Summary, October 1, 1989, box 42, folder 7, TBAP. On moral panics and racialized fears, see Macek, *Urban Nightmares*; Craig Reinarman and Harry Gene Levine, eds., *Crack in America: Demon Drugs and Social Justice* (Berkeley: University of California Press, 1997); Reeves and Campbell, *Cracked Coverage*.

80. Susan Moffat, "'No!' Is Their Rallying Cry: 6,000 Youths at Meeting Loudly Pledge to Avoid Gangs and Drugs," *Los Angeles Times*, April 22, 1994, B12.

81. Charles Hughes, interview by Max Felker-Kantor, December 30, 2022. Wausau was a predominantly white community of about 40,000 people in the early 1990s. As Hughes recalled, it was also undergoing significant demographic change as Southeast Asian refugees relocated to the city, which likely fueled the larger anxieties about external threats among many white residents.

82. DARE Unit, "Fact Sheet," [ca. December 1984], box 40945, folder 26, AAMI; Los Angeles Police Department and Los Angeles Unified School District, "Drug Abuse Resistance Education (DARE)," Office of Criminal Justice Planning, Grant Award, September 11, 1985, box C-1154, City Council File No. 85–1757, LACCF.

83. Chief Legislative Analyst to Grants, Housing and Community Development Committee, "Agreement with ETI for Evaluation of DARE Project," January 28, 1986, box C-1154, City Council File No. 85–1757," 1986.

84. U.S. Congress, House of Representatives, Committee on Education and Labor, *Hearing on Drug Abuse Prevention and Education*, 99th Cong., 2nd sess., August 6, 1986, 55. On the LAPD's war on gangs and the connection to DARE, see Daryl F. Gates and Robert K. Jackson, "The Situation in Los Angeles," *The Police Chief*, November 1990, 20–22.

85. Los Angeles Police Department and Los Angeles Unified School District, "DARE High School," Office of Criminal Justice Planning, Project Summary, October 1, 1989, box 42, folder 7, TBAP.

86. Ruth Rich, "Testimony Provided by Dr. Ruth Rich Director, Drug Free Schools and Communities Act Program Los Angeles Unified School District for Congress of the United States, House of Representatives Committee on Government on the Drug Crisis in America and the Proposals to Fight It," July 2, 1990, box 288, folder 15, TBAP. On the LAPD's data related to drugs and gangs, which found that gangs did not dominate drug trafficking in Los Angeles, see Felker-Kantor, *Policing Los Angeles*, 194–97; Donna Murch, "Crack in Los Angeles: Crisis, Militarization, and Black Response to the Late Twentieth-Century War on Drugs," *Journal of American History* 102, no. 1 (June 1, 2015): 162–73. DARE, in other words, was implicated in the aggressive policing targeting sellers and users on the streets of Los Angeles and America's cities. Independent researchers also commented on DARE's effort to reshape the perception of the police in the city's communities of color. As two researchers found, "The D.A.R.E. curriculum was designed to respond to the specific needs of African American and Mexican American neighborhoods in California's largest city. D.A.R.E. sought to reduce distrust of law enforcement officers in communities where the police often were viewed as an alien, racist presence. It also tried to counter the influence of drug-selling gangs." Michael J. Stoil and Gary Hill, "Problem: Preparing the Ground for Prevention in Early Adolescence," in *Preventing Substance Abuse: Interventions That Work* (New York: Springer, 1996), 55–70.

87. Dennis P. Rosenbaum and Gordon S. Hanson, "Assessing the Effects of School-Based Drug Education: A Six-Year Multilevel Analysis of Project D.A.R.E.," *Journal of Research in Crime and Delinquency* 35, no. 4 (November 1998): 381–412.

88. Anne Driscoll, "Policeman as Teacher and Model," *New York Times*, February 19, 1989, 51; DARE officer quoted in David L. Carter, *Community Policing and D.A.R.E.®: A Practitioner's Perspective*, Bureau of Justice Bulletin: Community Policing Series, NCJ 154275 (Washington, D.C.: Department of Justice, July 1995), 5.

89. DARE likely helped facilitate the acceptance of school resource officers (SROs) in the 1990s, but evidence of educators or policymakers connecting the two is scarce. In the first two decades of the program, DARE officers were explicitly not trained as SROs to maintain the distinction, however blurred, between the DARE officer as teacher and the SRO as the enforcer of punitive disciplinary policy. Following 9/11, however, all DARE officers were also trained as SROs. For instance, see DARE America, "The New D.A.R.E. Program," January 2, 2006, accessed May 28, 2022, https://web.archive.org/web/20060102103240/http://www.dare.com/home/newdareprogram.asp.

90. Independent Commission, "Transcript from I.C. Public Hearing," May 13, 1991, box 10, folder 4, Independent Commission on the Los Angeles Police Department Records, Collection no. 0229, Regional History Collections, Special Collections, USC Libraries, University of Southern California, Los Angeles.

91. Bernard C. Parks to Honorable Budget and Finance Committee City Council, City of Los Angeles, June 28, 1999, box B-2572, City Council File No. 98–1086, LACCF.

Chapter Two

1. *Crime File*, "Drug Education," directed by W. P. Fowler (the Police Foundation and National Institute of Justice, 1986), videocassette (VHS), 28 min. Some students commented that the tactic was "Walking Away" to which Boles corrected them, asserting it was saying "No Thanks." However, watching the scene actually suggests that both students were correct, and Boles clearly missed the point that two refusal tactics had been used by the student.

2. William Sturkey, interview by Max Felker-Kantor, December 29, 2022.

3. *Crime File*, "Drug Education."

4. Joshua Reeves, "Recognize, Resist, Report: D.A.R.E. America and the Kid Police," in *Citizen Spies: The Long Rise of America's Surveillance Society* (New York: New York University Press, 2017), 109–36.

5. On the disproportionate and discriminatory policing in Black and Latinx neighborhoods in Los Angeles, see Mike Davis, *City of Quartz: Excavating the Future in Los Angeles* (New York: Vintage Books, 1992); Max Felker-Kantor, *Policing Los Angeles: Race, Resistance, and the Rise of the LAPD* (Chapel Hill: University of North Carolina Press, 2018); Donna Murch, "Crack in Los Angeles: Crisis, Militarization, and Black Response to the Late Twentieth-Century War on Drugs," *Journal of American History* 102, no. 1 (June 1, 2015): 162–73.

6. The Safe and Drug Free Schools Act of 1988 required uniformed police officers to deliver antidrug education in order for schools to receive federal prevention funds.

See chapter 3 for a discussion of the ways the federal government and policy supported the expansion of DARE.

7. Chief of Police to Stanley Sheinbaum, "Invitation to Observe D.A.R.E. Program in Classroom," January 29, 1992, box 211, folder D.A.R.E. (Drug Abuse Resistance Education)—Martin Peretz, SSC.

8. Superintendent of Schools to Los Angeles Board of Education, "Los Angeles Police Department/Los Angeles Unified School District Cooperation Substance Abuse Prevention Education Program," June 20, 1983, box 1,424, folder 5, LAUSD; Chief of Police to Honorable Board of Police Commissioners, "Memorandum of Understanding between Los Angeles Police Department and Los Angeles Unified School District of the Drug Abuse Resistance Education (DARE) Program," September 13, 1985, box 117, folder 2, TBAP.

9. "Bureau of Special Investigation" [ca. 1986], box 3247, folder Why BSI Should Have a Deputy Chief, AAMI.

10. See DARE's Organizational Chart in Los Angeles Police Department and Los Angeles Unified School District, "Drug Abuse Resistance Education," Office of Criminal Justice Planning, Suppression of Drug Abuse in Schools Program, Grant Award, June 29, 1984, box 116, folder 1, TBAP.

11. Los Angeles Police Department, "Drug Abuse Resistance Education Regional Training Center Criteria Categorical Grant Progress Report," August 4, 1988, box C-2130, City Council File No. 88–1494, LACCF.

12. Andy Furillo, "DARE: It's Working and in Trouble: Police Anti-Drug Project at Schools Praised but Council Is Cool," *Los Angeles Times*, April 28, 1985, B1.

13. Los Angeles Police Department and Los Angeles Unified School District, "Drug Abuse Resistance Education (DARE)," Office of Criminal Justice Planning, Project Summary [ca. 1986], box C-805, City Council File No. 84–1431, LACCF. A Bureau of Justice manual on the DARE program would later describe the characteristics of a DARE officer as the following:

a. Is one who refrains from sexual, racial, gender, ethnic, or other inappropriate and insensitive remarks.
b. Is an exemplary role model in both formal and informal situations.
c. Is able to receive and act upon positive criticism.
d. Is flexible and can handle the unexpected.
e. Is able to interact with a wide variety of persons.
f. Is committed to a careful replication of the parent project.
g. Is able to consider audience sensitivities.
h. Is able to demonstrate:
   (1) Effective lesson preparation.
   (2) The incorporation of necessary lesson elements.
   (3) Effective classroom management techniques.
   (4) The ability to speak and write effectively.

Bureau of Justice Assistance, *The DARE Regional Training Center Policy Board's Manual for Training Law Enforcement Officers in the DARE Program*, Department of Justice, Office of Justice Programs, Bureau of Justice Assistance, NCJ 129758 (Washington, D.C., October 1991), 5.

14. "DARE to Keep Kids off Drugs," *Law and Order*, December 1987, 22–24; Daryl F. Gates, "LAPD's Project DARE Tells Youths to Resist Drugs," *School Safety*, Spring 1986, 26–27.

15. On the 200-hour training, see Sharon Greengold, "Teaching Kids to Turn Down Drugs: 'Operation DARE' Is at It Again," *Valley View*, October 3, 1984, box 116, folder 2, TBAP. On the development of the pilot-year program, see Superintendent of Schools to Los Angeles Board of Education, "Los Angeles Police Department/Los Angeles Unified School District Cooperative Substance Abuse Prevention Education Program," Communication No. 3, June 20, 1983, box 1,831, folder 3, LAUSD. For a copy of the eighty-hour training curriculum, see Los Angeles Unified School District, Office of Instruction, *Manual for Training Law Enforcement Officers in the D.A.R.E. Program*, Publication No. GC-113 (Los Angeles, 1987), box C-2130, City Council File No. 88–1494, LACCF.

16. Robert Reinhold, "Police, Hard Pressed in Drug War, Are Turning to Preventive Efforts," *New York Times*, December 28, 1989, A1.

17. David L. Carter, *Community Policing and D.A.R.E.®: A Practitioner's Perspective*, Bureau of Justice Bulletin: Community Policing Series, NCJ 154275 (Washington, D.C.: Department of Justice, July 1995), 7.

18. Los Angeles Police Department and Los Angeles Unified School District, "Drug Abuse Resistance Education (DARE): Project Summary," Office of Criminal Justice Planning, Grant Award [ca. 1986], box C-805, City Council File No. 84–1431, LACCF.

19. "DARE: Selecting the Right Officer," *FBI Law Enforcement Bulletin*, May 1990, 11–12.

20. "DARE Officer Training 2002," *Idaho Drug War News*, December 2002, L3000.91, ISA. On counterinsurgency and policing, see Stuart Schrader, *Badges without Borders: How Global Counterinsurgency Transformed American Policing* (Oakland: University of California Press, 2019).

21. Jeffrey Merrill, Tracey Dilascio, and Ilana Pinsky, "Law Enforcement and Drug Prevention: A Profile of the DARE Officer," *The Police Chief*, August 2002, 81–88.

22. On the ways that the police have always been militarized and developed in conjunction with imperial projects, see Julian Go, *Policing Empires: Militarization, Race, and the Imperial Boomerang* (New York: Oxford University Press, 2023).

23. Peter J. Meyer and Clare Ribando Seelke, *Central America Regional Security Initiative: Background and Policy Issues for Congress*, Congressional Research Service, R41731, December 17, 2015, 21. Thank you to Stuart Schrader for this document. On the history of counterinsurgency and policing, see Schrader, *Badges without Borders*.

24. U.S. Congress, House of Representatives, Committee on Education and Labor, *Drug Abuse Resistance Education Act of 1990: Report Together with Additional Views (to Accompany H.R. 5064)*, 101 Cong. 2nd sess., July 6, 1990, 2.

25. William DeJong, *Arresting the Demand for Drugs: Police and School Partnership to Prevent Drug Abuse*, Department of Justice, National Institute of Justice, Office of Communication and Research Utilization, NCJ 105199 (Washington, D.C., November 1987), 17; National School Safety Center, "DARE: Protecting the Future through Prevention Today," *School Safety*, April 1992, 7.

26. DARE America, "D.A.R.E. Will Teach Over 5.5 Million Children Drug Resistance Skills in 1994," press release, ca. 1994, Domestic Policy Council and Jose Cerda, "D.A.R.E. [Drug Abuse Resistance Education]," *Clinton Digital Library*, accessed January 18, 2023, https://clinton.presidentiallibraries.us/items/show/96852. Thank you to my research assistant Emily McGuire who worked extensively with the Clinton digital archives and found invaluable examples of the administration's continued support.

27. Los Angeles Unified School District, "Project DARE: Police-in-Classroom Anti-Drug Program Inaugurated at 50 Elementary Schools," *Spotlight*, no. 6, October 31, 1983, 2–3, box 1,424, folder 5, LAUSD.

28. Furillo, "DARE: It's Working."

29. Daryl F. Gates to Honorable Board of Police Commissioners, "Transmittal of 1989 City Innovations Awards Report (with attachments)," February 21, 1989, box C-2223, City Council File No. 89–0574, LACCF.

30. Jim Newton, "DARE Marks a Decade of Growth and Controversy," *Los Angeles Times*, September 9, 1993, WB.

31. For various places where policymakers stressed the use of police in schools, see U.S. Congress, House of Representatives, Subcommittee on Elementary, Secondary, and Vocational Education, Committee on Education and Labor, *Oversight Hearing on Drug Abuse Education Programs*, 101st Cong., 2nd sess., September 6, 1990; U.S. Congress, House of Representatives, Committee on Education and Labor, *Drug Abuse Resistance Education Act of 1990: Report Together with Additional Views (to Accompany H.R. 5064)*, 101st Cong. 2nd sess., July 6, 1990; Bureau of Justice Assistance, *An Introduction to DARE: Drug Abuse Resistance Education*, Department of Justice, Office of Justice Programs, Bureau of Justice Assistance, NCJ 129862 (Washington, D.C., October 1991).

32. Rose Matsui Ochi to Mayor Tom Bradley, "Transmittal of Drug Abuse Resistance Education (DARE) Program Semifinalist Application to the Innovations in State and Local Government, 1991 Awards Program (with attachments)," April 22, 1991, box D-197, City Council File No. 91–0703, LACCF.

33. Phyllis Q. Marquardt letter to Daryl F. Gates, January 31, 1986, box 108644, folder 6, AAMI.

34. Los Angeles Police Department and Los Angeles Unified School District, "Drug Abuse Resistance Education (DARE)," Office of Criminal Justice Planning, Suppression of Drug Abuse in Schools Program, Grant Award, April 4, 1984, box C-805, City Council File No. 84–0566, LACCF.

35. Glenn Nyre, *Project DARE Interim Evaluation Report, 1984–85* (Los Angeles: Evaluation and Training Institute, March 1985), box 132, folder 4, TBAP.

36. Glenn F. Nyre, "Drug Abuse Resistance Education (Project DARE) in Elementary Schools: Police as Teachers," in *Expanding Mental Health Interventions in Schools*, ed. Irving H. Berkovitz (Los Angeles: Kendall/Hunt, 1985), 101, 102.

37. In general, most educators viewed the DARE program in a positive light. For studies on educator perceptions of the DARE officer, see Joseph F. Donnermeyer, "Educator Perceptions of the D.A.R.E. Officer," *Journal of Alcohol & Drug Education* 44, no. 1 (Fall 1998): 1–17; Joseph F. Donnermeyer and Todd N. Wurschmidt, "Educators'

Perceptions of the D.A.R.E. Program," *Journal of Drug Education* 27, no. 3 (September 1997): 259–76.

38. Ahmad Roberts and Romel Mallard, "Our Interview with Dr. Melba Coleman," *DARE to Read* no. 3 (March 1988), box 1,424, folder 4, LAUSD.

39. Naomi Aragon and Ronica Hsu, "We 'D.A.R.E.' to Interview Mrs. Dore Wong," *DARE to Read* no. 5 (May 1988), box 1,424, folder 6, LAUSD.

40. *Crime File*, "Drug Education."

41. For one evaluation that found teachers both supported having police in the school but were also critical of the lack of training, see Wisconsin Survey Research Laboratory, *An Evaluation of the Drug Abuse Resistance Education Program in Wisconsin Schools: An Evaluation* (Madison: University of Wisconsin-Madison, July 1998), box 1, Records of the Superintendent's AODA Council, 1995–1999, WHS.

42. Donnermeyer, "Educator Perceptions of the D.A.R.E. Officer," 15.

43. Charles Hughes, interview by Max Felker-Kantor, December 30, 2022.

44. The DARE officer training manual went to great lengths to address the role of the police officer as a teacher and how to strengthen the relationship with the school. Los Angeles Unified School District, Office of Instruction, *Manual for Training Law Enforcement Officers in the D.A.R.E. Program*, Publication No. GC-113 (Los Angeles, 1987), box C-2130, City Council File No. 88–1494, LACCF.

45. "DARE Regional Training Center Conference Minutes," January 29–31, 1989, 11–20, box C-2143, City Council File No. 88-1962-S2, LACCF.

46. DARE Regional Training Center Advisory Committee, "Accreditation of DARE Training Centers," Spring 1989, box C-2143, City Council File 88–1962, LACCF.

47. Rich Connell, "Los Angeles Police, Schools Move Drug War into Elementary Classrooms," *Los Angeles Times*, August 28, 1983, V1.

48. Furillo, "DARE: It's Working." See also William Overend, "DARE Survives Early Doubts: L. A. Drug Effort Takes on International Dimensions," *Los Angeles Times*, May 30, 1989, 1–3.

49. Los Angeles City Council, "Item 21," May 13, 1986, box C-1108, City Council File No. 85-0214-S1, LACCF.

50. Lisa Jennings, "Schools and the Police: 'We Need Each Other,'" *Education Week*, April 12, 1989, accessed June 4, 2019, www.edweek.org/ew/articles/1989/04/12/08250011.h08.html.

51. Bureau of Justice Assistance, *Implementing Project DARE: Drug Abuse Resistance Education*, Department of Justice, Office of Justice Programs, Bureau of Justice Assistance, NCJ 115417 (Washington, D.C., June 1988), 69.

52. Eva Marx and William DeJong, *An Invitation to Project DARE: Drug Abuse Resistance Education*, Department of Justice, Office of Justice Programs, Bureau of Justice Assistance, NCJ 114802 (Washington, D.C., June 1988), ii.

53. City Administrative Officer to Tom Bradley, "Subgrant Agreement for the DARE Program with the Los Angeles Unified School District (LAUSD)," March 3, 1992, box 2947, folder 10, TBAP.

54. Councilmember Marvin Braude, Chairperson Public Safety Committee to the Council of the City of Los Angeles, "Communication," April 4, 1992, box C-2411, City Council File No. 90–1129, LACCF.

55. Los Angeles Police Department and Los Angeles Unified School District, "Drug Abuse Resistance Education (DARE)," Office of Criminal Justice Planning Grant Award, Suppression of Drug Abuse in Schools Program, April 4, 1984, box C-805, City Council File No. 84–0566, LACCF; Rich Connell, "Police Receive A's in Drug Abuse Class," *Los Angeles Times*, April 1, 1984, WS1.

56. Barry McCaffrey, "DARE Cares: Drug Prevention Protects America's Youth," August 29, 1999, box 9, folder D.A.R.E., RG 581.

57. Glenn Levant, "President's Message," *DareLine International*, 1998, 4, box 26, folder 16, accretion 19147–06, NYSA.

58. Daryl F. Gates and Harry Handler, "Substance Abuse Education for Los Angeles City Schools," June 14, 1983, box 4,205, folder 3, TBAP.

59. Jennifer Gonnerman, "Truth or D.A.R.E.—The Dubious Drug-Education Program Takes New York," *Village Voice*, April 6, 1999, accessed January 28, 2019, www.villagevoice.com/1999/04/06/truth-or-d-a-r-e/.

60. See Felker-Kantor, *Policing Los Angeles*.

61. Joelle Cohen, "Students Give Police Drug Program Poor Grades," *Los Angeles Herald Examiner*, February 12, 1984, box 4,205, folder 3, TBAP; Joelle Cohen, "Undercover Agent with Sense of Purpose," *Los Angeles Herald Examiner*, February 12, 1984, box 4,205, folder 3, TBAP.

62. Los Angeles Police Department and Los Angeles Unified School District, "Project Summary: Drug Abuse Resistance Education (DARE)," Office of Criminal Justice Planning, Grant Award [ca. 1986], box C-805, City Council File No. 84–1431, LACCF.

63. Glenn F. Nyre, *Project DARE: Interim Evaluation Report* (Los Angeles: Evaluation and Training Institute, March 12, 1984), box 1,424, folder 6, LAUSD.

64. Los Angeles Police Department and Los Angeles Unified School District, "Drug Abuse Resistance Education," Office of Criminal Justice Planning, Suppression of Drug Abuse in Schools Program, Grant Award, June 29, 1984, box 116, folder 1, TBAP.

65. Marx and DeJong, *An Invitation to Project DARE*, 4.

66. Bernal F. Koehrsen, Jr. and Dennis L. Damon, "Collectible Cop Cards," *FBI Law Enforcement Bulletin*, February 1993, 4.

67. Glenn F. Nyre, *An Evaluation of Project DARE* (Los Angeles: Evaluation and Training Institute, July 1984), folder 2, box 116, TBAP.

68. Everett M. Rogers, "Diffusion and Re-Invention of Project D.A.R.E.," in *Organizational Aspects of Health Communication Campaigns: What Works?*, ed. Thomas E. Backer and Everett M. Rogers (Newbury Park, CA: SAGE Publications, 1993), 149–50.

69. Daryl F. Gates to Honorable Board of Police Commissioners, "Transmittal of 1989 City Innovations Awards Report (with attachments)," February 21, 1989, box C-2223, City Council File No. 89–0574, LACCF.

70. Nyre, "Drug Abuse Resistance Education (Project DARE) in Elementary Schools," 101, 102.

71. Nyre, *Project DARE: Interim Evaluation Report*, A9.

72. Sally Ann Stewart, "L.A. Kids 'DARE' to Just Say No," *USA Today*, December 19, 1986, box 19, folder DARE [Drug Abuse Resistance Education] (2), OA18765, Office of the First Lady, Projects Office, RRPL.

73. William DeJong, "Project DARE: Teaching Kids to Say 'No' to Drugs and Alcohol," U.S. Department of Justice, National Institute of Justice, *NIJ Reports*, March 1986, 2–5.

74. D. Aldahl, Bilingual Teacher, Cheremoya Ave. School to City Council Members (with attached letters), May 8, 1985, box C-1108, City Council File No. 85–0214, LACCF.

75. "Fourth-Graders Write Essays on D.A.R.E. Program's Lessons," *Telegraph-Forum*, April 17, 2000, 5, Newspapers.com.

76. "DARE Fact," *Sioux City Journal*, June 24, 1993, 4, Newspapers.com. For other student essays and opinions on DARE, see, for instance, "Focus on Education: Schoolhouse and Drug Prevention," *Star Tribune*, May 10, 1995, 13, Newspapers.com; Erie Bratcher, "Student Submits DARE Essay," *McLean County News*, March 24, 1994, 9, Newspapers.com; "D.A.R.E. Essay Contest Winners Honored by Bucyrus City Council," *Telegraph-Forum*, June 24, 2000, 6, Newspapers.com; "Lincoln-Irving Elementary Student Writers," *The Dispatch*, December 6, 2009, 2, Newspapers.com.

77. Aryn Kelly & "The D.A.R.E. Squad" to Daryl Gates, February 28, 1988, box 3259, folder Projects March 1988, AAMI; Aryn Kelly, "DARE Squad Speaks," Volume 2, Nov. 1987, box 3259, folder Projects March 1988, AAMI.

78. Sue Templeton, "Students Become Role Models for DARE," *The Messenger*, May 24, 1990, 27, Newspapers.com. See also Aubrey Woods, "Role Models Steer Kids Away from Drugs," *The Tribune*, December 23, 1995, 1, Newspapers.com; Sarah Fuellemann, "School Selects Role Models," *Globe-Gazette*, May 12, 1997, 12, Newspapers .com. DARE America would later establish a Youth Advisory Board that brought fifty "outstanding young people" together for two-year terms to lead the fight against drugs. DARE America, "D.A.R.E. America Youth Advisory Board," July 10, 2000, box 9, folder D.A.R.E., RG 581.

79. William Sturkey, interview by Max Felker-Kantor, December 29, 2022.

80. "The DARE Program," *The Messenger*, March 7, 1990, 21, Newspapers.com.

81. Charlie Hughes and Erik Rajek, "DARE to Be Unnecessary," *Rib Mountain Gazette*, ca. 1992, in author's possession. Thank you to Charles Hughes for this source.

82. City of Cape Girardeau, *DARE—Drug Abuse Resistance Education in Cape Girardeau* (City of Cape Girardeau, Mo., 2011), accessed February 17, 2023, http://archive .org/details/DARE_-_Drug_Abuse_Resistance_Education_in_Cape_Girardeau.

83. *Police Officer Teaches Drug Education to Children ca. 1983* (WPA Film Library, Distributed by Films Media Group, 2007).

84. Bob Hanson, interview by Kim Winters, October 16, 2010, box 2, accession 560001, Wyoming Energy Boom Sublette County Natural Gas Oral History Project, American Heritage Center, University of Wyoming, Laramie, Wyo.

85. Arthur G. Sharp, "Special Report: Is DARE a Sacred Lamb?" *Law and Order*, April 1998, 42–47, here 46.

86. Gonnerman, "Truth or D.A.R.E." (emphasis mine).

87. Patrick Boyle, "A DAREing Rescue," *Youth Today*, April 2001, 1, 16–19.

88. The idea for a national DARE Officer Association originated in 1986 by the Crime Prevention Advisory Council (CPAC) in Los Angeles. See "Fact Sheet: DARE Requested Personnel Expansion," [ca. October 1986], box 108641, folder 25, AAMI.

89. National D.A.R.E. Officers Association, *Bylaws* [ca. 1988], box C-2130, City Council File No. 88–1494, LACCF. See also Los Angeles Police Department, "Drug Abuse Resistance Education Regional Training Center Criteria Categorical Grant Progress Report," August 4, 1988, box C-2130, City Council File No. 88–1494, LACCF.

90. National DARE Officers Association, "National D.A.R.E. Officers Association: Officers," 1988, box C-2130, City Council File No. 88–1494, LACCF; National DARE Officers Association, "National D.A.R.E. Officers Association: Executive Committee," 1988, box C-2130, City Council File No. 88–1494, LACCF.

91. National D.A.R.E. Officers Association, *Bylaws*.

92. Debbie Myers, "3,500 DARE Officers Gather for Updates on Drug," *USA Today*, July 15, 1992.

93. Christopher L. Ringwalt, Jody M. Greene, Susan T. Ennett, Ronaldo Iachan, Richard R. Clayton, and Carl G. Leukefeld, *Past and Future Directions of the D.A.R.E.® Program: An Evaluation Review Research in Brief*, Department of Justice, Office of Justice Programs, National Institute of Justice, NIJ 152055 (Washington, D.C., September 1994). For state level officer associations and conferences, see, for instance, Roy C. Klingler, "Notes from the President," *D.A.R.E. Idaho*, 1, no. 1 (January 1996), 7, L3000.93, ISA; John W. Herritage to Richard H. Girgenti, "NYS DARE Officers Association (NYS DOA) Conference," December 27, 1991, box 12, folder 10, accretion 19147–98, NYSA.

94. Merrill et al., "Law Enforcement and Drug Prevention: A Profile of the DARE Officer," 81–88.

95. Reeves, *Citizen Spies*, 125.

96. William Bennett and Richard G. Darman, "Press Briefing by Director of National Drug Control Policy William J. Bennett and Director of Office of Management and Budget Richard G. Darman," press briefing, September 5, 1989, folder Drug Free Schools, OA 13263, Judy Smith Files, White House Press Office, GBPL.

97. Daryl F. Gates, "A Partnership against Crime," *FBI Law Enforcement Bulletin*, August 1986, 6–9.

98. Carter, *Community Policing and D.A.R.E.®*. See also Richard R. Clayton et al., "DARE (Drug Abuse Resistance Education): Very Popular but Not Very Effective," in *Intervening with Drug-Involved Youth* (Thousand Oaks, Calif.: SAGE Publications, 1996), 101–9.

99. "DARE to Keep Kids off Drugs," *Law and Order*, December 1987, 22–24.

100. U.S. Congress, House of Representatives, Subcommittee on Elementary, Secondary, and Vocational Education, Committee on Education and Labor, *Oversight Hearing on Drug Abuse Education Programs*, 101st Cong., 2nd sess., September 6, 1990, 36–37.

101. *Oversight Hearing on Drug Abuse Education Programs*, 53.

102. *Oversight Hearing on Drug Abuse Education Programs*, 37.

103. DARE America, "D.A.R.E. Teachers News," accessed June 30, 2020, https://web.archive.org/web/20011218001739fw_/http://www.dare.com/D_NEWS/DN_TEACH/Dn_teach.htm.

104. DARE America, "About D.A.R.E.," January 3, 2006, accessed June 30, 2020, https://web.archive.org/web/20060103170718/http://www.dare.com/home/about_dare.asp.

105. "Otterstrom Earns Top DARE Officer Status," *D.A.R.E. Idaho*, 1, no. 3, July 1996, 5, L3000.93, ISA.

106. Anne Driscoll, "Policeman as Teacher and Model," *New York Times*, February 19, 1989, 51.

107. California Office of Criminal Justice Planning, "Suppression of Drug Abuse in Schools Program" (Sacramento, Calif., 1989), 11–12.

108. Lee P. Brown, "Building a Partnership between Police and Community," March 19, 1983, box 31, folder 38, LBP; Lee P. Brown, "Neighborhood Oriented Policing: A New Style of Policing," October 15, 1988, box 34, folder 19, LBP. For background on Lee P. Brown, see "The Honorable Lee P. Brown," *The History Makers*, November 4, 2004, accessed February 20, 2023, www.thehistorymakers.org/biography/honorable-lee-p-brown.

109. Lee P. Brown, "DARE Board Meeting Address," December 7, 2000, box 62, folder 127, LBP.

110. "Violent Crime Control and Law Enforcement Act of 1994," Pub. L. No. H.R. 3355, 42 U.S.C. § 14141 (1994); U.S. Department of Justice, Community Oriented Policing Services, *Community Policing Defined* (Washington, D.C., 2014).

111. Kevin Joy, "Former Members of Police Band Think Message Still Relevant," *The Columbus Dispatch*, November 9, 2013, accessed January 18, 2023, www.dispatch.com/story/entertainment/music/2013/11/09/former-members-police-band-think/23801149007/.

112. William Sturkey, interview by Max Felker-Kantor, December 29, 2022; Joe B. McKnight, "Rock Band Sends Anti-Drug Message: Ohio Cops Play 'Hot Pursuit' to Teen-Agers' Rave Reviews," *Los Angeles Times*, May 15, 1988.

113. Jim Gillie, "Hot Pursuit: D.A.R.E.," Danny and The Linders, YouTube, August 4, 2014, accessed July 10, 2019, https://www.youtube.com/watch?v=bQt1yjZeVvs.

114. Joy, "Former Members of Police Band"; McKnight, "Rock Band."

115. Minnesota Institute of Public Health, "Drug Abuse Resistance Education Program Evaluation Final Report" (St. Paul: Minnesota Institute of Public Health, July 16, 1997).

116. Minnesota DARE, "DARE Is Community Policing—Latest News," 2018, accessed August 27, 2020, www.mndare.org/WordPress/blog/2018/10/03/dare-is-community-policing/.

117. Merrill et al., "Law Enforcement and Drug Prevention: A Profile of the DARE Officer," 86.

118. Earl Wysong, Richard Aniskiewicz, and David Wright, "Truth and DARE: Tracking Drug Education to Graduation and as Symbolic Politics," *Social Problems* 41, no. 3 (1994): 448–72.

119. Gerald Regier memo to AG, "Drug Abuse Resistance Education (DARE) Program Supported by OJP's Bureau of Justice Assistance," September 5, 1991, box 707, folder Programs D.A.R.E. (Drug Abuse Resistance Education) 1991, RG 60.

120. DARE, "DARE Workbook," June 20, 1983, box 2,669, folder 10, LAUSD.

121. Reeves, *Citizen Spies*, 110.

122. DeJong, *Arresting the Demand for Drugs*, 3.

123. Glenn Nyre, *Project DARE Interim Evaluation Report, 1984–85* (Los Angeles: Evaluation and Training Institute, March 1985), box 132, folder 4, TBAP.

124. Vaughan Shubert, "Rationalizations within Neoliberalism: Public Schools, Protection, and the 1980s–1990s Culture Wars in Whatcom County, Washington" (master's thesis, Western Washington University, 2020), 97.

125. Los Angeles Police Department and Los Angeles Unified School District, "Drug Abuse Resistance Education (DARE)," Office of Criminal Justice Planning, Grant Award, October 11, 1985, box 117, folder 1, TBAP.

126. Overend, "DARE Survives Early Doubts."

127. Los Angeles Police Department and Los Angeles Unified School District, "Drug Abuse Resistance Education (DARE)," Office of Criminal Justice Planning, Grant Award, October 11, 1985, box 117, folder 1, TBAP.

128. Colleen F. Montoya et al., eds., *Evaluating School-Linked Prevention Strategies: Alcohol, Tobacco, and Other Drugs* (La Jolla: UCSD Extension, University of California, San Diego, 1993), 70. See also Paul Gordon, "The Truth about DARE," *Buzz: The Talk of Los Angeles*, September 1995, 72–77, 115.

129. "The Nation," *Asbury Park Press*, September 17, 1989, 57, Newspapers.com; Ellen Warren, "Teenager Disputes President," *The Charlotte Observer*, September 14, 1989, A1, Newspapers.com; "Cartel 'Medic' Warns U.S.," September 14, 1989, *Democrat and Chronicle*, 1A.

130. Merrill et al., "Law Enforcement and Drug Prevention: A Profile of the DARE Officer," 87.

131. DeJong, *Arresting the Demand for Drugs*, 8.

132. White House Conference for a Drug Free America, *Final Report* (Washington, DC, 1988), 40. See also Prevention Committee, "Narrative for Drug Prevention Recommendations (Draft)," April 28, 1988, box 1, folder Drug Abuse Prevention (4), OA 16408, Drug Free America White House Conference Files, RRPL.

Chapter Three

1. "Local Suppression of Drug Abuse in the Schools Advisory Committee Meeting Summary," September 18, 1984, box 108649, AAMI.

2. "Fact Sheet: DARE Requested Personnel Expansion," [ca. 1986], box 108641, folder 25, AAMI. See also Kathleen M. Wulf, *Executive Summary: A Study of the Implementation of the D.A.R.E. Program in Law Enforcement Agencies in the United States Presented to the Crime Prevention Advisory Council* (Los Angeles, June 1987), box 3247, folder Department Drug, Abuse, Prevention, Program, AAMI.

3. On the number of agencies sending personnel to be trained, see Bureau of Justice Assistance, *The DARE Regional Training Center Policy Board's Manual for Training Law Enforcement Officers in the DARE Program*, U.S. Department of Justice, Office of Justice Programs, Bureau of Justice Assistance, NCJ 129758 (Washington, D.C., October 1991), v. On the interest in DARE from other departments, see Marty Coyne, Director of Projects to Jack Courtemanche, Chief of Staff, "DARE Program," January 5, 1987, box 19, folder DARE [Drug Abuse Resistance Education] (2), OA18766, Office of the First Lady, Projects Office, RRPL. For an example of Minnesota's interest in DARE, see John D. Erskine to Frederick R. Colgan, "Project DARE," February 2, 1987, box 19, folder DARE [Drug Abuse Resistance

Education] (1), OA18766, Office of the First Lady, Projects Office, RRPL. For Las Vegas, see Clark County School District, "Project DARE Final Report," 1986, box 17, folder 1, JLLV.

4. Everett M. Rogers, "Diffusion and Re-Invention of Project D.A.R.E.," in *Organizational Aspects of Health Communication Campaigns: What Works?*, ed. Thomas E. Backer and Everett M. Rogers (Newbury Park, CA: Sage Publications, 1993), 143, 153; William J. Clinton, Proclamation 6588—National D.A.R.E. Day, 1993 and 1994, APP, accessed January 15, 2023; www.presidency.ucsb.edu/node/268943; William J. Clinton, Proclamation 6882—National D.A.R.E. Day, 1996, APP, accessed January 15, 2023, www.presidency.ucsb.edu/node/223168.

5. Rogers, "Diffusion and Re-Invention of Project D.A.R.E.," 143, 153.

6. Statistics on officers and classrooms compiled from Barry McCaffrey, "Remarks by Barry R. McCaffrey Director, Office of National Drug Control Policy before the First Annual Criminal Justice and Substance Abuse Conference Albany, New York" (June 29, 1999), box 2, folder Safe and Drug Free Schools; Barry McCaffrey, "DARE Cares: Drug Prevention Protects America's Youth" (August 29, 1999), box 9, folder D.A.R.E.; DARE America, "D.A.R.E. © at a Glance" [ca. 1999], box 9, folder D.A.R.E., all in RG 581. The numbers of DARE students is often an estimate, and there are differences between the data for students who received the core fifth- or sixth-grade curriculum and those who received other forms of the program, such as one-day presentations to grades K–12 by DARE officers. The 36 million number accounts for all these presentations. DARE America, *DARE America Form 990—Return of Organization Exempt from Income Tax*, 2001, accessed May 15, 2020, https://projects.propublica.org/nonprofits/organizations/954242541. For a list of countries using the DARE program, see DARE America, "D.A.R.E. International Programs," March 23, 2006, accessed June 30, 2020, https://web.archive.org/web/20060323110816/http://www.dare.com/home/International/Story1d4d.asp?N=International&M=9&S=6. DARE's International Programs had a presence in Antigua & Barbuda, Australia, Barbados, Belgium, Bolivia, Brazil, Canada, Cayman Islands, Colombia, Costa Rica, Curacao, Dominica, El Salvador, Falkland Islands, Finland, Germany, Grenada, Guatemala, Guyana, Honduras, Hungary, Iceland, Italy, Jamaica, Japan, Martinique, Mexico, Micronesia, Netherlands, Philippines, Norway, Panama, St. Christopher & Nevis, St. Lucia, St. Vincent & Grenadines, South Korea, Spain, Thailand, Trinidad & Tobago, Turkey, United Kingdom, and Wales.

7. Barry R. McCaffrey, "Remarks of Barry R. McCaffrey, Director, Office of National Drug Control Policy 13th Annual National D.A.R.E. Officers Association Dinner," July 7, 2000, in Office of National Drug Control Policy, "Drug Control Policy Speeches, 1996–2000" (Washington, D.C.: Executive Office of the President, 2000).

8. On the media and moral panic, see Jimmie L. Reeves and Richard Campbell, *Cracked Coverage: Television News, The Anti-Cocaine Crusade, and the Reagan Legacy* (Durham, N.C.: Duke University Press Books, 1994). On political attention, see David R. Farber, "Crackdown: The Politics and Laws of Drug Enforcement," in *Crack: Rock Cocaine, Street Capitalism, and the Decade of Greed* (New York: Cambridge University Press, 2019), 129–62. On moral panics more generally, see Stanley Cohen, *Folk Devils and Moral Panics* (New York: Routledge, 2011).

9. Donald R. Lynam et al., "Project DARE: No Effects at 10-Year Follow-Up," *Journal of Consulting and Clinical Psychology* 67, no. 4 (August 1999): 593. See also Earl Wysong, Richard Aniskiewicz, and David Wright, "Truth and DARE: Tracking Drug Education to Graduation and as Symbolic Politics," *Social Problems* 41, no. 3 (1994): 448–72.

10. Rick Aniskiewicz and Earl Wysong, "Evaluating DARE: Drug Education and the Multiple Meanings of Success," *Policy Studies Review* 9, no. 4 (Summer 1990): 741.

11. Rogers, "Diffusion and Re-Invention of Project D.A.R.E.," 157.

12. Daryl F. Gates and Harry Handler, "Substance Abuse Education for Los Angeles City Schools," June 14, 1983, box 4,205, folder 3, TBAP.

13. Daryl Gates to G. Albert Howenstein, Jr., June 7, 1984, City Council File No. 84–1431, box C-805, folder 84–1431, LACCF.

14. Los Angeles Police Department, "Drug Abuse Resistance Education Regional Training Center Criteria—Categorical Grant Progress Report," August 1, 1988, box C-2130, City Council File No. 88–1494, LACCF.

15. Daryl F. Gates to Mrs. Ronald Reagan, December 19, 1983, box 40929, folder 13, AAMI.

16. Daryl F. Gates to Admiral Daniel J. Murphy, April 4, 1984, box 108649, folder Bureau of Special Investigation 01–05 1984, AAMI.

17. Robert L. Vernon letter to Mrs. Ronald Reagan, September 18, 1984, box 40945, folder 26, AAMI; Robert L. Vernon letter to Honorable Edwin Meese III, September 20, 1984, box 40945, folder 26, AAMI; Robert L. Vernon letter to The Honorable George Bush, October 23, 1984, box 40945, folder 26, AAMI.

18. "DARE Promotion/Fund Raising Goals 1983/1984," 1983, box 40931, folder 20, AAMI.

19. Gates and Handler, "Substance Abuse Education for Los Angeles City Schools."

20. Rich Connell, "Los Angeles Police, Schools Move Drug War into Elementary Classrooms," *Los Angeles Times*, August 28, 1983, V1.

21. Joy Picus letter to Assistant Chief Robert L. Vernon, March 28, 1984, box 40945, folder 25, AAMI.

22. Councilman Hal Bernson, Chairman Police, Fire and Public Safety Committee to Los Angeles City Council, "Communication File No. 86–0620," September 5, 1986, box C-1346, City Council File No. 86–0620, LACCF. For examples of the ordinances approved by the City Council allowing police to affix DARE bumper stickers to their patrol cars, see documents in City Council File No. 85-0214-S2, LACCF. DARE bumper stickers continue to be affixed on LAPD and other Los Angeles city vehicles. If anyone visits the Los Angeles City Records Office at the Piper Technical Center, they will likely see faded DARE bumper stickers on a range of city vehicles.

23. Los Angeles City Council, "Motion," April 28, 1992, box D-237, City Council File No. 91-1503-S3, LACCF; Los Angeles City Council, "Resolution: Project D.A.R.E.," April 2, 1986, box C-1346, City Council File No. 86–0620, LACCF.

24. Daryl F. Gates, "LAPD's Project DARE Tells Youths to Resist Drugs," *School Safety*, Spring 1986, 26–27; Daryl F. Gates, "Project DARE—A Challenge to Arm Our Youth," *The Police Chief*, October 1987, 100–101; Daryl F. Gates, "A Partnership against Crime," *FBI Law Enforcement Bulletin*, August 1986, 6–9.

25. Daryl F. Gates, "Pertinent Matters of Interest in Police Affairs," April 22, 1985, box 3178, folder 4, TBAP.

26. Harold Johnson, "D.A.R.E. to Be Different," *Los Angeles Sentinel*, April 10, 1986, A3.

27. Daryl F. Gates, "Pertinent Matters of Interest in Police Affairs," April 22, 1985, box 3178, folder 4, TBAP.

28. Jim Brunner, "How DARE They? Cities Buck Trend of Support for Anti-Drug Program," *The Item*, October 3, 1996, 6A. On the DARE Lion, see the DARE website archives, DARE America, "D.A.R.E. Overview," 1999, accessed June 30, 2020, https://web.archive.org/web/20011107023418fw_/http://www.dare.com/D_EDUC/D_edu_Frame.htm (site archived). On the DARE Lion as a stuffed toy, see Sara to GDK, January 15, 1996, box 27, folder DARE-Sacred Heart School, Gerald D. Kleczka papers, 1969–2004, WHS.

29. "D.A.R.E. Vehicles," *Law and Order*, December 1991, 34. See also "Police Vehicle," *Law and Order*, July 1999, 30.

30. William Overend, "DARE Survives Early Doubts: L. A. Drug Effort Takes On International Dimensions," *Los Angeles Times*, May 30, 1989, 1–3.

31. Department of Justice, Bureau of Justice Assistance, "Drug Abuse Resistance Education Training and Technical Assistance—Grant Award," 1986, City Council File No. 86–1634, box C-1372, folder 86–1634, LACCF.

32. Assembly Bill No. 1983, Pub. L. No. 1983 (1983). See also CA Penal Code, Part 4, Prevention of Crimes and Apprehending Criminals, Title 6 California Council on Criminal Justice, Chapter 7 Suppression of Drug Abuse in Schools, accessed February 15, 2023, https://leginfo.legislature.ca.gov/faces/codes_displayText.xhtml?lawCode=PEN&division=&title=6.&part=4.&chapter=7.&article=.

33. Office of Criminal Justice Planning, State of California, *Suppression of Drug Abuse Schools Program: Program Guidelines* (Sacramento, Calif.: Office of Criminal Justice Planning, February 1984), box 116, folder 2, TBAP. For an example of the ways the LAPD and LAUSD used the funding the legislation provided to facilitate partnerships between schools and the police, see Chief Legislative Analyst to Grants, Housing and Community Development Committee, "Proposed Agreement between the City and the Evaluation and Training Institute (ETI) for Evaluation of the Drug Abuse Resistance Education (DARE) Program," February 2, 1985, 42–43, box C-805, City Council File No. 84–0566. See also Office of Criminal Justice Planning, State of California, *Suppression of Drug Abuse in Schools Program: Third Year Evaluation*, National Council on Crime and Delinquency (Sacramento, Calif.: State of California, Office of Criminal Justice Planning, 1988).

34. Overend, "DARE Survives Early Doubts."

35. State of California, Office of Criminal Justice Planning, *Suppression of Drug Abuse in Schools Program: Annual Report to the Legislature* (Sacramento, Calif.: May 1987), 9–10, box 104, folder Crime, Gang, Hearings, AHP.

36. Los Angeles Police Department and Los Angeles Unified School District, "Drug Abuse Resistance Education," Office of Criminal Justice Planning, Suppression of Drug Abuse in Schools Program, Grant Award, June 29, 1984, box 116, folder 1, TBAP. For a report on the distribution of grant funds, see Grants, Housing and

Community Development to the council of the City of Los Angeles, 2–3, box C-1154, City Council File No. 85–1757, LACCF. See also Daryl F. Gates to G. Albert Howenstein, Jr., June 7, 1984, box 116, folder 2, TBAP.

37. Pamela Moreland, "LAPD Schools Drug Education Program to Expand with $478,443 State Grant," *Los Angeles Times*, September 30, 1984, box 4,205, folder 3, TBAP; Harry Handler to Members, Board of Education, "Drug Abuse Resistance Education (DARE)," June 29, 1984, box 1,424, folder 5, LAUSD.

38. Sharon Greengold, "Teaching Kids to Turn Down Drugs: 'Operation DARE' Is at It Again," *Valley View*, October 3, 1984, 3A, box 116, folder 2, TBAP.

39. Commanding Officer, Juvenile Division to Commanding Officer, Bureau of Special Investigation, "1984/85 Recommended Strategy Change for the DARE Program," December 15, 1983, box 108649, folder DARE Drug Abuse Resistance Education Program, 1984, AAMI.

40. Los Angeles City Board of Education, "Report of Correspondence: Resolution Regarding the DARE Program," July 1985, box 1,424, folder 4, LAUSD. For the private school program, see Los Angeles Police Department and Archdiocese of Los Angeles Department of Schools, "Office of Criminal Justice Planning Project Summary," 1989, box C-2231, City Council File No. 89–0819, LACCF. For the high school program, see Los Angeles Police Department and Los Angeles Unified School District, "DARE High School," Office of Criminal Justice Planning, Project Summary, October 1, 1989, box 42, folder 7, TBAP.

41. Glenn F. Nyre, *An Evaluation of Project DARE* (Los Angeles: Evaluation and Training Institute, July 1984), box 116, folder 2, TBAP. For an example of a request for DARE information, see Glenn A. Levant to Alice Waller, November 22, 1988, box 6, folder 12, Series II, William Lee Robinson Papers, Richard B. Russell Library for Political Research and Studies, University of Georgia, Athens, Ga.

42. DARE, "Two-Week DARE Seminar Training Syllabus" [ca. 1986], box C-805, City Council File No. 84–1431, LACCF.

43. Harry Handler to Members, Board of Education, "Project DARE Final Evaluation Report, 1983–84," September 21, 1984, with attachment Glenn F. Nyre, *Project DARE Final Evaluation Report—1983–1984* (Los Angeles: Evaluation and Training Institute, 1984), box 1,424, folder 6, LAUSD.

44. "Outside Agencies Trained in DARE" [ca. 1986], box C-805, City Council File No. 84–1431, LACCF; Los Angeles Police Department and Los Angeles Unified School District, "Project Summary: Drug Abuse Resistance Education (DARE)," Office of Criminal Justice Planning, Grant Award [ca. 1985], 21, box C-1372, City Council File No. 86–1634, LACCF.

45. U.S. Congress, House of Representatives, Select Committee on Narcotics Abuse and Control, *Drug Abuse and Drug Trafficking along the Southwest Border (Tucson)*, 99th Cong., 2nd sess., January 14, 1986, 8–9. See also U.S. Congress, House of Representatives, Select Committee on Narcotics Abuse and Control, *Drug Trafficking and Abuse along the Southwest Border (El Paso)*, 99th Cong., 2nd sess., January 13, 1986; U.S. Congress, House of Representatives, Select Committee on Narcotics Abuse and Control, *Drug Abuse and Drug Trafficking along the Southwest Border (San Diego)*, 99th Cong., 2nd sess., January 16, 1986. For the same argument from the LAPD,

see Daryl F. Gates, "Project DARE—A Challenge to Arm Our Youth," *The Police Chief*, October 1987.

46. Mathea Falco, *The Making of a Drug-Free America: Programs That Work* (New York: Crown, 1992), 86.

47. Robert Reinhold, "Police, Hard Pressed in Drug War, Are Turning to Preventive Efforts," *New York Times*, December 28, 1989, A1.

48. When Las Vegas adopted the program, officials reflected on their reasoning, stating, "Traditional law enforcement efforts to control the distribution and sale of illicit drugs on school campuses are largely unsuccessful at this time. It was felt at the beginning of the project that a more hands-on approach between law enforcement and students was a better solution." Junior League of Las Vegas, "The 1988 President's Volunteer Action Awards Application," 1988, box 17, folder 1, JLLV.

49. As discussed, DARE officials provided training for programs in places such as Washington and Hawaii prior to Virginia. However, Virginia was one of the first places where entire school districts and systems adopted the program. For the "DARE Program Agreement Signing Ceremony," May 14, 1986, box 108641, folder 26, AAMI.

50. Virginia DARE, "Drug Abuse Resistance Education Project Virginia," 1985, box 19, folder DARE [Drug Abuse Resistance Education] (1), OA18765, Office of the First Lady, Projects Office, RRPL. See also B.S. Allsbrook letter to Barry Wade, May 30, 1986, box108641, folder 25, AAMI.

51. "DARE Regional Training Center Conference Minutes," January 29–31, 1989, 11–20, box C-2143, City Council File No. 88-1962-S2, LACCF.

52. B. S. Allsbrook to Frederick R. Colgan, "Project DARE," February 2, 1987, box 19, folder DARE [Drug Abuse Resistance Education] (1), OA18766, Office of the First Lady, Projects Office, RRPL. The Virginia DARE program became one of the examples the BJA reviewed before committing federal funding to the DARE program. See "Regional Training Center Advisory Committee Meeting Minutes," July 24, 1989, box C-2143, City Council File No. 88–1962, LACCF; Bureau of Justice Assistance, *Drug Abuse Resistance Education (DARE)—Fact Sheet*, Department of Justice, Office of Justice Programs, Bureau of Justice Assistance, NCJ FS000039 (Washington, D.C., September 1995).

53. Andy Furillo, "DARE: It's Working and in Trouble: Police Anti-Drug Project at Schools Praised but Council Is Cool," *Los Angeles Times*, April 28, 1985, B1.

54. *Crime File*, "Drug Education," directed by W. P. Fowler (the Police Foundation and National Institute of Justice, 1986), videocassette (VHS).

55. William DeJong, "Project DARE: Teaching Kids to Say 'No' to Drugs and Alcohol," U.S. Department of Justice, National Institute of Justice, *NIJ Reports*, March 1986, 2–5; William DeJong, *Arresting the Demand for Drugs: Police and School Partnership to Prevent Drug Abuse*, Department of Justice, National Institute of Justice, Office of Communication and Research Utilization, NCJ 105199 (Washington, D.C., November 1987); William DeJong, "A Short-Term Evaluation of Project Dare (Drug Abuse Resistance Education): Preliminary Indications of Effectiveness," *Journal of Drug Education* 17, no. 4 (December 1, 1987): 279–94.

56. William DeJong, interview by Max Felker-Kantor, January 14, 2021.

57. U.S. Congress, Senate, Committee on Labor and Human Resources, *Drug Abuse: Prevention, Education, and Treatment*, 100th Cong., 2nd sess., June 16, 1988, 198. See also Grants, Housing and Community Development Committee, "Report to the Council of the City of Los Angeles," September 8, 1987, box C-1372, City Council File No. 86-1634-S1, LACCF.

58. The seven recipients selected by the Bureau of Justice Assistance to participate in the DARE-TAP program were City of Portland, Maine Police Department; Phoenix, Arizona Department of Public Safety; Springfield, Illinois Department of State Police; Syracuse, New York Police Department; City of Huntsville, Alabama Police Department; Commonwealth of Massachusetts, MA Committee on Criminal Justice; Boston, Massachusetts Public Schools. City of Los Angeles Police Department, *Drug Abuse Resistance Education Training and Technical Assistance Categorical Grant Progress Report*, U.S. Department of Justice, Office of Justice Assistance, Research, and Statistics, July 16, 1987, box C-1372, City Council File No. 86-1634-S1, LACCF.

59. City Clerk to Grants, Housing and Community Development Committee, "Proposed Grant Application for the Drug Abuse Resistance Education and Training and Technical Assistance Program (DARE-TAP)," September 2, 1986, 1–4, box C-1372, City Council File No. 86–1634, LACCF.

60. City of Los Angeles Police Department, *Drug Abuse Resistance Education Training and Technical Assistance Categorical Grant Progress Report*, U.S. Department of Justice, Office of Justice Assistance, Research, and Statistics, October 28, 1987, 8–9, box C-1372, City Council File No. 86–1634, LACCF.

61. Grants, Housing and Community Development Committee to the Council of the City of Los Angeles, *Report*, March 24, 1987, 71, box C-1372, City Council File No. 86–1634, LACCF.

62. Rose Matsui Ochi to Mayor Tom Bradley, "Transmittal of: Grant Award for the City of Los Angeles Drug Abuse Resistance Education (DARE) Training and Technical Assistance Program," October 30, 1986, 103, box C-1372, City Council File No. 86–1634, LACCF.

63. DARE Training Center Policy Advisory Board, *Drug Abuse Resistance Education (DARE) Training Center Policies and Procedures*, Department of Justice, Office of Justice Programs, Bureau of Justice Assistance, NCJ 129395 (Washington, D.C., October 1991), i–iii. For information on the training to become a DARE mentor and trainer see Bureau of Justice Assistance, *The DARE Regional Training Center Policy Board's Manual for Training Law Enforcement Officers in the DARE Program*, Department of Justice, Office of Justice Programs, Bureau of Justice Assistance, NCJ 129758 (Washington, D.C., October 1991). For an example of state-level training and regional training centers, see Massachusetts Executive Office of Public Safety, *Summer D.A.R.E. Program Training Manual*, 1996, accessed February 17, 2023, http://archive.org/details/daresummerdaycamoomass; DARE Midwest Regional Training Center, *Missouri and Midwest Regional Training Center* (2003); Florida DARE Training Center, *Drug Abuse Resistance Education Annual Report FY 06–07* (Florida Department of Law Enforcement, January 2008). My understanding of the RTCs came from the research conducted by my graduate assistant, Will Connolly. For a reflection on the importance of the RTCs, see Nick DeMauro and John Lindsay, interview by Max Felker-Kantor, December 21,

2020; Nick DeMauro and Glenn Levant, interview by Max Felker-Kantor, January 14, 2021.

64. DARE Regional Training Center Advisory Committee, "Accreditation of DARE Training Centers," Spring 1989, box C-2143, City Council File No. 88–1962, LACCF.

65. Wulf, *Executive Summary*.

66. Bureau of Justice Assistance, *Edward Byrne Memorial State and Local Law Enforcement Assistance Program: FY 1990 Discretionary Program Announcement*, U.S. Department of Justice, Office of Justice Programs, NCJRS 123015 (Washington, D.C., March 1990); Bureau of Justice Assistance, *Edward Byrne Memorial State and Local Law Enforcement Assistance Program: FY 1996 Discretionary Program Plan*, U.S. Department of Justice, Office of Justice Programs, SL153 (Washington, D.C., May 1996); Bureau of Justice Assistance, *Program Brief: Edward Byrne Memorial State and Local Law Enforcement Assistance Program: Fiscal Year 2002*, U.S. Department of Justice, Office of Justice Programs (Washington, D.C., August 2002).

67. Los Angeles Police Department, DARE Western Regional Training Center, "D.A.R.E.—Western Regional Training Center," Bureau of Justice Assistance/D.A.R.E. America, Grant Application, 1996, box 729604, folder Fund 477 96–97 DARE RTC, Mayor Antonio R. Villaraigosa Files, Los Angeles City Archives, Los Angeles; Los Angeles Police Department, DARE Western Regional Training Center, "D.A.R.E.—Western Regional Training Center," Bureau of Justice Assistance/D.A.R.E. America Grant Application, 1997, box 729604, folder Fund 477 10th yr, DARE RTC, Mayor Antonio R. Villaraigosa Files, Los Angeles City Archives, Los Angeles. Other material related to the DARE RTC is available in City Council File No. 98–1086, LACCF.

68. DARE, "Drug Abuse Resistance Education Regional Training Centers Policy and Procedures," March 13, 1989, 32–38, box C-2143, City Council File No. 88-1962-S2, LACCF. See also DARE Regional Training Center Commission, "Accreditation of DARE Training Centers: Criteria and Requirements for Self-Study," Spring 1989, 39–63, box C-2143, City Council File No. 88-1962-S2, LACCF.

69. Rogers, "Diffusion and Re-Invention of Project D.A.R.E.," 150–51.

70. Los Angeles Police Department, DARE Western Regional Training Center, "D.A.R.E.—Western Regional Training Center," Bureau of Justice Assistance/D.A.R.E. America Grant Award, July 26, 1995, box 35, folder 15, Series 5 Mayoral Programs, Mayor Richard J. Riordan Administrative Papers, CSLA-17, Department of Archives and Special Collections, William H. Hannon Library, Loyola Marymount University, Los Angeles.

71. "R.T.C. Statistics," 1989, box C-2143, City Council File 88–1962, LACCF.

72. Jim Newton, "DARE Marks a Decade of Growth and Controversy: Youth: Despite Critics, Anti-Drug Program Expands Nationally. But Some See Declining Support in LAPD," *Los Angeles Times*, September 9, 1993, WB1; Department of Justice, Office of Justice Programs, Bureau of Justice Assistance, *An Introduction to DARE: Drug Abuse Resistance Education*, U.S. Department of Justice, Office of Justice Programs, Bureau of Justice Assistance, NCJ 129862 (Washington, D.C., October 1991).

73. Bureau of Justice Assistance, *Drug Abuse Resistance Education (DARE)–Fact Sheet*, 4.

74. Rogers, "Diffusion and Re-Invention of Project D.A.R.E.," 139.

75. Paul Gordon, "The Truth about DARE," *Buzz: The Talk of Los Angeles*, September 1995, 72–77, 115. The 70 percent figure comes from a number of reports; see Dennis P. Rosenbaum and Gordon S. Hanson, "Assessing the Effects of School-Based Drug Education: A Six-Year Multilevel Analysis of Project D.A.R.E.," *Journal of Research in Crime and Delinquency* 35, no. 4 (November 1, 1998): 381–412; DARE America, *DARE America Form 990—Return of Organization Exempt from Income Tax*, 2001, accessed May 15, 2020, https://projects.propublica.org/nonprofits/organizations/954242541. See supra note 5 for a discussion of DARE student data.

76. Everett M. Rogers, "Diffusion of Drug Abuse Prevention Programs: Spontaneous Diffusion, Agenda Setting, and Reinvention," in *Reviewing the Behavioral Science Knowledge Base on Technology Transfer. NIDA Research Monograph 155*, ed. Thomas E. Backer, Susan L. David, and Gerald Saucy, vol. 155 (Rockville, Md.: National Institute on Drug Abuse, 1995), 90–105.

77. Augustus Hawkins, "Augustus Hawkins Statements on the Omnibus Drug Abuse Act of 1986," 1986, box 120, folder Memoranda, 1987 [1], Augustus F. Hawkins Papers. See also U.S. Congress, House of Representatives, Committee on Education and Labor, *Drug Abuse Resistance Education Act of 1986: Report Together with Additional Views (to Accompany H.R. 5378)*, 99th Cong., 2nd sess., September 9, 1986, 2.

78. Farber, *Crack*, 134–36.

79. U.S. Congress, House of Representatives, Select Committee on Narcotics Abuse and Control, *Drug Abuse Education*, 99th Cong., 2nd sess., May 20, 1986, 1.

80. U.S. Congress, House of Representatives, Committee on Education and Labor, *Hearing on Drug Abuse Prevention and Education*, 99th Cong., 2nd sess., August 6, 1986, 10.

81. *Hearing on Drug Abuse Prevention and Education*, 89.

82. Crime Control Act of 1990, Pub. L. No. 101–647, 104 Stat. 4790 (1990). For an overview of the political support for DARE, see Earl Wysong and David W. Wright, "A Decade of DARE: Efficacy, Politics and Drug Education," *Sociological Focus* 28, no. 3 (1995): 283–311.

83. Budget numbers from The White House, National Drug Control Strategy: A Nation Responds to Drug Use (Washington, D.C.: The White House, January 1992); The White House, National Drug Control Strategy: Progress in the War on Drugs, 1989–1992 (Washington, D.C.: The White House, January 1993).

84. Susan T. Ennett et al., "How Effective Is Drug Abuse Resistance Education? A Meta-Analysis of Project DARE Outcome Evaluations," *American Journal of Public Health* 84, no. 9 (September 1994): 1394–401.

85. Drug-Free Schools and Communities Act Amendments of 1989, Pub. L. No. 101–226, 103 Stat. 1928 (1989).

86. "Wilson Backs Drug Campaign," *The Signal*, October 12, 1989, 6, Newspapers.com.

87. U.S. Congress, House of Representatives, Subcommittee on Elementary, Secondary, and Vocational Education, Committee on Education and Labor, *Oversight Hearing on Drug Abuse Education Programs*, 101st Cong., 2nd sess., September 6, 1990, 7, 1, 3, 5. See also U.S. Congress, House of Representatives, Committee on Education and Labor, *Drug Abuse Resistance Education Act of 1990: Report Together with Additional Views (to Accompany H.R. 5064)*, 101st Cong., 2nd sess., July 6, 1990.

88. Crime Control Act of 1990, Pub. L. No. 101 647, 104 Stat. 4790 (1990).

89. Zell Miller to Lee Robinson, June 24, 1971, box 6, folder 12, Series II, William Lee Robinson Papers, Richard B. Russell Library for Political Research and Studies, University of Georgia, Athens, Ga.

90. J. R. Berggren, Jr. to Tommy F. Thompson, July 7, 1994, box 38, folder DPI—DARE Program, Wisconsin. Governor (1987–2001: Thompson): Constituent Correspondence Dealing with the Budget and Specific Subjects, Part 1 (1999/126): Original Collection, 1987–1995, WHS. Parents also urged the governor to support DARE. Dolores Radtke to Tommy F. Thompson, July 7, 1994, box 38, folder DPI—DARE Program, Wisconsin. Governor (1987–2001: Thompson): Constituent Correspondence Dealing with the Budget and Specific Subjects, Part 1 (1999/126): Original Collection, 1987–1995, WHS.

91. Crime Control Act of 1990.

92. "D.A.R.E.—Program Growth Nationwide," *D.A.R.E. Idaho*, January 1996, L3000.93, ISA.

93. "House Keeps Govs. in School Drug-Fund Loop," *Alcoholism & Drug Abuse Weekly* 6, no. 11 (March 14, 1994): 1–2.

94. Wysong and Wright, "A Decade of Dare," 283–311.

95. Improving America's Schools Act of 1994, Pub. L. No. 103–761 (1994). For an overview of the legislative changes, see E. Suyapa Silvia and Judy Thorne, *School-Based Drug Prevention Programs: A Longitudinal Study in Selected School Districts. Final Report* (Washington, D.C.: U.S. Department of Education, Planning and Evaluation Service, 1997).

96. Improving America's Schools Act of 1994.

97. The White House, *National Drug Control Strategy*, 163.

98. Silvia and Thorne, *School-Based Drug Prevention Programs*, 4–30.

99. On asset stripping see Clyde Woods, "Les Misérables of New Orleans: Trap Economics and the Asset Stripping Blues, Part 1," *American Quarterly* 61, no. 3 (2009): 769–96. On racial disparity and asset forfeiture and seizure see Michael D. Makowsky, Thomas Stratmann, and Alex Tabarrok, "To Serve and Collect: The Fiscal and Racial Determinants of Law Enforcement," *Journal of Legal Studies* 48, no. 1 (January 2019): 189–216; Kelsey Shoub et al., "Fines, Fees, Forfeitures, and Disparities: A Link Between Municipal Reliance on Fines and Racial Disparities in Policing," *Policy Studies Journal* 49, no. 3 (2021): 835–59.

100. Daryl F. Gates to Senator Edward M. Davis, April 16, 1984, box 40945, folder 25, AAMI.

101. U.S. General Accounting Office, *Asset Forfeiture: Improved Guidance for Use of Shared Assets* (Washington, D.C., December 1993).

102. Lt. Roger Coombs, City of LA Police Department, "Grant Manager's Memorandum, Pt. 1: Project Summary: Drug Abuse Resistance Regional Educational Training Centers," September 15, 1988, 361, box C-2143, City Council File No. 88–1962, LACCF.

103. "Police Bemoan Loss of D.A.R.E.," *Idaho Cops for Kids*, vol. 2, September 2004, L3000.90, ISA.

104. For the first National DARE Day proclamation, see Ronald Reagan, "National DARE Day, 1988," 1988, box 66, file National D.A.R.E. Day, 1988, Anne Higgins Files, Series V, RRPL.

105. Nathan Shapell to Ronald Reagan, "591937," September 6, 1988, box 41, folder HE006-01 (591661–592699), WHORM: Subject File, HE006-01, RRPL. For an example of a state-level DARE Day, see Mario M. Cuomo, "DARE Day," September 14, 1989, box 45, folder 13, accretion 19147–95, NYSA.

106. Garry Abrams, "Pupils Polish an Apple for the First Lady," *Los Angeles Times*, February 11, 1987, F1.

107. DARE America, "Reagan Named Honorary D.A.R.E. Graduate Following Signing of Omnibus Anti-Substance Abuse Act," press release, ca. 1988, box OA18771, folder DARE to Keep Kids off Drugs [Information Kit], Office of the First Lady, Press Office, RRPL; Ronald Reagan, Proclamation 5854—National D.A.R.E. Day, 1988, September 8, 1988, APP, accessed January 18, 2023, www.presidency.ucsb.edu/node/253938. Every president through Barack Obama named a day in September National DARE Day. See Barack Obama, "Presidential Proclamation–National D.A.R.E. Day," April 8, 2010, https://obamawhitehouse.archives.gov/the-press-office/presidential-proclamation-national-dare-day.

108. Mel Levine, "National Drug Abuse Resistance Education Day," *Congressional Record*, March 29, 1990, v. 136 no. 36, E895. See also Mel Levine, "National Drug Abuse Resistance Education Day," *Congressional Record Daily Edition*, April 14, 1988, v. 134, E1065, 6997.

109. "$50 Million Increase for D.A.R.E. Proposed," *Alcoholism & Drug Abuse Weekly* 4, no. 24 (June 10, 1992): 7.

110. DARE America, *DARE Honors Greg Penske* (Los Angeles: April 20, 1993), box 148, folder 681, RLA.

111. "Nancy Reagan Comes to Muir Junior High," *Los Angeles Sentinel*, October 12, 1989, B9; "Photo Standalone 22—Ways to Say No," *Los Angeles Sentinel*, July 6, 1989, B9; Scott Harris, "Students Let Out a Cheer Fit for Royalty: Union Avenue: Princess Alexandra of Great Britain Visits the Downtown Elementary School to Learn about the DARE Drug Program," *Los Angeles Times*, October 17, 1990, B1; "Visit of Her Royal Highness Princess Alexandra Union Elementary," October 16, 1990, box 329, folder 2, TBAP; "News Advisory: Drug Czar Bennett to Address D.A.R.E. Class," *PR Newswire*, June 6, 1989, folder Drug Abuse Resistance Education (DARE) Reception, 9/13/89, OA 13684, Chron File, 1989–1993, Speech File Backup Files, White House Office of Speechwriting, GBPL.

112. Rogers, "Diffusion and Re-Invention of Project D.A.R.E.," 139–62.

113. "Bush: 'No' to Drugs; 'Yes' to Opening Up Teaching—Education Week," *Education Week*, March 29, 1989, accessed June 4, 2019, www.edweek.org/ew/articles/1989/03/29/08230038.h08.html.

114. George H. W. Bush, "National D.A.R.E. Day, 1989—A Proclamation," September 13, 1989, folder National D.A.R.E. Day 1989 0/13/1989, OA 31444, Presidential Proclamation Files, Susan Griffith Files, White House Office of Correspondence, GBPL.

115. Chris Smith to Chriss Winston, "September 13, D.A.R.E. Remarks," September 12, 1989, folder DARE Ceremony, 9/13/89, OA 13502, Chron File, 1989–1993, Speech File Draft Files, White House Office of Speechwriting, GBPL.

116. George H. W. Bush, "Remarks by the President during Signing Ceremony for Drug Abuse Resistance Education Day Proclamation," September 13, 1989, folder DARE Ceremony, 9/13/89, OA 13502, Chron File, 1989–1993, Speech File Draft Files, White House Office of Speechwriting, GBPL.

117. See correspondence in OA 08683, folder DARE, Shiree Sanchez Files, White House Office of Public Liaison, GBPL; "DARE Teacher Telegrams," 1989, folder DARE, OA 08683-003, Shiree Sanchez Files, White House Office of Public Liaison, GBPL.

118. Andy Wolfford, "Bells Ring to Reaffirm Commitment to Anti-Drug Program," *The Advocate-Messenger*, September 15, 1989, 1, Newspapers.com. Local DARE programs routinely developed their own programming surrounding National DARE Day. See discussions of DARE Day activities in Las Vegas in Project D.A.R.E., "Project D.A.R.E. Minutes of Special Meeting," August 18, 1988, box 17, folder 2, JLLV; Project D.A.R.E., "Project D.A.R.E. Minutes of Regular Meeting," October 19, 1988, box 17, folder 2, JLLV.

119. Boyle, "A DAREing Rescue," 16.

120. Office of National Drug Control Policy, *National Drug Control Strategy: 1998* (Washington, D.C.: Office of National Drug Control Policy, Executive Office of the President, 1998); The White House, *National Drug Control Strategy* (Washington, D.C.: The White House, February 1995).

121. Earl Wysong, Richard Aniskiewicz, and David Wright, "Truth and DARE: Tracking Drug Education to Graduation and as Symbolic Politics," *Social Problems* 41, no. 3 (1994): 448–72.

122. "In Support of DARE Day," *Congressional Record Daily Edition*, May 9, 1989, v. 135, S 5059; "In Recognition of National DARE Day," *Congressional Record Daily Edition*, September 13, 1990, v. 136, H 7509; "National DARE Day," *Congressional Record Daily Edition*, September 10, 1992, v. 138, S 13298; "Honoring the DARE Program," *Congressional Record Daily Edition*, April 21, 1994, v. 140 Cong Rec S 4598.

123. Mike Sullivan, "Meeting the Challenge of Drug Free Schools: Remarks of Governor Mike Sullivan, Wyoming D.A.R.E. Officers Association Conference," Pinedale, Wyoming, April 6, 1990, box 9, folder 8, Michael J. Sullivan Papers, Collection #10348, American Heritage Center, University of Wyoming.

124. George H. W. Bush to Daryl Gates, 1989, Daryl Gates Alphabetical File, White House Office of Records Management (WHORM), GBPL.

125. Bush had similar words of praise for Glenn Levant when he retired from the LAPD and went to work for DARE America full time. See George H. W. Bush to Glenn Levant, October 19, 1992, Glenn Levant Alphabetical File, White House Office of Records Management (WHORM), GBPL.

126. Patrick Boyle, "A DAREing Rescue," *Youth Today*, April 2001, 1, 16–19.

127. "DARE: Selecting the Right Officer," *FBI Law Enforcement Bulletin*, May 1990, 11–12.

128. Richard R. Clayton et al., "DARE (Drug Abuse Resistance Education): Very Popular but Not Very Effective," in *Intervening with Drug-Involved Youth* (Thousand Oaks, Calif: SAGE Publications, 1996), 101–9.

Chapter Four

1. DARE America, *DARE Honors Greg Penske* (Los Angeles: April 20, 1993), box 148, folder 681, RLA.

2. Daryl F. Gates, "A Partnership against Crime," *FBI Law Enforcement Bulletin*, August 1986, 6–9.

3. On public-private partnerships, see Lily Geismer, *Left Behind: The Democrats' Failed Attempt to Solve Inequality* (New York: Public Affairs, 2022).

4. Michael Massing, *The Fix* (New York: Simon & Schuster, 1998), 161–62; David F. Musto, *The American Disease: Origins of Narcotic Control*, 3rd ed. (New York: Oxford University Press, 1999), 267; Arnold S. Trebach, *The Great Drug War, and Radical Proposals That Could Make America Safe Again* (New York: Macmillan, 1987), 170–78.

5. Joel Brinkley, "Fighting Narcotics Is Everyone's Issue Now," *New York Times*, August 10, 1986. On the early federal strategy, see Drug Abuse Policy Office, Office of Policy Development, The White House, *Federal Strategy for Prevention of Drug Abuse and Drug Trafficking 1982* (Washington, D.C., 1982).

6. Ronald Reagan, "The President's News Conference," March 6, 1981, APP, accessed January 18, 2023, www.presidency.ucsb.edu/node/247096; Drug Abuse Policy Office, "The Reagan Administration Five-Point Plan to Prevent and Control Drug Abuse in the United States," March 31, 1982, box 24, folder Drug Abuse Policy Reference 1981–1982, OA 16998, Richard Williams Files, RRPL. On law-and-order rhetoric and the rise of the New Right, see Katherine Beckett, *Making Crime Pay: Law and Order in Contemporary American Politics* (New York: Oxford University Press, 1997).

7. Carlton E. Turner to Herbert Ellingwood and Edwin J. Gray, "Points for Presidential Speech on Crime, Drugs, Etc.," September 17, 1981, box 23, folder Drug Police Documents (5 of 8), Carlton E. Turner Files, RRPL; Turner praised the Parent Movement, for example, precisely because it did not use federal resources: "Significantly, the Parent Movement has grown with little financial support from the government." Drug Abuse Policy Office, Office of Police Development, The White House, *Federal Strategy for Prevention of Drug Abuse and Drug Trafficking 1982* (Washington, D.C., 1982), 3. Turner believed that the government should reduce its role in drug treatment and education and that the private sector should fill in on the demand side; Massing, *The Fix*, 153–54.

8. U.S. Congress, House of Representatives, Select Committee on Narcotics Abuse and Control, *Drug Abuse Prevention in America's Schools*, 100th Cong., 1st sess., June 9, 1987, 14–15; U.S. Congress, House of Representatives, Select Committee on Narcotics Abuse and Control, *Oversight of the Anti-Drug Abuse Act of 1986 and the Federal Drug Strategy*, 100th Cong., 1st sess., December 8, 1987, 20–21; U.S. Congress, House of Representatives, Select Committee on Narcotics Abuse and Control, *Implementation of Provisions of the Anti-Drug Abuse Act of 1986: Report*, 100th Cong., 1st sess., 1988, 6; Elaine Woo, "Public School Programs: Fighting Drugs: The Big Question Is How to Do It," *Los Angeles Times*, January 19, 1987, V1; Bud Newman, "The $2.9 Billion Anti-Drug Abuse Act," *UPI*, January 8, 1987, UPI Archives, https://www.upi.com/Archives/1987/01/08/The-29-billion-Anti-Drug-Abuse-Act-that-President

-Reagan/3078537080400/; David F. Musto, "Historical Perspectives," in *Substance Abuse: A Comprehensive Textbook*, ed. Joyce H. Lowinson et al. (Philadelphia, Pa.: Wolters Kluwer Health, 2004), 12.

9. "Project DARE Development Strategy," 1984, box 108649, folder DARE Drug Abuse Resistance Education Program 1984, AAMI. See also "DARE Promotion/Fund Raising Goals 1983/1984," 1983, box 40931, folder 20, AAMI.

10. Robert L. Vernon to Donald W. Crocker, March 16, 1984, box 108649, folder DARE Drug Abuse Resistance Education Program 1984, AAMI.

11. Raymond Ziegler to Robert L. Vernon, May 16, 1984, box 108649, folder DARE Drug Abuse Resistance Education Program 1984, AAMI.

12. Los Angeles Police Department, *1985–1986 Annual Report* (Los Angeles, 1986), 11, box 30, folder 5, Los Angeles Webster Commission Records, Collection no. 0244, Regional History Collections, Special Collections, University of Southern California Libraries, Los Angeles, CA.

13. Los Angeles Police Department, Bureau of Special Investigation, "News Release: New LAPD Advertising Campaign for DARE," April 3, 1086, box 108641, folder 26, AAMI.

14. Peter O'Malley to Lt. Pat Froehle, September 27, 1984, box 108649, folder DARE Drug Abuse Resistance Education Program 1984, AAMI; Jack R. Sheridan to Chief Daryl F. Gates, February 24, 1988, box 3259, folder Projects Match 1988, AAMI; Steven M. Ramsey to Lt. Roger Coombs, January 16, 1986, box 108641, folder 26, AAMI; Margaret A. Merrett to Lt. Roger Coombs, November 15, 1985, box 108641, folder 26.

15. Daryl F. Gates to Robert Baker, Xerox Corporation, November 21, 1984, box 108649, folder DARE Drug Abuse Resistance Education Program 1984, AAMI.

16. "Locals Give Gates $50,000 for DARE," *Los Angeles Sentinel*, August 18, 1988. For other examples of local donations, see "LAPD Gets $500,000 Grant for School Anti-Drug Program," *Los Angeles Times*, June 28, 1985, B6; "Grant Money to Buy Anti-Drug School Aids," *Los Angeles Times*, July 25, 1985, oc_a5. Nancy Reagan also supported the program using her Nancy Reagan Foundation to provide a $50,000 grant; "Nancy Reagan Comes to Muir Junior High," *Los Angeles Sentinel*, October 12, 1989, B9. For discussions about accepting private donations, see Keith Comrie to Tom Bradley, "Request from the Police Department for Acceptance of Funds Donated to the City for the Drug Abuse Resistance Education (DARE) Program," June 24, 1986, box 2,805, folder 1, TBAP; Chief of Police to Honorable Board of Police Commissioners, "Proposed Resolution to Accept Funds Donated to the City of Los Angeles," May 19, 1986, box 2,805, folder 1, TBAP. Gates wrote to Senator Edward Kennedy about how DARE met its cost through private funding and the business community's support; U.S. Congress, Senate, Committee on Labor and Human Resources, *Drug Abuse: Prevention, Education, and Treatment*, 100th Cong., 2nd sess., June 16, 1988, 198. Other local organizations also gave funds to DARE, including the Rotary Club of Los Angeles, which donated $100,000 in 1989; Mary Lou Loper, "On View," *Los Angeles Times*, June 18, 1989, folder Drug Abuse Resistance Education (DARE) Reception, 9/13/89, OA 13684, Chron File, 1989–1993, Speech File Backup Files, White House Office of Speechwriting, GBPL.

17. Tom Bradley to the Board of Police Commissioners, June 12, 1984, box 108649, folder DARE Drug Abuse Resistance Education Program 1984, AAMI.

18. Daryl Gates to Lew R. Wasserman, October 11, 1984, box 108649, folder DARE Drug Abuse Resistance Education Program 1984, AAMI; Daryl F. Gates to Robert J. Clark, Northrop Corporation, December 4, 1984, box 108649, folder DARE Drug Abuse Resistance Education Program 1984, AAMI.

19. Gates, "A Partnership against Crime," 6–9.

20. Crime Prevention Advisory Council, "By-Laws," box C-1712, City Council File No. 87–1127 (Part 1 of 2), LACCF.

21. Tom Bradley to the Council, "Donation to DARE," March 19, 1986, box 2,805, folder 4, TBAP.

22. Junior League of Las Vegas, "Contract between Las Vegas Metropolitan Police Department and Junior League of Las Vegas, Clark County School District, Las Vegas, Nevada" [ca. 1986], box 17, folder 1, JLLV; Clark County School District, "Coalition Guidelines Project D.A.R.E. (Drug Abuse Resistance Education)," 1986, box 17, folder 1, JLLV; Junior League of Las Vegas, "DARE Info Sheet" [ca. 1986], box 17, folder 1, JLLV.

23. Las Vegas Metropolitan Police Department, Clark County School District, and Junior League of Las Vegas, "Agreement: Project D.A.R.E.," 1986, box 17, folder 1, JLLV; Clark County School District, "1989–1990 Budget" (1989), box 17, folder 1, JLLV.

24. DARE Inc., "Articles of Incorporation of D.A.R.E. Inc." [ca. 1986], box 17, folder 1, JLLV; DARE Inc., "Bylaws of D.A.R.E. Inc." [ca. 1986], box 17, folder 1, JLLV.

25. Junior League of Las Vegas, "Committee Planning and Evaluation: Drug Abuse Resistance Education (DARE)" [ca. 1989], box 17, folder 2, JLLV; "DARE to Hold Fundraiser at EXPO," *Henderson Home News*, October 1989, box 17, folder 1, JLLV. For more information on DARE and the role of the JLLV in raising funds and developing political support from state legislators, see Project D.A.R.E., "Project D.A.R.E. Minutes of Regular Meeting," April 10, 1989, box 17, folder 2, JLLV; Project D.A.R.E., "Project D.A.R.E. Minutes of Regular Meeting," January 30, 1989, box 17, folder 2, JLLV.

26. "Local Businessman Sponsors WH&B Golf Tournament," *Las Vegas Review-Journal*, October 4, 1989, box 17, folder 1, JLLV. Individuals often donated cash directly to DARE. See Adele Koot and Terri Patton to Diane & Danny Shaw, May 16, 1989, box 17, folder 2, JLLV.

27. U.S. Congress, House of Representatives, Committee on Education and Labor, *Hearing on Drug Abuse Prevention and Education*, 99th Cong., 2nd sess., August 6, 1986, 86.

28. On the Reagan era and governance, see Gil Troy, *Morning in America: How Ronald Reagan Invented the 1980s* (Princeton, N.J.: Princeton University Press, 2005).

29. Center for Court Innovation, *Lessons from the Battle over D.A.R.E.: The Complicated Relationship between Research and Practice*, Bureau of Justice Assistance, Office of Justice Programs, U.S. Department of Justice (Washington, D.C., 2009), 2–3. On DARE America's tax exempt status, see State of California, Franchise Tax Board to DARE America, December 26, 1990, box 148, folder 681, RLA. See also Frank Pegueros, interview by Max Felker-Kantor, July 25, 2019.

30. DARE America, *DARE Honors Greg Penske*; DARE America, *DARE to Make Your Dreams Come True—Auction Book* (Los Angeles: April 20, 1993), box 148, folder 682, RLA.

31. U.S. Congress, Senate, Committee on Labor and Human Resources, *Drug Abuse: Prevention, Education, and Treatment*, 100th Cong., 2nd sess., June 16, 1988, 193.

32. DARE America, "D.A.R.E. Will Teach 3 Million Children Drug Resistance Skills in 1989."

33. "Group Organized to Promote DARE," *Law and Order*, December 1987, 24.

34. DARE America, "DARE: Teaching Kids to Never Take Drugs," pamphlet, ca. 1993, box 148, folder 681, RLA.

35. Officer-in-Charge to Commanding Officer, Bureau of Special Investigation, "'DARE America' Budget," March 25, 1987, box 3247, folder Department Drug, Abuse, Prevention, Program, AAMI.

36. Glenn A. Levant, *Keeping Kids Drug Free: D.A.R.E. Official Parent's Guide*, First Edition (San Diego, Calif.: Laurel Glen, 1998), x.

37. DARE America, "D.A.R.E. Will Teach 1.5 Million Children Drug Resistance Skills in 1988," press release, ca. 1988, box OA18771, folder DARE to Keep Kids off Drugs [Information Kit], Office of the First Lady, Press Office, RRPL.

38. Levant, *Keeping Kids Drug Free*, x.

39. "DARE Regional Training Center Conference Minutes," January 29–31, 1989, 11–20, box C-2143, City Council File No. 88-1962-S2, LACCF.

40. DARE America, "DARE America Conference," brochure, 1988, 8, box C-1712, City Council File No. 87–1127 (Part 1 of 2), LACCF.

41. "DARE Regional Training Center Conference Minutes."

42. Christopher L. Ringwalt et al., "Past and Future Directions of the D.A.R.E.® Program: An Evaluation Review Draft Final Report" (Research Triangle Institute, September 1994).

43. "DARE Opens D.C. Office: Seeks to Be Prevention 'Partner,'" *Alcoholism & Drug Abuse Weekly* 6, no. 5 (January 31, 1994), 4.

44. DARE America, *DARE America Form 990—Return of Organization Exempt from Income Tax*, 2008, accessed May 15, 2020, https://projects.propublica.org/nonprofits/organizations/954242541.

45. Loeb & Troper, *DARE America Financial Statements and Auditors Reports* (New York: December 31, 2000), box 729604, folder Fund 477 DARE RTC 12th Year, Mayor Antonio R. Villaraigosa Files, Los Angeles City Archives, Los Angeles.

46. DARE America, "DARE Bumper Sticker," 1993, box 148, folder 681, RLA.

47. "News: Mattel Toy Modeled after DARE Van," *Law and Order*, September 2000, 6.

48. Kate Zernike, "Antidrug Program Says It Will Adopt a New Strategy," *New York Times*, February 15, 2001, A1; Everett M. Rogers, "Diffusion and Re-Invention of Project D.A.R.E.," in *Organizational Aspects of Health Communication Campaigns: What Works?*, ed. Thomas E. Backer and Everett M. Rogers (Newbury Park, Calif.: SAGE Publications, 1993), 139–62.

49. Loeb & Troper, *DARE America Financial Statements and Auditors Reports*.

50. Paul Gordon, "The Truth about DARE," *Buzz: The Talk of Los Angeles*, September 1995, 72–77, 115.

51. Bureau of Justice Assistance, *Implementing Project DARE: Drug Abuse Resistance Education*, Department of Justice, Office of Justice Programs, Bureau of Justice Assistance, NCJ 115417 (Washington, D.C., June 1988), 1.

52. DARE America, "Publication Information," *DareLine International*, no. 6, 1998, box 26, folder 16, accretion 19147–06, NYSA.

53. DARE Unit pamphlet in *Hearing on Drug Abuse Prevention and Education*, 133.

54. DARE America, "DARE: Teaching Kids to Never Take Drugs," pamphlet, RLA; DARE, *Drugs Are Everyone's Problem*, pamphlet, 1985, box 19, folder DARE [Drug Abuse Resistance Education] (1), OA18765, Office of the First Lady, Projects Office, RRPL.

55. Emily Dufton, *Grass Roots: The Rise and Fall and Rise of Marijuana in America* (New York: Basic Books, 2017), 168.

56. "Security Pacific Donates $1 Million to DARE," *Los Angeles Times*, December 19, 1989. On Idaho and corporate sponsors, see Rick Otterstrom, "Bingham County D.A.R.E. Day," *D.A.R.E. Idaho*, July 1996, 4; "D.A.R.E. Fundraising," *Law and Order*, September 1988, 4; "D.A.R.E. Hotline," *Law and Order*, October 1988, 4. For donations by Shell Oil Company see Justus Spillner to Los Angeles Police Department, Public Affairs, November 4, 1986, box 108644, folder 6, AAMI. For an overview of the various stakeholders in DARE, see Earl Wysong and David W. Wright, "A Decade of Dare: Efficacy, Politics and Drug Education," *Sociological Focus* 28, no. 3 (1995): 283–311.

57. "Restaurant Supports Anti-Drug Program," *Los Angeles Times*, September 14, 1989, 7HD; Clay Harden, "KFC/D.A.R.E. Celebrate Graduation of Forty-Millionth Student," *Cloverdale Reveille*, July 6, 1994, 10; "Photo Standalone 24—Actor Michael Warren," *Los Angeles Sentinel*, September 22, 1988, C7; "Photo Standalone 24—Daring Do," *Los Angeles Sentinel*, December 1, 1988, B9.

58. Harden, "KFC/D.A.R.E. Celebrate Graduation of Forty-Millionth Student."

59. DARE America, *DARE Honors Greg Penske*; DARE America, *DARE to Make Your Dreams Come True—Auction Book*.

60. DARE, *Drugs Are Everyone's Problem*, pamphlet.

61. DARE America, "D.A.R.E. Will Teach 3 Million Children Drug Resistance Skills in 1989," press release, 1989, folder Drug Abuse Resistance Education (DARE) Reception, 9/13/89, OA 13684, Chron File, 1989–1993, Speech File Backup Files, White House Office of Speechwriting, GBPL.

62. DARE America, "Yogi Bear Becomes D.A.R.E. America Spokesbear as Hanna-Barbera Joins Fight against Drug Abuse," press release, February 15, 1989, folder Drug Abuse Resistance Education (DARE) Reception, 9/13/89, box 30, Chron Files, 1989–1993, Speech File Backup Files, White House Office of Speechwriting, GBPL.

63. "DARE Bear Yogi," directed by Don Jurwich, animation (United States: Hannah Barbera Productions, 1989).

64. "Restaurant Supports Anti-Drug Program," *Los Angeles Times*, September 14, 1989, 7HD.

65. In general, see Geismer, *Left Behind*; Nicole Hemmer, *Partisans: The Conservative Revolutionaries Who Remade American Politics in the 1990s* (New York: Basic Books, 2022).

66. Janice Strauss, interview by Danette Turner, August 2, 2002, 15–16, OH ST82A, Mesa Room Oral History Series, Mesa Public Library, Mesa, Ariz.

67. Paul Gordon, "The Truth about DARE," *Buzz: The Talk of Los Angeles*, September 1995, 72–77, 115; DARE America, *DARE America Form 990—Return of Organization Exempt from Income Tax*, 2001, accessed May 15, 2020, https://projects.propublica.org/nonprofits/organizations/954242541.

68. Tom Adams and Barbara West, "The Private Sector: Taking a Role in the Prevention of Drug and Alcohol Abuse for Young People," *Journal of Drug Education* 18, no. 3 (September 1, 1988): 186–88.

69. DARE, *Drugs Are Everyone's Problem*, pamphlet.

70. "Drug Abuse Program Background," 1986, box 21, folder Background Working Papers—August 1986 Presidential Drug Briefings (1), OA 16997, Richard Williams Files, RRPL.

71. Glenn Levant, "President's Message," *DareLine International*, no. 6, 1998, 4, box 26, folder 16, accretion 19147–06, NYSA.

72. Reverend Thomas Kilgore, Jr., Chair, Commission on the Prevention of Drug and Alcohol Abuse, *Attorney General's Commission on the Prevention of Drug and Alcohol Abuse: Final Report* (Sacramento, Calif.: Office of the Attorney General, 1986), 62.

73. DARE, *Drugs Are Everyone's Problem*, pamphlet.

74. U.S. Congress, Senate, Committee on Labor and Human Resources, *Drug Abuse: Prevention, Education, and Treatment*, 100th Cong., 2nd sess., June 16, 1988, 199.

75. Glenn F. Nyre, *DARE Evaluation for 1985–1989* (Los Angeles: Evaluation and Training Institute, January 1990), box 5021, folder 6, TBAP.

76. Michael Wagman, "DARE Program Gets L.A. Club Support," *Advertising Age*, September 29, 1986, box 21, folder D.A.R.E. [Drug Abuse Resistance Education], Carlton E. Turner Files, RRPL.

77. Ronald Reagan, "Remarks at a White House Briefing for Service Organization Representatives on Drug Abuse," July 30, 1986, APP, accessed January 18, 2023, www.presidency.ucsb.edu/node/259325.

78. Drug Abuse Policy Office, Office of Policy Development, The White House, *Federal Strategy for Prevention of Drug Abuse and Drug Trafficking 1982* (Washington, D.C., 1982).

79. Chantal d'Aulnis to Carlton E. Turner, "Super Hero and Teen Titans Special Editions," March 4, 1985, box 18, folder DC Comics, Inc., Carlton E. Turner Files, RRPL.

80. DC Comics, "The New Teen Titans," comic, no date, box 18, folder DC Comics, Inc., Carlton E. Turner Files, RRPL.

81. Robert L. Vernon, Associate Chief to Daniel F. Leonard, Deputy Director, Drug Abuse Police Office, March 7, 1984, box 108649, folder Drug Abuse Resistance Program 1984, AAMI.

82. *Hearing on Drug Abuse Prevention and Education*, 54.

83. Wysong and Wright, "A Decade of Dare," 299–300; DARE America, "Board of Directors," 1993, box 148, folder 681, RLA.

84. "Lakers Debut New Anti-Drug Rap and Video: The World Champion Lakers Debut Rap Single 'Just Say No,'" *Los Angeles Sentinel*, September 17, 1987, A1; "Lakers Say Yes to Video, No to Drugs," *Los Angeles Times*, September 4, 1987; "New Laker Video

Raps Drug Use," *Los Angeles Times*, October 18, 1987, V_D22; *Just Say No* (CBS/FOX Video Sports, 1987). The Lakers were not the only NBA players to engage in such activities. Similar anti-drug programs across the country also received extensive corporate funding and sponsorship from athletes. In Massachusetts, for example, Bank of Boston sponsored a "Stand Tall against Drugs" program in schools using former Boston Celtic M. L. Carr as a spokesperson and ambassador; *Hearing on Drug Abuse Prevention and Education*, 30–31, 108–11.

85. "Lakers to Take Anti-Drug Walk," *Los Angeles Sentinel*, October 15, 1987, B1; "Lakers, Wives to Lead Walk against Drugs," *Los Angeles Times*, October 15, 1987, A6.

86. Office of Criminal Justice Planning, *Suppression of Drug Abuse in Schools Program Annual Report to the Legislature* (Sacramento, Calif.: Office of Criminal Justice Planning, 1989), 19. Similar fundraisers benefiting DARE were held in other California cities as part of the state's DSP program. These events promoted DARE's message and helped fund local programs.

87. Harold Johnson, "D.A.R.E. to Be Different," *Los Angeles Sentinel*, April 10, 1986.

88. U.S. Congress, House of Representatives, Subcommittee on National Security, International Affairs, and Criminal Justice of the Committee on Government Reform and Oversight, *Shattering the Myths of the Drug Culture: Celebrity Role Models Just Say No*, 105th Cong., 2nd sess., June 18, 1998, 16–17.

89. U.S. Congress, *Shattering the Myths*, 18.

90. Art Marroquin, "Stars Come Out to Mark School's 1st DARE Carnival," *Los Angeles Times*, May 11, 1999; DARE America, "Table of Contents," *DareLine International*, 2000, https://web.archive.org/web/20011123061945/http://www.dare.com/D_LINE/dec2000/index.htm.

91. "Arsenio Hall Becomes D.A.R.E.'s First Ambassador to Keep Kids off Drugs," *Jet*, February 4, 1991, 56–58; John L. Mitchell, "'The Blame Must Be Shared': Many Blacks Fear Police Are the Enemy," *Los Angeles Times*, August 27, 1982, A1.

92. Debra Gendel, "Are We Not Babes in Shoes?" January 14, 1994, E3; Debra Gendel, "Playing It Totally Cool," February 25, 1994, E3. Alongside these news articles, I found many of the attendees in a Getty Images search: "Drug Abuse Resistance Education," Getty Images, 1994, accessed January 11, 2023, www.gettyimages.com/photos/drug-abuse-resistance-education?assettype=image&family=editorial&phrase=drug%20abuse%20resistance%20education&sort=mostpopular.

93. See Geismer, *Left Behind*.

Chapter Five

1. "Gambling: Bennett: Virtue Is as Virtue Does?" *Newsweek*, May 11, 2003, accessed December 7, 2022, www.newsweek.com/gambling-bennett-virtue-virtue-does-136961.

2. Bennett's worldview was a good fit with Reagan, who tapped him in 1981 to be chair of the National Endowment for the Humanities (NEH). From the NEH he moved to direct the National Humanities Center, where he became a critic of the perceived liberal/left leaning in academia. Bennett's moral crusading took center stage when Reagan appointed him as secretary of education in 1985 and would continue under

George H. W. Bush as the nation's first drug czar. On Bennett generally, see Andrew Hartman, *A War for the Soul of America: A History of the Culture Wars* (Chicago: University of Chicago Press, 2015), 216–18; Steve Macek, *Urban Nightmares: The Media, The Right, and the Moral Panic over the City* (Minneapolis: University of Minnesota Press, 2006), 103–6; Michael Massing, *The Fix* (New York: Simon & Schuster, 1998), 195–98. On the Christian Right, see Emily Suzanne Johnson, *This Is Our Message: Women's Leadership in the New Christian Right* (New York: Oxford University Press, 2019).

3. Bennett continued with a point about the ways the state cannot fill in for "traditional" institutions of family, church, and community. He wrote, "The state does not, cannot, and even should not always pick up where families and individuals leave off. . . . The American people understand that the institutions of family, church, and neighborhood will bring about more positive change than is within the power of governments . . . to do." William J. Bennett, *The De-Valuing of America: The Fight for Our Culture and Our Children* (New York: Summit Books, 1992), 32–33, 36, 103. For the ways Bennett was portrayed in media at the time, see Paul M. Barrett, "Behind Antidrug Plan Is the '60s Odyssey of 'Czar' Bill Bennett: Once-Liberal Academic Saw Dope Ruin Many Lives, Got Thoroughly Fed Up; His Date with Janis," *Wall Street Journal*, September 6, 1989, A1; Rowland Evans and Robert Novak, "Bill Bennett: Secretary for Education," *Reader's Digest*, March 1988, 104–9; Michael Massing, "The Two William Bennetts," *New York Review of Books*, March 1, 1990, accessed May 11, 2020, www.nybooks.com/articles/1990/03/01/the-two-william-bennetts/.

4. Charles A. Murray, *The Underclass Revisited* (Washington, D.C.: American Enterprise Institute, 1999).

5. William J. Bennett, Director, Office of National Drug Control Policy, *National Drug Control Strategy* (Washington, D.C.: The White House, September 1989), 8.

6. As Bennett along with criminologist John Dilulio and future drug czar John Walters explained, the roots of this "moral poverty"—that "of being without loving, capable, responsible adults who teach the young right from wrong"—was not unemployment, the decimation of social programs, or racial discrimination but "the enfeebled condition—in some places in our society, the near collapse—of our character-forming institutions." William J. Bennett, John J. Dilulio, and John P. Walters, *Body Count: Moral Poverty—and How to Win America's War against Crime and Drugs* (New York: Simon & Schuster, 1996), 13, 196. As the historian Michael Katz argued, Murray, Bennett, and other conservative intellectuals promoted the message that social programs "reinforced values and behaviors that varied from those of the rest of American society. They were the source of a new culture defined by behavior rather than income." Michael Katz, *The Underclass Debate: Views from History* (Princeton, N.J.: Princeton University Press, 1993), 15.

7. Andrew Hartman has suggested that "so-called gangsta rap seemed bent on making a mockery of Reagan's America." Hartman, *A War for the Soul of America*, 177–82; Austin McCoy, "NWA—'F- Tha Police'(1988)," in *One-Track Mind: Capitalism, Technology, and the Art of the Pop Song*, ed. Asif Siddiqi (London: Routledge, 2022), 172–89; Felicia Angeja Viator, *To Live and Defy in LA: How Gangsta Rap Changed America* (Cambridge, Mass.: Harvard University Press, 2020), 210–18.

8. Jeff Chang, *Can't Stop, Won't Stop: A History of the Hip-Hop Generation* (New York: St. Martin's Press, 2005), 319.

9. On hip-hop as resistance, see Robin D. G. Kelley, "Kickin' Reality, Kickin' Ballistics," in *Race Rebels: Culture, Politics, and the Black Working Class* (New York: Free Press, 1994), 183–227; McCoy, "NWA—'F- Tha Police'(1988)"; Viator, *To Live and Defy in LA*.

10. DARE presumed to teach youth to alter their behavior by emphasizing personal responsibility, promoting family values, and enhancing students' self-esteem. In so doing, DARE presented drug use as a matter of individual choice and morality and fed into a broader punitive ethos and governing logic during the Reagan era. In general, see David R. Farber, *Crack: Rock Cocaine, Street Capitalism, and the Decade of Greed* (New York: Cambridge University Press, 2019); Gil Troy, *Morning in America: How Ronald Reagan Invented the 1980s* (Princeton, N.J.: Princeton University Press, 2005), 286–90.

11. In general, see Emily Dufton, *Grass Roots: The Rise and Fall and Rise of Marijuana in America* (New York: Basic Books, 2017).

12. For a discussion of color blindness and how messages of personal transformation rather than social inequality were used to explain problems in Black communities, see Keeanga-Yamahtta Taylor, *From #BlackLivesMatter to Black Liberation* (Chicago: Haymarket Books, 2016); Marisa Chappell, *The War on Welfare: Family, Poverty, and Politics in Modern America* (Philadelphia: University of Pennsylvania Press, 2010). On the "underclass debates," see Katz, *The Underclass Debate*.

13. On Bennett's approach to values and morality in education, see Bennett, *The De-Valuing of America*, 56–62.

14. William Bennett, "Drugs: Consequences and Confrontation," speech, May 3, 1989, folder Drug Strategy: William Bennett Speech, OA 021312, Kristen Gear Files, White House Office of Public Affairs, GBPL.

15. U.S. Congress, House of Representatives, Select Committee on Narcotics Abuse and Control, *Drug Abuse Education*, 99th Cong., 2nd sess., May 20, 1986, 2.

16. William H. Bennett, *What Works: Schools without Drugs* (Washington, D.C.: U.S. Department of Education, 1986), vi, 11.

17. Howard Kohn, "Cowboy in the Capital: Drug Czar Bill Bennett," *Rolling Stone*, November 12, 1989, accessed February 17, 2023, www.rollingstone.com/politics/politics-news/cowboy-in-the-capital-drug-czar-bill-bennett-45472/.

18. "Drug Czar Urges Pupils to Turn In Parents, Says It's Not 'Snitching,'" *Los Angeles Times*, May 18, 1989, L2.

19. Bennett, *What Works*, 36.

20. George H. W. Bush, "Presidential Remarks: Drug Address Bennett Swearing-In," speech, March 13, 1989, folder Swearing-in of Director of National Drug Control Policy William Bennett Swearing-in, 3/13/89 [1], OA 13479, Chron File, 1989–1993, Speech File Backup Files, White House Office of Speechwriting, GBPL; George H. W. Bush, "Remarks by the President and Director of the Office of National Drug Control Policy William Bennett," speech, March 13, 1989, folder Swearing-in of Director of National Drug Control Policy William Bennett Swearing-in, 3/13/89 [1], OA 13479, Chron File, 1989–1993, Speech File Backup Files, White House Office of Speechwriting, GBPL.

21. "Talking Points on Anti-Drug Abuse Efforts," March 24, 1989, folder Talking Points-Drug Abuse, 3/24/89, OA 13480, Chron File, 1989–1993, Speech File Backup Files, White House Office of Speechwriting, GBPL. On Bennett's views, see Bennett, "Drugs: Consequences and Confrontation."

22. Terry Johnson to the President, February 24, 1992, folder DARE, OA 06391-055, William Caldwell Files, White House Office of Public Liaison, GBPL.

23. Ken Franckling, "Drugs in America . . . : A Society 'Awash in Drugs': No Easy Answers to Anti-Drug Education," *New Pittsburgh Courier*, September 3, 1988, 1.

24. Los Angeles Police Department, DARE Unit, "Los Angeles Police Department Training Seminar Project D.A.R.E." [ca. 1985], folder 2, box 19, OA18765, Office of the First Lady, Projects Office, RRPL.

25. Chief Legislative Analyst to Grants, Housing and Community Development Committee, "Drug Abuse Resistance Education," July 31, 1984, box 116, folder 2, TBAP; Harry Handler to Members, Board of Education, "Drug Abuse Resistance Education (DARE)," August 22, 1983, box 1,424, folder 5, LAUSD.

26. Los Angeles Police Department, *1983 Annual Report* (Los Angeles, 1983), 11.

27. Las Vegas Metropolitan Police Department, Clark County School District, and Junior League of Las Vegas, "DARE to Say No! Student Workbook" [ca. 1989], box 17, folder 3, JLLV.

28. Greg Braxton, "Students Learn Drug Resistance," *Los Angeles Times*, February 19, 1984, GB1, box 116, folder 2, TBAP.

29. DARE, "DARE Lessons" [ca. 1984], box C-1154, City Council File No. 85-1757, LACCF.

30. DARE, "DARE Workbook," June 20, 1983, box 2,669, folder 10, LAUSD.

31. Eva Marx and William DeJong, *An Invitation to Project DARE: Drug Abuse Resistance Education*, Department of Justice, Office of Justice Programs, Bureau of Justice Assistance, NCJ 114802 (Washington, D.C., June 1988), 9.

32. DARE America, "DARE Workbook," 1992, in author's possession.

33. "DARE: Selecting the Right Officer," *FBI Law Enforcement Bulletin*, May 1990, 12.

34. John R. Faine, *DARE in Nashville Schools 1988–89: An Evaluation of the Drug Abuse Resistance Program* (Social Research Laboratory, Western Kentucky University, September 1, 1989), 59, 57, Paper 498, WKU Archives Records, accessed October 20, 2020, https://digitalcommons.wku.edu/dlsc_ua_records/498.

35. DARE America, "Workbook," January 1991, box 148, folder 681, RLA.

36. The DARE Report, *Land of Decisions and Choices*, directed by Tricia Garcia and Mike Frank Polcino (DARE America, 1990).

37. Ronald Reagan, "Remarks at a White House Briefing for Service Organization Representatives on Drug Abuse," July 30, 1986, APP, accessed January 18, 2023, www.presidency.ucsb.edu/node/259325.

38. Malcolm K. Sparrow, Mark H. Moore, and David M. Kennedy, *Beyond 911: A New Era for Policing* (New York: Basic Books, 1990), 66; DARE America, "Parents Guidebook," 1993, box 148, folder 681, RLA; Office of the Superintendent, "Observance of Red-Ribbon Week, October 25–31, 1987," December 9, 1987, box 1,424, folder 4, LAUSD; Melinda Cooper, *Family Values: Between Neoliberalism and the New Social Conservatism* (New York: Zone Books, 2017), 179. Cooper explains how the consequences of irresponsible behavior were deserved in the context of the AIDS crisis. She argues that

neoliberal responses to AIDS drew lines around the insurable and uninsurable based on whether one engaged in risky behavior after the full knowledge of the mode of transmission was widespread. Those who continued to engage in risky behavior were undeserving of insurance. I make a similar point about drugs. Those who continued to use drugs with the knowledge that no level of drug use was acceptable were undeserving of intervention and subject to punishment.

39. Los Angeles Police Department and Los Angeles Unified School District, "DARE High School," Office of Criminal Justice Planning, Project Summary, October 1, 1989, box 42, folder 7, TBAP.

40. Robert Vernon, "Salt for Chrisis Concerns," NAE Convention, 1985, box 121, item 55, tape 173, National Association of Evangelicals Records, Wheaton College Archives and Special Collections. Vernon's evangelical Christian beliefs led to controversy when allegations that Vernon promoted officers in the LAPD who aligned with his church or were evangelical themselves. See Bill Boyarsky, "Bible Bob, the LAPD and Freedom," *Los Angeles Times*, November 15, 1991, www.latimes.com/archives/la-xpm-1991-11-15-me-1342-story.html. See also Vernon's book on the LAPD and the 1992 rebellion published by Focus on the Family Publishers Robert L. Vernon, *L.A. Justice: Lessons from the Firestorm* (Colorado Springs, Co: Focus on the Family Publishers, 1993).

41. "Happy Birthday D.A.R.E.," *DARE to Read*, no. 1 (September 1988), box 1,424, folder 6, LAUSD; Paul Gordon, "The Truth About DARE," *Buzz: The Talk of Los Angeles*, September 1995.

42. Presidential Messages to Officer Philip Fazzino, "Project DARE," September 28, 1989, folder Publication: National Drug Control Strategy, OA 08203, Beverly Ward Files, White House Office of Correspondence, GBPL; George H. W. Bush, "Presidential Remarks: Address to Students," September 7, 1989, folder Address to Students Re: Drugs, 9/12/89 [1], OA 13501, Chron File, 1989–1993, Speech File Backup Files, White House Office of Speechwriting, GBPL.

43. Colleen F. Montoya et al., eds., *Evaluating School-Linked Prevention Strategies: Alcohol, Tobacco, and Other Drugs* (La Jolla, Calif.: UCSD Extension, University of California, San Diego, 1993), 70.

44. Max Felker-Kantor, *Policing Los Angeles: Race, Resistance, and the Rise of the LAPD* (Chapel Hill: University of North Carolina Press, 2018), 227–32.

45. David L. Carter, *Community Policing and D.A.R.E.®: A Practitioner's Perspective*, Bureau of Justice Bulletin: Community Policing Series, NCJ 154275 (Washington, D.C.: Department of Justice, July 1995), 4.

46. U.S. Congress, House of Representatives, Subcommittee on Elementary, Secondary, and Vocational Education, Committee on Education and Labor, *Oversight Hearing on Drug Abuse Education Programs*, 101st Cong., 2nd sess., September 6, 1990, 38.

47. Carter, *Community Policing and D.A.R.E.*, 6.

48. Michael J. Manos, Keith Y. Kameoka, and Joyce H. Tanji, *Evaluation of Honolulu Police Department's Drug Abuse Resistance Education Project*, Report No. 329 (Honolulu, Hawaii: Youth Development and Research Center, July 1986), 18.

49. Superintendent of Schools to Los Angeles City Board of Education, "Continuation of the 'Drug Free Schools and Communities Act Program' Funded under the Provisions of P.L. 99–570," October 3, 1988, box 1,424, folder 4, LAUSD.

50. Melody Lark, "The Drug-Free Schools and Communities Act of 1986: Policy, Formation, Causation, and Program Implementation" (paper prepared for the 1995 AERA Conference, San Francisco, CA, Division H: School Evaluation and Program Development Roundtable Discussion, April 22, 1995), 1.

51. "Drug-Free Schools and Communities Act Amendments of 1989," Pub. L. No. 101–226, 103 STAT. 1928 (1989).

52. Board of Education of the City of Los Angeles, "Implementation of Drug-Free Schools Program," April 10, 1991, box 1,424, folder 7, LAUSD. For a similar statement about the complementary nature of enforcement and prevention measures, see Los Angeles Police Department, "Drug Abuse Resistance Education (DARE)," December 26, 1986, box 117, folder 3, TBAP.

53. Los Angeles Police Department and Los Angeles Unified School District, "Drug Abuse Resistance Education," Office of Criminal Justice Planning, Suppression of Drug Abuse in Schools Program, Grant Award, June 29, 1984, box 116, folder 1, TBAP; Ruth Rich, "Testimony Provided by Dr. Ruth Rich Director, Drug Free Schools and Communities Act Program Los Angeles Unified School District for Congress of the United States, House of Representatives Committee on Government on the Drug Crisis in America and the Proposals to Fight It," July 2, 1990, box 288, folder 15, TBAP. For stories of using expulsions as a means to wage the war on drugs in schools, see Richard Holguin, "Just Say 'Go': Downey Schools Wage War on Drug Use with Wave of Expulsions," *Los Angeles Times*, November 20, 1986, SE1.

54. Rose Matsui Ochi, Executive Director Criminal Justice Planning Office to Mayor Tom Bradley, "Transmittal of Grant Proposal/Award Fact Sheet for the Drug Abuse Resistance Education (DARE) Private Schools Program (with attachments)," April 24, 1989, box C-2231, City Council File No. 89–0819, LACCF.

55. Los Angeles Police Department and Los Angeles Unified School District, "DARE High School," Office of Criminal Justice Planning, Project Summary, October 1, 1989, box 42, folder 7, TBAP; Chief of Police to Honorable Board of Police Commissioners, "Transmittal of the Year-End Evaluation on the Drug Abuse Resistance (DARE) High School Program," August 22, 1989, box 4,435, folder 3, TBAP. The LAPD also believed "continuance of the DARE program and advancement of drug resistant DARE students to the higher grade levels is expected to reduce the demand for drugs. This cumulative effect will complement enforcement efforts on or near area school campuses." Los Angeles Police Department and Los Angeles Unified School District, "Project Summary: Drug Abuse Resistance Education (DARE)," Office of Criminal Justice Planning, Grant Award [ca. 1986], box C-805, City Council File No. 84–1431, LACCF.

56. Commanding Officer, DARE Division to Commanding Officer, Bureau of Special Investigation, "Activities Report—Ending March 1, 1989," February 29, 1989, box 13580, folder 15, AAMI.

57. Rose Matsui Ochi, Executive Director Criminal Justice Planning Office to Mayor Tom Bradley, "Transmittal of: (1) Proposed Fifth-Year Grant Proposal/Award for the City of Los Angeles Drug Abuse Resistance Education (DARE) Program; and (2) Subgrant Agreement with the Los Angeles Unified School District (LAUSD) to provide for Program Implementation (with attachments)," March 28, 1988, box C-1698, City Council File No. 87–0667, LACCF; Los Angeles Police Department, "Drug Abuse

Resistance Education (DARE)," December 26, 1986, box 117, folder 3, TBAP; Los Angeles Police Department and Los Angeles Unified School District, "Drug Abuse Resistance Education," Office of Criminal Justice Planning, Suppression of Drug Abuse in Schools Program, Grant Award, June 29, 1984, box 116, folder 1, TBAP.

58. Jodie Needle, "They DAREd to Be There," *South Florida Sun Sentinel*, May 22, 1999, 3B, Newspapers.com.

59. U.S. Congress, House of Representatives, Select Committee on Narcotics Abuse and Control, *Drug Abuse Prevention in America's Schools*, 100th Cong., 1st sess., June 9, 1987, 8.

60. Mathea Falco, *The Making of a Drug-Free America: Programs That Work* (New York: Crown, 1992), 87.

61. William DeJong, *Arresting the Demand for Drugs: Police and School Partnership to Prevent Drug Abuse*, U.S. Department of Justice, National Institute of Justice, Office of Communication and Research Utilization, OJP-86-C-002 (Washington, D.C.: November 1987), iv.

62. Charles A. Gruber, "A Positive Evaluation of DARE," *Law and Order*, April 1998, 52.

63. Los Angeles City Task Force on Immigration, *Interim Report of the Los Angeles City Task Force on Immigration* (Los Angeles: Los Angeles City Council, April 1987), box 1172, folder 13, TBAP.

64. Lynell George and David Dante Troutt, "Guns No Butter," *L.A. Weekly*, January 5, 1989, 24–27, 28, 30, Newspapers.com.

65. Minnesota Institute of Public Health, *Drug Abuse Resistance Education Program Evaluation Final Report*, Minnesota Drug Abuse Resistance Education Advisory Council (St. Paul: Minnesota Institute of Public Health, July 16, 1997), 19.

66. Faine, *DARE in Nashville Schools 1988–89*, 30.

67. Andy Furillo, "DARE: It's Working and in Trouble: Police Anti-Drug Project at Schools Praised but Council Is Cool," *Los Angeles Times*, April 28, 1985, B1.

68. "Student/Parent Orientation—DARE+Plus," September 1, 1993, box 148, folder 681, RLA.

69. DARE America, *DARE America Form 990—Return of Organization Exempt from Income Tax*, 2002, accessed May 15, 2020, https://projects.propublica.org/nonprofits/organizations/954242541.

70. See attached document on D.A.R.E.+PLUS and DARE in DARE America, *DARE America Form 990—Return of Organization Exempt from Income Tax*, 2002.

71. DARE America, "New DARE After-School Program Introduced Today in Los Angeles," press release, June 14, 1993, box 148, folder 682, RLA.

72. DARE America, "New DARE After-School Program."

73. Doug Besharov to Chris DeMuth, "Out-of-Wedlock Births and Poverty," April 15, 1992, box 148, folder 682, RLA.

74. On race, poverty, and welfare in the Reagan era, see Julilly Kohler-Hausmann, "Welfare Crises, Penal Solutions, and the Origins of the 'Welfare Queen,'" *Journal of Urban History* 41, no. 5 (2015): 756–71; Julilly Kohler-Hausmann, "'The Crime of Survival': Fraud Prosecutions, Community Surveillance, and the Original 'Welfare Queen,'" *Journal of Social History* 41, no. 2 (Winter 2007): 329–54.

75. DARE America, "New DARE After-School Program."

76. Nick DeMauro and Glenn Levant, interview by Max Felker-Kantor, January 14, 2021.

77. DARE America, "New DARE After-School Program."

78. Osamu Inoue to Joel Rubenstein, September 27, 1993, box 148, folder 681, RLA; Nella Charles to Glenn Levant, October 5, 1993, box 148, folder 681, RLA. For examples of RLA's facilitating connections between DARE Plus and corporations such as Kodak, Fujifilm, Laguna Clay, and the Great Western Forum for Lakers tickets, see Glenn Levant to Ian D. Campbell, November 22, 1993, box 148, folder 681, RLA; Glenn Levant to Bob Steiner, December 3, 1993, box 148, folder 681, RLA.

79. Tim to Ed, "DARE Plus," December 3, 1993, box 148, folder 681, RLA.

80. Jonathan Moses, "Milken to Work in Antidrug Program," *Wall Street Journal*, June 4, 1993, B8, box 148, folder 681, RLA; DARE America, "Prepared by DARE America," April 23, 1993, box 148, folder 681, RLA; DARE America, "New DARE After-School Program"; Joel Rubenstein to Mike Milken, June 2, 1993, box 148, folder 681, RLA.

81. DARE America, "DARE Plus Rally," program, June 16, 1993, box 148, folder 681, RLA. On press attention to Michael Jackson's involvement in the launch, see clippings attached to DARE America, "Prepared by DARE America," April 29, 1993, box 148, folder 681, RLA.

82. DARE America, "New DARE After-School Program."

83. Susan Gonzalez et al., "DARE Plus Marina Del Rey Middle School," 1993, box 148, folder 681, RLA.

84. For some examples of other cities that adopted DARE Plus, see Anne Lindberg, "School Program Works to Keep Pupils Interested," *Tampa Bay Times*, August 6, 1994, 90, Newspapers.com; Paul Powell, "DARE PLUS Program an Alternative in Wharton," *Victoria Advocate*, May 9, 1995, 2, Newspapers.com.

85. Quayle also criticized Time Warner, Inc. for distributing Body Count's, Ice-T's group, records. Dan Quayle, *Address during DARE Conference*, July 17, 1992, 19920717 ROTVP during DARE Conference, Louisville, KY, White House Communications Agency Audio, GBPL.

86. Malcolm K. Sparrow, Mark H. Moore, and David M. Kennedy, "Daryl Gates and Los Angeles: Community Crime Prevention," in *Beyond 911* (Basic Books, 1990), 66, box 22, folder 16, Independent Commission on the Los Angeles Police Department Records, Collection no. 0229, Regional History Collections, Special Collections, USC Libraries, University of Southern California, Los Angeles.

87. Katz, ed., *The Underclass* Debate; Cooper, *Family Values*, 38–46.

88. For the DARE triad logo including school, police, and parents see DARE America, "Eight Ways to Say No!" 1993, box 148, folder 681, RLA.

89. DARE America, *Parents Guidebook* (Los Angeles: 1993), box 148, folder 681, RLA.

90. Los Angeles Police Department, "Grant Award: Drug Abuse Resistance Education (DARE)," Office of Criminal Justice Planning, October 11, 1985, box 117, folder 1, TBAP; *Hearing on Drug Abuse Prevention and Education*, 56.

91. Bureau of Justice Assistance, *An Introduction to the National DARE Parent Program*, Department of Justice, Office of Justice Programs, Bureau of Justice Assistance, NCJ 142422 (Washington, D.C.: June 1993), 2–3.

92. Los Angeles Police Department, "Drug Abuse Resistance Education Regional Training Center Criteria Categorical Grant Progress Report," U.S. Department of Justice, Office of Justice Assistance, Research and Statistics, August 4, 1988, box C-2130, City Council File No. 88–1494, LACCF.

93. Glenn A. Levant, *Keeping Kids Drug Free: D.A.R.E. Official Parent's Guide*, 1st ed. (San Diego, Calif.: Laurel Glen, 1998), 25, 38.

94. On skeptical parents, see Garry Abrams, "Turning In Parents for Using Drugs: The Great Debate: Adults Have Doubts, but Many Youngsters Say Such Drastic Action May Be Needed," *Los Angeles Times*, September 12, 1986, G1; "DARE Called a Mockery," *La Crosse Tribune*, September 30, 1993, B1.

95. Glenn Nyre, *Project DARE Final Evaluation Report* (Los Angeles: Evaluation and Training Institute, October 9, 1985), box 1,424, folder 6, LAUSD.

96. *The MacNeil/Lehrer NewsHour*, April 11, 1988, NewsHour Productions, American Archive of Public Broadcasting (GBH and the Library of Congress), Boston, Mass. and Washington, D.C., accessed January 24, 2020, http://americanarchive.org/catalog/cpb-aacip-507-rv0cv4cm12.

97. Robert Vernon, "Salt for Chrisis Concerns," NAE Convention, 1985, box 121, item 55, tape 173, National Association of Evangelicals Records, Wheaton College Archives and Special Collections.

98. On the suburban crisis and fears of the city, see Kyle Riismandel, *Neighborhood of Fear: The Suburban Crisis in American Culture, 1975–2001* (Baltimore, Md.: Johns Hopkins University Press, 2020); Matthew D. Lassiter, "Impossible Criminals: The Suburban Imperatives of America's War on Drugs," *Journal of American History* 102, no. 1 (June 2015): 126–40.

99. Levant, *Keeping Kids Drug Free*, 9–11. While DARE officials did not refer to when children became responsible for their actions or explicitly differentiate between racialized "super-predators" and threatened innocent white youth, there was a general decline in the presumption of limited criminal responsibility among kids during the 1970s. The consequences created a two-tiered juvenile justice system. As Geoff Ward has shown, by the 1980s the Black kids in the juvenile justice system were treated as dangerous and undeserving offenders compared to white kids, who were often viewed as deserving and routed to rehabilitation rather than punitive institutions. See Geoff K. Ward, *The Black Child-Savers: Racial Democracy and Juvenile Justice* (Chicago: University of Chicago Press, 2012), 239–43. See also Erica Meiners, *For the Children?* (Minneapolis: University of Minnesota Press, 2016). DARE's emphasis on the importance of family values similarly reflects the effort to shore up parental control of kids to address the perceived problem of runaway youth and child kidnapping in white neighborhoods and the irredeemable youth of color, who deserved punishment described by historian Paul Renfro. For instance, Levant's implicit message about the threat of drugs to innocent suburban kids played on messages of the unredeemable "inner-city" gang members mentioned by Vernon. See Paul M. Renfro, "Kids in Custody: Protection and Punishment in the Reagan Era," in *Stranger Danger: Family Values, Childhood, and the American Carceral State* (New York: Oxford University Press, 2020), 143–70.

100. Arthur G. Sharp, "Special Report: Is DARE a Sacred Lamb?" *Law and Order*, April 1998, 44.

101. Earl Wysong, Richard Aniskiewicz, and David Wright, "Truth and DARE: Tracking Drug Education to Graduation and as Symbolic Politics," *Social Problems* 41, no. 3 (1994): 448–72.

102. William J. Bennett, "America's New 'Invisible Man,'" speech, July 18, 1989, folder Drug Strategy: Drug Proposal, OA 021312, Kristen Gear Files, White House Office of Public Affairs, GBPL.

103. George H. W. Bush, "Remarks by the President during Signing Ceremony for Drug Abuse Education Day Proclamation," speech, September 13, 1989, folder Publication: National Drug Control Strategy, OA 08203, Beverly Ward Files, White House Office of Correspondence, GBPL.

104. Ellen Flax and Reagan Walker, "Cavazos Pledges $2 Million to Enhance Anti-Drug Efforts," *Education Week*, April 12, 1989, accessed March 3, 2020, www.edweek.org/education/cavazos-pledges-2-million-to-enhance-anti-drug-efforts/1989/04.

105. DARE, "Teaching Kids to Never Take Drugs," pamphlet, n.d., Domestic Policy Council and Jose Cerda, "D.A.R.E. [Drug Abuse Resistance Education]," *Clinton Digital Library*, accessed January 18, 2023, https://clinton.presidentiallibraries.us/items/show/96852.

106. Hillary Clinton, "First Lady Hillary Rodham Clinton Speech at DARE Event, Mott Elementary School, Flint, Michigan," speech, October 8, 1996, First Lady's Office, Speechwriting, and Laura Schiller, "HRC Clinton/Gore Speeches 1996: [10/8 D.A.R.E. [Drug Abuse Resistance Education] Event, Flint, MI]," *Clinton Digital Library*, accessed January 18, 2023, https://clinton.presidentiallibraries.us/items/show/55400.

107. William J. Clinton, "Speeches [1]" (n.d.), Domestic Policy Council, Bruce Reed, and Crime Series, "Speeches [1]," *Clinton Digital Library*, accessed July 23, 2020, https://clinton.presidentiallibraries.us/items/show/22619.

108. U.S. Congress, House of Representatives, Subcommittee on Select Education and Civil Rights of the Committee on Education and Labor, *Hearing on the Reauthorization of the Drug Free Schools and Communities Act*, 103rd Congress, 1st sess., March 31, 1993, 32.

109. U.S. Congress, House of Representatives, Subcommittee on National Security, International Affairs, and Criminal Justice of the Committee on Government Reform and Oversight, *Shattering the Myths of the Drug Culture: Celebrity Role Models Just Say No*, 105th Cong., 2nd sess., June 18, 1998, 31.

110. Lily Geismer, *Left Behind: The Democrats' Failed Attempt to Solve Inequality* (New York: Public Affairs, 2022), 173.

111. DARE America, *DARE America Form 990—Return of Organization Exempt from Income Tax*, 2002, accessed May 15, 2020, https://projects.propublica.org/nonprofits/organizations/954242541.

112. Wisconsin Department of Public Instruction, *An Evaluation of the Drug Abuse Resistance Education Program in Wisconsin Schools* (Madison, Wis., March 1999), 2, box 1, Records of the Superintendent's AODA Council, 1995–1999, WHS.

113. Minnesota Institute of Public Health, *Drug Abuse Resistance Education Program Evaluation Final Report*, 17.

Chapter Six

1. Kristina Marlow and Steven Rhodes, "DARE under Fire: Despite Popularity, Program Fails to Stop Kids from Using Drugs, Study Says," *Chicago Tribune*, November 1, 1994, 117, Newspapers.com.

2. Susan Moffat, "'No!' Is Their Rallying Cry: 6,000 Youths at Meeting Loudly Pledge to Avoid Gangs and Drugs," *Los Angeles Times*, April 22, 1994, WB4; "Violent Crime Control and Law Enforcement Act of 1994," Pub. L. No. H.R.3355, 42 U.S.C. § 14141 (1994).

3. "Violent Crime Control and Law Enforcement Act of 1994."

4. Rick Aniskiewicz and Earl Wysong, "Evaluating DARE: Drug Education and the Multiple Meanings of Success," *Policy Studies Review* 9, no. 4 (Summer 1990): 733. Or, as another scholar suggested, findings of ineffectiveness did not matter when compared to the perception among parents that DARE represented a positive effort by schools and the police to address drug use. "It is unlikely that drug education will ever be withdrawn from the schools, even if it is shown to be ineffective," Bangert-Drowns suggested. "It appears to serve other functions . . . such as the reassurance of parents that the schools are at least trying to control substance abuse among students." Robert L. Bangert-Drowns, "The Effects of School-Based Substance Abuse Education—A Meta-Analysis," *Journal of Drug Education* 18, no. 3 (September 1, 1988): 243–64.

5. Kerman Maddox to Tom Bradley, "DARE Program Update," June 25, 1985, box 1596, folder 2, TBAP.

6. Chief of Police to Honorable Board of Police Commissioners, "Drug Abuse Resistance Education (DARE) Longitudinal Evaluation Annual Report July, 1988," August 11, 1988, box C-805, City Council File No. 84–0566, LACCF.

7. Dennis Cauchon, "Studies Find Drug Program Not Effective," *USA Today*, October 11, 1993, A01; Harold K. Becker, Michael W. Agopian, and Sandy Yeh, "Impact Evaluation of Drug Abuse Resistance Education (DARE)," *Journal of Drug Education* 22, no. 4 (1992): 283–91.

8. Christopher Ringwalt, Susan T. Ennett, and Kathleen D. Holt, "An Outcome Evaluation of Project DARE (Drug Abuse Resistance Education)," *Health Education Research* 6, no. 3 (1991): 327–37.

9. Richard R. Clayton and Anne Cattarello, "Prevention Intervention Research: Challenges and Opportunities," in *Drug Abuse Prevention Intervention Research: Methodological Issues*, ed. William J. Bukoski and Carl G. Leukefeld, NIDA Research Monograph 107 (Washington, D.C.: U.S. Department of Health and Human Services, 1991); Richard R. Clayton et al., "Persuasive Communication and Drug Prevention: An Evaluation of the DARE Program," in *Persuasive Communication and Drug Abuse Prevention*, ed. Lewis Donohew, Howard E. Sypher, and William J. Bukoski, (New York: Routledge, 1991), 295–313; Richard R. Clayton, Anne Cattarello, and Katherine P. Walden, "Sensation Seeking as a Potential Mediating Variable for School-Based Prevention Intervention: A Two-Year Follow-Up of DARE," *Health Communication* 3, no. 1 (October 1991): 229–39.

10. Christopher L. Ringwalt et al., *Past and Future Directions of the D.A.R.E.® Program: An Evaluation Review Research in Brief*, Department of Justice, Office of Justice

Programs, National Institute of Justice, NIJ 152055 (Washington, D.C., September 1994); Christopher Ringwalt, interview by Max Felker-Kantor, December 22, 2020; Susan Ennett, interview by Max Felker-Kantor, January 22, 2021.

11. Patrick Boyle, "A DAREing Rescue," *Youth Today*, April 2001, 16. See also Dennis Cauchon, "Study Critical of D.A.R.E. Rejected," *USA Today*, October 4, 1994, A01; Laura Miller, "Study Critical of Anti-Drug Program Called Flawed," *Education Week*, October 12, 1994, accessed June 4, 2019, www.edweek.org/ew/articles/1994/10/12/06dare.h14.html.

12. Christopher L. Ringwalt et al., *Past and Future Directions of the D.A.R.E.® Program: An Evaluation Review Draft Final Report* (Research Triangle Institute, September 1994), 1–3.

13. Colleen F. Montoya et al., eds., *Evaluating School-Linked Prevention Strategies: Alcohol, Tobacco, and Other Drugs* (La Jolla, Calif.: UCSD Extension, University of California, San Diego, 1993), 59.

14. Montoya et al., eds., *Evaluating School-Linked Prevention Strategies*, 62.

15. Montoya et al., eds., *Evaluating School-Linked Prevention Strategies*, 44.

16. Montoya et al., eds., *Evaluating School-Linked Prevention Strategies*, 70.

17. Ringwalt et al., *Past and Future Directions of the D.A.R.E.® Program*, 8–21.

18. Kristina Marlow and Steven Rhodes, "DARE Fails to Stop Drug Use, Study Says," *Corvallis Gazette-Times*, November 6, 1994; Kristina Marlow and Steven Rhodes, "Study: DARE Teaches Kids about Drugs but Doesn't Prevent Use," *Herald-Journal*, November 6, 1994.

19. Sylvester Monroe and Lisa H. Towle, "D.A.R.E. Bedeviled," *Time*, October 17, 1994, 49.

20. Cauchon, "Studies Find Drug Program Not Effective"; Miller, "Study Critical of Anti-Drug Program Called Flawed." On the reactions of the researchers involved in the study, see Christopher Ringwalt, interview by Max Felker-Kantor, December 22, 2020; Susan Ennett, interview by Max Felker-Kantor, January 22, 2021; "Deposition of Susan Ennett," D.A.R.E. America and Glenn Levant vs. Rolling Stone Magazine, et al., No. 99–01132 RAP (United States District Court, Central District of California, February 2, 2000), in author's possession.

21. U.S. Department of Justice, Office of Justice Programs, National Institute of Justice, "The D.A.R.E Program: A Review of Prevalence, User Satisfaction, and Effectiveness," *National Institute of Justice Update* (Washington, D.C.: October 1994).

22. Cauchon, "Study Critical of D.A.R.E. Rejected."

23. Susan T. Ennett et al., "How Effective Is Drug Abuse Resistance Education? A Meta-Analysis of Project DARE Outcome Evaluations," *American Journal of Public Health* 84, no. 9 (September 1994): 1399.

24. Ennett et al., "How Effective Is Drug Abuse Resistance Education?" 1398. On some of the hesitancy from academics about the efficacy of the use of police officers as teachers see Allan Cohen, interview by Max Felker-Kantor, January 26, 2021.

25. Jeff Elliott, "Drug Prevention Placebo: How DARE Wastes Time, Money, and Police," *Reason*, March 1995, 14–21, accessed August 7, 2019, https://reason.com/1995/03/01/drug-prevention-placebo/.

26. Cauchon, "Study Critical of D.A.R.E. Rejected."

27. Marlow and Rhodes, "Study: DARE Teaches Kids about Drugs but Doesn't Prevent Use."

28. Elliott, "Drug Prevention Placebo."

29. Cauchon, "Study Critical of D.A.R.E. Rejected."

30. "D.A.R.E. Graduates Say Program Has Helped Them Avoid Drugs, Alcohol," *Los Angeles Sentinel*, July 22, 1993, F16.

31. Marlow and Rhodes, "Study: DARE Teaches Kids about Drugs but Doesn't Prevent Use."

32. Paul Gordon, "The Truth about DARE," *Buzz: The Talk of Los Angeles*, September 1995, 72–77, 115.

33. Jim Newton, "DARE Marks a Decade of Growth and Controversy: Youth: Despite Critics, Anti-Drug Program Expands Nationally. But Some See Declining Support in LAPD," *Los Angeles Times*, September 9, 1993, WB1.

34. Cauchon, "Studies Find Drug Program Not Effective"; Elliott, "Drug Prevention Placebo."

35. Gordon, "The Truth about DARE."

36. Cauchon, "Studies Find Drug Program Not Effective."

37. Billy Webster and Leslie Thornton to Mack McLarty, Chief of Staff, "Presidential Crime/Violence Initiatives," March 1, 1994, "1994 Cabinet Crime Bill Activities" (1994), Office of Speechwriting and Jonathan Prince, "1994 Cabinet Crime Bill Activities," *Clinton Digital Library*, accessed July 24, 2020, https://clinton.presidentiallibraries.us/items/show/34273.

38. Gordon, "The Truth About DARE."

39. Earl Wysong, Richard Aniskiewicz, and David Wright, "Truth and DARE: Tracking Drug Education to Graduation and as Symbolic Politics," *Social Problems* 41, no. 3 (1994): 464.

40. Marlow and Rhodes, "DARE under Fire."

41. Newton, "DARE Marks a Decade of Growth and Controversy."

42. Ringwalt et al., *Past and Future Directions of the D.A.R.E.® Program*, 3.

43. Richard R. Clayton et al., "DARE (Drug Abuse Resistance Education): Very Popular but Not Very Effective," in *Intervening with Drug-Involved Youth* (Thousand Oaks, Calif: Sage Publications, 1996), 101–9. For information on the scientific advisory board on DARE's website, see DARE America, "D.A.R.E. Scientific Advisory Board," August 10, 2002, https://web.archive.org/web/20020810191947/http://www.dare.com/InsideDARE/Story.asp?N=InsideDARE&M=13&S=45.

44. Earl Wysong and David W. Wright, "A Decade of DARE: Efficacy, Politics and Drug Education," *Sociological Focus* 28, no. 3 (1995): 283–311; Aniskiewicz and Wysong, "Evaluating Dare."

45. National Institute of Justice, "The D.A.R.E Program: A Review of Prevalence, User Satisfaction, and Effectiveness," 2.

46. On estimates of funding and a story about Snohomish County, Washington, dropping DARE, see *The NewsHour with Jim Lehrer*, April 25, 1997, NewsHour Productions, American Archive of Public Broadcasting (GBH and the Library of Congress), Boston and Washington, D.C., accessed January 16, 2023, http://americanarchive.org/catalog/cpb-aacip-507-hh6c24rb63.

47. Associated Press, "Girl's Tip Leads to 'Pot' Seizure at Home," *San Bernardino County Sun*, September 10, 1986, 20, Newspapers.com; Aniskiewicz and Wysong, "Evaluating DARE," 738.

48. Los Angeles Police Department and Los Angeles Unified School District, "Drug Abuse Resistance Education (DARE)," Office of Criminal Justice Planning, Grant Award, September 11, 1985, box C-1154, City Council File No. 85–1757, LACCF.

49. Marie Gottschalk, *Caught: The Prison State and the Lockdown of American Politics* (Princeton, N.J.: Princeton University Press, 2014); Todd R. Clear, *Imprisoning Communities: How Mass Incarceration Makes Disadvantaged Neighborhoods Worse* (New York: Oxford University Press, 2009).

50. James Bovard, "Unsafe at Any Speed: Turning Kids into Druggies and Snitches," *American Spectator*, April 1996, 48–49.

51. Students took the message of the Three Rs to heart in their DARE essays. "Students Write Top DARE Essays," *Telegraph-Forum*, December 22, 1994, 2, Newspapers.com; Andy Wolfford, "Bells Ring to Reaffirm Commitment to Anti-Drug Program," *Advocate-Messenger*, September 15, 1989, 1, Newspapers.com; Joshua Reeves, *Citizen Spies: The Long Rise of America's Surveillance Society* (New York: New York University Press, 2017), 109–12, 122–30. In general, see Ryan Grim, *This Is Your Country on Drugs: The Secret History of Getting High in America* (Hoboken, N.J.: Wiley, 2009), 89–102.

52. Sara to GDK, January 15, 1996, box 27, folder DARE-Sacred Heart School, Gerald D. Kleczka papers, 1969–2004, WHS.

53. For a discussion of the wariness among communities of color that DARE officers and school resources officers might be used as intelligence gatherers for the police see Allan Cohen, interview by Max Felker-Kantor, January 26, 2021.

54. James Bovard, "A Look at . . . The Child Protection Debate: Kids, Cops and Caseworkers: America's Newest Parent Traps DARE Scare: Turning Children into Informants?" *Washington Post*, January 30, 1994, a25.

55. Crystal Grendell, Plaintiff v. James Gillway, et al., 974 F. Supp. 46 (United States District Court for the District of Maine 1997).

56. Grendell v. Gillway, et al.

57. Joseph Pereira, "The Informants: In a Drug Program, Some Kids Turn In Their Own Parents: Police Teach DARE Classes, Get Tips from Students; Girl's Case Splits Town; 'I Would Never Tell Again,'" *Wall Street Journal*, April 20, 1992, A1.

58. Elliott, "Drug Prevention Placebo."

59. Pereira, "The Informants."

60. Stephen Glass, "Don't You D.A.R.E.," *New Republic*, March 3, 1997, 18–28; Stephen Glass, "Truth & D.A.R.E.," *Rolling Stone*, March 5, 1998, 42–43; Glenn Levant and Stephen Glass, "Double DARE," *New Republic*, August 4, 1997, 4. Glass wrote a letter of apology and admitted his wrongdoing; see Stephen Glass, "Letter to DARE from Stephen Glass," *National Families in Action: A Guide to the Drug-Prevention Movement*, January 25, 1999.

61. Keith W. Strandberg, "Truth about D.A.R.E.," *Law Enforcement Technology*, May 1999, box 14, folder 14, Mary Panzer Papers, 1981–2004, WHS. On Parsons and leadership transitions at DARE America see DARE America, "Change of Leadership at D.A.R.E.," January 10, 2013, https://dare.org/change-of-leadership-at-d-a-r-e/.

62. D.A.R.E. America v. Rolling Stone Magazine, 101 F. Supp. 2d 1270 (United States District Court for the Central District of California 2000). The United States Court of Appeals upheld the verdict. See D.A.R.E. America v. Rolling Stone Magazine, 270 F.3d 793 (United States Court of Appeals for the Ninth Circuit 2001). See also "Deposition of Susan Ennett." Some state officials followed the story and decided to keep DARE in operation. Johnnie Smith, Division of Narcotics Enforcement and JoAnna Richard, Legislative Liaison to State Legislator, "Drug Abuse Resistance Education Program (DARE)," June 11, 1999, box 14, folder 14, Mary Panzer Papers, 1981–2004, WHS.

63. Joseph Pereira, "Busting Mom and Dad," *The Sacramento Bee*, April 26, 1992, 141, 146, Newspapers.com.

64. Frank Fisher, "Maine Teenager Complains DARE Officer 'Let Me Down,'" *Valley News*, September 21, 1997, B6, Newspapers.com.

65. Jimmie L. Reeves and Richard Campbell, *Cracked Coverage: Television News, The Anti-Cocaine Crusade, and the Reagan Legacy* (Durham, N.C.: Duke University Press Books, 1994), 159. For a more recent example of a student informing on their parents, see Radley Balko, "D.A.R.E.: Ripping Families Apart Since 1983," *Reason*, October 17, 2010, accessed December 12, 2021, https://reason.com/2010/10/17/dare-ripping-families-apart-si/.

66. Andre Henderson, "All Parent Groups Aren't High on DARE," *Governing*, September 1, 1992, 16.

67. Steven K. Paulson, "Campaign against DARE Program Launched: Drug Education: Opponents Say Psychological Technique—Letting Children Make Choices—Is Harmful," *Los Angeles Times*, June 14, 1992, 5.

68. Newton, "DARE Marks a Decade of Growth and Controversy."

69. Associated Press, "Drug Abuse Resistance Education Program Has Supporters, but Critics Question Effectiveness," *Valley News*, September 21, 1997, B6, Newspapers.com.

70. Sylvester Monroe and Lisa H. Towle, "D.A.R.E. Bedeviled," *Time*, October 17, 1994, 49.

71. Judy McLemore, "DARE a 'Sham' or a 'Crime?'" pamphlet [ca. 1991], box 10, folder DARE Program, Gary Patton Political Papers, MS 81, Special Collections and Archives, University Library, University of California, Santa Cruz, Santa Cruz, Calif.

72. Parents Against DARE, "An Effective Drug Education Program . . ." [ca. 1992], box 10, folder DARE Program, Gary Patton Political Papers, MS 81, Special Collections and Archives, University Library, University of California, Santa Cruz, Santa Cruz, Calif.

73. Henderson, "All Parent Groups Aren't High on DARE."

74. Newton, "DARE Marks a Decade of Growth and Controversy."

75. Pereira, "The Informants."

76. Associated Press, "DARE Called a Mockery," *La Crosse Tribune*, September 30, 1993, 9, Newspapers.com.

77. Claudia Miller, "Survey Finds DARE Program May Be Falling Short," *Oakland Tribune*, November 13, 1994, A15–16, Newspapers.com.

78. *The NewsHour with Jim Lehrer*, April 25, 1997.

79. Associated Press, "Man Protests School Anti-Drug Program," *Daily Sentinel,* April 23, 1992, B5, Newspapers.com; Dana Nunn, "Fort Collins Group Goes Anti-DARE," *Daily Sentinel,* June 2, 1992, 9, Newspapers.com.

80. *The NewsHour with Jim Lehrer,* April 25, 1997.

81. Deborah Saathoff, "Bad Habits: School Anti-Drug Programs Sometimes Fall Short—and May Even Increase Abuse," *Dallas Morning News,* May 13, 1997, 20A, File Safe, Disciplined, Drug-Free Schools That Instill Values, William "Bill" Kincaid's Files, 1997–1997, WJC-DPC: Records of the Domestic Policy Council (Clinton Administration), ca. 1992–1/20/2001, William J. Clinton Library (Little Rock, Ark.), accessed January 15, 2023, https://catalog.archives.gov/id/122243248.

82. Travis Jordan to Stanley Sheinbaum, "D.A.R.E. Drug Education Program [with Attached Articles Critical of D.A.R.E.]," July 15, 1999, box 211, folder D.A.R.E. (Drug Abuse Resistance Education)—Martin Peretz, SSC.

83. Travis Jordan to Stanley Sheinbaum, "D.A.R.E. Drug Education Program." Parents also questioned the blind devotion to the program by the police regardless of its effectiveness. "There are national studies indicating that it doesn't work, but there's also this almost religious attachment to it, mainly from the local police," explained a parent and representative from the Massachusetts American Civil Liberties Union. "I don't think it's helping my son." See news articles attached to the source for more.

84. Newton, "DARE Marks a Decade of Growth and Controversy."

85. Los Angeles Times, "Seattle Rethinks Drug Education," *Boston Globe,* December 1, 1996; Kim Murphy, "Seattle Dares to Seek DARE Alternatives: City Is Latest to Defect from Venerable Anti-Drug Program, Saying It Wants Better Results," *Los Angeles Times,* November 19, 1996; Travis Jordan to Stanley Sheinbaum, "D.A.R.E. Drug Education Program."

86. Jacob Sullum, "DARE Aware," *Reason,* January 2001, 14–15.

87. DARE America, Worldwide to DARE supporters, "NBC Dateline Story on D.A.R.E.," *D.A.R.E. Idaho,* 2, no. 2, April 1997, 2, L3000.93, ISA.

88. "How to Save Your D.A.R.E. Program," *D.A.R.E. Idaho,* 4, no. 2, December 1996, 4, L3000.93, ISA.

89. Boyle, "A DAREing Rescue," 1, 16–19.

90. Julia C. Mead, "DARE Program: Sacred Cow or Fatted Calf?" *New York Times,* February 1, 2004, LI1, www.nytimes.com/2004/02/01/nyregion/dare-program-sacred-cow-or-fatted-calf.html.

91. Travis Jordan to Stanley Sheinbaum, "D.A.R.E. Drug Education Program."

92. Violent Crime Control and Law Enforcement Act of 1994, 42, 66.

93. William J. Clinton, "Address before a Joint Session of the Congress on the State of the Union," speech, January 23, 1996, APP, www.presidency.ucsb.edu/node/223046.

94. Office of Speechwriting and Michael Waldman, "1996 DNC [Democratic National Convention] Platform," *Clinton Digital Library,* accessed January 13, 2023, https://clinton.presidentiallibraries.us/items/show/45382.

95. Mead, "DARE Program: Sacred Cow or Fatted Calf?"

96. E. Suyapa Silvia and Judy Thorne, *School-Based Drug Prevention Programs: A Longitudinal Study in Selected School Districts. Final Report* (Washington, D.C.: U.S. Department of Education, Planning and Evaluation Service, 1997).

97. "D.A.R.E. Expands Program to Include Violence Prevention," *Alcoholism & Drug Abuse Weekly*, 6, no. 35 (September 12, 1994), 1.

98. DARE, "DARE Teaching Kids to Never Take Drugs," pamphlet, n.d., Domestic Policy Council and Jose Cerda, "D.A.R.E. [Drug Abuse Resistance Education]," *Clinton Digital Library*, accessed January 18, 2023, https://clinton.presidentiallibraries.us/items/show/96852.

99. Lee P. Brown, "D.A.R.E. Press Conference," August 26, 1998, box 58, folder 100, LBP.

100. Barry R. McCaffrey, "DARE Cares: Drug Prevention Protects America's Youth," *D.A.R.E. Idaho*, 4, no. 2, October 1999, 6, L3000.93, ISA.

101. Barry R. McCaffrey, "Remarks of Barry R. McCaffrey, Director, Office of National Drug Control Policy 13th Annual National D.A.R.E. Officers Association Dinner," July 7, 2000, in Office of National Drug Control Policy, "Drug Control Policy Speeches, 1996–2000" (Washington, D.C.: Executive Office of the President, 2000). On the Clinton administration support for DARE, see John Carnevale, interview by Max Felker-Kantor, January 7, 2021.

102. Boyle, "A DAREing Rescue," 17.

103. Millicent Lawton, "Study of Calif. Anti-Drug Education Programs Stirs Debate—Education Week," *Education Week*, November 22, 1995, accessed June 4, 2019, www.edweek.org/ew/articles/1995/11/22/12calif.h15.html; Millicent Lawton, "New Guide Gives A's to Six of 47 National Anti-Drug Programs—Education Week," *Education Week*, June 12, 1996, accessed June 4, 2019, www.edweek.org/ew/articles/1996/06/12/38drug.h15.html.

104. Dennis P. Rosenbaum and Gordon S. Hanson, "Assessing the Effects of School-Based Drug Education: A Six-Year Multilevel Analysis of Project D.A.R.E.," *Journal of Research in Crime and Delinquency* 35, no. 4 (November 1, 1998): 381–412; Adrienne D. Coles, "Discontented, Some Districts Shifting Gears on Anti-Drug Programs," *Education Week*, January 20, 1999, 5. Other studies found that in suburban schools, DARE's effectiveness was marginal. Donna S. Kochis, "The Effectiveness of Project DARE: Does It Work?" *Journal of Alcohol & Drug Education* 40, no. 2 (Winter 1995): 40. A 1994 study also conducted by Rosenbaum and a team of researchers in Illinois found that suburban kids who went through the DARE curriculum also had a higher likelihood of using drugs and a less negative attitude toward drug use. However, this study did not receive the national media attention of the 1998 study. Susan T. Ennett et al., "Long-Term Evaluation of Drug Abuse Resistance Education," *Addictive Behaviors* 19, no. 2 (March 1, 1994): 113–25.

105. *NBC Evening News*, "In Depth (Kids and Illegal Drugs: D.A.R.E.)," aired March 18, 1998 on NBC.

106. Dennis P. Rosenbaum, "Just Say No to D.A.R.E.," *Criminology & Public Policy* 6, no. 4 (2007): 815–24.

107. Jim Avila and Tom Brokaw, "In Depth (Kids and Illegal Drugs: D.A.R.E.)," *NBC Evening News*, NBC, March 18, 1998, Vanderbilt Television News Archive, accessed June 23, 2020, https://tvnews.vanderbilt.edu/broadcasts/623318.

108. DARE America, "Program Communications Quarterly Activities Report, October 1-December 30, 1997," 1997, box B-2572, City Council File No. 98–1086, LACCF.

109. *The NewsHour with Jim Lehrer*, April 25, 1997.

110. "Young, White and Middle-Class," *The Economist*, December 6, 1997, 26.

111. Charles A. Gruber, "A Positive Evaluation of DARE," *Law and Order*, April 1998, 42.

112. Center for Court Innovation, *Lessons from the Battle over D.A.R.E.: The Complicated Relationship between Research and Practice*, Bureau of Justice Assistance, Office of Justice Programs, U.S. Department of Justice (Washington, D.C., 2009), 5; one Ohio University study conducted in 1999 found positive results. See evaluation in Los Angeles City Council, City Council File No. 98–1086, box B-2572, LACCF.

113. John H. Hough, "DARE: An Opponent's View," *Law and Order*, April 1998, 48–50, here 50, 49.

114. Eamon Clifford, "Taking a Bite out of DARE: Why Not More Cops in Clown Suits?" *Law and Order*, April 1998, 51.

115. Lily Geismer, *Left Behind: The Democrats' Failed Attempt to Solve Inequality* (New York: Public Affairs, 2022); Nicole Hemmer, *Partisans: The Conservative Revolutionaries Who Remade American Politics in the 1990s* (New York: Basic Books, 2022).

116. National Health Policy Forum, "Issue Brief: Substance Abuse Prevention: Could an Improved D.A.R.E. Program Help Bridge the Gap between Research and Practice?" (Washington, D.C.: National Health Policy Forum, April 15, 1999); Office of National Drug Control Policy, *National Drug Control Strategy: 1999* (Washington, D.C.: Office of National Drug Control Policy, Executive Office of the President, 1999), 38–39.

117. Silvia and Thorne, *School-Based Drug Prevention Programs*, 20.

118. National Health Policy Forum, "Issue Brief: Substance Abuse Prevention."

119. Safe, Disciplined, and Drug-Free Schools Expert Panel, *Exemplary and Promising: Safe, Disciplined and Drug-Free Schools Programs* (Washington, D.C.: U.S. Department of Education, June 2002).

120. United States Congress, Senate, Committee on Appropriations, *Departments of Commerce, Justice, and State, the Judiciary, and Related Agencies Appropriation Bill, 1998: Report (to Accompany S. 1022)*, No. 105–48 (Washington, D.C., 1997).

121. Boyle, "A DAREing Rescue," 1, 16–19.

122. Boyle, "A DAREing Rescue"; Joetta L. Sack, "DARE Anti-Drug Program to Shift Strategy," *Education Week*, February 21, 2001, 5; Laura Fording, "DARE-Ing to Be Different," *Newsweek*, February 17, 2001; Claudia Kalb, Andrew Murr, Karen Springen, and Adam Rogers, "DARE Checks into Rehab," *Newsweek*, February 26, 2001; Mary Lord, "Truth or D.A.R.E.," *U.S. News & World Report*, February 26, 2001. Crucial background for the role of RWJF and the relationship between the scientific community and DARE came from John Carnevale, interview by Max Felker-Kantor, January 7, 2021. For background on the meeting in Washington, D.C. and perception of DARE as an effective delivery mechanism see Allan Cohen, interview by Max Felker-Kantor, January 26, 2021.

123. Jennifer Gonnerman, "Truth or D.A.R.E.—The Dubious Drug-Education Program Takes New York," *Village Voice*, April 6, 1999, accessed January 28, 2019, www.villagevoice.com/1999/04/06/truth-or-d-a-r-e/.

124. Boyle, "A DAREing Rescue," 1.

125. Robert Wood Johnson Foundation, *A New DARE Curriculum Gets Mixed Reviews* (Robert Wood Johnson Foundation, March 2010), 3.

126. National Health Policy Forum, "Issue Brief: Substance Abuse Prevention: Could an Improved D.A.R.E. Program Help Bridge the Gap between Research and Practice?" (Washington, D.C.: National Health Policy Forum, April 15, 1999).

127. Jeffrey Merrill, Tracey Dilascio, and Ilana Pinsky, "Law Enforcement and Drug Prevention: A Profile of the DARE Officer," *The Police Chief*, August 2002, 81.

128. Robert Wood Johnson Foundation, *A New DARE Curriculum Gets Mixed Reviews*.

129. University of Akron's Institute for Health and Social Policy, *The University of Akron's Adolescent Substance Abuse Prevention Study: A Longitudinal Evaluation of the New Curricula for the D.A.R.E Middle (7th Grade) and High School (9th Grade) Programs:* TAKE CHARGE OF YOUR LIFE: *Year Four Progress Report* (Akron, Ohio: University of Akron's Institute for Health and Social Policy, March 2006), https://web.archive.org/web/20060323112745/http://www.dare.com/home/Resources/documents/DARE March06ProgressReport.pdf.

130. DARE America, *DARE America Form 990—Return of Organization Exempt from Income Tax*, 2002, accessed May 15, 2020, https://projects.propublica.org/nonprofits/organizations/954242541.

131. Marjorie E. Kanof, *Youth Illicit Drug Use Prevention: DARE Long-Term Evaluations and Federal Efforts to Identify Effective Programs*, GAO-03-172R (Washington, D.C.: U.S. General Accounting Office, January 15, 2003), 2; "GAO Literature Review Reiterates Ineffectiveness of Original D.A.R.E.," *Alcoholism & Drug Abuse Weekly* 15, no. 4 (January 27, 2003), 1–2; Brian Vastag, "GAO: DARE Does Not Work," *JAMA* 289, no. 5 (February 5, 2003): 539.

132. Safe, Disciplined, and Drug-Free Schools Expert Panel, *Exemplary and Promising*.

133. Allison Gruner Gandhi et al., "The Devil Is in the Details: Examining the Evidence for 'Proven' School-Based Drug Abuse Prevention Programs," *Evaluation Review* 31, no. 1 (February 1, 2007): 43–74.

134. Carol Hirschon Weiss, Erin Murphy-Graham, and Sarah Birkeland, "An Alternate Route to Policy Influence: How Evaluations Affect D.A.R.E.," *American Journal of Evaluation* 26, no. 1 (March 1, 2005): 12–30.

135. DARE America, "The New D.A.R.E. Program," June 6, 2004, https://web.archive.org/web/20040906073423/http://dare.com/home/newdareprogram.asp.

136. DARE America, "Curriculum," March 23, 2006, https://web.archive.org/web/20060323110211/http://www.dare.com/home/Curriculum/default66d2.asp?N=Curriculum&M=10&S=0; "D.A.R.E. Curriculum Gets High Marks," *Akron Update*, February 21, 2003, https://web.archive.org/web/20080906231613/http://www.uakron.edu/aupdate/Feb212003/Feature_58.php; DARE America, "D.A.R.E America Thanks the Robert Wood Johnson Foundation and University of Akron," 2001, https://web.archive.org/web/20011107023418fw_/http://www.dare.com/D_EDUC/D_edu_Frame.htm. See also Zili Sloboda, interview by Max Felker-Kantor, December 14, 2020.

137. "The New D.A.R.E. Program," *Idaho Cops for Kids*, June 2006, 1, L3000.90, ISA.

138. "D.A.R.E. Curriculum Gets High Marks."

139. DARE America, "New DARE Program," January 2, 2006, https://web.archive.org/web/20060102103240/http://www.dare.com/home/newdareprogram.asp.

140. Merrill et al., "Law Enforcement and Drug Prevention," 87.

141. Merrill et al., "Law Enforcement and Drug Prevention," 88.

142. DARE America, "Curriculum," March 23, 2006, https://web.archive.org/web/20060323110211/http://www.dare.com/home/Curriculum/default66d2.asp?N=Curriculum&M=10&S=0. See also, DARE America, "New DARE Program" January 2, 2006, https://web.archive.org/web/20060102103240/http://www.dare.com/home/newdareprogram.asp. For a discussion of school resource officers and police in schools in the twenty-first century, see Kathleen Nolan, *Police in the Hallways: Discipline in an Urban High School* (Minneapolis: University of Minnesota Press, 2011).

143. DARE America, "The New D.A.R.E. Program," pamphlet, [ca. 2005], in author's possession.

144. See, for instance, *Idaho Cops for Kids*, vol. 1, June 2004, L3000.90, ISA.

145. "Marti's Message," *Idaho Cops for Kids*, May 2005, 3, L3000.90, ISA.

146. There are numerous news articles and testimonies on DARE America's website (via the Internet Archive's Wayback Machine) from the early 2000s about school police officers and DARE officers crediting the program with helping to stop potential school shooters, bomb threats, and potential child abductions. See DARE America, "D.A.R.E. News," August 10, 2002, https://web.archive.org/web/20020810200341/http://www.dare.com/NewsRoom/StoryPage.asp?N=NewsRoom&M=14&S=34&RecordID=17; DARE America, "D.A.R.E. Kids News," 1999, accessed June 30, 2020, https://web.archive.org/web/20011107023424fw_/http://www.dare.com/D_NEWS/D_news_Frame.htm. Thank you to Emily McGuire for her work finding and summarizing DARE.com websites using the Wayback Machine.

147. Glenn Levant, "Terrorism Must Also Be Fought on the Battlefield of Drug Abuse," 2001, https://web.archive.org/web/20011107014211fw_/http://www.dare.com/common/narco_terrorism.htm.

148. Thomas Feiling, *Cocaine Nation* (New York: Pegasus Books, 2012).

149. Wysong, Aniskiewicz, and Wright, "Truth and DARE."

150. Gonnerman, "Truth or D.A.R.E."

151. Reeves, *Citizen Spies*, 130–31.

152. Gonnerman, "Truth or D.A.R.E."

153. Howard Blume, "No Joking Matter: Spoof on D.A.R.E. Draws Ire from Cops, Prosecution by D.A.," *L.A. Weekly*, November 23, 1995, 19, Newspapers.com.

154. Howard Blume, "Hawking Hemp in Claremont," *L.A. Weekly*, December 28, 1995, 26, Newspapers.com.

155. Briony Wright, "The Unlikely Story behind 'D.A.R.E. to Keep Kids off Drugs' T-shirts," i-D, April 20, 2017, https://i-d.vice.com/en_uk/article/j5mmqp/the-unlikely-story-behind-dare-to-keep-kids-off-drugs-t-shirts; DailyMail.com, "Keeping a Low Profile! Dakota Johnson Cuts Grungy Figure in Graphic Print Black Top and Frayed Jeans as She Gets in Some Retail Therapy," *Daily Mail*, March 25, 2017, www.dailymail.co.uk/~/article-4348024/index.html.

156. Justin Kirkl, "Serena Williams' Husband Turned a Vintage T-Shirt into a Brilliant Fashion Troll," *Esquire*, August 27, 2019, www.esquire.com/style/a28820657/serena-williams-alexis-ohanian-maria-sharapova-us-open-dare-shirt/.

157. Gabriella Miyares, Dilara Balkan, and Marisa Hetzler, "The Iconic, Ironic D.A.R.E. Shirt," accessed January 9, 2023, Drug Policy Alliance, https://drugsandstuff.libsyn.com/episode-45-puff-or-pass-the-iconic-ironic-dare-shirt.

158. DARE America, "D.A.R.E. Logo and Shirt—One of the Most Recognized Logos in the World," DARE.org, May 16, 2022, https://dare.org/d-a-r-e-logo-and-shirt-one-of-the-most-recognized-logos-in-the-world/.

159. Rosenbaum, "Just Say No to D.A.R.E.," 820.

160. Andy Furillo, "DARE: It's Working and in Trouble: Police Anti-Drug Project at Schools Praised but Council Is Cool," *Los Angeles Times*, April 28, 1985, B1.

Epilogue

1. Anthony Petrosino et al., "US State Government and DARE: The Story in Four States," *Evidence & Policy: A Journal of Research, Debate and Practice* 2, no. 3 (2006): 291–319. For the impact of the closing of the RTCs on DARE, see Nick DeMauro and John Lindsay, interview by Max Felker-Kantor, December 21, 2020.

2. Carol Hirschon Weiss, Erin Murphy-Graham, and Sarah Birkeland, "An Alternate Route to Policy Influence: How Evaluations Affect D.A.R.E.," *American Journal of Evaluation* 26, no. 1 (March 1, 2005): 12–30; Carol H. Weiss et al., "The Fairy Godmother—and Her Warts: Making the Dream of Evidence-Based Policy Come True," *American Journal of Evaluation* 29, no. 1 (March 1, 2008): 29–47.

3. Sarah Birkeland, Erin Murphy-Graham, and Carol Weiss, "Good Reasons for Ignoring Good Evaluation: The Case of the Drug Abuse Resistance Education (D.A.R.E.) Program," *Evaluation and Program Planning*, 28, no. 3 (August 1, 2005): 247–56.

4. On Parsons, Pegueros, and leadership transitions at DARE America see DARE America, "Change of Leadership at D.A.R.E.," January 10, 2013, https://dare.org/change-of-leadership-at-d-a-r-e/.

5. Frank Pegueros, interview by Max Felker-Kantor, July 25, 2019; Nick DeMauro and Glenn Levant, interview by Max Felker-Kantor, January 14, 2021.

6. Dennis P. Rosenbaum, "Just Say No to D.A.R.E.," *Criminology & Public Policy* 6, no. 4 (2007): 815–24.

7. DARE America, "Dare Presentation to the DCs," February 26, 2013, LA Records Request #20-8027; DARE America, "DARE Memorandum of Agreement," 2013, LA Records Request #20-8027; DARE America, "DARE Preamble," 2013, LA Records Request #20-8027; DARE America, "LAPD DARE Press Release—May 2013," May 2013, LA Records Request #20-8027, all in author's possession. City and police officials had started discussions about removing uniformed officers from DARE to place them back on patrol in early 2002. See Roberta M. Yang to Rick Caruso, March 26, 2002; Commanding Officer, DARE Division to Chief of Police, "Report for the Police Commission on Alternative Deployments for DARE Division," April 16, 2002, both in box 651558, folder LAPD—DARE, Mayor Hahn Records, Los Angeles City Archives, Los Angeles, CA.

8. On keepin' it REAL, see DARE America, "Curricula," 2023, accessed February 27, 2023, https://dare.org/education/.

9. DARE America, "The History of DARE," accessed May 28, 2022, https://dare.org/history/.

10. DARE America, "Homepage," accessed July 5, 2023, https://dare.org/; Fred Kight, "Anti-Drug Program Dares to Change," *Athens News*, April 7, 2014, 1, 22–23.

11. LEAD, "About," accessed May 28, 2022, www.leadrugs.org/. See Nick DeMauro and John Lindsay, interview by Max Felker-Kantor, December 21, 2020; Nick DeMauro and Glenn Levant, interview by Max Felker-Kantor, January 14, 2021; Zili Sloboda, interview by Max Felker-Kantor, December 14, 2020. I do not intend to weigh in on what became a conflict between DARE leaders in New Jersey and DARE America, which led to DARE's removal in many New Jersey schools. See Michael Hill, "D.A.R.E. New Jersey Loses Fight with National Organization," *NJ Spotlight News*, May 21, 2015, accessed January 17, 2023, www.njspotlightnews.org/video/d-a-r-e-new-jersey-loses-fight-with-national-organization/; Jeanette Rundquist, DARE anti-drug program looks to withdraw from N.J. schools amid feud," *NJ.com*, December 20, 2012, accessed May 28, 2022, www.nj.com/news/2012/12/widely_used_anti-drug_program.html. See also Nick DeMauro and John Lindsay, interview by Max Felker-Kantor, December 21, 2020.

12. DARE America, "Homepage," accessed August 27, 2020, https://dare.org. On the shifts in DARE's curriculum, I am relying on an informal conversation with Frank Pegueros of DARE America, June 25, 2019. Theodore L. Caputi and A. Thomas McLellan, "Truth and D.A.R.E.: Is D.A.R.E.'s New Keepin' It REAL Curriculum Suitable for American Nationwide Implementation?" *Drugs: Education, Prevention and Policy* 24, no. 1 (January 2, 2017): 49–57.

13. Kight, "Anti-Drug Program Dares to Change."

14. I visited the DARE America office in Culver City in the summer of 2019 where I spoke with CEO Frank Pegueros about DARE's history and evolution. Frank Pegueros, interview by Max Felker-Kantor, July 25, 2019.

15. DARE America, *DARE America Form 990—Return of Organization Exempt from Income Tax*, 2018, accessed May 15, 2020, https://projects.propublica.org/nonprofits/organizations/954242541. See also DARE America, *DARE America Form 990—Return of Organization Exempt from Income Tax*, 2019, accessed March 3, 2023, https://projects.propublica.org/nonprofits/organizations/954242541/202043219349322464/full.

16. DARE America, "Homepage," 2023, accessed March 3, 2023, https://dare.org.

17. On social media, see Kelly M. Hayes (@MsKellyMHayes), 2022, "I was in the D.A.R.E. program in the 5th grade. That cop was shady as hell and lied all the fucking time. Even as a fifth grader, I could tell he was just making shit up," Twitter, August 13, 2022, 9:09 A.M., https://twitter.com/MsKellyMHayes/status/1558440568673411078. On TikTok parody, see, for instance, Mason (@chickendelicious), "he's always like, 'wheres my money and family photos' and I'm like 'retrace ur steps,'" TikTok, 2022, www.tiktok.com/@chickendelicious/video/7164251329781566762/. Thank you to my research assistant Ciera Boyes for her work investigating Twitter and TikTok for parodies of DARE.

18. Ellie (@elliewelliebobellie), "5th grade me who won the dare essay and pledged to never do drugs or drink alcohol," 2022, www.tiktok.com/@elliewelliebobellie/video/7156799671925542190?is_copy_url=1&is_from_webapp=v1.

19. Savannah Walsh, "*Euphoria* Recklessly Glorifies Drug Use and Sex, Says DARE," *Vanity Fair*, January 26, 2022, accessed January 27, 2022, www.vanityfair.com/hollywood/2022/01/euphoria-recklessly-glorifies-drug-use-and-sex-says-dare; Gil Kaufman, "Zendaya Responds to D.A.R.E.'s 'Euphoria' Criticism: 'Our Show Is in No Way a Moral Tale,'" *Billboard*, February 8, 2022, accessed February 17, 2023, www.billboard.com/culture/tv-film/zendaya-responds-dare-euphoria-criticism-drug-use-1235028486/.

20. KCTV5 Staff and Emily Van de Riet, "AR-15 Raffle Pulled from School's DARE Fundraiser following Recent Mass Shootings," accessed January 8, 2023, www.nbc29.com/2022/06/02/ar-15-raffle-pulled-schools-dare-fundraiser-following-recent-mass-shootings/.

21. Dayton 24/7 Now Newsroom, "Former D.A.R.E. Officer sentenced for child pornography charges," *Dayton 24/7 Now*, April 6, 2023, https://dayton247now.com/amp/news/local/former-dare-officer-sentenced-for-child-pornography-charges; William Morris, "Plymouth deputy, a DARE officer, sentenced to 40 years for prescription drug thefts," *Des Moines Register*, June 14, 2022, www.desmoinesregister.com/story/news/crime-and-courts/2022/06/14/iowa-deputy-dare-officer-sentenced-stealing-prescription-drugs-plymouth-county/7627977001/; Maggie Mancini, "Former Bucks County D.A.R.E. officer sentenced to decades in prison for sexually assaulting teenage boys," *Philly Voice*, March 22, 2023, www.phillyvoice.com/bucks-county-dare-officer-james-carey-sentencing-state-prison-55-years-sexual-assault-boys/.

22. On violence work see Micol Seigel, *Violence Work: State Power and the Limits of Police* (Durham, N.C.: Duke University Press, 2018).

23. George H. W. Bush to Daryl Gates, 1989, Daryl Gates Alphabetical File, White House Office of Records Management (WHORM), GBPL.

24. Daryl F. Gates, *Chief: My Life in the LAPD* (New York: Bantam Books, 1993), 1–2.

25. Gates, *Chief*, 309–10.

26. Thank you to Monica Muñoz Martinez for suggesting this reference. Keith Chapman, *Paw Patrol*, directed by Jamie Whitney (Toronto, Canada: Spin Master Entertainment, 2013), television. On copaganda, see Paul Kaplan and Daniel LaChance, *Crimesploitation: Crime, Punishment, and Pleasure on Reality Television*, (Stanford, Calif.: Stanford University Press, 2022).

Archival Sources and Interviews

Archives Consulted

Archiving the Age of Mass Incarceration Project, LAPD Records, UCLA, Los Angeles, Calif.
George H. W. Bush Presidential Library, College Station, Tex.
- Beverly Ward Files, White House Office of Correspondence
- Judy Smith Files, White House Press Office
- Kristen Gear Files, White House Office of Public Affairs
- Presidential Proclamation Files
- Shiree Sanchez Files, White House Office of Public Liaison
- Susan Griffith Files, White House Office of Correspondence
- WHORM Alphabetical File
- WHORM Subject File
- White House Communications Agency Audio
- White House Office of Speechwriting
- William Caldwell Files, White House Office of Public Liaison

Idaho State Archives, Boise
- DARE Idaho
- Idaho Cops for Kids
- Idaho Drug War News

Los Angeles City Archives, Calif.
- City Council Files
- Mayor Antonio R. Villaraigosa Files

Loyola Marymount University, Department of Archives and Special Collections, William H. Hannon Library, Los Angeles, Calif.
- Mayor Richard J. Riordan Administrative Papers, CSLA-17
- Rebuild LA Collection, CSLA-6

National Archives and Records Administration, College Park, Md.
- RG 581 Office of National Drug Control Policy Subject Files
- RG 60 Subject Files of the Attorney General, 1974–93, General Records of the Department of Justice.

New York State Archives, Albany
- Division of Criminal Justice Services Commissioner's Subject and Correspondence Files

Ronald Reagan Presidential Library, Simi Valley, Calif.
- Anne Higgins Files
- Carlton E. Turner Files
- Drug Free America White House Conference Files

Office of the First Lady, Press Office
Office of the First Lady, Projects Office
Richard Williams Files
WHORM: Subject File

Southern California Library, Los Angeles, Calif.
Clippings File

University of Nevada, Las Vegas, Special Collections
Junior League of Las Vegas Records, 1946–2010, MS-00179

University of California, Los Angeles, Special Collections, Charles E. Young Research Library
Los Angeles Unified School District Board of Education Records (Collection 1923)
Mayor Tom Bradley Administration Papers (Collection 293)

University of California, Santa Barbara, Department of Special Collections, Davidson Library
Stanley K. Sheinbaum Collection, MSS 217

University of Georgia, Richard B. Russell Library for Political Research and Studies, Athens
William Lee Robinson Papers

University Library, University of California, Santa Cruz, Special Collections and Archives
Gary Patton Political Papers, MS 81

University of Southern California, Regional History Collections, Special Collections, USC Libraries, Los Angeles
Los Angeles Webster Commission Records, Collection no. 0244
Independent Commission on the Los Angeles Police Department Records, Collection no. 0229

University of Wyoming, American Heritage Center, Laramie
Michael J. Sullivan Papers, Collection #10348
Wyoming Energy Boom Sublette County Natural Gas Oral History Project

William J. Clinton Presidential Library, Little Rock, Ark.
Clinton Digital Archives

Wisconsin Historical Society, Madison
Mary Panzer Papers, 1981–2004
Records of the Superintendent's AODA Council, 1995–1999
Gerald D. Kleczka papers, 1969–2004

Woodson Research Center, Fondren Library, Rice University, Houston, Tex.
Dr. Lee P. Brown Papers, 1960–2004, MS 509

Interviews Conducted

Carnevale, John. Interview by Max Felker-Kantor, January 7, 2021.

Cohen, Allan. Interview by Max Felker-Kantor, January 26, 2021.

DeJong, William. Interview by Max Felker-Kantor, January 14, 2021.

DeMauro, Nick, and Glenn Levant. Interview by Max Felker-Kantor, January 14, 2021.

DeMauro, Nick, and John Lindsay. Interview by Max Felker-Kantor, December 21, 2020.
Ennett, Susan. Interview by Max Felker-Kantor, January 22, 2021.
Hansen, Bill. Interview by Max Felker-Kantor, January 27, 2021.
Hughes, Charles. Interview by Max Felker-Kantor, December 30, 2022.
Johnson, Anderson C. Interview by Max Felker-Kantor, April 29, 2022.
Pegueros, Frank. Interview by Max Felker-Kantor, July 25, 2019.
Ringwalt, Christopher. Interview by Max Felker-Kantor, December 22, 2020.
Rohrbach, Luanne. Interview by Max Felker-Kantor, December 20, 2021.
Sloboda, Zili. Interview by Max Felker-Kantor, December 14, 2020.
Sturkey, William. Interview by Max Felker-Kantor, December 29, 2022.

Index

Note: Pages in italics denote an image.